Texts and Monographs in Computer Science

P2?
P1!

Fairness

Nissim Francez

With 147 Illustrations

Springer-Verlag
New York Berlin Heidelberg Tokyo

Nissim Francez
Department of Computer Science
Technion–Israel Institute of Technology
Haifa 32000
Israel

Series Editor

David Gries
Department of Computer Science
Cornell University
Ithaca, NY 14853
U.S.A.

ACM Classifications: D.1.3, D.2.4, D.3.1, D.4.1, F.1.2, F.3.1, F.3.3

Library of Congress Cataloging in Publication Data
Francez, Nissim.
Fairness.
(Texts and monographs in computer science)
Bibliography: p.
Includes index.
1. Electronic digital computers–Programming.
2. Programming languages (Electronic computers)–
Semantics. 3. Parallel processing (Electronic computers)
I. Title. II. Series.
QA76.6.F7226 1986 005.4′3 86–6565

Media conversion by House of Equations Inc., Newton, New Jersey.
Printed and bound by R.R. Donnelley & Sons, Harrisonburg, Virginia.
Printed in the United States of America.

9 8 7 6 5 4 3 2 1

ISBN 0-387-96235-2 Springer-Verlag New York Berlin Heidelberg Tokyo
ISBN 3-540-96235-2 Springer-Verlag New York Berlin Heidelberg Tokyo

To Tikva,
the fairest of them all

Two roads diverged in a yellow wood,
And sorry I could not travel both
And be one traveler, long I stood
And looked down one as far as I could
To where it bent in the undergrowth;

Then took the other, as just as fair,
And having perhaps the better claim,
Because it was grassy and wanted wear;
Though as for that the passing there
Had worn them really about the same,

And both that morning equally lay
In leaves no step had trodden black.
Oh, I kept the first for another day!
Yet knowing how way leads on to way,
I doubted if I should ever come back.

I shall be telling this with a sigh
Somewhere ages and ages hence:
Two roads diverged in a wood, and I-
I took the one less traveled by,
And that has made all the difference.

–Robert Frost,
The Road Not Taken

Preface

The main purpose of this book is to bring together much of the research conducted in recent years in a subject I find both fascinating and important, namely *fairness*. Much of the reported research is still in the form of technical reports, theses and conference papers, and only a small part has already appeared in the formal scientific journal literature.

Fairness is one of those concepts that can intuitively be explained very briefly, but bear a lot of consequences, both in theory and the practicality of programming languages. Scientists have traditionally been attracted to studying such concepts. However, a rigorous study of the concept needs a lot of detailed development, evoking much machinery of both mathematics and computer science.

I am fully aware of the fact that this field of research still lacks maturity, as does the whole subject of theoretical studies of concurrency and nondeterminism. One symptom of this lack of maturity is the proliferation of models used by the research community to discuss these issues, a variety lacking the invariance property present, for example, in universal formalisms for sequential computing.

I was personally involved in much of the research reported in the book, in the form of original contribution, refereeing, discussions with others active in the subject, and have closely followed the developments. I did my best to present as uniformly as I could both my (and my colleagues') results as well as results by others. At the current state of the art I have found this to be a very difficult task. Thus, in many cases I drew heavily on the original presentations, often copying much of their text and making changes appropriate to the framework.

The book is mainly intended for the graduate student and active researcher level. Much of it needs only the usual computer science undergraduate background in program verification and some mathematical and logical maturity. Parts of the needed background are reviewed briefly. Chapters 6, 7, and (part of) 8 need more knowledge in mathematical logic, set theory, and some knowledge of algebra and topology.

In deciding how to organize the book, I made two major decisions:

(1) Choose (fair) *termination* as the basic property under investigation. Termination is a good representative of all other properties that depend on fairness.
(2) Choose *proof-obligations* (and rules) as the main tool used in the investigation.

The organization of the book is as follows:

- Chapter 0 gives a very general background and introduces the programming language used in most of the discussion in the book.
- Chapter 1 reviews the standard method of proving termination of programs.
- Chapter 2 presents one proof method for fair termination (the helpful directions) in two variants, which are interrelated.
- Chapter 3 presents the other prevailing method for fair termination proofs (explicit schedulers) and also deals with random assignments.

  Chapters 2 and 3 are the core of the book. Later chapters present extensions in various directions.
- Chapter 4 preserves the same programming language and presents a variety of extensions and generalizations of the fairness notions involved.
- Chapter 5 preserves the simple fairness notions and extends the programming language constructs to cover various aspects of concurrency and communication.
- Chapter 6 presents a formalized logical presentation of the issues dealt with semantically in Chapter 2.
- Chapter 7 presents yet another logical framework with a different paradigm.
- Chapter 8 uses a functional approach and is concerned with rules generating fairness while all previous chapters were concerned with the consequences of assuming it. The chapter also briefly discusses one other fairness-like concept—the finite delay.

I am definitely sure that we are far away from having said the last word on the fairness issue. I hope that this book will present the scientific community with a tool for relating to past research and a stimulus of carrying on further research.

Acknowledgments

I started to write the book while on sabbatical at the IBM–T.J. Watson Research Laboratories in Yorktown Heights. I wish to thank the mathematics department there for providing the time and means for embarking on such a project.

I would like to thank David Gries for encouraging me in this project, suggesting to publish the book in the series edited by him, and for critically reading some chapters of the early versions.

With the following colleagues I had many stimulating discussions and arguments both about the subject and about the book: K.R. Apt., R.J. Back, E.M. Clarke, A. Emerson, R. Gerth, O. Grumberg, D. Harel, S. Katz, D. Kozen, R. Kurki-Suonio, D. Lehmann, J.A. Makowsky, R. Milner, E.-R. Olderog, D. Park, A. Pnueli, S. Porat, J. Siffakis, C. Sterling, W. P. deRoever, and A.P. Sistla.

I especially thank Frank Stomp for critically reading the whole manuscript and having many useful suggestions.

At Yorktown Heights, Nancy A. Perry and Barbara White were more than helpful in typing a preliminary version. The artwork was also done at Yorktown Heights, by the art department. Raya Anavi, at the Computer Science Department, Technion, did a fine job, very devoutedly, in typing and formatting the final version.

I also thank Anat Ha-Levi for the frontispiece drawing.

While at the Technion, the work on the book was partially supported by the Fund for the Promotion of Research in the Technion.

Table of Contents

CHAPTER 0
Introduction

0.1 Motivation and Background

One of the main trends in recent developments in computer systems and programming languages is the inclusion of *concurrency (or parallelism)* and *nondeterminism.* Consequently, much recent research is devoted to the theory of these two modes of computation. A major direction within this theory is concerned with the *semantics* of programming languages expressing concurrency and nondeterminism and with *verification* of concurrent and nondeterministic programs. Among the new problems that the study of concurrency and nondeterminism encountered is that of *fairness.* This issue has revealed itself in many different contexts, as many facets of some very basic phenomenon. Some research directions, such as *denotational semantics,* had to solve some difficult mathematical problems (e.g. the *power domain* [PL 76, S 78, LE 76]); others, such as partial correctness proofs, needed some new insights (e.g. the discovery of *noninterference* [OG 76], [LA 77] and of *cooperation* [AFR 80], [LG 81] embodying relations among proofs). No research topic, however, raised controversy as much as the issue of fairness: Is it a "legitimate" (whatever that may mean) feature to be included in a programming language? Is it a "legitimate" area of study within computer science (as opposed to pure mathematics)?

The reason for the opposition to fairness-like constructs is a common property of all of them, again appearing in different light in different contexts:

- In denotational semantics, their study revealed the phenomenon of *non-($\omega-$)continuity* of the semantic functions, and hence, by *Scott's-thesis,* their non-computability.
- In proof theory, they called for the use of higher *countable ordinals* in proofs, transcending the natural numbers.

All this is caused by the fact that fairness-like constructs introduce what is known as *unbounded nondeterminism. A program may always terminate and still produce infinitely many different possible results!*

Thus, the opponents to fairness claimed that since it is impossible for an implementation to produce all and only fair computations, fairness should be banned from programming languages, and each programmer should "code his/her own fairness".

This argument of non-implementability borders with one's cosmological viewpoints, which may or may not forbid primitives with an infinite fan-out of results. Here we are not going to argue with such claims; we leave them to be resolved by prevailing theories of physics. Our main justification for studying fairness, besides the mathematical interest and elegance resulting, is that it *is* relevant to computer science in general, and programming in particular, at *a certain level of abstraction!*

Thus, it may well be the case that at a low level of abstraction, some electronic circuitry is not capable of producing all and only fair behaviors (will it cause a glitch. . . ?). It may even be the case that no nondeterminism, whether fair or unfair, is possible at that level, again depending on the answer to the cosmological question of the determinacy of the universe. On the other hand, it is hardly conceivable that properties of programs at some high-level application level should explicitly depend on some implementation-dependent choices of resolving nondeterminism. Should the correctness of an airline reservation system depend on the fact that 17 pointers with some strange relationship to each other are used for the internal structuring of the queue? Should the correctness of a simulation program depend on the fact that the random number generator cannot produce some "crazy" natural number because of the specific use of COMMON block in the FORTRAN program implementing it?

Another argument arises when one tries to abstract away from *probabilities* that occur at low levels of execution. One would not like the operating system to depend on the fact that the probability of drift between two local clocks is that or another or the correctness of a bank-account system to depend on the difference between the probability distribution of usage of after-hours banking by two subsets of physically-remote customers.

Thus, our basic belief is that at the appropriate level of abstraction one should identify one common property that generalizes all actual behaviors of a program and adopt it as a starting point for design and reasoning. Fairness is such a generalization. Of course, there may be several (and conflicting) viewpoints regarding the right level of abstraction for doing so. Since this is neither an issue of principle nor an issue of technical mathematical treatment but rather an engineering issue, we do not dwell on it here.

The following analogy, borrowed from [PA 82], may be used to stress the point:

> The fair set. . . has the same questionable status as many similarly defined sets of real numbers. To the strict constructivist such sets should play no part in reasoned argument or specification. But its implication must be recognized—that fairness, unbounded nondeterminism, are "unspecifiable". They are constraints. . . that may not, in their general form, be expressed—or, if expressed, may not be used in reasoned argument. Since it does seem possible [*as shown in this book—N.F.*] to reason usefully with such constraints, this is not the position to be taken here. . .

Following is a brief survey of some of the contexts in which fairness-like constructs are encountered.

- The most basic context (and the one on which we concentrate for the rest of the book) is that of a *repetitive choice among alternatives.* In this context, fairness means that having to repeatedly choose among a set of alternatives, no alternative will be postponed forever. Such choices may occur on many occasions:
  - i. In a nondeterministic program, the choice as to which alternative to pursue next.
  - ii. In a multiprogrammed system, the choice as to which process should be granted the next allocated slice of processor-time.
  - iii. Generalizing (ii), in a resource-allocation system, the choice as to which user should be granted a resource next. In this context, the problem is occasionally referred to as "freedom from starvation".
  - iv. In a mutual exclusion system, the choice of which process should be granted entry next.
- Another important family of contexts involves the issue of *idling,* also known as *finite delay.*
  - i. In a resource-allocation system, a user "stuck" without the resource, will eventually proceed.
  - ii. In using synchronization primitives such as semaphores, critical regions, monitors, entry calls, etc. no process will wait forever while other processes advance.
- In the context of unsynchronized communication, it is common to assume that each message sent will eventually arrive at its destination.
- In data-flow computations and related contexts, one often encounters the problem of a *fair merge,* where several infinite sequences are merged into one, and no input sequence should have an infinite tail not appearing in the output.
- In the context of *repeated retrial,* one assumes that eventually one trial will be successful. This is a classic assumption in many network protocols for remote communication.
- Related to the previous issue is an assumption basic to fault tolerance: no fault occurs infinitely often.

As mentioned above, these, and several others, are all aspects of the same basic phenomenon. Had formal models been given to them, one could reduce them all to the first one, which is chosen in this book to be formally modeled and investigated.

0.2 A Taxonomy of Fairness Concepts

Since *fairness* is used as a generic name for a multitude of concepts, it is useful to distinguish more carefully between them. In this section we informally describe several of them. Formal definitions are given in later chapters and sections.

A basic property that distinguishes a subclass of fairness notions is that of *eventuality:* fairness is defined as a restriction on some infinite behavior according to *eventual occurrence* of some events. In this book, we shall be concerned *only* with these. At the end of this taxonomy we briefly describe some fairness notions that do not fall under this category.

A common property of the fairness notions *within* this category is that they all imply that, under certain conditions, each of a number of alternative (or even competing) events occur infinitely-often in every infinite behavior of the system considered. Thus, whenever such an event occurs, it is bound *eventually* to occur again. Obviously, the concepts of "behavior", "event" and "occurrence", as well as "alternative", are all taken in an informal sense, since their exact definition depends on the model of computation and programming language constructs used. Within this category, we may distinguish three main subclasses, depending on the condition guaranteeing the eventual occurrence.

i. Unconditional Fairness. As suggested by its name, this kind of fairness implies that for each behavior each event occurs infinitely often without any further qualification. This is a strong requirement, which fits situations where every event can unconditionally occur. In a more refined situation, where an event occurrence can be either *enabled* or *disabled,* unconditional fairness is not a useful requirement. As an example of a programming context in which it is useful, consider multiprogrammed *non-communicating concurrency: n processes,* totally independent of each other, conceptually are executed in parallel but use one common processor. An event is the execution of an atomic step in one process. In this case, unconditional fairness means that along an infinite execution each process is allocated processor-time infinitely many times. Note, in particular, that nothing (except finiteness) is assumed about the length of the interval between consecutive processor-time allocations to any given process, or about the length of time the processor is allocated to any given process. Such measures transcend the eventuality-kind of fairness assumed here.

In a "fair carpool", for example, this kind of fairness implies (assuming that every driver shows up every time) that each driver will drive infinitely often.

Another characterization of the same behavior is that of an "even dice", by which every face will appear infinitely often in any infinite sequence of throws.

ii. Weak Fairness. A more interesting concept takes into account an *enabledness* of the relevant events. Thus, in a carpool, if some driver is occasionally sick, it is no excuse for relieving any other driver of his duties.

In concurrent programming, most often processes are communicating with each other and may need to synchronize by waiting for some condition on their state to become true. Or processes may compete for resources, thereby delaying each other. For example, for mutual exclusion, processes may compete to enter a "critical region". According to *weak fairness,* an event will not be indefinitely postponed provided that it remains *continuously enabled* from some time instant until occurring. Weak fairness is most often associated with busy waiting, or simple queue-implementations of scheduling or resource-allocation: once a process has entered a queue, it stays there until it is scheduled or forever, if this never happens. . . A weakly-fair scheduler will guarantee eventual exit of every *process entering* such queue. Thus, every driver showing up continuously will eventually have to drive. . .

Consider a similar situation where processes are queued for entry to a "conditional critical region" or a semaphore passage. A "malicious" scheduler may cause a process to leave the waiting queue only to find out that the condition for region entry is false, or the semaphore is zero, at that moment. To prevent this kind of malicious scheduling, we have

iii. Strong Fairness. Strong fairness guarantees eventual occurrence under the condition of being *infinitely-often enabled,* but not necessarily continuously. Thus, if the semaphore is positive infinitely often, each waiting process will eventually pass it. Similarly, if the critical region's entry condition is true infinitely often, each attempting process will eventually enter it. Such a policy is tricky to implement, but is the needed abstraction in many cases.

Strong fairness arises also when a process may wait disjunctively for *one* of a set of enabled events to occur, with the occurrence of one canceling the readiness to accept others. This occurs in constructs like CSP's guarded commands or ADA's *select* construct.

These three levels may be also distinguished within *equifairness.* This is a stronger notion, requiring an even higher commitment of the scheduler: not only does each event occur infinitely often, but among each subset of *jointly-enabled* events, it is infinitely often the case that the numbers of occurrences of each event in the subset are equal. This is a useful concept when roughly equi-fast processors assigned to different processes. Though this seems to be a somewhat more quantitative requirement, note that nothing is assumed about the length of intervals between consecutive equalizations. Other state-dependent properties may replace equality, generating various generalizations of fairness.

Another criterion for distinction between fairness notions within the category of eventualities arises in case the events considered are not flat, but rather have a hierarchical structure. For example, in a language for concurrent programming, one level of alternation might be to choose a process to execute its next step, while within each process there might be an internal choice as to which step is the next. Or in case of guarded loops, there may be *nesting of tests* within a guarded command. In this case, one can distinguish between *top-level* fairness, flattening the events as far as fairness is considered, and *all-levels* fairness, taking into consideration simultaneously all levels of nesting. We shall deal mainly with the first, and devote only one section to the second.

Another interesting family, *extreme fairness,* arises when one distinguishes among conditions holding at the time of an occurrence of an event and requires infinitely many occurrences for each condition that held infinitely often at times of enabledness. This turns out to be a natural approximation to *probabilistic properties* of programs, which are independent of *specific probability distributions* among alternative event occurrences.

One way of relaxing pure eventualities is to take relative ordering into account. The most frequently encountered example of such fairness requires an "order of arrival", where events occur in the order they become enabled. This is also a by-product of queue implementations.

A much more demanding order-oriented fairness property is the requirement that any finite sequence (though sometimes of bounded length) occur infinitely often. A simple example (J.A. Makowsky) is a "fair Billiard game", in which it is not the case that player A always plays immediately after player B, who is the *worst* player at the table. Thus, the relative order permutes infinitely often. This is called "absolute fairness" in [QS 82], where a distinction is also made between fairness with respect to transitions vs. fairness with respect to state predicates reachability. The second is shown capable of simulating the first using auxiliary variables.

Obviously, eventualities are not the only possible kind of fairness properties. More quantitative methods exist, based on more "economic-oriented" approaches. One can start with "bounded-delay" fairness, in which there exists a (hopefully "small") bound on the length of the interval between consecutive occurrences of the same event. These fairness properties occur in many real-time applications, where time really matters.

Other approaches require even more: a "weight", or "price" , is introduced with the resources, whose integral is required to become 0 infinitely often–something like a "fair loan", where there is an advantage of first getting the money and only later returning it. In term of the carpool, one could have a (person $\times$ mileage) measure to optimize in some way (see [FW 82] for an "economically fair" car-pool algorithm).

In this book, we confine our attention to eventualities only, since we are not interested in analytic methods, but rather discrete ones. For convenience and uniformity, we select one representative property, that of *termination,* as a prototype property on which the effects of fairness are studied. It is known that other properties such as reachability, starvation-freedom, finite delay, etc. (mentioned in the previous subsection) can all be reduced to termination of derived programs. This reduction will be explicit in our treatment of strong fairness.

0.3 The Language of Guarded Commands (*GC*)

In this section we define the programming language used throughout most of the book for describing nondeterministic programs. It is known as the language of *guarded commands* (*GC*) [DIJ 75, DIJ 76]. There are several reasons for preferring this language in the context of our study:

a. It is concise, concentrating on the issues of nondeterministic choice among alternatives and avoiding more general features that might be useful in "real" programming, but are irrelevant in our context.
b. It has well-defined semantics, definable by several of the current methods of defining the semantics of programming languages.
c. It is well-known in the research community of the theory of programming and programming languages.
d. It has had an extensive influence on the development of programming languages for concurrent and distributed programs.

We start by specifying the syntax of *GC* using standard BNF notation. We deviate from its original syntax, and use a more concise version, inspired by CSP [HO 78], as shown in the table *GC*_SYNTAX in Figure 0.1.

```
<statement>::=<assignment>|skip|<selection>|<repetition>
                                           |<composition>
<composition>::=<statement>;<statement>
<assignment>::=<variable>:=<expression>
<selection>::=[<Boolean-expression> → <statement>
              {[]
              <Boolean-expression> → <statement>}*
              ]
<repetition>::=*<selection>
```

Figure 0.1 *GC*-SYNTAX.

Remarks About the Syntax: We do not further specify the structure of variables, expressions and Boolean expressions. We assume that expressions are *terms* in an underlying, uninterpreted *signature* containing constants, function symbols and predicate symbols. We assume the existence of two Boolean constants **true** and **false.** In the examples, we usually use simple variables and the signature of Arithmetic (addition, multiplication, equality, etc.). We are concerned with a typical repetitive statement, which will be denoted by

$$S{::}\ *[B_1 \rightarrow S_1\ [\,]\ \cdots\ [\,]\ B_n \rightarrow S_n],$$

often abbreviated as

$$S{::}\ *[\ \underset{i \in I}{[\,]}\ B_i \rightarrow S_i]\ ,\quad \text{where } I = \{1,\ \cdots\ ,n\}, \text{ for some } n \geqslant 0.$$

In case $n = 0$, S is identified with *skip.*

The Boolean expression B_i, $i \in I$, are referred to as *guards.* We find it convenient to add some redundancy to the syntax, considering a repetition of the form $S{::=}\ *[\ \underset{i \in I}{[\,]}\ i{:}\ B_i \rightarrow S_i]$. We refer to $i{:}\ B_i \rightarrow S_i$ as the i-th *direction* in S, and occasionally also as the i-th *move.*

We now turn to the *semantics* of *GC.* We assume an implicit *interpretation* **I,** which assigns in a standard way functions to the function symbols, predicates to the predicate symbols, etc., over a *domain.* Since the details of the underlying interpretation are irrelevant, we do not explicitly refer to them in the discussion to follow.

Definition: A *state* is a mapping from the family of variables to their domain of interpretation.

We use lower case Greek letters σ, ξ, to denote states. For a fixed *GC* program S, we denote by Σ_S the collection of all possible states of S. We assume that a fixed state **fail** is included in Σ_S, for any S, mapping each variable to an element in the domain of interpretation also denoted by **fail.** When S is clear from context, we use Σ. We use $\sigma[x]$ to denote the value of x in state σ. Similarly, for an expression e, $\sigma[e]$ denotes the value of e in state σ.

Definition: A guard B is *enabled* in a state σ, iff $\sigma[B]$ is true, denoted by $\sigma \models B$. Given the signature, there is a standard inductive definition for defining the truth of Boolean (quantifier-free) expression, which is omitted here. A guard **true** is always enabled (i.e. in any state $\sigma \in \Sigma$), while a guard **false** is never enabled.

Definition: For a state σ and term e, the *variant* state $\sigma' = \sigma[e/x]$ is the state given by

$$\sigma'[x] = \sigma[e]$$

$$\sigma'[v] = \sigma[v], \quad \text{for any variable } v \text{ other than } x.$$

We now describe informally the semantics of a *GC* program. The meaning of each statement is given relative to an *initial state* σ_0.

assignment: The meaning of $x := e$ is assigning to x the value $\sigma_0[e]$, creating the variant state $\sigma' = \sigma_0[e/x]$.

skip: This statement "does nothing"; the final state is equal to the initial state.

composition: The meaning of $S_1;S_2$ is executing S_1 in σ_0, and if it terminates in a state σ', executing S_2 in σ'. If S_1 does not terminate on σ_0, neither does the composition. Note that since nondeterminism is involved, S_1 may be executed (starting in σ_0) in several ways, resulting possibly in different final states.

selection: Here nondeterminism emerges. Let S:: $[\ \underset{i \in I}{[]}\ i\text{: } B_i \rightarrow S_i\ ]$. In order to execute S in σ_0, first determine $A = \{i \in I \mid \sigma_0 \models B_i\}$ i.e. the set of all guards enabled in σ_0. If $A = \emptyset$, the final state is **fail.** Otherwise, an *arbitrary* $i \in A$ is selected and S_i is executed on σ_0. No assumptions are made about the element of A chosen.

repetition: Let S:: $*[\ \underset{i \in A}{[]}\ i\text{: } B_i \rightarrow S_i\ ]$ be a repetition statement. To execute S, first determine A as above. If $A = \emptyset$ execution terminates, resulting in the initial state as the final state. Otherwise, again an arbitrary $i \in I$ is selected, S_i is executed in σ_0, resulting in some state σ', for which the *whole procedure is repeated.* Note that multiple choices of elements of A (possibly infinitely many) occur, and again no assumption is made about this sequence of choices.

The purpose of the book is to study the effect of adding such assumptions.

In the literature on semantics of programming languages, there are numerous ways of formally defining the semantics of *GC* programs, with and without reference to the operational interpretation of execution. The original semantics was introduced by means of *weakest-precondition* predicate-transformers [DIJ 75, DIJ 76]; later, denotational approaches using *power-domains,* various operational semantics, and others (see [deB

80] for formal definitions of the semantics of "standard", unfair nondeterminism), were developed.

For our purposes, we assign a semantics to *GC* by which every pair S,ξ_0, where S is a *GC* program and ξ_0 is an initial state , is mapped into a *tree* $T_S(\xi_0)$ reflecting all possible executions of S beginning in ξ_0, especially all the nondeterministic choices involved.

Intuitively, for a typical repetition statement $S{::}\ *[\ \underset{i\in I}{[]}\ i{:}\ B_i \rightarrow S_i]$, the tree $T_S(\xi_0)$ should have the form as in Figure 0.2.

Here $A = \{i \in I \mid \xi_0 \models B_i\} = \{i_1, \cdots ,i_k\}$ is the index-set of all guards satisfied by ξ_0. The states ξ'_j, ξ''_j are leaves of the subtrees T_j, $1 \leqslant j \leqslant k$, what represents all the terminating computations of S_j on ξ_0. These subtrees may contain infinite paths, in case S_j has non-terminating computations on ξ_0. Every leaf ξ_j of T_j has as a subtree the tree $T_S(\xi_j)$ representing the execution of the "rest of the loop S" (after one iteration) on ξ_j. This reflects the circularity in defining the semantics of iteration (or recursion).

Thus, the nodes of the required trees are labeled with states, while the arcs are labeled with direction-indices. A node labeled with a state (associated with the looping point) has a subtree for each direction enabled at that state. We use π to denote paths (finite or infinite) in computation trees. With every (finite or infinite) path in $T_S(\xi_0)$

$$\pi : \xi_0 \underset{i_0}{\rightarrow} \ldots \xi_j \underset{i_j}{\rightarrow} \xi_{j+l} \rightarrow \quad \cdots$$

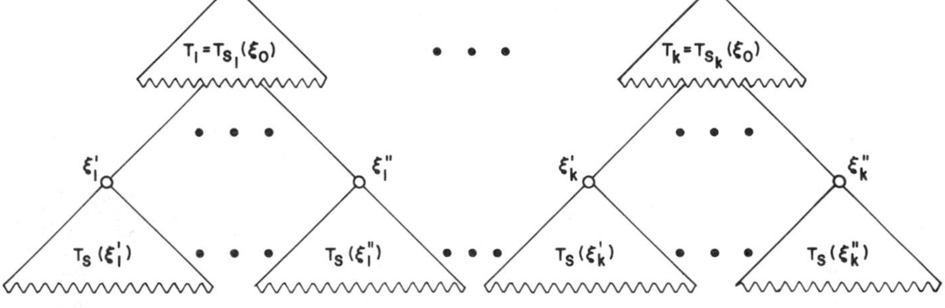

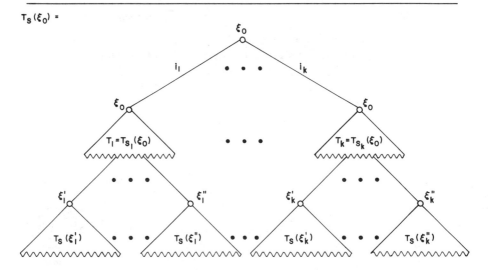

Figure 0.2 The tree $T_S(\xi_0)$. [GFMR 81].

we may associate a corresponding computation of S on ξ_0, where the ξ_j's are the intermediate states of the loop top level and the i_j's reflect the choices to resolve nondeterminism. We refer to such states, occurring at the top-level of S as *marked*, abstracting away from an explicit inclusion of a location counter as part of the state. In these terms, enabledness always refers to marked states. Nested loops have their own, independent, marking. For $j \geqslant 0$, ξ_{j+1} is *one of* the possible results obtained by executing S_{i_j} on ξ_j. Internal choices within S_{i_j}, similarly to intermediate states between ξ_j and ξ_{j+1} are "hidden" in this notation. In case some S_j has an infinite computation starting from some (marked) state ξ_k, which, therefore, is never reaching another marked state, we use the notation

$$\xi_0 \rightarrow \ldots \xi_k \rightarrow .$$

Obviously, a tree $T_S(\xi_0)$ is infinite if and only if S has a nonterminating computation on ξ_0. Note that the computation trees are *finitely-branching* (actually, *boundedly-branching* by $|I|$, the number of guards). Thus, by Konig's lemma [KO 27], $T_S(\xi_0)$ is infinite if and only if it contains an infinite path.

The discussion in the sequel does not depend on the exact machinery used to define such trees. The usual formal definition of $T_S(\xi_0)$ is by induction on the structure of S. We omit the (rather standard) details and present two examples instead.

Example: (random natural-number generator) Consider the program P (taken from [DIJ 76]) shown in Figure 0.3. Let the initial state be ξ_0: $x = 0 \wedge b = true$. Then the tree $T_P(\xi_0)$ is as in Figure 0.4. This program is non-terminating. For every $i \geqslant 0$ it contains a terminating computation ending with $x = i$ (and $b = false$), obtained by choosing i times direction 1 and then once direction 2. It also contains a nonterminating computation, choosing direction 1 forever. All these computations are reflected as paths in the corresponding tree.

Example: (4-sorting) As a second example, consider the program $S4$ (see Figure 0.5) over natural numbers (where simultaneous assingment is introduced for brevity, in its obvious interpretation). Let ξ_0 be the initial

```
P::*[1: b → x := x+1
     []
     2: b → b := false
    ].
```

Figure 0.3 Random-number generator.

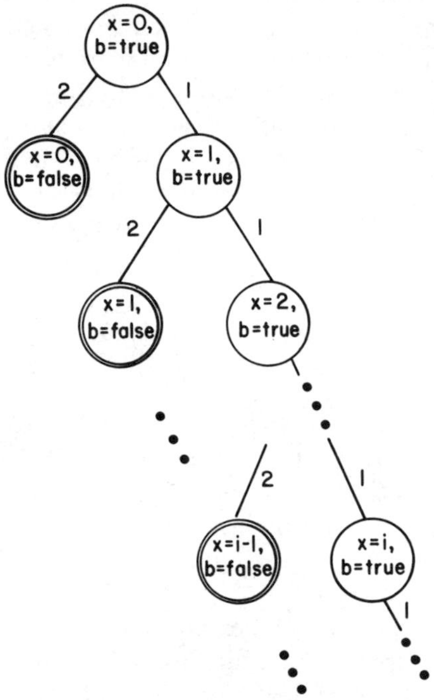

Figure 0.4 The tree $T_S(\xi_0)$.

state ξ_0: $x_1 = 1$, $x_2 = 4$, $x_3 = 3$, and $x_4 = 2$. Then, the tree $T_{S4}(\xi_0)$ is as in Figure 0.6, where states are represented as 4-tuples (x_1, x_2, x_3, x_4). As we shall prove later, $S4$ is a terminating program, and $T_{S4}(\xi)$ is finite for every $\xi \in \Sigma_{S4}$. It is easy to see that upon termination $x_1 \leqslant x_2 \leqslant x_3 \leqslant x_4$ holds.

Definition: For a given domain of states Σ, let $\mathbf{T}_\Sigma$ be the domain of all computation-trees over Σ.

```
S4:: *[1: x1 > x2 → (x1, x2) := (x2, x1)
      []
      2: x2 > x3 → (x2, x3) := (x3, x2)
      []
      3: x3 > x4 → (x3, x4) := (x4, x3)
      ].
```

Figure 0.5 Program $S4$.

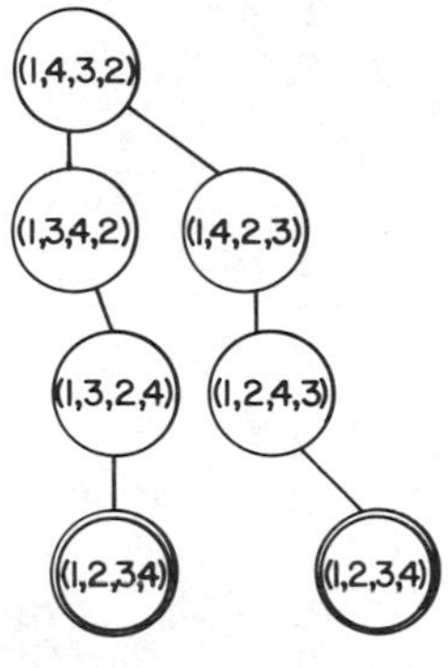

Figure 0.6 The tree $T_{S4}(\xi_0)$.

0.3.1 A partial-correctness proof system for *GC*

Since termination proofs need also some partial-correctness reasoning, involving establishing precondition-postcondition relationships, we make use of the following set of axioms and proof rules, without elaboration on their soundness and completeness. See [A 84] for details. We use the notation $\{p\}\ S\ \{q\}$ for a partial-correctness assertion, where: S is any *GC* program, p, q are predicates (over Σ_S) usually expressed in a first-order predicate logic (over the given signature) with equality, **L**.

Definition: $\models \{p\}\ S\ \{q\}$ holds (under an implicit interpretation **I** of **L**) iff for every computation tree $T_S(\xi_0)$: if $\xi_0 \models p$, then for every state ξ labeling a leaf of $T_S(\xi_0)$, $\xi \models q$ holds.

This definition conforms with the usual interpretation of truth of $\{p\}\ S\ \{q\}$: if p is satisfied by an initial state and the execution of S terminates, then q is satisfied by any final state.

*A*1. $\{p\}\ skip\ \{p\}$ (skip-axiom)

*A*2. $\{p_e^x\}x := e\{p\}$ (assignment-axiom)

where p_e^x is the predicate obtained by substituting e for all free occurrences of x in p. We assume that e is total.

$$(R1)\ \frac{\{p\}S_1\{r\},\{r\}S_2\{q\}}{\{p\}S_1;S_2\{q\}}$$ (composition-rule)

$$(R2)\ \frac{p \rightarrow \bigvee_{i=1,n} B_i,\ \{p \wedge B_i\}S_i\{q\}, i=1, \cdots, n}{\{p\}[\ \underset{i=1,n}{[\,]}\ B_i \rightarrow S_i]\{q\}}$$ (selection-rule)

$$(R3)\frac{\{p \wedge B_i\}S_i\{p\},\quad i=1,\ \cdots\ ,n}{\{p\}*[\ [\ ]_{i=1,n}B_i \rightarrow S_i]\{p \wedge \bigwedge_{i=1,n} \neg B_i\}} \qquad \text{(repetition-rule)}$$

(p is called the *loop invariant*)

$$(R4)\frac{p \rightarrow p',\quad \{p'\}S\{q'\},\quad q' \rightarrow q}{\{p\}S\{q\}}. \qquad \text{(consequence-rule)}$$

Note that by this rule, all the true statements (under the implicit interpretation) are axioms of our proof system.

Definition: $\vdash \{p\}S\{q\}$ iff there exists a proof using the axioms and derivation rules stated above of $\{p\}S\{q\}$.

In the examples, we reason freely about partial correctness and do not always bother about a presentation of the reasoning as a proof in the given system, but such a formalized proof always underlies the reasoning.

Note that partial-correctness properties are independent of any fairness assumptions, and hence the same deductive system for partial correctness is used across the whole discussion.

The reader is referred to [A 84] for a more detailed discussion (and examples) of partial correctness proofs for *GC* programs.

CHAPTER 1

Termination and Well-Foundedness

1.0 Overview

The original proof method for termination of programs originated in [FL 67], for a family of flowchart-like programs, and it still underlies proof-methods for more elaborate kinds of programs. The basic idea is to associate some kind of a *measure* or *ranking*, with intermediate states of a computation, *which decreases as the computation proceeds.* The ranking has to be such that *no infinite strictly decreasing sequence of ranks is possible.* As a result, no infinite computation is possible.

We start by reviewing some of the basic notions involved. Then the original Floyd-method is explained in terms of a deterministic sub-language of *GC*, after which the method is extended to nondeterministic *GC* programs.

Definition: For a set A, a relation $R \subseteq A \times A$ is a *partial-ordering* of A, iff:

1) for every $a \in A$: aRa (reflexivity)
2) for every $a_1, a_2 \in A$: $a_1 R a_2 \wedge a_2 R a_1 \rightarrow a_1 = a_2$ (antisymmetry)
3) for every $a_1, a_2, a_3 \in A$: $a_1 R a_2 \wedge a_2 R a_3 \rightarrow a_1 R a_3$ (transitivity)

Furthermore, we say that R is a *total-ordering* of A in case

4) for every $a_1, a_2 \in A$: $\neg a_1 R a_2 \rightarrow a_2 R a_1$.

We use $\leqslant$ as a generic partial-ordering in the sequel, and write $a_1 \leqslant a_2$ for $a_1 R a_2$, when the specific order involved is determined by context. We use $a_1 \geqslant a_2$ for $a_2 \leqslant a_1$ when convenient. The strict ordering corresponding to $\leqslant$ is denoted by $<$.

Definition: A partial ordering $\leqslant$ (over A) is *well-founded* iff there does not exist an infinite decreasing sequence of elements in A, i.e. a sequence

$$a_0 > a_1 > \cdots > a_i > \cdots .$$

This definition extends to an arbitrary relation $R \subseteq A \times A$, which is well-founded in case there exists no sequence $<a_i>$ $i = 0,1,\ldots$ such that $a_i R a_{i+1}$ and $a_i \neq a_{i+1}$, $i = 0, 1, \cdots$

Definition: An element $a \in A$ is *minimal* iff there exists no $a' \in A$ such that $a' < a$. We use 0 as a generic minimal element for any A.

For example, the natural numbers under the usual ordering are well-founded, while the rational numbers are not:

$$\left\{ \frac{1}{2} > \frac{1}{3} > \frac{1}{4} > \cdots > \frac{1}{n} > \cdots \right\}.$$

In our context, we are interested in the "most general" well-founded set. This set is known in set theory as the *ordinals*, a natural generalization of the natural numbers. We briefly review here its construction and the intuition behind it. A comprehensive discussion of the ordinals, their properties and the *transfinite induction* induced by them may be found in the standard mathematical literature on set theory.

The basic idea results from viewing *N*, the set of natural numbers, as a *set of sets*. Consider the following recursive definition:

$$0 \overset{def.}{=} \emptyset$$

$$n + 1 \overset{def.}{=} n \cup \{n\}.$$

It is easy to verify by ordinary induction that one gets, for every $n \geqslant 0$,

$$n = \{0, 1, \cdots, n - 1\}.$$

Using this observation, it is possible to construe the usual ordering of *N* as:

$$m < n \quad \textit{iff} \quad m \in n.$$

Thus, the well-foundedness of *N* under its natural ordering is cast as the *transitivity* of the set membership relation ϵ on the "new" *N*. This is possible in view of the following transitivity property of the "new" natural numbers, induced by the definition:

$$x \in y \in z \rightarrow x \in z, \qquad x, y, z \in N.$$

This viewpoint can be extended by looking for a most general transitive set of sets. Indeed, *N* itself is transitive, and we may define

$$\omega \overset{def.}{=} \cup_{n \in N}\, n = \{0, 1, \cdots \}.$$

Thus, we can identify two basic operations taking part in extending this sequence. The first is the *successor*, obtained by unifyng any member with the singleton set of that member; the second is the *limit*, obtained by taking the union of all smaller elements (than a given one). Continuing this way, we obtain

$$\omega + 1 \stackrel{def.}{=} \omega \cup \{\omega\} = \{0, 1, \cdots, \omega\},$$

$$\omega + 2 \stackrel{def.}{=} \omega + 1 \cup \{\omega + 1\} = \{0, 1, \cdots, \omega, \omega + 1\}.$$

In the next limit step we obtain

$$\omega + \omega \stackrel{def.}{=} \cup_{n \in \omega} \omega + n = \{0, 1, \cdots, \omega, \omega + 1, \omega + 2, \cdots\}.$$

This procedure can be carried out indefinitely. We thus take as the ordinals the set of all ϵ*−transitive* sets, well-ordered by $\in$. In other words,

$$\alpha < \beta \ \textit{iff} \ \alpha \in \beta.$$

1.1 Termination Proofs for Deterministic Programs

In order to present (a variant of) Floyd's original rule, we consider GC_D (deterministic guarded commands), a sublanguage of GC with the following two restrictions:

(1) every repetition statement is of the form $*[B \rightarrow S]$ i.e. has one alternative only,
(2) every selection statement is of the form

$$[B \rightarrow S_1 \ [\,] \ \neg B \rightarrow S_2].$$

(Alternatively, one could impose the restriction $B_i \wedge B_j \equiv false$, $1 \leqslant i \neq j \leqslant n$, on the original formulation).

It can clearly be seen that for $S \in GC_D$ and any $\xi \in \Sigma_S$, the tree $T_S(\xi)$ degenerates to a single (possibly infinite) path.

Since only the repetition statement is a source of nontermination, we alter the rule concerning it, as explained intuitively above. We introduce the following notation, where p, q are as in the partial-correctness case, $S \in GC_D$.

Definition: $\models <p> S <q>$ holds (under the underlying interpretation **I** of the given signature) iff every computation tree $T_S(\xi_0)$, where $\xi_0 \models p$, is *finite* and ξ', the state labeling its leaf, satisfies $\xi' \models q$. We call $\models$ $<p>\ S\ <q>$ a *total-correctness* assertion.

Lemma: $<p>\ S\ <q>\ \equiv \{p\}\ S\ \{q\}\ \wedge\ <p>\ S\ <true>$.

Proof: Immediate from the definitions. []

In view of the (relative) completeness of the system for partial correctness, it is enough to consider assertions of the form $<p>\ S\ <true>$, called *termination assertions,* as we do in most examples. Let $S{::}\ *[B \rightarrow S_1]$. We obtain the rule **DT** shown in the table in Figure 1.1.

Thus, in order to establish termination of S, we have to find a partially-ordered, well-founded set W, and an invariant *pi* parametrized by elements of W, that is established by the initial state (INIT), that implies that the computation may proceed as long as the parameter is not a minimal element (CONT), that implies termination when the parameter is a minimal element (TERM), and, most importantly, is preserved with a *strictly smaller* value of the parameter after each traversal of the body S_1 (DEC).

Note that in (DEC) the two occurrences of ξ refer, respectively, to an initial state and final state in an execution of S, which are traditionally denoted by the same state-variable, always denoting a "current state". On many occasions, the state-variables are completely omitted and left implicit. Remember that 0 denotes a generic minimal element in W, without loss of generality. Requiering termination only upon reaching a minimal value in the well-founded set is only a matter of convenience. Note also, that S_1 may contain nested repetition statements, and (DEC) will generate a subproof.

For several examples of termination proofs of deterministic programs, the reader is referred to [MA 74].

Notation: If, for a GC_D program S, a proof of $<p>\ S\ <q>$ using the **DT**-rule exists, we denote it by $\vdash_{\mathbf{DT}} <p>\ S\ <q>$ (of course, the whole system for partial correctness might be used while proving termination).

To prove $<p>\ S\ <q>$:

Find a well-founded, partially-ordered, set $(W, \leqslant)$, and a *parametrized-invariant* $pi{:}\Sigma_S \times W \rightarrow \{true, false\}$, satisfying:

1. (INIT) $p(\xi) \rightarrow \exists w{:}\ pi(\xi, w)$.
2. (CONT) $pi(\xi, w) \wedge w \neq 0 \rightarrow B$.
3. (TERM) $pi(\xi, 0) \rightarrow (\neg B \wedge q)$.
4. (DEC) $<pi(\xi, w) \wedge w \neq 0 \wedge B>\ S_1\ <\exists v{:}\ v<w \wedge pi(\xi, w)>$.

Figure 1.1 Rule **DT** (deterministic termination).

Theorem: (soundness of the rule DT) For a typical repetition statement $S \in GC_D$

$$\text{if } \vdash_{\mathbf{DT}} <p>\ S\ <q> \text{ then } \models <p>\ S\ <q>.$$

Proof: Suppose, by way of contradiction, that $\vdash_{\mathbf{DT}} <p>\ S\ <q>$, but not $\models\ <p>\ S\ <q>$. By the soundness of the partial-correctness proof-system for *GC*, we may assume that $\models\ <p>\ S\ <true>$ does not hold. In other words, there exists an initial state ξ_0 satisfying p and an infinite computation of S on ξ_0, satisfying all clauses of the rule.

By (INIT), $pi(w_0)$ holds initially, for some $w_0 \in W$.
By (TERM), w_0 is not minimal (since the computation is infinite).
By (CONT), B holds.
By (DEC), after executing S_1 once, there exist a $w_1 < w_0$, satisfying $pi(w_1)$.
By induction, we obtain an infinite sequence of W-elements $w_0 > w_1 > \cdots$, all satisfying $pi(w_k)$, $k = 0,1, \cdots$ which contradicts the well-foundedness of W.

Hence, $\models\ <p>\ S\ <q>$ holds. []

The soundness theorem guarantees that whenever termination is established using the **DT**-rule, termination is indeed the case. An application of the rule is, thus, a sufficient condition for termination. We now show that the opposite also holds, and a successful application of the rule is also necessary for termination. Here we deal only with what is known as *semantic completeness*. We show that $(W, \leqslant)$ and $pi(w)$ exist satisfying all the clauses of **DT**, in the set-theoretical sense. In other words, we are interested here in *pi* as a set of pairs (ξ, w), and ignore the question of its *expressibility* in some formal assertion language. This kind of *syntactic completeness* is dealt with in a later chapter.

Theorem: (semantic completeness of the DT rule) For a typical repetition statement $S \in GC_D$

$$\text{if } \models <p>\ S\ <q> \text{ then } \vdash_{\mathbf{DT}} <p>\ S\ <q>.$$

Proof: Assume $\models\ <p>\ S\ <q>$. We have to find $(W, \leqslant)$ and $pi(w)$ satisfying all the clauses of the rule. Take $W = N$, the natural numbers, with $\leqslant$ their usual ordering. Let $T_p(S)$ be the family of all computation trees (paths, actually) of S whose root is labeled with an (initial) state satisfying p. By assumption, every such path $\pi \in T_p(S)$ has the form $\pi = \xi_0 \underset{S_1}{\rightarrow} \xi_1 \underset{S_1}{\rightarrow} \cdots \underset{S_1}{\rightarrow} \xi_i \underset{S_1}{\rightarrow} \cdots \xi_m$, for some $m \geqslant 0$. Since S is deterministic and terminates, $\xi_i \neq \xi_j$ whenever $i \neq j$ (otherwise, an infinite loop is inevitable). Also, if two different paths π, π', where

$$\pi = \xi_0 \to \xi_1 \to \cdots \to \xi_i \to \cdots \xi_m$$

$$\pi' = \xi'_0 \to \xi'_1 \to \cdots \to \xi'_i \to \cdots \xi'_{m'}$$

have a state in common, say $\xi_i = \xi'_{i'}$, then they have in common the tail from that state onwards, and $m-i = m'-i'$. Hence, the following ranking is well-defined:

$\rho(\xi) = k$ iff there exists a computation path of S on some initial state satisfying p on which the state ξ occurs at distance k from the leaf.

We may now define the parametrized-invariant as $pi(\xi, k) \overset{def.}{\equiv} (\rho(\xi) = k)$.

We now check that all the clauses of **DT** hold for the invariant as defined above:

(ad INIT) Take any initial state ξ_0 satisfying p. Let k be the length of the whole computation of S on ξ_0. Then, $pi(k)$ holds by definition.
(ad CONT) Assume $pi(k)$ for $k \neq 0$. Thus, the computation executes the loop body at least once more, hence B must be true on the state.
(ad TERM) Assume $pi(0)$. Since the state has no descendants, $\neg B$ must be satisfied.
(ad DEC) Assume $pi(k) \wedge k > 0 \wedge B$. Then, after another execution of the loop body, the resulting state is at distance $k' = k-1$ on the same computation path, hence $pi(k')$ holds. [ ]

Note that both theorems are independent of the underlying interpretation of the signature. As the completeness proof shows, the natural numbers are sufficient for termination proofs of deterministic programs.

The two theorems, formulated above for deterministic programs, are to be extended for a variety of fairness assumptions. We first extend the rule for (bounded) nondeterministic programs.

1.2 Termination Proofs for Nondeterministic Programs

In this section, we extend the basic idea of a well-founded ranking to nondeterministic programs, namely to full *GC*. We first recall that if a repetition statement S:: $*[\ \underset{i \in I}{[]}\ i\colon B_i \to S_i]$ does not terminate on an initial state $\xi_0 \in \Sigma_S$, then the computation-tree $T_S(\xi_0)$ has at least one infinite path. In other words, for a terminating S, all its computation trees are *finite*. This suggests

Definition: $\models$ $<p>$ S $<true>$ iff every $T \in \mathbf{T}_{\Sigma_S}$ having a root labeled with a state ξ_0 such that $\xi_0 \models p$, is a finite tree.

The basic idea of the proof-method extension is the following: *since any enabled direction may be chosen for execution (in each loop-traversal), show that the ranking decreases along every direction!*

Thus, we obtain the rule **NDT** shown in Figure 1.2.

Before presenting the soundness and semantic completeness theorems, we prove termination of the 4-sorting program $S4$.

Example: (termination of the 4-sorting program) Reconsider the program $S4$ in a previous example rewritten as

$$S4:: *[\ \underset{i=1,2,3}{[]}\ i: x_i > x_{i+1} \rightarrow (x_i, x_{i+1}) := (x_{i+1}, x_i)]$$

We want to establish $<true>$ $S4$ $<true>$ using **NDT**. Take as W the set of all quadruples of natural numbers $(x_1^0, x_2^0, x_3^0, x_4^0)$, ordered *lexicographically* among permutations and unrelated otherwise. Thus, the minimal elements are all the ordered permutations. We check that the clauses apply, with

$$pi(x_1^0, x_2^0, x_3^0, x_4^0) \overset{def.}{=} (x_1, x_2, x_3, x_4) \text{ is a permutation of } (x_1^0, x_2^0, x_3^0, x_4^0).$$

(INIT) choose $x_i^0 = \xi_0[x_i]$, the initial value of x_i.
(CONT), (TERM)–obvious.
(DEC)

$$< pi(x_1^0, x_2^0, x_3^0, x_4^0) \wedge x_i > x_{i+1} >$$

$$(x_i, x_{i+1}) := (x_{i+1}, x_i)$$

$$< \exists y_1, y_2, y_3, y_4: (y_1, y_2, y_3, y_4) < (x_1^0, x_2^0, x_3^0, x_4^0) \wedge pi(y_1, y_2, y_3, y_4) >$$

To prove $<p>$ S $<true>$:

Find a well-founded, partial ordered, set $(W, \leqslant)$, and a *parametrized-invariant* pi: $\Sigma_S \times W \rightarrow \{true, false\}$, satisfying:

1. (INIT) $p(\xi) \rightarrow \exists w: pi(\xi, w)$.
2. (CONT) $pi(\xi, w) \wedge w \neq 0 \rightarrow \bigvee_{i \in I} B_i$.
3. (TERM) $pi(\xi, 0) \rightarrow \neg \bigvee_{i \in I} B_i$.
4. (DEC) $<pi(\xi,w) \wedge w \neq 0 \wedge B_i> S_i < \exists v: v<w \wedge pi(\xi, v)>, i \in I$.

Figure 1.2 Rule **NDT** (nondeterministic termination).

This obviously holds by choosing the y_j's as the "old" x_j's for $j \neq i,\ i+1$ and $y_i(y_{i+1})$ as the "old" $x_{i+1}(x_i)$, since the resulting permutation is lexicographically smaller, having $x_i < x_{i+1}$ where initially $x_i > x_{i+1}$ was the case.

One can choose a more "quantitative" measure, by defining

$$\rho(x_1, x_2, x_3, x_4) = \sum_{i=1,4} \delta_i,$$

where δ_i is the distance of x_i from its place in the ordered permutation of (x_1, x_2, x_3, x_4), and taking $W = \{0,1, \cdots ,8\}$ naturally ordered.

Theorem: (soundness of the NDT rule) For a typical repetition statement $S \in GC$

$$\text{if } \vdash_{\mathbf{NDT}} <p>\ S\ <true>, \text{ then } \models <p>\ S\ <true>.$$

Proof: Assume that $\vdash_{\mathbf{NDT}} <p>\ S\ <true>$ holds and $<p>\ S\ <true>$ is false, i.e. S has an infinite computation on some initial state ξ_0, such that $\xi_0 \models p$.

By (INIT), $pi(w_0)$ holds initially, for some $w_0 \in W$.
By (TERM), w_0 is not minimal.
By (CONT), for some B_{i_0}, $i_0 \in I$, is true.
By (DEC), there exists a w_1, $w_1 < w_0$, such that $pi(w_1)$ holds for the state resulting after executing S_{i_0}. By induction, we obtain the following decreasing sequence of elements of W:

$$w_0 > w_1 > \cdots > w_i > \cdots$$

such that $pi(\xi_j, w_j)$ and $\xi_j \underset{S_{i_j}}{\rightarrow} \xi_{j+1}$. This contradicts the fact that $(W, \leqslant)$ is well-founded. Hence, $\models <p>\ S\ <true>$. []

This establishes the sufficiency of a successful application of **NDT** for termination of a nondeterministic program. Once again, we turn our attention to the necessity.

Theorem: (semantic completeness of the NDT rule) For a typical repetition statement $S \in GC$

$$\text{if } \models <p>\ S\ <true>, \text{ then } \vdash_{\mathbf{NDT}} <p>\ S\ <true>.$$

Proof: We have to show the existence of a well-founded set $(W, \leqslant)$, and a $pi(w)$ (a set of pairs $<\xi, w>$), satisfying **NDT**.

The proof is similar to the **DT** case. For a computation tree $T_S(\xi)$, we define:

$\rho(\eta) = k$ if k is the maximal distance of nodes labeled η from a leaf in $T_S(\xi)$.

Thus, under the standard *GC* semantics, it is always possible to choose $W = N$ for **NDT**. The fact that an *apriori* bound on the size of the tree exists is crucial for this definition. This depends, by Konig's lemma [KO 27], on the fact that all trees in $\mathbf{T}_{\Sigma_S}$ are boundedly branching. Overcoming this restriction is a main theme in the sequel. Thus, the parametrized invariant is, once again, pi(ξ, k) $\overset{def.}{\equiv}$ $(\rho(\xi) = k)$. We leave out most of the details of showing that the **NDT** rule applies.

(ad DEC). If $pi(w) \wedge B_i$ holds for a non-minimal w, then by executing S_i we obtain a state labeling a subtree, with the maximal distance decreased at least by 1, reestablishing the invariant with a strictly smaller parameter.

Thus, $\vdash_{\mathbf{NDT}}$ $<p>$ S $<true>$ has been shown. []

We end this section with the following

Definition: ***NDT*** is the class of all terminating *GC* programs.

This class is properly contained in all the classes of fairly terminating *GC* programs defined in the sequel.

CHAPTER 2
The Method of Helpful Directions

2.0 Introduction to Fair Termination

In this chapter we extend the use of direct well-foundedness arguments to prove termination of *GC* programs under a variety of *scheduling policies* for repeated choices among the guards of a repetitive statement.

Recall that the basic proof principle **NDT** required a decrease in a well-founded ranking on *every* enabled direction. We shall relax this strict decreasing-requirement and replace it with the following intuitive alternative: At each intermediate stage of execution (of a typical repetition statement), choose a (nonempty) subset of I (called *helpful directions*) such that:

i. Whenever a helpful direction is taken, a well-founded ranking of the state decreases.
ii. The scheduling policy forces a helpful direction to be chosen eventually.

Thus, along an infinite computation adhering to the given policy, infinitely often a helpful direction must be followed, which would imply an infinite decreasing sequence of ranks, contradicting well-foundedness. It is due to this intuition that we coined the name in the chapter's title. The meaning of what we are doing is as follows: we are relativizing the notion of termination by making certain infinite sequences of the standard semantics as "not counting" and showing that all others, that do count, are finite. Had we a different semantics, which generates only these computations that adhere to the given scheduling-policy, then such a program would be properly terminating.

There are two possible natural ways of choosing the helpful directions at intermediate stages and both have been developed independently, about the same time.

i. The one bases the selection upon the *rank,* measuring some abstract "distance" from termination. Each rank will have its own set of helpful directions ([G 84], [GFMR 81]).
ii. The other is based upon a state predicate, and each such predicate determines directions which are "helpful" (i.e. cause a rank decrease) when it holds on a given state [LPS 81].

We present both methods as well as a mutual reduction among them. In a later chapter another solution to the same problem, based on a different intuition, is presented. We build the rules for three kinds of fair-scheduling policies gradually complicating the proof burden the rule has to meet.

Definition: For a typical repetition statement $S \in GC$ and an infinite path $\pi \in T_S(\xi)$ (for any initial state ξ): π is

1. *unconditionally fair,* iff *every direction* is chosen infinitely often along π.
2. *weakly fair,* iff *every direction continuously enabled* along π is chosen infinitely often along π.
3. *strongly fair,* iff *every direction infinitely-often enabled* along π is chosen infinitely often along π.

A *finite* path is unconditionally, weakly and strongly fair.

In the terminology of [LPS 81] these are: *impartial, just* and *fair,* respectively. We prefer our names, which occur more often in the literature.

It is instructive to describe explicitly the negations of the various fairness classes. Thus, a path π is *unconditionally unfair* iff it is infinite and contains only finitely many occurrences of some direction $i_0 \in I$. In other words, it contains a suffix (or tail) not containing *any* occurrence of direction i_0. We refer to such a π as *unconditionally* i_0*-unfair.* Furthermore, π is *weakly unfair* iff there is a direction $i_0 \in I$, that is continuously enabled along π but taken only finitely-often . Again, such a π contains a suffix along which direction i_0 is continuously enabled but *never taken.* Such a path is referred to as *weakly* i_0*-unfair.* Finally, π is *strongly unfair* iff there is a direction $i_0 \in I$ that is infinitely-often enabled along π but taken only finitely many times. Such a π contains a suffix along which direction i_0 is infinitely often enabled but *never* taken, referred to as *strongly* i_0*-unfair.* (Compare this definition with the taxonomy in the introduction.) Note that these definitions have a strong syntactic flavor in that fairness is confined to direction selections at a given syntactic location of the program. We shall later return to this issue.

Our aim is, for each such fairness criterion, to prove that a *given repetition statement S does not have infinite paths satisfying that fairness criterion.* Thus, under a semantics enforcing the policy determined by the given criterion, S is properly terminating.

Definition: A typical repetition statement $S \in GC$ is:

1. *unconditionally-fair terminating* (abbreviated ***UFT***), iff all the unconditionally-fair paths on any computation tree $T_S(\xi_0)$ are finite.
2. *weakly-fair terminating* (abbreviated ***WFT***), iff all the weakly-fair paths of any $T_S(\xi_0)$ are finite.
3. *strongly-fair terminating* (abbreviated ***SFT***), iff all the strongly-fair paths on any $T_S(\xi_0)$ are finite.

We use the notation $\ll p \gg S \ll \mathit{true} \gg$ as generic for fair termination of a *GC* program *S* (under a precondition *p*), and put **u**, **w** or **s**, as the case may be, to distinguish between the exact fairness assumed. Thus, we have

$$\overset{\mathbf{u}}{\ll} p \gg S \ll \mathit{true} \gg : \text{S is } \textbf{\textit{UFT}}.$$

$$\overset{\mathbf{w}}{\ll} p \gg S \ll \mathit{true} \gg : \text{S is } \textbf{\textit{WFT}}.$$

$$\overset{\mathbf{s}}{\ll} p \gg S \ll \mathit{true} \gg : \text{S is } \textbf{\textit{WFT}}.$$

Definition: A computation path $\pi \in T_S(\xi)$ is *i-avoiding* if it contains no occurrences of direction $i \in I$.

2.1 Ordinal Directed Choice of Helpful Directions

As mentioned in the Introduction, unconditional fairness is not very useful and is less frequently encountered. However, the proof rule corresponding to the termination property it induces will be basic for all the rest. Therefore, we start with its presentation.

2.1.1 A proof rule for unconditionally-fair termination

Example: Consider again Dijkstra's example program *P* for a random generator of natural numbers (in Figure 2.1). As argued before this is a possibly non-terminating program. It has only one infinite computation sequence, namely $(1)^\omega$. Obviously, this computation is not unconditionally fair, since direction 2 is never taken. Hence this program is ***UFT***. Had direction 2 been taken, *P* would immediately terminate. In this sense, direction 2 is "helpful".

The intuition behind the suggested proof rule is as follows: at any stage, let us *choose* the directions along which a certain well-founded variant decreases; let the other directions be non-increasing w.r.t. to that variant. Then, by the unconditional fairness assumption, eventually a decreasing

```
P:: x := 0; b := true;
  *[ 1: b → x := x+1
     []
     2: b → b := false
  ].
```

Figure 2.1 Dijkstra's example: random (natural) number generator.

move has to occur, since every direction is taken infinitely often. Thus, all unconditionally fair computation sequences are guaranteed to be finite. We generalize this reasoning to the following rule, **UFT** (see Figure 2.2). We also leave out all state arguments, which are implicit.

Here D_w stands for Decreasing (at "distance" w), while S_w stands for Steady (or, non-decreasing).

Explanation:

(ad 1–3) These clauses guarantee that the parametrized invariant is initially established and that the program terminates only when reaching a minimal element of $(W, \leqslant)$.

(ad 4) This clause guarantees that along every direction in D_w, if it is taken, then there is a decrease in the well-ordering. Note that at least one decreasing direction is required.

(ad 5) This clause guarantees that along every direction in S_w, if it is taken, there is no increase in the well-ordering. Thus, an infinite computation, proceeding along S_w directions only, and not decreasing, is possible. Such a sequence, however, is unconditionally unfair.

To prove $\overset{u}{\ll} p \gg S \ll true \gg$:

Choose a well-founded, partially-ordered, set $(W, \leqslant)$, a *parametrized invariant* pi: $\Sigma_S \times W \rightarrow \{true, false\}$ and, for each $w \in W$, $w > 0$, a partition of I into $\emptyset \neq D_w \cup S_w$, all satisfying:

1. (INIT) $p \rightarrow \exists w: pi(w)$.
2. (CONT) $(pi(w) \wedge w > 0) \rightarrow \bigvee_{i=1,n} B_i$.
3. (TERM) $pi(0) \rightarrow \neg \bigvee_{i=1,n} B_i$,
4. (DEC) $\overset{u}{\ll} pi(v) \wedge w > 0 \wedge B_j \gg S_j \ll \exists v: v < w \wedge pi(v) \gg$, for all $j \in D_w$.
5. (NOINC) $\overset{u}{\ll} pi(w) \wedge w > 0 \wedge B_i \gg S_i \ll \exists v: v \leqslant w \wedge pi(v) \gg$, for all $i \in S_w$.

Figure 2.2 Rule **UFT** (unconditionally-fair termination).

Remarks:

(1) If we take $S_w = \emptyset$ (and hence $D_w = I = \{1,\ldots,n\}$) for all $w \in W$, $w > 0$, the rule reduces to the usual termination rule **NDT**.

(2) In proving clauses (1)–(5) of the rule, application of the ordinary partial-correctness rules (for assignments, etc.) is allowed.

(3) Without loss of generality, since enabledness does not influence unconditional fairness, assume $B_1 = \cdots = B_n = B$.

We now present a formal **UFT** proof for *P* as above.

We prove $\overset{u}{\ll} true \gg P \ll true \gg$. Choose the well-founded set $W = \{0,1\}$ with $0 < 1$, $S_1 = \{1\}$, $D_1 = \{2\}$, and as the parametrized invariant

$$pi(x, b, w) \overset{def.}{\equiv} (w = 1 \to b) \wedge (w = 0 \to \neg b).$$

We now check that all clauses of the proof rule are satisfied.

Ad INIT: if $b = true$ holds initially, take $w=1$ to establish *pi*; otherwise, take $w=0$.
Ad CONT, TERM: immediate.
Ad DEC: *b* changes from *true* to *false* upon executing direction 2: $b := false$, and hence *w* drops from 1 to 0.
Ad NOINC: *b* remains *true* under direction 1: $x := x + 1$, and $pi(w)$ is independent of *x*, so *pi* stays true with $w = 1$.

Next, we prove the soundness of the suggested proof rule w.r.t. the computation trees, as before, and its completeness. We again do not deal in this section with the specification language needed to express $pi(w)$ and the partitions, an issue dealt with in a later chapter.

Theorem: (soundness of rule UFT) For a typical repetition statement $S \in GC$:

$$\text{if} \vdash_{\text{UFT}} \overset{u}{\ll} p \gg S \ll true \gg, \text{ then} \models \overset{u}{\ll} p \gg S \ll true \gg.$$

Proof: Assume that for a program *S* we have a well-founded, partially-ordered, set $(W, \leqslant)$, a partition of *I* into S_w, $D_w \neq \emptyset$ for each $w > 0$, and a parametrized invariant $pi(w)$ satisfying the clauses (1)–(5) of the UFT-rule.

Assume, by way of contradiction, that for some state ξ_0, $T_S(\xi_0)$ contains an infinite unconditionally-fair path with marked states $<\xi_i>_{i=0}^{\infty}$ (where ξ_i is the state after the i-th traversal of the body of *S*). Consider the corresponding sequence of directions taken, $<d_i>_{i=0}^{\infty}$. It cannot contain an infinite subsequence $<d_{i_j}>_{j=0}^{\infty}$ of *D*-moves, since by clause (DEC) this would imply the existence of an infinite decreasing sequence of elements in *W*, contradicting *W*'s well-foundedness. Thus from some *k* onwards, $pi(\xi_k, w)$ holds for the same $w \in W$, and all moves d_{i_j} for $j > k$ are S_w-moves (by clause (NOINC)), contradicting the assumption that $<\xi_i>_{i=0,\infty}$ is unconditionally fair. [ ]

Theorem: (semantic completeness of rule UFT) For a typical repetition statement $S \in GC$:

$$\text{if} \models \overset{\mathbf{u}}{\ll} p \gg S \ll true \gg, \quad \text{then} \vdash_{\overline{\mathbf{UFT}}} \overset{\mathbf{u}}{\ll} p \gg S \ll true \gg.$$

Proof: This part is harder. Assume $\overset{\mathbf{u}}{\ll} p \gg S \ll true \gg$ holds. Then we have to find a well-founded, partially-ordered, set $(W, \leqslant)$, partitions S_w, $D_w \neq \emptyset$ of I for each $w > 0$ and a parametrized invariant $pi(w)$ (given by a collection of pairs (w,ξ)) such that clauses (1)–(5) hold.

Since all we have at hand is the computation tree, we have to derive everything needed from that tree (compare also [deR 76] for another well-foundedness argument based on the operational object, the computation stack, for nondeterministic recursive procedures).

We are given that the computation tree $T_S(\xi_0)$, for every state ξ_0 satisfying p, either is finite or contains at least one infinite, hence unconditionally-unfair, computation sequence. The basic idea is to construct another (possibly countably infinitely branching) tree $T_S^*(\xi_0)$, some of whose nodes are obtained by collapsing certain infinite families of nodes in $T_S(\xi_0)$, all lying on unconditionally-unfair sequences originating in nodes $\xi \in T_S(\xi_0)$, such that $T_S^*(\xi_0)$ *is well-founded,* i.e. contains finite paths only. Then we use a standard ranking of $T_S^*(\xi_0)$ by means of (countable) *ordinals* to obtain the parametrized invariant. A direction originating in ξ and remaining in the same infinite family belongs to S_w, for the corresponding rank w. A move that leaves such a family belongs to D_w. Special care must be taken that these partitions do not depend on the initial state labeling ξ_0, the root of the computation tree. Rather, all the initial states satisfying the precondition should induce the same partitions, as the rule requires. We now present the details of the construction. Let $T_S(\xi_0)$ be given. Throughout, we refer to *marked* states, which are the only ones to be considered, as states.

Case (a): $T_S(\xi_0)$ is finite (this means that S always terminates in ξ_0, independently of any fairness assumptions). This reduces basically to **NDT**. Choose a ranking of the nodes by means of an initial segment of the ordinals (actually, of the natural numbers), ranking leaves by 0, and proceeding inductively level by level from leaves till root; furthermore, choose uniformly $S_w = \emptyset$, $D_w = I$ for $w > 0$. It is easy to verify that clauses (1)–(5) of the rule hold.

Case (b): $T_S(\xi_0)$ contains at least one infinite, hence unconditionally unfair, computation path π. This case is dealt with below.

Definition: Let $\xi \in T_S(\xi_0)$, $d \in I$. Define ξ's d-cone $CONE_d(\xi)$ as follows:
$CONE_d(\xi)$ = the set of all *occurrences* of states in $T_S(\xi_0)$ residing on infinite d-avoiding computation paths starting in ξ. Direction d is called the cone's *directive*.

A computation path is said to *leave* a d-cone $CONE_d(\xi)$ at node $\eta \in CONE_d(\xi)$, if the next (marked) state-occurrence of the path, following η, is outside $CONE_d(\xi)$. Recall that a move may consist of several arcs, passing through unmarked states. Only the final marked state is of concern here. In case a move does not reach any marked state (which happens when this direction contains an internal loop with an unfair computation), that move is considered as remaining within the cone.

Lemma: (cone-exit) Let $\xi \in T_S\ \xi_0)$, and let $\eta \in CONE_d(\xi)$ for some $d \in I$. Then, a computation sequence leaves $CONE_d(\xi)$ (at some node η) if and only if it is either finite or contains a d-move.

Proof: Suppose not. Then an infinite path π starts at η and contains d-move. Since $\eta \in CONE_d(\xi)$, there is some finite path π' joining ξ to η, along which no d-move was taken. Hence the concatenation $\pi'\pi$ is contained in $CONE_d(\xi)$, contradicting the assumption that π leaves $CONE_d(\xi)$ at node η.
The other direction is trivial. []

The situation is described in Figure 2.3, where a triangle denotes a finite tree. In the figure, η_1,η_2 are two occurrences of exit points from the cone (as stated in the cone-exit lemma). The state-occurrences ξ_1',ξ_2' are the ones resulting by the first move leaving the cone. Note that every path leaving the cone is either finite or contains a d-move, in accordance with the cone-exit lemma.

Next we define inductively a hierarchy **A** of families of states A_i, covering $T_S(\xi_0)$. Here i denotes the level at which the family A_i is defined. Actually, at each such level there may be countably many such A_i's. To simplify the notation we avoid the extra index distinguishing them, leaving the distinction to the context. The role of such a family A_i is to be contracted to a (single) node in the well-founded tree $T_S^*(\xi_0)$. Some A_i's are cones, while others, having no direction-avoiding infinite paths leaving them, are singletons.

Base Step: We distinguish between two possibilities:

(a) The root ξ_0 is the origin of a d_0-avoiding computation path, for some $d_0 \in \{1, \ldots, n\}$. In this case take $A_0 = CONE_{d_0}(\xi_0)$.
(b) Otherwise, take $A_0 = \{\xi_0\}$, a singleton.

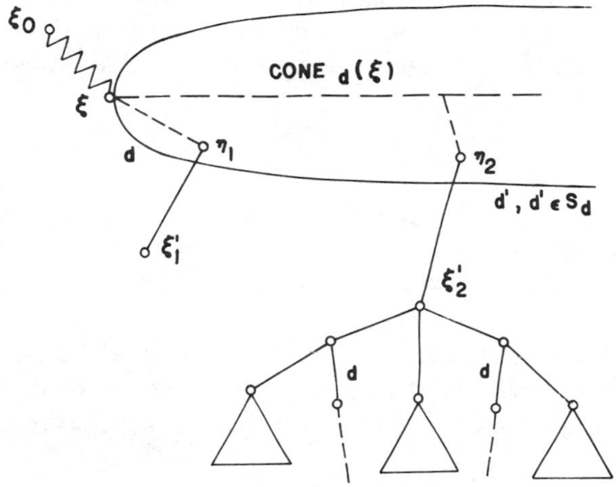

Figure 2.3 Cone exit [GFMR 81].

In both cases, we say that A_0 is at level 0, with root ξ_0.

Induction Step: Let A_i be at level i, with root ξ_i. We distinguish between four cases.

(a) $A_i = CONE_{d_i}(\xi_i)$ and π is an infinite path leaving A_i. By the cone-exit lemma it is not d_i-avoiding. Let ξ_{i+1} be the state resulting from the first d_i-move after π leaves A_i.
(b) $A_i = CONE_{d_i}(\xi_i)$ and π is a *finite* path leaving the cone. Let ξ_{i+1} be the first state after π left the cone.
(c) $A_i = \{\xi_i\}$ where ξ_i is not a leaf. Consider any ξ_{i+1} which is a child of ξ_i in $T_S(\xi_0)$.
(d) If $A_i = \{\xi_i\}$ and ξ_i is a leaf, A_i has no descendants.

After determining ξ_{i+1}, we again distinguish between two possibilities in constructing A_{i+1}.
(1) There is no infinite d-avoiding path originating in ξ_{i+1} for any $d \in \{1, \ldots, n\}$. In that case, let the singleton $A_{i+1} = \{\xi_{i+1}\}$ be a *descendant* of A_i at level i+1.
(2) Otherwise, consider the collection D of all d's for which there is an infinite d-avoiding path originating at ξ_{i+1}. Let d_{i+1} be the direction chosen least recently, possibly not at all, as a cone directive along $\xi_0 - \xi_1 - \cdots - \xi_{i+1}$, and define $A_{i+1} = CONE_{d_{i+1}}(\xi_{i+1})$ to be a descendant of A_i at level $i + 1$. In case of a tie, the direction with the smallest index is chosen. By "least recently" is meant, that if d has been chosen as a cone-direction at ξ_k, $0 \leqslant k \leqslant i+1$, then every other $d' \in D$ (and not d) has been chosen as a directive along

$\xi_{k+1}, \ldots, \xi_{i+1}$. Thus, when iterating, we vary the cone-directive maximally, which means that if some direction d may serve as a cone-directive again and again along some path, eventually it will be selected as such.

Remarks:

1. By assumption $T_S(\xi_0)$ is infinite, and therefore contains an infinite unconditionally-unfair path. Thus, this path has an infinite tail which is d-avoiding for some $d \in I$, and hence at least one A_i is a cone.
2. If some A_i is a cone it always has decendents (either cones or singletons), i.e. it is never a leaf in the contracted tree. This is important in establishing clause (4) of the rule. This does not hold when applying the cone construction to arbitrary programs (not neccessarily fairly terminating).

Lemma: (cone-chain) In the hierarchy **A** there does not exist an infinite sequence of descendant cones $CONE_{d_i}(\xi_i)$ s.t. $<\xi_i>_{i=0}^{\infty}$ reside on an infinite path of $T_S(\xi_0)$.

Remark: If we describe the construction of cones as in Figure 2.4, we have by the cone-chain lemma only finite chains of cones. It can be verified that all leaves are of the form $\{\xi_i\}$ (singletons, not cones).

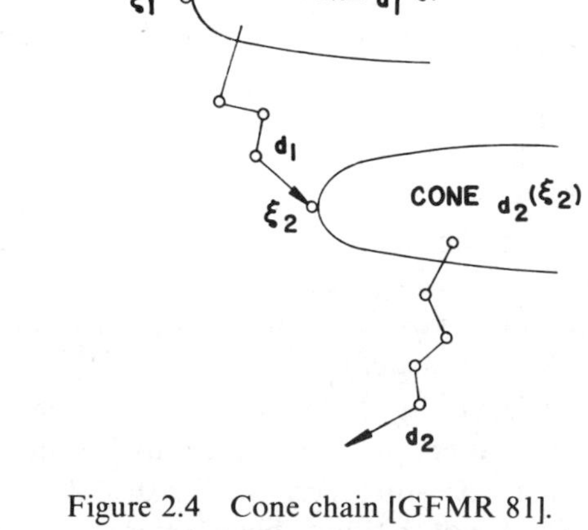

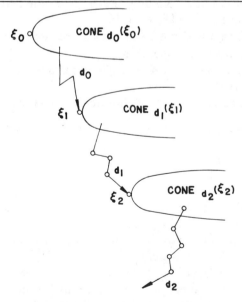

Figure 2.4 Cone chain [GFMR 81].

Proof: The main idea is to show that an infinite path cannot "cross" (enter and exit) infinitely many different cones. Rather, it has an infinite tail that remains within some cone. The proof utilizes the maximal variability as described in the inductive construction of **A**.

Suppose such an infinite sequence of states $<\xi_i>$, $i \geqslant 0$, exists. Then it is unconditionally-unfair by the assumption of unconditionally-fair termination of the given program. Thus, there is some $\bar{d} \in I$ s.t. the path $<\xi_i>$ is $\bar{d}$-unconditionally-unfair. Take the least such $\bar{d}$. Then there is an i_0 such that the infinite tail originating at ξ_{i_0} is $\bar{d}$-avoiding. Hence, there is also a $j_0 \geqslant i_0$, such that either $\bar{d}$ did not occur at all on the initial subpath $\xi_0 \to \ldots \to \xi_{j_0}$ or it occurred less recently than any other move. Hence $\bar{d} = d_{j_0}$ in the inductive construction of $CONE_{d_{j_0}}(\xi_{j_0})$, (by the directive choice criterion of maximal variability), and the path $<\xi_i>$ would have an infinite tail contained in $CONE_{d_{j_0}}(\xi_{j_0})$, contrary to assumption.

Now we define $T_S^*(\xi_0)$ as suggested above. Its nodes are all the families A_i in the hierarchic construction, and its edges are either original edges entering cones, or original edges leaving cones, and, otherwise, edges outside cones. By the cone-chain lemma, the tree $T_S^*(\xi_0)$ is well-founded, i.e. contains finite paths only (though, possibly, infinitely many of them). Note again that by the previous remark a leaf is never a cone.

In order to get rid of undesired ξ_0-dependence of W, S_w, D_w and pi, we do one more construction: Combine all the trees $T_S^*(\xi_0)$ s.t. $\xi_0 \models p$ into the infinitary well-founded tree T_S^* (see Figure 2.5).

Next, the nodes of T_S^* are ranked. All leaves are ranked with 0; an intermediate node is ranked with the successor of the least upper bound of the ranks of its (at most countably many) immediate descendants. Call this rank the *basic rank*

A problem that may arise, and has to be avoided, is the following: by the basic ranking of T_S^* it may be the case that two different nodes, being cones with *different directives,* have received the *same* rank. This would

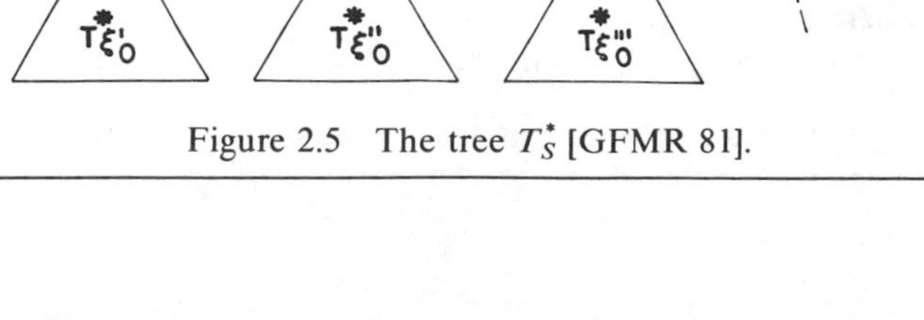

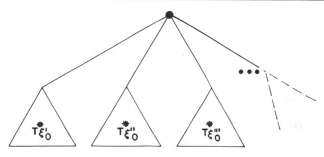

Figure 2.5 The tree T_S^* [GFMR 81].

destroy the uniqueness of the choice of the decreasing directions as depending on the rank only, required by the proof rule. Thus, uniqueness has to be restored.

In order to achieve this we perform a *rank-shift:* Suppose that at some level of the basic ranking, say λ, there are equiranked cones with different directives, say of ordertype α. Then rerank these consecutively by $\lambda+1, \ldots, \lambda+\alpha$, and proceed to the next level $\lambda+\alpha+1$.

Let ρ denote the resulting ranking function of T_S^*. Then we define the parametrized invariant *pi* and partitions (S_w, D_w) (see Figure 2.6). As W we choose the ordinals ranking T_S^*, an initial segment of the countable ordinals, with their usual ordering.

Thus, states are ranked according to the cone in which their occurrences reside, and $pi(w,\xi)$ may be satisfied by ξ with more than one w. Note that the rank-shift of T_S^* assures that S_w is well-defined, while the fact that **A** is a *cover* guarantees that *pi* is well-defined. []

Next, we show that clauses (1)–(5) of the rule **UFT** hold.

Lemma: *W, pi,* (S_w, D_w) satisfy clauses (1)–(5) of the rule **UFT**.

Proof: *Clauses* (INIT), (CONT), (TERM): immediate.

Clause (DEC): assume $pi(w) \wedge w > 0 \wedge B_i$ holds in ξ, for $i \in D_w$. Without loss of generality (by the rank-shift), assume $\xi \in T_S^*(\xi_0)$ and $p(\xi_0)$ holds. We distinguish between two cases:

a. There is a cone containing ξ and ranked w, say $CONE_d(\eta)$. In this case, $D_w = \{d\}$, and hence $i = d$. By the cone-exit lemma, the d-move leaves the cone at some $\delta \in CONE_d(\eta)$, and hence reached a state with a lower rank, since the ranking was bottom-up in T_S^*.

$$pi(\xi, w) \overset{def.}{\equiv} \exists\eta\colon \xi \in CONE_d(\eta) \wedge \rho(CONE_d(\eta)) = w$$
$$\vee$$
$$\forall\eta,d\colon \xi \notin CONE_d(\eta) \wedge \rho(\xi) = w.$$

and, for $w > 0$:

$$S_w = \begin{cases} S_d & \text{if } \exists\eta\colon \rho(CONE_d(\eta)) = w \\ \varnothing & \textit{otherwise} \end{cases}$$

where $S_d = I - \{d\}$.

Hence, $D_w = \{d\}$, a singleton set, or $D_w = I = \{1, \ldots, n\}$.

Figure 2.6 Parametrized invariant and partitions.

---

b. The state-occurrence ξ is not contained in a cone, and is ranked w. Hence $D_w = \{1, \ldots, n\}$, and indeed any enabled move leads to a descendant node with a smaller rank.

Clause (NOINC): assume $pi(w) \wedge w > 0 \wedge B_i$ holds in ξ, for $i \in S_w$. Again assume $\xi \in T_S^*(\xi_0)$ and $p(\xi_0)$ holds. Then $\xi \in CONE_d(\eta)$ for some η and d (since, otherwise, $S_w = \varnothing$), and $d \neq i$. If move S_i remains in the cone, by construction the rank remains the same. Otherwise, it leaves the cone, and hence the rank decreases.

Thus, we establish the applicability of **UFT**, and hence its semantic completeness. []

Applying the completeness to the tree $T_P(\xi_0)$ of the random natural-number generator example (with $\xi_0 \models x = 0 \wedge b = true$), yields the cone and exits in Figure 2.7, which yield the collapsed tree $T_P^*(\xi_0)$ in Figure 2.8.

In order to see that unconditional-fairness is not very useful in the context of nondeterminism (or concurrency, for that matter), consider the following *GC* program *F*:

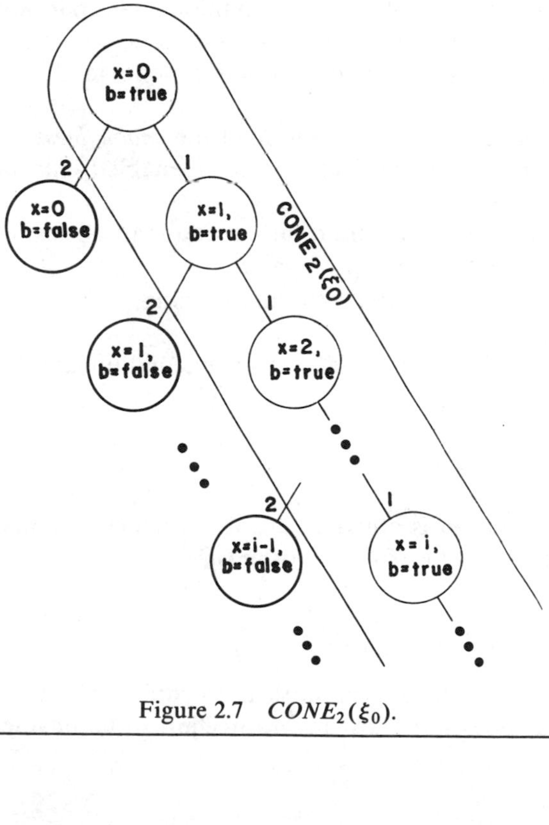

Figure 2.7 $CONE_2(\xi_0)$.

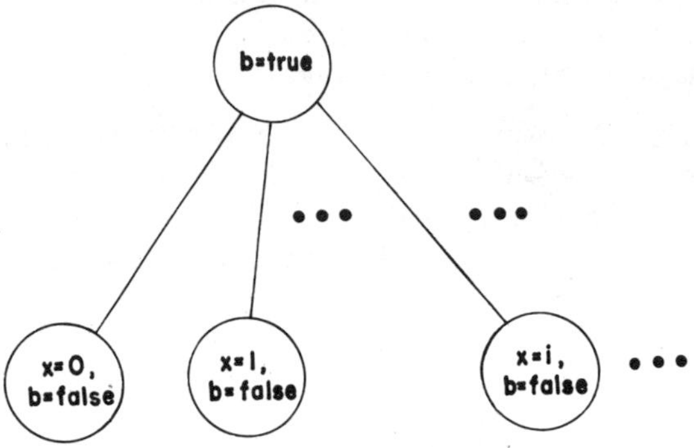

Figure 2.8 $T_P^*(\xi_0)$.

F:: *[1: *true* → *skip*
[]
2: *false* → *skip*
].

The program F is obviously nonterminating, but *is* ***UFT***! The only infinite computation of F (actually, the only computation at all) is 1^ω (note the state-independence), which is unconditionally-unfair, not having a single occurrence of direction 2. Applying our cone construction would collapse its whole computation into a single node in T_F^* (with countably many decendants).

The catch, of course, is the ignoring of the *enabledness* of the directions in the *UF*-policy. Direction 2 in F is *never* enabled, and no wonder it is never taken.

This motivates more elaborate fair-scheduling policies, which take into account the enabledness of the directions.

We sum up this subsection with the following:

Definition: Let ***UFT*** be the class of all unconditionally-fair terminating *GC*-programs.

Theorem: ***NDT*** $\subset$ ***UFT***.

Proof: Weak inclusion is obvious, and the strictness follows from the fact that the program P is in ***UFT*** but not in ***NDT***. []

2.1.2 Weakly-fair termination

In this section we are dealing with a scheduler that takes into account *enabledness*. It does not allow for a direction to be enabled continuously along an infinite computation, but only finitely often taken. Consider the program T in Figure 2.9.

This program is not in ***NDT***, since it has an infinite computation $(1)^{\omega}$. However, along this computation direction 2 is always enabled, and never taken; hence, it is not a *WF* infinite computation, and can be ignored. In a *WF* computation, direction 1 may be taken for a while, but eventually direction 2, continuously enabled, must be taken. It decreases x and, hence, is a helpful direction at this stage. Then both directions 1, 2 become disabled, but directions 3, 4 have the same relationship. Direction 4 is helpful; though it does not directly decrease x, it reenables the pair of directions $\{1, 2\}$, repeating the same behavior and eventually causing $x = 0$ to become true, terminating the program T.

Abstracting from this example, the intuitive factor to be included in a **WFT** rule is: show that for each infinite computation a helpful direction (at that stage) is *continuously enabled!*

We get the rule **WFT** in Figure 2.10.

Part i of **WFT** requires W, pi, D_w, S_w as for **UFT**; however, $pi(w)$ has to satisfy an additional property, guaranteeing *continuous-enabledness* (CE).

Theorem: (soundness of WFT) For a typical repetition statement $S \in GC$:

$$\text{if } \vdash_{\mathbf{WFT}} \overset{\mathbf{w}}{\ll} p \gg S \ll true \gg, \quad \text{then} \quad \models \overset{\mathbf{w}}{\ll} p \gg S \ll true \gg .$$

T:: $b := true$; $c := false$;
*[1: $b \wedge x > 0 \rightarrow skip$
[]
2: $b \wedge x > 0 \rightarrow b := false;\ c := true;\ x := x - 1$
[]
3: $c \rightarrow skip$
[]
4: $c \rightarrow c := false;\ b := true$
].

Figure 2.9 Program T.

To prove $\overset{\mathbf{w}}{\ll} p \gg S \ll true \gg$:

i. Prove clauses (1)–(5) of rule **UFT** are satisfied, with **w** replacing **u**.
ii. Show that the following additional clause holds:

6. (CE) $pi(w) \wedge w > 0 \rightarrow B_j$, for some $j \in D_w$.

Figure 2.10 Rule **WFT** (weakly-fair termination).

Proof: (D. Lehmann [LE 81]) Suppose there are $(W, \leqslant)$, pi, D_w and S_w satisfying all clauses of **WFT**. Let $\xi_0, \xi_1, \cdots, \xi_i, \cdots$ be a sequence of (marked) states (finite or infinite) describing a computation of S, starting in a state satisfying p. By (INIT) $\xi_0 \models pi(w_0)$ for some w_0. By (DEC), (NOINC) and (CONT) there is a non-increasing sequence: $w_0 \geqslant w_1 \geqslant \cdots \geqslant w_j \geqslant \cdots$ such that $\xi_j \models pi(w_j)$, and $w_{j-1} > w_j$ if the j-th move was from $D_{w_{j-1}}$. If the sequence is finite, the last state ξ_m satisfies $\neg \bigvee_{i \in I} B_i$ and, by (TERM), S terminates.

We must now show that no infinite execution of S may be weakly-fair. If the sequence of w_i's is infinite then, from a certain point onwards, they all are equal: $w_m = w_{m+1} = \cdots$. Therefore *no* move from D_{w_m} was taken an infinite number of times. Since D_{w_m} is not empty there is a $d \in D_{w_m}$ and move d was taken only a finite number of times. By (CE), since $\forall n \geqslant m$: $\xi_n \models pi(w_m)$ and $\xi_n \models \bigvee_{i \in I} B_i$, we have $\xi_n \models B_d$ for every $n \geqslant m$. This establishes the (weak) unfairness of the path. [ ]

Theorem: (semantic completeness of WFT) For a typical repetition statement $S \in GC$:

$$\text{if } \models \overset{w}{\ll} p \gg S \ll \mathit{true} \gg, \text{ then } \vdash_{\mathbf{WFT}} \overset{w}{\ll} p \gg S \ll \mathit{true} \gg .$$

Proof: We have to find, given that $\overset{w}{\ll} p \gg S \ll \mathit{true} \gg$, a parametrized invariant $pi(w)$, $w \in W$, a well-founded, partially ordered, set and partitions D_w, S_w of I for each $w > 0$, satisfying **WFT**.

The basic idea is to apply a similar construction to that in the completeness proof of **UFT** and "shrink" every $T_S(\xi_0)$ into a well-founded $T_S^*(\xi_0)$. However, we have to take care that the additional clause (CE) of *continuous-enabledness* is also satisfied. To achieve this, we slightly modify (but with significant consequences) the inductive definition of the cone chains.

We consider only d's for which there is an infinite d-avoiding path originating at ξ_i, *and along which d is continuously enabled.* This modification preserves the cone-chain lemma, and we can proceed as before.

The invariant π and partitions D_w, S_w are taken as before. Hence, all clauses of **UFT** hold. We now have to show that (CE) also holds, due to the change in the definition of cone chains. Suppose there is a $w > 0$, such that $pi(w)$ implies $\bigvee_{j \in S_w} B_j$, but not B_k, for any $k \in D_w$. Then, an infinite computation of S consisting solely of S_w moves (preserving $pi(w)$) will be weakly-fair, contradicting the assumption that no infinite weakly-fair computations of S (on p-initial states) exist. Thus, all clauses of **WFT** apply, and the rule is semantically complete. [ ]

We do not present concrete proofs applying **WFT**, since the next section contains several detailed proofs using the related rule **SFT** for strongly-fair termination.

We conclude this section by relating the termination classes discussed so far.

Definition: Let ***WFT*** be the class of all *WFT GC*-programs.

Theorem: ***NDT*** $\subset$ ***WFT*** $\subset$ ***UFT***.

Proof: Obvious. [ ]

2.1.3 Strongly-fair termination

In this section we consider proving termination under the assumption of strong-fairness, i.e. a direction is infinitely taken along an infinite computation if it is *infinitely-often enabled*, not necessarily continuously. To see the difference between weak and strong fair termination, consider the program C in Figure 2.11.

Consider the computation path $(1)^\omega$:

$$b = true,\ c = true \xrightarrow{1} b = true,\ c = false \xrightarrow{1} b = true,\ c = true \xrightarrow{1} b = true,\ c = false$$

Along this computation, the truth-value of c alternates between 'true' and 'false'. Therefore the guard of direction 2, namely $b \wedge c$, is not continuously enabled, and hence this infinite computation is weakly fair, and C *is not in* ***WFT***. On the other hand, it is the case that $b \wedge c$ is infinitely-often true along that computation; thus a strongly-fair scheduler would have necessarily taken direction 2, terminating C. Indeed, using the rule to be introduced in this section, we shall prove formally that C is in ***SFT***.

The rule is again based on the same intuition of choosing helpful directions (decreasing a well-founded variant); this time we have to add a clause that takes care of the new extra condition, namely infinitely-often enabledness. The basic new idea is to reduce an eventual-enabledness of a

---

```
C:: b := true; c := true;
          *[ 1: b → c := ¬c
             [ ]
             2: b ∧ c → b := false
          ].
```

Figure 2.11 Program C [GFMR 81].

---

helpful direction to (strongly-fair) termination of an auxiliary program. This program will have as its computations the subset of computations of the original program that advance only along S-moves, and *terminates as soon as a helpful direction is needed.* This is achieved by adjoining the negation of the disjunction of the guards of the helpful directions to the guard of every other direction. A variant approach for achieving the same goal, that turns to be more useful for other situations, is described at the end of this section. Thus, we obtain the rule **SFT** in Figure 2.12.

The role of the new clause is to establish an eventual enabledness of some decreasing direction in D_w, as long as $pi(w)$ holds. This ensures infinitely often enabledness of such a direction, or a decrease in $pi(w)$. It imposes a recursive application of the rule to an auxiliary program $\overline{S}_w$ (called also the *derived program*), and hence requires a subproof. The derived program $\overline{S}_w$ terminates because of one of two reasons:

(a) $\bigwedge_{i \in S_w} \neg B_i$ is true, hence no S_w- move is possible and (possibly) only D_w-moves are left.
(b) For some $j \in D_w$, B_j is true, i.e. a D_w- move is enabled. Hence, this clause guarantees that along infinite S_w-computations, D_w-moves are infinitely often enabled, that is, such computations are strongly-unfair. By convention, $\overline{S}_w = skip$ if $S_w = \varnothing$.

Note that the derived program has less guarded commands (directions) than the original one. This is why the proof itself terminates, not entering an infinite sequence of recursive applications of the rule. The similar problem for rules discussed in the sequel is handled in a more complicated way. A typical boundary condition in the chain of recursive applications of **SFT** is obtaining an empty program ($skip$), which terminates by definition. Other boundary conditions are obtaining a terminating (i.e. in ***NDT***) program and appealing to **NDT**, without generating a recursive application, or even obtaining a deterministic program and using **DT**.

Actually, the use of the derived program is a "coding trick" by means of which the eventual occurrence (of a condition) in one program is reduced to termination of another program. We appeal to it in order to remain strictly within the framework of termination. Furthermore, its use

---

To prove $\overset{\mathbf{s}}{\ll} p \gg S \ll true \gg$:

i. prove clauses (1)–(5) of rule **UFT** are satisfied, with **s** replacing **u**.
ii. prove the additional clause

6. (IOE) $\overset{\mathbf{s}}{\ll} pi(w) \wedge w > 0 \gg \overline{S}_w :: *[\underset{j \in S_w}{[]} (B_j \wedge \neg \bigvee_{k \in D_w} B_k) \rightarrow S_j] \ll true \gg.$

Figure 2.12 Rule **SFT** (strongly-fair termination).

---

depends on some "closure properties" of the underlying programming language (GC in our case), allowing the expression of the derived program. As we shall see in a later chapter, this "closure" property is a major obstacle to the direct adoption of the proof method to a language for concurrent programming. At the end of this chapter we introduce another technique for establishing IOE, which avoids the closure problem. For GC, the two techniques coincide.

We now proceed with some example proofs.

Example: Consider again the program C, in which *D-moves are only eventually enabled,* and clause (IOE) is indeed needed. We prove

$$\overset{s}{\ll} \textit{true} \gg C \ll \textit{true} \gg .$$

Choose W, pi, S_1, D_1, as for the unconditionally-fair termination of the random natural number generator. As for clause (IOE), the derived program is

$$\overline{C}_1 :: *[\ b \wedge \neg (b \wedge c) \rightarrow c := \ \neg c],$$

which is deterministic and terminates after one step at most. We omit details of subproofs, which reduces to use of **DT**.

This example is still trivial, but it should give the reader a feeling for the spirit of the rule, which captures eventual enabling of a D-move by means of a proof of termination of the derived program.

Example: Next, we consider an example program CC (see Figure 2.13) which displays a richer well-founded set and several different derived programs. Let x, y, z range over N.

To prove $\overset{s}{\ll} \textit{true} \gg CC \ll \textit{true} \gg$, choose $W = \omega + 1$, with $n < \omega$ for all $n \in N$,

$$pi(w, x, y, z) \overset{def.}{\equiv} (w = \omega \rightarrow x = 0) \wedge (w \neq \omega \rightarrow x \neq 0 \wedge y = w),$$

$$S_\omega = \{1,3,4\}, \qquad D_\omega = \{2\}, \qquad S_n = \{1,2,4\}, \qquad D_n = \{3\}.$$

For clause (IOE) we get as auxiliary programs CC_n, CC_ω (see Figure 2.14). Note the renumbering of alternatives.

```
CC:: x := 0; y := 0;
  *[ 1: x=0 → y := y + 1 [] 2: x=0 ∧ even(y) → x := 1
   []
   3: x≠0 ∧ y≠0 → y := y−1 [] 4: x≠0 ∧ y≠0 → z := z + 1
  ].
```

Figure 2.13 Example program CC [GFMR 81].

$$
\begin{aligned}
CC_\omega :: *[&1: x=0 \wedge odd(y) \rightarrow y := y+1 \\
&[\,] \\
&2: x\neq 0 \wedge y\neq 0 \rightarrow y := y-1 \\
&[\,] \\
&3: x\neq 0 \wedge y\neq 0 \rightarrow z := z+1 \\
].&
\end{aligned}
$$

$$
\begin{aligned}
CC_n :: *[&1: x=0 \rightarrow y := y+1 \\
&[\,] \\
&2: x=0 \wedge even(y) \rightarrow x := 1 \\
&[\,] \\
&3: x\neq 0 \wedge y\neq 0 \wedge \neg(x\neq 0 \wedge y\neq 0) \rightarrow \cdots \\
].&
\end{aligned}
$$

Figure 2.14 Derived programs CC_ω, CC_n [GFMR 81].

To prove $\overset{s}{\ll} pi(n) \wedge n>0 \gg CC_n \ll true \gg$ is trivial since $pi(n)$ implies $x \neq 0$, and hence CC_n terminates immediately. The proof will use $W = \{0\}$ and all clauses hold vacuously, except INIT and TERM, which are also clear.

To prove $\overset{s}{\ll} x=0 \gg CC_\omega \ll true \gg$, choose $W' = \{0,1\}$ and let

$$S'_w = \{2,3\}, \qquad D'_w = \{1\}$$

and $pi'(w, x, y, z) \overset{def.}{\equiv} x=0 \wedge ((even(y) \rightarrow w=0) \wedge (odd(y) \rightarrow w=1))$.

To show clause (DEC), for direction 1, note that $w=1$ implies $odd(y)$. Hence afterwards $even(y)$ holds, hence $pi'(0)$.

To show clause (NOINC), for direction 2, a similar argument applies. Direction (3) does not modify y at all. To show clause (IOE) the only derived program is $CC_{\omega,1}$ (see Figure 2.15). Termination under $pi'(1)$ is again immediate, as $pi'(1)$ implies $x = 0$.

Finally, consider the program PR in Figure 2.16. This program strongly-fair terminates if and only if the conjecture that there exist infinitely many "twin" primes is true.

We would like to draw the reader's attention to the fact that our proof rule deals with what might be called "top-level fairness". In other words, it considers fair choices among guards at the top-level of the iterative statement only, while allowing arbitrary choices for inner guards, except for nested-loops, which again are fairly executed. Thus, the program (suggested by Shmuel Katz) L in Figure 2.17 is *not* strongly-fair terminating for an initial state $b=true$.

The infinite computation $(1,2)^\omega$, in which direction 2 is always taken as 2.1 (and never as 2.2) is fair according to our definition. A discussion of *all-levels fairness* and its induced fair termination proofs appears in section 3.3. Note that the distinction between "*all-levels*" fairness and "*top-level*" fairness cannot be captured by merely attributing fairness to choices in conditionals (as opposed to iterations). Figure 2.18 contains a program *LL* which does not contain any "inner" conditionals, only loops.

The computation $\pi = ((1)^* \, 2.2)^\omega$ *is* an infinite fair computation by our definitions. Each of the inner loops is treated fairly *whenever entered*, but fairness does not carry to consecutive executions of the same loop. This computation is, of course, *unfair* under the *all-levels* fairness approach.

$$
\begin{array}{l}
CC_{\omega,1}:: *[\ 1: x\neq 0 \wedge y\neq 0 \rightarrow y := y-1 \\
\qquad\qquad [\,] \\
\qquad\qquad 2: x\neq 0 \wedge y\neq 0 \rightarrow z := z+1 \\
\qquad\qquad].
\end{array}
$$

Figure 2.15 Derived program $CC_{\omega,1}$ [GFMR 81].

$$
\begin{array}{l}
PR:: y := 1;\ b := \mathit{true}; \\
\qquad *[\ 1: b \rightarrow y := y+1 \\
\qquad\quad [\,] \\
\qquad\quad 2: b \wedge \mathit{prime}(y) \wedge \mathit{prime}(y+2) \rightarrow b := \mathit{false} \\
\qquad\quad].
\end{array}
$$

Figure 2.16 Program *PR* [GFMR 81].

$$
\begin{array}{l}
L:: *[\ 1: b \rightarrow \mathit{skip} \\
\qquad [\,] \\
\qquad 2: b \rightarrow [2.1: b \rightarrow \mathit{skip} \\
\qquad\qquad\quad [\,] \\
\qquad\qquad\quad 2.2: b \rightarrow b := \mathit{false} \\
\qquad\qquad\quad] \\
\qquad].
\end{array}
$$

Figure 2.17 The Program *L* [GFMR 81].

$$
\begin{array}{l}
LL:: *[\ 1: b \rightarrow c := \mathit{true} \\
\qquad [\,] \\
\qquad 2: b \rightarrow *[2.1: c \rightarrow b := \mathit{false} \\
\qquad\qquad\quad [\,] \\
\qquad\qquad\quad 2.2: c \rightarrow c := \mathit{false} \\
\qquad\qquad\quad]\ ].
\end{array}
$$

Figure 2.18 All-level fairness with no conditionals [GFMR 81].

Theorem: (soundness of the rule SFT) For a typical repetition statement $S \in GC$:

$$\text{if } \vdash_{\mathbf{SFT}} \overset{s}{\ll} p \gg S \ll true \gg, \text{ then } \models \overset{s}{\ll} p \gg S \ll true \gg .$$

Proof: The reasoning is similar to the previous soundness proofs. Suppose an infinite computation $\pi = <\xi_i>$, $i=0,1,\ldots$ of S on an initial state $\xi_0 \models p$ exists, and all clauses of **SFT** apply. Then, there exists a sequence of elements of W, $w_0 \geqslant w_1 \geqslant w_2 \cdots$, such that $pi(\xi_j, w_j)$ holds, $j=0,1,\ldots$ By well-foundedness, there exists a $k > 0$, such that $w_k = w_{k+1} = \cdots$. Hence, by (DEC), the moves taken along the tail of π starting in ξ_k are S_{w_k} moves only. However, by (IOE) on this tail, $\bigvee_{j \in D_w} B_j$ is infinitely often true, so some $i \in D_w$ is infinitely often enabled, but never taken, hence π is not strongly-fair. [ ]

Theorem: (semantic completeness of the rule SFT) For a typical repetition statement $S \in GC$:

$$\text{if } \models \overset{s}{\ll} p \gg S \ll true \gg, \text{ then } \vdash_{\mathbf{SFT}} \overset{s}{\ll} p \gg S \ll true \gg .$$

Proof: Suppose $\models \overset{s}{\ll} p \gg S \ll true \gg$. With analogy to previous proofs, we modify the inductive definition of cone-chains, so as the cone-chain lemma is preserved, while condition (IOE) is also enforced.

We refer again to the inductive definition of the A_i's. Here we consider only d's for which there is an infinite d-avoiding path originating at ξ_i, and *along which d is infinitely often enabled!*

We leave it to the reader to verify that cone-chain lemma mentioned above holds. We now define S_w, D_w, $pi(w)$ as for **UFT** and show that (IOE) also holds, due to the modification in the inductive definition of cone-chains. Suppose that there is a $w > 0$, such that the derived program $\overline{S}_w$ is not in **SFT**. Then, it contains an infinite path π, strongly-fair (relative to $\overline{S}_w$'s directions). However, by the cone-chain lemma, this path must have an infinite tail completely residing in some cone with directive d.

Note that $d \notin S_w$ by the assumption that π is strongly-fair in $\overline{S}_w$. Thus, $d \in D_w$, and by the way the derived program $\overline{S}_w$ is constructed, π must have terminated. This establishes that

$$\models \overset{s}{\ll} pi(w) \wedge w > 0 \gg \overline{S}_w \ll true \gg .$$

However, since $\overline{S}_w$ has only a proper subset of the directions of S, we obtain by an obvious inductive argument that

$$\vdash_{\mathbf{SFT}} \overset{s}{\ll} pi(w) \wedge w > 0 \gg \overline{S}_w \ll true \gg .$$

Definition: Let *SFT* be the class of all *SFT GC* programs.

Theorem: $NDT \subset WFT \subset SFT \subset UFT$.

Proof: Immediate from the definitions and examples above. [ ]

2.2 State Directed Choice of Helpful Directions

In this section we present another method for proving termination based on fairness-properties, due to [LPS 81]. Though the original method is described in terms of an abstract model of unstructured concurrent programs, we adapt it here to *GC* programs. The method is also based on choosing helpful directions at intermediate stages of the computation. However, the choice of which direction is helpful depends on state predicates, rather than on abstract distance from termination. Another slight difference between the two methods is the use of a *ranking function* in [LPS 81], instead of the parametrized invariant in [GFMR 81]. We present the original semantic completeness proofs, since they differ from these of [GFMR 81], and then show inter-reducibility between the two approaches.

2.2.1 Unconditionally-fair termination

Let $S::*[\underset{i \in I}{[\,]} B_i \rightarrow S_i]$ be a typical *GC* repetition statement. The rule **M** (see Figure 2.19) is used for proving *UFT*.

Explanation: The predicate Q_i, $i \in I$, is intended to characterize states for which direction i is helpful. The condition $Q = \bigvee_{i \in I} Q_i$ should be invariant during the whole computation, implying that at any stage there exists a helpful direction. We again may assume $B_1 = B_2 = \cdots = B_n = B$.

To prove $\overset{u}{\ll} p \gg S \ll true \gg$:

Find a well-founded, partially-ordered set, $(W, \underset{def.}{\leqslant})$, a *ranking function* $\rho: \Sigma_S \rightarrow W$, *direction-predicates* $Q_i \subseteq \Sigma_S$, $i \in I$, where $Q = \bigvee_{i \in I} Q_i$, such that

M1. $p \rightarrow Q \wedge \exists w: \rho = w, (Q \wedge \rho > 0) \rightarrow \bigvee_{i \in I} B_i, (Q \wedge \rho = 0) \rightarrow \neg \bigvee_{i \in I} B_i$.

M2. $\overset{u}{\ll} Q \wedge \rho = w \wedge B_i \gg S_i \ll Q \wedge \rho \leqslant w \gg, i \in I, w > 0$.

M3. $\overset{u}{\ll} Q_i \wedge \rho = w \wedge B_j \gg S_j \ll \rho = w \rightarrow Q_i \gg, i \in I, j \neq i, w > 0$.

M4. $\overset{u}{\ll} Q_i \wedge \rho = w \wedge B_i \gg S_i \ll \rho < w \gg, i \in I, w > 0$.

Figure 2.19 Rule **M** (impartial termination).

M1—boundary conditions;
M2—the rank *never increases* after taking an enabled direction;
M3—when i is the helpful direction, but some other enabled direction has been taken, preserving the rank, then i is still a helpful direction for the resulting state;
M4—when an enabled helpful direction is taken, the rank decreases.

We now turn to soundness and semantic completeness of rule **M**.

Theorem: (soundness of the rule M) For a typical repetition statement $S \in GC$:

$$\text{if } \overset{\mathbf{u}}{\vdash_{\mathbf{M}}} \ll p \gg S \ll \mathit{true} \gg, \text{ then } \overset{\mathbf{u}}{\models} \ll p \gg S \ll \mathit{true} \gg .$$

Proof: Assume $\overset{\mathbf{u}}{\vdash_{\mathbf{M}}} \ll p \gg S \ll \mathit{true} \gg$, and assume that an unconditionally-fair infinite computation of S on an initial state ξ_0 satisfying p exists:

$$\xi_0 \rightarrow_{S_{i_0}} \xi_1 \rightarrow_{S_{i_1}} \cdots \xi_j \rightarrow_{S_{i_j}} \cdots .$$

By M1 and M2, $Q(\xi_j), j = 0,1. \ldots$ By M2,

$$\rho(\xi_0) \geqslant \rho(\xi_1) \geqslant \cdots \geqslant \rho(\xi_i) \geqslant \cdots .$$

Since W is well-founded, there exist some $k \geqslant 0$ such that $\rho(\xi_k) = \rho(\xi_{k+1}) = \cdots$, i.e. the value of ρ stopped decreasing at ξ_k. Since $Q(\xi_k)$ holds, there is some $m \in I$ such that $Q_m(\xi_k)$ holds, and since ρ does not decrease after ξ_k, $Q_m(\xi_j)$ holds for all $j \geqslant k$ by M3. Thus, by (M4), direction m is never taken beyond ξ_k, and thus the given sequence is not unconditionally-fair, contradicting the assumption. [ ]

Theorem: (semantic completeness of the rule M) For a typical repetition statement $S \in CG$:

$$\text{if } \overset{\mathbf{u}}{\models} \ll p \gg S \ll \mathit{true} \gg, \text{ then } \overset{\mathbf{u}}{\vdash_{\mathbf{M}}} \ll p \gg S \ll \mathit{true} \gg .$$

Proof: Suppose that $\overset{\mathbf{u}}{\models} \ll p \gg S \ll \mathit{true} \gg$. We have to show how to define W, ρ, Q_i, $i \in I$, satisfying M1–M4. Define a relation $R \subseteq \Sigma_S \times \Sigma_S$ as follows: $R(\xi, \xi') \overset{def.}{\equiv}$ there exists a computation path of S of the form $\xi = \xi_0 \rightarrow_{S_{i_0}} \xi_1 \rightarrow_{S_{i_1}} \xi_2 \cdots \xi_m = \xi'$, such that each direction $i \in I$ is taken along it at least once. An infinite chain $\xi_0 R \xi_1 R \xi_2 \cdots$ would imply an infinite unconditionally-fair computation, which is impossible by assumption. Hence R is a well-founded relation. For $A \subseteq \Sigma_S$, let

$\min(A)$, denote the set of all R-minimal elements in A. Then, we define a sequence of subsets of Σ_S by transfinite induction, as follows:

$$A_0 = \min(\Sigma_S)$$

$$A_{\alpha+1} = \min(\Sigma_S - A_\alpha), \textit{ for a successor ordinal,}$$

$$A_\beta = \min(\Sigma_S - \bigcup_{\alpha < \beta} A_\alpha), \textit{ for a limit ordinal.}$$

Note that every $\xi \in \Sigma_S$ belongs to some A_α. Now, the initial ranking is defined by: $\rho^0(\xi) = \alpha \longleftrightarrow \xi \in A_\alpha$.

Proposition: ρ^0 satisfies the following two properties:

a) if $\xi R \xi'$ then $\rho^0(\xi) > \rho^0(\xi')$
b) if, for every $\xi'' \in \Sigma_S$, $\xi' R \xi'' \to \xi R \xi''$, then $\rho^0(\xi) \geqslant \rho^0(\xi')$.

Consider two states ξ and ξ', such that ξ' results from ξ by taking direction i, for some $i \in I$. Then, every path from ξ' to some ξ'' on which each direction is taken at least once, can be extended to a similar path from ξ to the same ξ''. Thus, by property b) of ρ^0, $\rho^0(\xi) \geqslant \rho^0(\xi')$. Hence, ρ^0 is a non-increasing rank. However, it does not necessarily satisfy the decreasing conditions. Consider any finite computation path $\pi = \xi_0 \to_{i_0} \xi_1 \to_{i_1} \to \cdots \to_{i_k} \xi_{k+1}$, and denote by $\delta(\pi)$ the set of directions taken along it, i.e. $\delta(\pi) = \{i_0, \ldots, i_k\}$. Now define the *weight* of π by: $w(\pi) = \min_{i \in I}(i \notin \delta(\pi))$, i.e. the direction with the smallest index not taken in π. Using the weight, we now refine ρ^0 with another ranking, ρ^*:

$$\rho^*(\xi) = \max\{w(\pi) \mid \xi \overset{*}{\underset{\pi}{\to}} \xi', \quad \text{for some } \pi, \text{ such that } \rho^0(\xi) = \rho^0(\xi')\}.$$

That is, $\rho^*(\xi)$ is the maximal weight of all paths that connect ξ to another equiranked state ξ'. Clearly, $1 \leqslant \rho^*(\xi) \leqslant |I|$. Also, if $\xi \overset{*}{\underset{\pi}{\to}} \xi'$ and $\rho^0(\xi) = \rho^0(\xi')$, then $w(\pi) \neq |I|$, otherwise we would have $\xi R \xi'$ and thereby $\rho^0(\xi) > \rho^0(\xi')$.

Now, we are ready to define what we need for applying **M**. We take $W = \mathbf{ord} \times [1..|I|]$, ordered lexicographically. This is clearly a well-founded ordered set. As the ranking ρ, we take

$$\rho(\xi) \overset{def.}{=} (\rho^0(\xi), \rho^*(\xi)).$$

For the direction-predicates we take the *disjoint* predicates

$$Q_i(\xi) \overset{def.}{=} (\rho^*(\xi) = i).$$

It remains to verify that indeed (M1)–(M4) hold. M1 is immediate. Let $Q \wedge \rho = (\alpha, k) \wedge B_i$ hold in a state ξ, and execute S_i. Suppose the rank of the resulting state ξ' is (α', k'). We already know that $\alpha \geqslant \alpha'$. If $\alpha > \alpha'$, M2 is already established. Hence, assume $\alpha = \alpha'$. Let π' be any path leading from ξ' to some ξ'', such that $\rho^0(\xi') = \rho^0(\xi'')$. Consequently, $\delta'(\pi) \subseteq \delta(\pi)$, and hence $w(\pi') \geqslant w(\pi)$, for every such π. Thus, $\rho^*(\xi) \geqslant \rho^*(\xi')$, and M2 is established.

M3 is established easily, if i is the largest "yet missing" direction, then taking direction j, $j \neq i$, cannot change this fact. Similarly, for M4, taking direction i either leaves no direction missing, causing a decrease in ρ^0, or direction i is not the "largest missing" anymore, and a smaller one is. This completes the proof of the semantic completeness of **M**. []

2.2.2 Weakly-fair and strongly-fair termination

As we know from the previous section, passing from **UFT** to **WFT** and to **SFT** requires an additional property to be satisfied by the invariants and the ranking. It is not surprising that the extra property in each case is similar to the corresponding method in the ordinal-directed choices, since the main difference manifests itself in the treatment of the helpful conditions, belonging to the level of unconditional fairness. Thus, we obtain the rule **J** for weakly-fair termination (see Figure 2.20).

The additional clause requires the *continuous enabledness* of direction i while the direction predicate Q_i holds.

Theorem: (soundness of rule J) For a typical repetition statement $S \in GC$:

$$\text{if } \vdash_{\mathbf{J}} \overset{\mathbf{w}}{\ll} p \gg S \ll true \gg, \text{ then } \models \overset{\mathbf{w}}{\ll} p \gg S \ll true \gg .$$

Proof: Similar to previous soundness proofs. An infinite computation would give rise to an infinite strictly descending sequence of elements of W, the well-founded set, which is impossible. []

Theorem: (semantic completeness of rule J) For a typical repetition statement $S \in GC$:

To prove $\overset{\mathbf{w}}{\ll} p \gg S \ll true \gg$:

i. Prove clauses (1)–(4) of rule **M** with **w** replacing **u**.

ii. Prove $(Q_i \wedge \bigvee_{j \in I} B_j) \rightarrow B_i$, $i \in I$.

Figure 2.20 Rule **J** (just termination).

$$\text{if } \models \overset{\mathbf{w}}{\ll p \gg S \ll true \gg}, \text{ then } \vdash_{\mathbf{J}} \ll p \gg S \ll true \gg .$$

Proof: Again, a slight modification of the construction for rule **M** will suffice. For a finite computation path π, let

$$e(\pi) = \{j \in I \mid B_j \textit{ holds} \text{ for } \textit{every state along } \pi\}.$$

Thus, $e(\pi)$ is the set of all continuously-enabled directions along π. We say that π is *full* iff $e(\pi) \subseteq \delta(\pi)$ (where $\delta(\pi)$ is as for rule **M**). Then we let

$$\xi R \xi' \overset{def.}{\equiv} \text{there exists a full path from } \xi \text{ to } \xi'.$$

We also modify the definition of the *weight* of a path:

$$w(\pi) = \min_{i \in I}(i \notin e(\pi) - \delta(\pi)).$$

From this stage, the proof is the same as for rule **M**. [ ]

Finally, we present the rule **F** for strongly-fair termination in Figure 2.21. Again we see the familiar recursive application involved in strong fairness. We denote by (F1)–(F4) the four clauses in i (corresponding to (M1)–(M4) in **J**), and by (F5) the clause ii.

Theorem: (soundness of rule F) For a typical repetition statement $S \in GC$:

$$\text{if } \vdash_{\mathbf{J}} \overset{\mathbf{s}}{\ll p \gg S \ll true \gg}, \text{ then } \models \overset{\mathbf{s}}{\ll p \gg S \ll true \gg}.$$

Proof: Omitted (similar to previous soundness proofs). [ ]

Theorem: (semantic completeness of rule F) For a typical repetition statement $S \in GC$:

$$\text{if } \models \overset{\mathbf{s}}{\ll p \gg S \ll true \gg}, \text{ then } \vdash_{\mathbf{F}} \overset{\mathbf{s}}{\ll p \gg S \ll true \gg}.$$

To prove $\overset{\mathbf{s}}{\ll p \gg S \ll true \gg}$:

i. Prove clauses (1)–(4) of rule **M** with **s** replacing **u**.

ii. Prove that $\overset{\mathbf{s}}{\ll Q_i \gg \bar{S}_i \ll true \gg}$, where for every $i \in I$

$$\bar{S}_i :: *[\, \underset{j \in I}{[\,]} B_j \wedge \neg B_i \rightarrow S_j].$$

Figure 2.21 Rule **F** (fair termination).

Proof: Suppose $\overset{s}{\models} \ll p \gg S \ll true \gg$ holds. Then, certainly $\underset{u}{\models} \ll p \gg S \ll true \gg$ also holds, and by the completeness of rule **M**, we know that there exist $(W, \leqslant)$, ρ, Q_i, $i \in I$ such that $\overset{s}{\vdash}_{\mathbf{M}} \ll p \gg S \ll true \gg$, establishing the first clause. Furthermore, computations of $\bar{S}_i$ are also computations of S, restricted to initial states satisfying Q_i and along which direction i is never enabled. Hence, $\bar{S}_i$ also strongly fair terminates, establishing ii. Note again the inductive argument on the number of directions in $\bar{S}_i$, which is smaller by at least 1 then that of S. []

Figure 2.22 is an example of an application of the rule **F** to a program *GCD* representing a distributed computation of the greatest common divisor of two positive natural numbers. The distributedness is represented if we consider the first two guards to be executed by one processor, while the two last ones are executed by another processor. The example is a modification of a corresponding one in [LPS 81]. Clearly, this program is not in ***NDT***; we want to prove $\overset{s}{\ll} y_1>0 \wedge y_2>0 \gg GCD \ll true \gg$.

As the well-founded set we choose again $W = N$, the natural numbers, with their usual ordering. As the ranking function, we take

$$\rho(y_1, y_2) = \begin{cases} y_1 + y_2 & y_1 \neq y_2 \\ 0 & y_1 = y_2 \end{cases}.$$

As the direction predicates we define:

$$Q_1(y_1, y_2) \overset{def.}{=} y_1 \geqslant y_2 > 0$$

$$Q_2(y_1, y_2) \overset{def.}{=} false \text{ (i.e. this direction is helpful for no state)}$$

$$Q_3(y_1, y_2) \overset{def.}{=} false$$

$$Q_4(y_1, y_2) \overset{def.}{=} y_2 > y_1 > 0.$$

Thus, $Q = y_1 > 0 \wedge y_2 > 0$ and is clearly invariant; also, $Q \wedge \rho = 0$ implies $y_1 = y_2$ implying termination (M1). The value of $\rho(y_1, y_2)$ never increases, since the y's are either decremented or left unchanged (M2). In case ρ did not decrease, it is due to having taken directions {2,3}–executing a *skip*–and, hence, preserving the direction predicate (M3). Clause (M4) also holds, since decreasing y_i, $i = 1,2$, decreases also $y_1 + y_2$ (possibly reducing ρ to 0, in case $y_1 = y_2$ after decreasing any of the y's). Finally, the recursive application is immediate. Thus, we established the strongly-fair termination of *GCD*.

```
GCD:: *[ 1: y1 > y2 → y1 := y1 − y2
         []
         2: y2 > y1 → skip
         []
         3: y1 > y2 → skip
         []
         4: y2 > y1 → y2 := y2 − y1
       ].
```

Figure 2.22 Program *GCD*.

2.3 Inter-reducibility of the Two Methods

In this section we show the equivalence of ordinal-directed choice of helpful direction to the state-predicate-directed choice. In one sense this is clear, since both methods are complete. We show, however, a stronger relationship; namely, how to transform a proof in each system to a proof in the other one. As a representing case we shall deal with proofs of strongly-fair termination. One direction of the reduction is taken from [GFMR 81], and the other direction from [LE 81].

Theorem: (reduction of ordinal-directed choice to state-directed choice) For a typical repetition statement $S \in GC$:

Any proof of $\overset{s}{\ll} p \gg S \ll true \gg$ using rule **SFT** can be converted to a proof using rule **F**.

Proof: Assume that $(W, \leqslant)$, *pi*, $<(S_w, D_w)>_{w \in W}$, $w>0$ were found satisfying all clauses of **SFT**, relative to precondition p, and w.l.o.g that $|D_w| = 1$. In order to apply rule **F**, we have to:

(i) Find a partial ranking function $\rho: \Sigma_S \rightarrow W'$, where W' is also a well-founded ordering.
(ii) Find predicates Q_i, $i = 1, \ldots, n$ over states, where $Q = \bigvee_{i=1}^{n} Q_i$, satisfying (F1)–(F5) of **F**.

Take $W' = W$ (using the same ordering), and define $\rho(\xi) \underset{def.}{=} \min_w pi(\xi, w)$, $Q_i(\xi) \equiv i \in D_{\rho(\xi)}$. Hence $Q(\xi) \equiv \exists w\colon pi(\xi, w)$, its invariance following directly from the invariance of *pi*.

Next, we verify conditions (F1)–(F5) of **F**.

Condition (F1): $p(\xi) \rightarrow \exists w\colon pi(\xi, w)$ holds by clause (INIT) of **SFT**; the rest by (CONT), TERM).
Condition (F2): follows from clauses (NOINC) of **SFT**, guaranteeing that

$pi(v)$ holds for $v \leqslant w$; hence the minimal v s.t. $pi(v)$ does not increase, either.
Condition (F3): $Q_i \wedge \rho = w \wedge B_j$ implies that by executing S_j, $j \neq i$ an S-move is taken, and since ρ is the minimal w s.t. $pi(\xi, w)$, this S-move does not decrease the ordinal, hence $Q_i(\xi)$ still holds.
Condition (F4): follows directly from clause (DEC), since $Q_i \wedge B_i$ imply a D-move is taken.
Condition (F5): reduces to clause (IOE). []

Theorem: (reduction of state-directed choice to ordinal-directed choice) For a typical repetition statement $S \in GC$:

Any proof of $\ll p \gg S \overset{s}{\ll} true \gg$ using rule **F** can be converted to a proof using rule **SFT**.

Proof: Suppose $(W, \leqslant)$, ρ, Q_i, $i \in I$ have been found satisfying all clauses of **F**. We have to find $(W', \leqslant)$, pi, (D_w, S_w), $w > 0$, such that all clauses of rule **SFT** are satisfied.

We choose $W' = W \times (2^I - \{\varnothing\})$ with the following ordering: $(w, A) < (w', A')$ iff $w < w'$, or $w = w'$ and $A' \subset A$. This is clearly a well-founded ordering. The invariant and partitions of I into decreasing and steady directions are defined as follows:

$$D_{(w,A)} = A, \qquad S_{(w,A)} = I - A, \quad \text{for } w \in W,\ \varnothing \neq A \subseteq I.$$

$$pi(\xi, (w,A)) \overset{def.}{\equiv} (\rho(\xi) = w \wedge A = \{i \mid i \in I,\ \xi \models Q_i\}).$$

We now verify that all the clauses of **SFT** are satisfied.

(ad DEC) Suppose $pi(\xi, (w,A)) \wedge B_i$ holds, for some $i \in D_{(w,A)}$ i.e. $i \in A$. Then, $\xi \models Q_i$ by the definition of pi. By (F4), if ξ' is a state resulting from the execution of S_i on ξ, then $\rho(\xi') < \rho(\xi)$. Also, by (F2), $B = \{k \mid k \in I \wedge \xi' \models Q_k\} \neq \varnothing$. Thus, $pi(\xi', (\rho(\xi'),B))$ holds, reestablishing the parametrized invariant with a smaller parameter.

(ad NOINC) Suppose $pi(\xi, (w,A)) \wedge B_i$ holds, for some $i \in S_{(w,A)}$. The state ξ' resulting from executing S_i on ξ satisfies $\rho(\xi') \leqslant \rho(\xi)$. By (F2) we have $Q(\xi')$, and hence $B = \{k \mid \xi' \models Q_k\} \neq \varnothing$. Therefore, $pi(\xi', (\rho(\xi'),B))$ holds. If $\rho(\xi') < \rho(\xi)$ we are done. If $\rho(\xi') = \rho(\xi)$, then by (F3), $A \subseteq B$, and thus $(w, A) \geqslant (\rho(\xi'), B)$, and again we are done.

(ad IOE) If $|I| = 1$ then $S_w = \varnothing$ and the derived program is degenerated. Suppose $S_w \neq \varnothing$. Since every strongly-fair execution of $\overline{S}_{(w,A)}$ is also extensible to a strongly-fair execution of S (compare with a similar argument in the completeness proof of **UFT**),the property follows by the induction hypothesis, since $\bar{S}_{(w,A)}$ has less guards than S, by $D_{(w,A)} \neq \emptyset$. We leave the boundary conditions to be verified by the reader. []

2.4 Relativized Fair Termination

In this section an alternative approach is suggested, for proving the IOE condition (infinite enabledness) without the *derived program* construction. Instead, the notion of *relativized fair termination* (to a state-predicate I) is introduced, according to which computation paths that do not preserve the invariance of I are "ruled out" and the first violation of I is treated as a termination point. Consequently, the only computations which can interfere with fair termination relative to I are those infinite computations which preserve I and are fair.

The approach presented here establishes infinite enabledness by considering the *same* program, but with a different relativizing predicate I. The presentation follows basically that of [G 84]; though the discussion is in terms of *GC*, the same observation is valid for the [LPS 81] approach. In chapter 5 we show how this approach, which does not require any closure properties from the programming language, is extended to proving fair termination of *CSP* programs, lacking that kind of closure.

Below, a rule for proving relativized fair termination (called **I-FAIR**) is presented. Also, the modifications in the proofs of the soundness and semantic completeness of the previous rules that are needed for carrying the same properties to the current rule are indicated. We restrict the discussion to the case of strong fairness, the other cases being similar.

Definition: A *GC* program S is *I-fairly terminating* if every one of its infinite computations is either unfair, or contains a state which satisfies $\neg I$.

We use I: $\ll p \gg S \ll q \gg$ to denote that S I-fairly terminates w.r.t. a precondition p and a postcondition q. Fair termination of S is expressed in these terms by *true*-fair termination (choosing I to be *true*). Thus, the rule **I-FAIR**, presented in Figure 2.23, can be used to prove (unrelativized) fair termination as well.

The clauses of **I-FAIR**, except (TERM) and (IOE), are identical to those of **SFT**. The (IOE) clauses of the two rules, even though using different tools, basically prove the same property of the given program S. Consequently, the proofs of the respective soundness and semantic completeness are also closely related, as shown below.

Explanations:

1. (TERM) expresses that satisfying $\neg I$ is considered as termination.
2. (IOE) establishes that every computation of S either terminates or con-

To prove I: $\ll p \gg S \ll q \gg$:

Choose a well-founded, partially-ordered, set $(W, \leqslant)$, a parametrized invariant pi: $W \times \Sigma_S \to \{true, false\}$ and for every non-minimal $w \in W$ choose a decreasing direction $d_w \in \{1, \ldots, n\}$, satisfying:

(INIT), (CONT), (DEC), (NOINC)–as in **SFT**.

(TERM)

$$pi(0) \to ([\bigwedge_{i=1,n} \neg B_i \wedge q] \vee \neg I).$$

(IOE)

$$I': \ll pi(w) \wedge w > 0 \gg S \ll true \gg$$

where $I' \overset{def.}{=} I \wedge \neg B_{d_w}$.

Figure 2.23 The rule **I-FAIR** (relativized fair termination).

tains a state which satisfies $\neg I \vee B_{d_w}$ (which is $\neg I'$). That is, S either I-fairly terminates or reaches a state in which d_w is enabled.

Theorem: (soundness of I-FAIR)

If $\vdash_{\textbf{I-FAIR}} I$: $\ll p \gg S \ll q \gg$ then $\models$ I: $\ll p \gg S \ll q \gg$.

Proof: Similar to that of **SFT**. []

Theorem: (semantic completeness of rule I-FAIR)

If $\models$ I: $\ll p \gg S \ll q \gg$ then $\vdash_{\textbf{I-FAIR}} I$: $\ll p \gg S \ll q \gg$.

Proof: Only the differences w.r.t. the completeness proof of **SFT** are discussed in some detail. Following the completeness proof of **SFT**, the main idea is the contraction of states residing on infinite, unfair or *not I-preserving* computations in an execution tree into nodes of a new tree, which is well founded.

The proof differs from the corresponding proof for **SFT** in two respects:

a. Since states satisfying $\neg I$ are considered terminal, the original tree is first *truncated* at all nodes having such a state occurrence. Only then is the contraction applied. The effect of this truncation must be considered.
b. The proof rule is recursively applied during a proof. While for **SFT** the proof that only a finite sequence of such applications always exists involved a simple syntactic induction on the size of the derived pro-

gram, in the current context the recursive application is to the *same* program, but with a stronger invariant. Thus, a different reasoning is involved, ordering pairs of programs S and relativizing invariants I by the subsets of directions allowable anywhere in the execution tree T_S truncated according to I.

Let $T_S(\sigma_0)$ be the computation tree of a program S, for an initial state σ_0.

Definition: *The truncated tree* $\overline{T}_S^I(\sigma_0)$, of $T_S(\sigma_0)$, w.r.t. a predicate I (over Σ_S), is obtained from the original tree $T_S(\sigma_0)$, by truncating every computation path leaving a state satisfying $\neg I$. We omit the superscript I whenever it is clear from the context.

Note: Every final state of $\overline{T}_S(\sigma_0)$ satisfies either q or $\neg I$.

Next, a *ranked* well founded tree $\overline{T}_S^*(\sigma_0)$ is constructed out of the truncated tree $\overline{T}_S(\sigma_0)$, for every σ_0 satisfying p. All these trees are combined to one tree as before. The construction now proceeds as in the case of **SFT**.

Next, we have to show that W, pi and d_w, defined as above, satisfy the clauses of the rule **I-FAIR**. For most of the clauses the details are analogous to the **SFT** case. We consider here only the points in which an extra observation should be made.

(DEC) and (NOINC): Since pi is defined in terms of the truncated tree of S, it is not necessarily defined for every reachable state of S. Thus, for (DEC) and (NOINC) it must be shown not only that there is a decrease or a non increase, respectively, for the execution of every direction of S, but also that pi is *defined* for the resulting state after the execution . That is the purpose of the following lemma.

Definition: A reachable state of S is *pi-definable* if $pi(\sigma, w)$ holds for some $w \in W$.

Lemma: (hereditariness of *pi*-definability) If $pi(\sigma,w) \wedge w > 0 \wedge B_i(\sigma)$ holds for some state σ and direction i, then every σ' resulting from the execution of S_i on σ, is pi-definable.

Proof: Since σ is pi-definable for a non-minimal element of W, it occurs in some non-leaf node of the truncated tree. Thus, σ' is also on the truncated tree and σ' is pi-definable. [ ]

(TERM): Only the leaves on the truncated tree are ranked by 0, and at every such leaf there is an occurrence of a state which is either a terminal state of S or satisfies $\neg I$. Thus, whenever $pi(0,\sigma)$ holds, so does $(\bigwedge_{i=1,n} \neg B_i(\sigma) \wedge q(\sigma)) \vee \neg I(\sigma)$.

(IOE): The main concern regarding this clause is to show that the number of recursive applications of **I-FAIR**, derived from the application of (IOE) according to the completeness proof, is finite; therefore, the proof for I-fair termination of S is itself finite. To show this, we attach to each application of the rule a well founded rank, $\rho[I,S]$, and show that this rank decreases until, during applications to which the minimal rank is attached, no recursive application is needed and the proof terminates. That is established by the following two lemmata.

Definitions:

(1) A direction i of S is *denied* by a state predicate I if I implies $\neg B_i$.
(2) $\rho[I,S]$ s defined as the number of directions of S denied by I. If S is clear, we use $\rho[I]$.

To any application of the rule we now attach the rank $n - \rho[I,S]$, where n is the number of directions of S and I is the relativizing predicate.

Lemma: (rank-decrease) If in the completeness proof a decreasing direction d_w is chosen (for a non-minimal $w \in W$), then

$$\rho[I \wedge \neg B_{d_w}] < \rho[I].$$

Consequently, the rank attached to some application of the rule is smaller than the rank attached to the recursive application it generates.

Proof: We have to show that d_w is not denied by I. Assume the contrary. Then d_w is not enabled on the truncated tree $\overline{T}_S^I(\sigma_0)$, at non-leaf nodes. But it was chosen as a decreasing direction for w, therefore it is *pi-definable*, contradicting the assumption. [ ]

Lemma: (0 rank) No recursive application is generated by an application of **I-FAIR** to which a 0 rank is attached.

Proof: Let S and I be given such that $n - \rho[I,S] = 0$. Then, I denies every direction of S. Following the completeness proof, we derive W, pi and d_w. First, the truncated tree $\overline{T}_S^I(\sigma_0)$ is constructed for every initial state σ_0. It contains only one node, σ_0, and so is the well founded tree $\overline{T}_S^*(\sigma_0)$, obtained from $\overline{T}_S^I(\sigma_0)$. Next, the combined tree is constructed. It has all its nodes ranked by 0, except the dummy one, serving as its root. We now define W to be $\{0\}$; $pi(\sigma,w)$ to hold for every initial state and $w = 0$; we choose no decreasing direction since W contains only a minimal element. The application of **I-FAIR** is then trivial, except for (TERM) and (INIT), since for no $w \in W$ $w > 0$ holds. Thus, *no more recursive applications are generated.* [ ]

The two lemmata show that the application of **I-FAIR** is finite. This completes the completeness proof of this rule.

We avoid presenting here examples of the application of this rule to fair termination proofs of *GC* programs since such proof closely resemble proofs using **SFT**. Rather, we present in chapter 5 examples of the application of a generalization of this rule for proving fair termination of communicating processes.

CHAPTER 3

The Method of Explicit Scheduler

3.0 Overview

In this chapter we present an alternative method for proving termination of *GC* programs under various fairness assumptions. The presentation is based on [AO 83] and [APS 84]. The main idea of this approach is the following: *reduce the fair-termination problem of GC programs to ordinary (nondeterministic) termination of GC_R programs, an augmentation of GC with random assignments.* A similar idea is mentioned also in [B 82] and [PA 81].

The reduction method is such that it uses random-assignment (of natural numbers) to explicitly represent the fair scheduler within the program. Once this transformation is carried out, the resulting nondeterministic program will have a variant decreasing along *every direction* whenever the original program is fairly terminating. Finally, the effect of the transformation is simulated within a proof rule, which now serves for proving properties of the original, untransformed, program.

3.0.1 Random assignments

We add the following two definitions to the syntax of *GC* to obtain that of GC_R:

$$<statement> ::= ... \mid <rassignment>$$

$$<rassignment> ::= <var> := ?$$

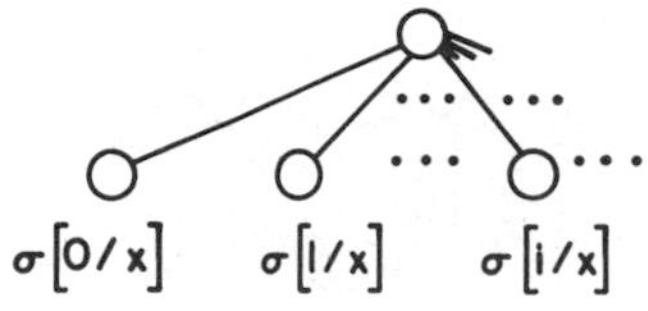

Figure 3.1 $\mathbf{T}_{x:=?}(\sigma)$.

The semantics of the random assignment statement $x:=?$, when executed in state σ, is to produce any variant of σ out of the set $\{\sigma[n/x] \mid n \in N\}$. In contrast to the rest of the language, which is uninterpreted, random assingments in this context are interpreted, using natural numbers. In other words, '$x:=?$' assigns to x a random natural number. This is a very strong primitive. In terms of computation-trees, it produces a countably-branching tree $T_{x:=?}(\sigma)$ (see Figure 3.1), which hints towards a connection with fairness, having the same property.

Taking such a primitive to always terminate transcends the effective semantics of *GC*.

As for partial-correctness, we add an appropriate axiom to capture the semantics of random assignments:

$$\text{A3.}\{\forall x\colon p\}\ x:=?\ \{p\}.$$

We do not have to modify the proof rule **NDT** for termination of iterative statements in GC_R, but it is no longer always applicable with natural numbers.

In this method, the countable ordinals are also needed, due to the presence of random assignments, which share with fairness the effect of preventing a priori bounds on the computation length. We present here a brief overview of the properties of random assingments needed for our purpose. A more thorough attempt to relate fairness and random assingments is postponed to a later section.

3.1 Unconditionally-Fair Termination

We start by presenting a *transformation* $T_u\colon GC \to GC_R$, which for a typical repetition statement $S \in GC$ produces a program $T_u(S) \in GC_R$, whose fair-scheduler is explicitly represented by means of random assignments. To overcome notational difficulties, we first discuss programs with two directions only. Since the fairness is unconditional, we may again assume that both directions have the same boolean expression as guard. Thus, we consider

$$
\begin{aligned}
&S::*[1: B \rightarrow S_1 \ [\,] \ 2: B \rightarrow S_2].\\
&T_u(S):: z_1:=? \ ; \ z_2:=?;\\
&\qquad *[1: B \wedge z_1 \leqslant z_2 \rightarrow S_1 \ ; \ z_1:=? \ ; \ z_2:=z_2-1\\
&\qquad\ \ [\,]\\
&\qquad\ \ 2: B \wedge z_2 < z_1 \rightarrow S_2 \ ; \ z_2:=? \ ; \ z_1:=z_1-1\\
&\qquad].
\end{aligned}
$$

The transformation introduces two *new* variables (not occurring in S), z_1 and z_2, which range over integers. The assignments to these variables and the extra inequalities added to the guards represent the fair-scheduling policy in the following way, informally expressed:

At every moment in a computation of $T_u(S)$ the values of the variables z_1 and z_2 represent the *priorities* assigned to the directions 1 and 2. Consequently, z_1 and z_2 are called *priority variables.* We say that S_1 has a higher priority than S_2 if $z_1 \leqslant z_2$ holds (and vice versa for $z_2 < z_1$). The guards $B \wedge z_1 \leqslant z_2$ and $B \wedge z_2 < z_1$ guarantee that the direction with the higher priority is scheduled for execution. If both directions have the same priority, S_1 gets executed. After every execution of a direction, say i, the priority of the other direction, which was not chosen, say j, gets *increased* (by decrementing z_j by 1) whereas the priority of direction i is reset to some arbitrary non-negative value. Gradually increasing the priority of direction j excludes the possibility of postponing j's right for execution forever. This guarantees unconditional fairness. At the very beginning of a computation of $T_u(S)$ both priority variables are initialized to arbitrary non-negative values. The value $z_j + 1$ describes also the maximum number of computation steps (iterations of the body of S) which may happen *before* direction j is eventually scheduled for execution. Therefore, the variables z_1, z_2 may also be called *counter variables* or (following [APS 84]) *delay variables.* But these are only informal explanations for showing that $T_u(S)$ allows all and only fair computations. The precise relationship between S and $T_u(S)$ is next stated.

Definition: For computation sequences

$$\pi = \sigma_0 \rightarrow_{i_0} \cdots \sigma_j \rightarrow_{i_j} \cdots \qquad \text{and}$$

$$\pi' = \sigma'_0 \quad {}_{i_0} \cdots \sigma'_j \rightarrow_{i_j} \cdots$$

1) π' is an *extension* of π to the variables $z_1, \cdots, z_n$ if the states σ'_j differ from σ_j at most in the variables $z_1, \cdots, z_n$.

2) π is a *restriction* of π' to the variables $x_1, \cdots, x_m$ if every state σ_j is obtained from σ'_j by resetting every variable $z \notin \{x_1, \cdots, x_m\}$ to its value in σ'_0, i.e. by defining:

$$\sigma_j[z] = \begin{cases} \sigma'_0[z] & \text{if } z \notin \{x_1, \ldots, x_m\} \\ \sigma'_j(z) & \textit{otherwise.} \end{cases}$$

Lemma: (faithfulness of T_u)

(i) If π is an unconditionally-fair computation sequence of S then there exists an extension π' of π to the (new) variables z_1 and z_2 so that π' is a computation sequence of $T_u(S)$.
(ii) Conversely, if π' is a computation sequence of $T_u(S)$ then its restriction π to the variables of S is an unconditionally-fair computation sequence of S.

This lemma states that T_u is a *faithful transformation* in the sense that for every program S of the form considered here, $T_u(S)$ simulates *exactly* all and only unconditionally-fair computation sequences of S.

Proof: (i) Consider an unconditionally-fair computation sequence

$$\pi = \sigma_0 \underset{i_0}{\rightarrow} \cdots \sigma_j \underset{i_j}{\rightarrow} \cdots$$

of S with $i_j \in \{1,2\}$. We show how to extend π to a sequence

$$\pi' = \sigma'_0 \underset{i_0}{\rightarrow} \cdots \sigma'_j \underset{i_j}{\rightarrow} \cdots$$

by providing values to the variables z_1 and z_2. For $l \in \{1,2\}$ we define

$$\sigma'_j(z_l) = \min \{k-j \mid k \geqslant j \wedge (i_k = l \vee \sigma_k \models \neg B)\} \in N.$$

Note that this minimum always exists because π is unconditionally fair. By construction in every state σ'_j (except the final state σ'_k with $\sigma'_k \models \neg B$ if π is finite) exactly one of the variables z_1 and z_2, namely z_{i_j}, has the value 0. The other variable has a positive value. Thus the scheduler built into the program $T_u(S)$ would indeed choose the direction i_j when started in the state σ'_j. Furthermore, the values of the variables z_1 and z_2 in the states σ'_j have been defined in a way which is consistent with the assignments to these variables in $T_u(S)$. This shows that π' is in fact a valid computation sequence of $T_u(S)$.

(ii) Let π' be a computation sequence of $T_u(S)$ and let π be its restriction to the variables of S. It is obvious that π is a valid computation sequence of S. But we have to prove that this computation sequence is unconditionally fair.

Suppose this is not the case. Then π is infinite, i.e. B is always true, but one direction of S, say i, is from a certain moment on never taken. By definition of $T_u(S)$ the value of the variable z_i becomes arbitrarily small and from some moment on smaller than -1. But this is impossible because it is easy to check that in every state σ'_j of π' the following invariant

$$IN \equiv (z_1 \geqslant -1 \wedge z_2 \geqslant -1) \wedge (z_1 = -1 \rightarrow z_2 \geqslant 0)$$
$$\wedge (z_2 = -1 \rightarrow z_1 \geqslant 0)$$

holds. []

Corollary: Let p be an assertion without z_1 and z_2 as free variables. Then

$$\overset{u}{\models} \ll p \gg S \ll true \gg \text{ iff } \models < p > T_u(S) < true > .$$

Thus, in order to prove termination of S under the unconditional-fairness assumption it suffices to prove termination of $T_u(S)$ in the usual sense. It is not needed that S be actually transformed into $T_u(S)$ as part of a proof method. This approach would correspond to Flon and Suzuki's idea to employ certain transformations as proof rules in a system for total correctness of parallel programs [FS 81], with the disadvantage of destroying the structure of the original program S. Instead–in a second step–we use the transformation conceptually in order to derive a direct proof rule for S. This derivation applies the proof rule of [AP 82] (which is actually **NDT** with W as an initial segment of the countable ordinals) to $T_u(S)$ and then reads back the ensuring rule in terms of the original program S. Thus, in order to apply the derived proof rule one never has to carry out the transformations of S into $T_u(S)$ explicitly.

We introduce some notational conventions. For a predicate $p \subseteq \Sigma_{T_u(S)}$, let p^{in} be an abbreviation for $p \wedge IN$, where IN is the invariant mentioned in the proof of the faithfulness-of-T_u lemma. In anticipation of the formulation of the rule for $n > 2$ guards, abbreviate $z_1 \leqslant z_2$ as $turn = 1$ and $z_2 > z_1$ as $turn = 2$. We thus obtain the rule **UFAIR**$_2$ in Figure 3.2, deviating slightly from [AO 83] in forbidding termination before the 0 parameter is reached. It is assumed that z_1, z_2 do not occur free in p or S.

Before presenting examples of application of this rule in proofs, a simplification of the rule is presented, which applies only to the case of two directions and makes many proofs easier. It is not known to date whether this simplification is complete. In general finding an invariant $pi(\alpha, z_1, z_2)$ means estimating the number α of iterations of the loop S. This estimation can be expressed in terms of the variables in S with additional help of the priority variables z_1 and z_2. Fortunately, in the case of two guards we can often represent this number α as a (lexicographically ordered) pair $\alpha = <\beta, z>$, where β counts the number of *rounds* the program S will still execute before termination and z counts the number of steps in the current round. A *round* is a maximal sequence of computation steps for which always direction 1 (subprogram S_1) or always direction 2 (subprogram S_2) is executed. Partitioning α into β and z is very helpful in those cases where the number β of rounds can be estimated

---

To prove $\overset{u}{\ll} p \gg S \ll \mathit{true} \gg$:

Find a *parametrized invariant* pi: $\mathbf{ord} \times \Sigma_{T_u(S)} \to \{\mathit{true}, \mathit{false}\}$ (referred to as $pi(\alpha, z_1, z_2)$), satisfying:

1. (INIT) $p \to \forall z_1, z_2 \geqslant 0 \exists \alpha: pi(\alpha, z_1, z_2)$.
2. (CONT) $(pi^{in}(\alpha, z_1, z_2) \wedge \alpha > 0) \to B$.
3. (TERM) $pi^{in}(0, z_1, z_2) \to \neg B$.
4. (DEC)

$\overset{u}{\ll} pi^{in}(\alpha, z_1, z_2) \wedge B \wedge turn = i \gg S_i \ll \forall z_1, z_2 \geqslant 0 \exists \beta: \beta < \alpha \wedge pi^{in}(\beta, \tilde{z}_1, \tilde{z}_2) \gg$,
$i = 1,2$ where

$$\tilde{z}_k = \begin{cases} z_k & k = i \\ z_k - 1 & k \neq i \end{cases}.$$

Figure 3.2 Rule **UFAIR$_2$**.

---

independently of their lengths z. To do this we use *turn* as an additional variable, and not just as an abbreviation for $z_1 \leqslant z_2$ or $z_2 < z_1$. This informal discussion is made precise in the rule **SIM-UFAIR$_2$** in Figure 3.3, where $\Sigma_S{}^*$ is an extension to the states of S with a variable $turn \in \{1,2\}$. It is assumed that the variable *turn* does not occur free in p or S.

Note that in (DEC) the value of α is decreased only if a switch of control to the other direction occurs. This formalizes the intuitive idea that α counts the number of rounds instead of the numbers of loop traversals.

Lemma: (soundness of SIM-UFAIR$_2$) If there is an invariant $pi^*(\alpha, turn)$ satisfying the premises of the simplified proof rule **SIM-UFAIR$_2$** then

---

To prove $\overset{u}{\ll} p \gg S \ll \mathit{true} \gg$:

Find a *parametrized invariant* pi^*: $\mathbf{ord} \times \Sigma_S{}^* \to \{\mathit{true}, \mathit{false}\}$, satisfying:

1. (INIT) $p \to \forall turn \exists \alpha: pi^*(\alpha, turn)$.
2. (CONT) $(pi^*(\alpha, turn) \wedge \alpha > 0) \to B$.
3. (TERM) $pi^*(0, turn) \to \neg B$.
4. (DEC)

$\overset{u}{\ll} pi^*(\alpha, i) \wedge B \gg S_i \ll \exists \gamma: \gamma \leqslant \alpha \wedge pi^*(\gamma, i) \wedge \exists \beta: \beta < \alpha \wedge pi^*(\beta, 3-i) \gg$,
$i = 1,2$.

Figure 3.3 Rule **SIM-UFAIR$_2$**.

---

there exists also an invariant $pi(\alpha, z_1, z_2)$ satisfying the premises of the original rule **UFAIR**$_2$.

Proof: Let $(W, \leqslant)$ be the well-founded set associated with the application of $pi^*(\alpha, turn)$, then $pi(\alpha, z_1, z_2)$ can be constructed from $pi^*(\alpha, turn)$ as follows:

$$\begin{aligned} pi(\alpha, z_1, z_2) \equiv & (B \wedge z_1 \leqslant z_2 \rightarrow \exists \beta{:}\ \beta > 0 \wedge \alpha = <\beta, z_2> \wedge pi^*(\beta, 1)) \\ & \wedge (B \wedge z_2 < z_1 \rightarrow \exists \beta{:}\ \beta > 0 \wedge \alpha = <\beta, z_1> \wedge pi^*(\beta, 2)) \\ & \wedge (\neg B \rightarrow \exists turn, z{:}\ \alpha = <0, z> \wedge pi^*(0, turn)), \end{aligned}$$

where pairs $<\beta, z>$ are ordered lexicographically:

$$<\beta_1, z_1> \; < \; <\beta_2, z_2> \;\longleftrightarrow\; \beta_1 < \beta_2 \vee (\beta_1 = \beta_2 \wedge z_1 < z_2).$$

Note that the standard invariant IN implies that always $z_1 \geqslant -1 \wedge z_2 \geqslant -1$ holds. Thus the pairs $<\beta, z>$ relevant to $pi^{in}(\alpha, z_1, z_2)$ are elements of $W \times \{z \mid z \geqslant -1\}$ which is indeed a well-founded structure under lexicographical order. It is now easy to check that $pi^{in}(\alpha, z_1, z_2)$ satisfies the clauses of rule **UFAIR**$_2$. Note that IN is crucial for verifying the premises (DEC). [ ]

There is no known proof of the relative completeness of the simplified rule **SIM-UFAIR**$_2$, i.e. the converse of the above lemma. The stumbling block is that there is no counter variable z to use. Nevertheless, the simplified rule is a very useful, sound proof rule which is rather easy to apply as is now shown.

Example:

$$\overset{u}{\vdash}_{\textbf{SIM-UFAIR}_2} \ll true \gg *[1{:}\ b \rightarrow skip [\,]\ 2{:}\ b \rightarrow b{:}=false] \ll true \gg.$$

Let us first apply the original rule **UFAIR**$_2$ where we need a parametrized invariant $pi(\alpha, z_1, z_2)$. As we know α is intended to count the numbers of *loop traversals*. To determine α, let us analyze the possible cases. First if b is *false* at the beginning, the program terminates immediately so that $\alpha = 0$ holds. Otherwise $\alpha > 0$ holds. Suppose we start with the second direction S_2:: $b{:}=false$. Then simply $\alpha = 1$ holds. A more interesting case is if we start with the first direction S_1:: *skip*. Now the exact number α of loop traversals is not predictable any more because S_1 may be executed arbitrarily often. However, unconditional fairness is assumed, which guarantees that S_1 will be executed only finitely many times, depending on how often S_2 may be neglected. The maximal number of times S_2 may be neglected is given by $z_2 + 1$, where z_2 is the priority variable associated with S_2. The "$+1$" is necessary here because S_1 may be executed once even if $z_2 = 0$ holds (as follows from the standard invariant IN). This discussion can be summarized in the following variant:

$$pi(\alpha, z_1, z_2)_0 \equiv (\neg b \longleftrightarrow \alpha = 0)$$
$$\wedge (b \wedge turn = 1 \rightarrow \alpha = 2+z_2)$$
$$\wedge (b \wedge turn = 2 \rightarrow \alpha = 1)$$

where the underlying well-founded structure is $(N, \leqslant)$.

As it turns out $pi(\alpha, z_1, z_2)$ satisfies indeed the premises of the proof rule **UFAIR**$_2$. Note how convenient it is to formalize the informal case analysis with the help of the "turn" notation. Also realize how the additional counter variable z_2 reflects the assumption of (unconditional) fairness. With z_2 it is possible to find an entity α which gets decreased with every loop execution, but without z_2 this is impossible (which accords with the fact that without a fairness assumption the program is not guaranteed to terminate).

Next, consider the simplified rule **SIM-FAIR**$_2$, where an invariant $pi^*(\alpha, turn)$ is needed–with α counting the number of *rounds* only. This time the program analysis is even simpler than the one before. If b is false, then $\alpha = 0$ holds. If b is true and direction S_1 is selected there will be two rounds: $\alpha = 2$. Otherwise, if we start with S_2 only one round is possible: $\alpha = 1$. This leads to

$$pi^*(\alpha, turn) \equiv (\neg b \longleftrightarrow \alpha = 0)$$
$$\wedge (b \wedge turn = 1 \rightarrow \alpha = 2)$$
$$\wedge (b \wedge turn = 2 \rightarrow \alpha = 1)$$

where the underlying well-founded structure is simply $(\{0,1,2\}, \leqslant)$. It is easy to check that $pi^*(\alpha, turn)$ satisfies the premises of the rule **SIM-UFAIR**$_2$. Note that it is the unconditional-fairness assumption which provides a meaningful interpretation of $pi^*(\alpha, turn)$: since in case $b \wedge turn = 1$ the first round is finite we need not bother about *how long* this round actually is.

Example:

$$\overset{u}{\vdash}_{\mathbf{SIM\text{-}UFAIR}_2} \ll true \gg S \ll true \gg,$$

where S is given as in Figure 3.4.

We wish to apply the simplified rule immediately. Thus the number α of rounds has to be estimated again. Observe that this time α is not uniformly bounded as in the previous example where $(\alpha \leqslant 2)$, but we can give a bound for α depending on the value of the variable x in the initial

```
*[1: x > 0→b:=true
 []
 2: x > 0→[b→x:=x−1; b:=false
            []
           ¬b→skip
            ]
].
```

Figure 3.4 Program *S*.

state: $\alpha \leqslant 2x + 1$. Thus we choose $(N, \leqslant)$ as the well-founded structure.

The following invariant analyzes the possible cases precisely:

$$\begin{aligned} pi^*(\alpha, turn) \equiv\ & (x \leqslant 0 \longleftrightarrow \alpha = 0) \\ & \wedge (x > 0 \wedge turn = 1 \rightarrow \alpha = 2x) \\ & \wedge (x > 0 \wedge turn = 2 \wedge b \rightarrow \alpha = 2x - 1) \\ & \wedge (x > 0 \wedge turn = 2 \wedge \neg b \rightarrow \alpha = 2x + 1). \end{aligned}$$

And indeed this invariant suffices to prove the above termination assertion via the rule **SIM-UFAIR$_2$**.

Example:

$$\overset{\mathbf{u}}{\vdash_{\mathbf{SIM-UFAIR_2}}} \ll true \gg P \ll true \gg,$$

where *P* is given as in Figure 3.5.

```
*[1: x > 0→b:=true;
              [c→x:=x + 1
              []
              ¬c→skip
              ]
 []
 2: x > 0→ c:=false;
               [b→x:=x−1; b:=false
               []
               ¬b→skip
               ]
 ].
```

Figure 3.5 Program *P*.

Again we wish to estimate the number of rounds in order to apply rule **SIM-UFAIR$_2$**. But this time we have augmented the program of the previous example in such a way that even if we know the initial state σ_0 we cannot predict the number of rounds in case that $x > 0 \wedge c$ holds in σ_0 and the first direction is selected. However, as soon as the first round has ended, the number of the remaining rounds is determined exactly as in the previous example. This suggests $\omega + 1$ as the well-founded set . Intuitively, ω represents the concept of an unknown number which will become precise as soon as ω gets decreased to some $n < \omega$. For an initial value of x satisfying $x > 0$ the maximal number α of rounds can now be estimated as

$$(\alpha = \omega) \vee (2x-1 \leqslant \beta \leqslant 2x + 1).$$

With this intuition the following invariant is understandable:

$$\begin{aligned} pi^*(\alpha,turn) &\equiv (x \leqslant 0 \longleftrightarrow \alpha = 0) \\ \wedge (x > 0 \wedge turn &= 1 \wedge c \rightarrow \alpha = \omega) \\ \wedge (x > 0 \wedge turn &= 1 \wedge \neg c \rightarrow \alpha = 2x) \\ \wedge (x > 0 \wedge turn &= 2 \wedge b \rightarrow \alpha = 2x-1) \\ \wedge (x > 0 \wedge turn &= 2 \wedge \neg b \rightarrow \alpha = 2x+1). \end{aligned}$$

Note the new part as compared with the invariant of the previous example. Again $pi^*(\alpha, turn)$ satisfies the premises of proof rule **SIM-UFAIR$_2$** and thus proves the desired termination assertion.

This is an example which we cannot prove without resorting to infinite ordinals in the well-founded structures even if we count the number of rounds only. Clearly by counting every single loop execution we would have encountered infinite ordinals already in the previous example. This is so because lexicographically ordered pairs $\alpha = <\beta,z>$ needed in the translation of $pi^*(\beta, turn)$ into $pi(\alpha', z_1, z_2)$ can be written equivalently as

$$\alpha' = \beta \times \omega + z.$$

Next we extend this approach of dealing with unconditional fairness to a typical repetition statement $S \in GC$ with any number of directions, all still guarded by the same Boolean expression B. Again we proceed in two steps, first looking for a transformation which simulates the unconditionally-fair computations of S and then using this transformation to derive a proof rule for termination under the unconditional-fairness assumption. The transformation $T_u(S)$ (see Figure 3.6) is a systematic extension of the one for the two directions case. The $z_1, \cdots, z_n$ are new variables not occurring in S which range over the integers. The expression $turn=i$ is an abbreviation defined by

$$turn = i \equiv (i = \min\{j \mid z_j = \min_{k \in I}\{z_k\}\})$$

$$
\begin{aligned}
T_u(S) \equiv\ & \text{for } all\ i \in I\ do\ z_i := ?; \\
& *[\ \underset{i \in I}{[\,]}\ i\!:\ B \wedge turn = i \rightarrow S_i; z_i := ?; \\
& \quad \text{for } all\ j \in I - \{i\}\ do\ z_j := z_j - 1 \\
& \quad].
\end{aligned}
$$

Figure 3.6 Transformation $T_u(S)$.

which holds if i is the smallest index such that z_i has the minimal value among $z_1, \cdots, z_n$. As in the case of two guards the variables $z_1, \cdots, z_n$ are *priority variables* used to realize a schedule in $T_u(S)$ which allows only unconditionally-fair computations. At every moment in the computation of $T_u(S)$ the direction with the smallest index and the maximal priority, say i, is executed. After this execution the priorities of all other directions j, $j \neq i$, get incremented (i.e. z_j decremented) by 1 whereas the priority of i gets reset to an arbitrary non-negative value. We do not bother here to code *for all ... do* in *GC*, which is a straightforward programming exercise.

Recall that in the transformed program in the two-directional case the variables z_1 and z_2 were always $\geqslant -1$. For $T_u(S)$ we can show analogously that $z_1, \ldots, z_n \geqslant -n+1$ is always true. In fact, this is a special case of the more general invariant (playing the same role *IN* played before)

$$INV \equiv \bigwedge_{i=1}^{n-1} |\,\{k \mid z_k \leqslant -i\}\,| \leqslant n-i$$

which holds in every state of a computation sequence of $T_u(S)$. This can be proved in a lemma analogous to the faithfulness lemma above. We shall not do this here because it will be a special case of the more general faithfulness lemma to follow. But we state:

Proposition: Let p be an assertion without $z_1, \cdots, z_n$ as free variables. Then

$$\overset{u}{\models} \ll p \gg S \ll true \gg \ \textit{iff}\ \models\ < p >\ T_u(S)\ < true >.$$

This proposition is the starting point for the second step where the proof rule **NDT** is applied to $T_u(S)$. This leads to the rule **UFAIR** in Figure 3.7.

Soundness and relative completeness of the rule **UFAIR** follows automatically from the faithfulness of T_u and the corresponding results for the proof rule **NDT** for GC_R. We remark that in the case $n = 1$, i.e. S:: $*[1\!: B \rightarrow S_1]$, the transformed program $T_u(S)$ is equivalent to S and the proof rule **UFAIR** becomes equivalent to the original proof rule **DT** for deterministic termination.

To prove $\overset{u}{\ll} p \gg S \ll true \gg$:

Find a parametrized invariant pi: $\mathbf{ord} \times \Sigma_{T_u(S)} \rightarrow \{true, false\}$, satisfying:

1. (INIT) $p \rightarrow \forall z_1, \cdots, z_n \geqslant 0 \exists \alpha: pi(\alpha, z_1, \cdots, z_n)$
2. (CONT) $pi^{in}(\alpha, z_1, \cdots, z_n) \wedge \alpha > 0 \rightarrow B$
3. (TERM) $pi^{in}(0, z_1, \cdots, z_n) \rightarrow \neg B$
4. (DEC)

$$\overset{u}{\ll} pi^{in}(\alpha, z_1, \cdots, z_n) \wedge B_i \wedge turn = i \gg$$
$$S_i$$
$$\ll \forall z_i \exists \beta: \beta < \alpha \wedge pi^{in}(\beta, \tilde{z}_1, \cdots, \tilde{z}_n) \gg,$$

$i \in I$, where

$$\tilde{z}_k = \begin{cases} z_k & k = i \\ z_k - 1 & k \neq i \end{cases}$$

Figure 3.7 Rule **UFAIR.**

In the case of two directions we were able to derive a sound simplified rule **SIM-UFAIR**$_2$ from **UFAIR**$_2$ which relied only on the notion of a round and was rather easy to apply. But in the case of $n \geqslant 3$ directions this simplification technique no longer works successfully. An attempted generalization would lead to a rule **SIM-UFAIR** with a premise

(*DEC*)

$$\overset{u}{\ll} pi^*(\alpha, i) \wedge B \gg$$

$$S_i$$

$$\ll \exists \gamma: \gamma \leqslant \alpha \wedge pi^*(\gamma, i) \wedge \forall j \in I - \{i\} \exists \beta: \beta < \alpha \wedge pi^*(\beta, j) \gg.$$

However, even in the simplest cases such an invariant $pi^*(\alpha, turn)$ satisfying (DEC) need not exist. Here is an example: we would like to prove

$$\overset{u}{\ll} true \gg *[\ 1{:}\, b \rightarrow skip\ [\,]\ 2{:}\, b \rightarrow skip\ [\,]\ 3{:}\, b \rightarrow b{:=}false]\ \ll true \gg,$$

a straightforward extension of a previous example. But this cannot be done with the proposed proof rule **SIM-UFAIR** because there is no bound for the number β of rounds if we start with $turn \in \{1,2\}$ *unless* the priority z_3 of the third direction S_3:: $b{:=}false$ is known. Thus one cannot achieve much without priority variables as soon as $n \geqslant 3$ directions are considered, and therefore we stick to the original proof rule **UFAIR**.

This section is ended with examples of the application of **UFAIR**.

Example: Previous examples were particularly simple because there was a fixed direction which was responsible for termination. Here is a more symmetric program which will be important in the next, more complicated example.

$$A:: *[\underset{i \in I}{[]} i: \neg \bigwedge_{i \in I} b_i \rightarrow b_i := true].$$

Here the Boolean variable b_i being true can be interpreted as reporting that some i-th subprogram S_i has already been executed. The program A terminates as soon as every direction has been executed at least once. The claim to be proved is

$$\overset{\mathbf{u}}{\vdash_{\mathbf{UFAIR}}} \ll true \gg A \ll true \gg .$$

To prove this claim an estimation of the maximal number of executions of the body of A is needed. So assume that currently the i-th direction S_i is being executed i.e. that $turn = i$ holds. Then α depends on how many times the other directions j, $j \neq i$, may still be neglected. But this can be measured in terms of the priority variables z_j, $j \neq i$. Taking the standard invariant INV for these variables into account a first estimation of α in case of $turn = i$ is

$$\alpha = n + \max_{j \in I} \{z_j \mid j \neq i\}.$$

This equation clearly holds at the beginning of a computation but is not kept invariant in the course of such a computation. The problem is that as soon as the j-th direction has been executed the corresponding priority variable z_j gets reset arbitrarily whereas the maximum number of times the loop is left to be executed decreases by at least 1. But this deficiency can be fixed easily by using the Boolean variables b_j which indicate whether direction j has already been executed. For $turn = i$ we set

$$q_i \equiv (\alpha = n + \max \{ \text{ if } b_j \textit{ then } -n + 1 \textit{ else } z_j \mid j \in I, j \neq i\})$$

where $-n + 1$ is the smallest value z_j can assume.

Finally, define

$$pi(\alpha, z_1, \cdots, z_n) \equiv (b_1 \wedge \cdots \wedge b_n \longleftrightarrow \alpha = 0)$$
$$\wedge \; (\bigwedge_{i \in I} \neg (b_1 \wedge \cdots \wedge b_n) \wedge turn = i \rightarrow q_i).$$

It turns out that $pi(\alpha, z_1, \ldots, z_n)$ indeed satisfies the premises of proof rule **UFAIR**.

We end this section with a more substantial example, involving some algebra.

Example: Let $(L, \subseteq)$ be a complete lattice which satisfies the *finite chain property*, i.e. every strictly increasing chain

$$x_1 \subset x_2 \subset x_3 \subset \cdots$$

in L is finite. Thus $(L, \subseteq)$ is a well-founded structure. Then the product $(L^n, \subseteq)$ with $n \geqslant 2$ is also a complete lattice with the finite chain property. Consider an operator monotonic w.r.t. $\subseteq$

$$F\colon L^n \rightarrow L^n$$

By Knaster–Tarski's theorem [TA 55] F has a least fixed point $\mu F \in L^n$ (more about this theorem in Chapter 6). We wish to compute μF asynchronously by employing n subprograms S_i each of which is allowed only to apply the i-th component function

$$F_i\colon L^n \rightarrow L$$

of F defined by $F_i(x_1, \cdots, x_n) = y_i$, where

$$F(x_1, \cdots, x_n) = (y_1, \cdots, y_n).$$

These subprograms arc activated nondeterministically by the following program

$$FIX{::}\ *[1\colon B \rightarrow x_1{:=}F_1(\bar{x})\ [\,]...[\,]\ n\colon B \rightarrow x_n{:=}F_n(\bar{x})]$$

where $\bar{x} \equiv (x_1, \cdots, x_n)$ and $B \equiv \neg(\bar{x} = F(\bar{x}))$. In general, FIX need not compute μF; the claim is that it will do so under the assumption of unconditional fairness:

$$\overset{\mathbf{u}}{\models} \ll \bar{x} = \perp \gg FIX \ll \bar{x} = \mu F \gg \qquad \text{(C)}$$

where $\perp$ is the least element in L^n. This correctness result is a special case of a more general theorem proved by Cousot [C 77] while the formalized proof is due to [AO 83]. We would like to prove (C) with the help of the proof rule **UFAIR**. To this end we proceed in two steps.

Step 1) We start with an informal analysis of program FIX. Consider a computation sequence

$$\pi = \sigma_0 \rightarrow_{i_0} \cdots \sigma_j \rightarrow_{i_j} \cdots$$

of FIX and define $\sigma_j[\bar{x}] \equiv (\sigma_j[x_1], \cdots, \sigma_j[x_n])$ for $j \geqslant 1$ and

$$F_i[\bar{x}] = (x_1, \cdots, x_{i-1}, F_i(\bar{x}), x_{i+1}, \cdots, x_n)$$

for $1 \leqslant i \leqslant n$. Since $\sigma_0[\ \bar{x}\ ] = \perp$ holds and the component functions F_i are monotonic, the assertion

$$\perp \subseteq \bar{x} \subseteq F_i[\ \bar{x}\ ] \subseteq \mu F \qquad (+)$$

is true for every $i \in \{1, \cdots, n\}$ in every state σ_j of π. Thus, $\bar{x} = \mu F$ will hold as soon as *FIX* has terminated with $\bar{x} = F(\ \bar{x}\ )$. But why does *FIX* terminate? Note that by $(+)$ the program *FIX* produces an increasing chain

$$\sigma_0[\ \bar{x}\ ] \subset \cdots \subset \sigma_j[\ \bar{x}\ ] \subset \cdots .$$

The existence of some state σ_j with $\bar{x} = F(\ \bar{x}\ )$ is implied by two facts:

1° By the finite chain property of L^n the values $\sigma_j[\ \bar{x}\ ] \in L^n$ cannot be increased infinitely often.
2° By the unconditional-fairness assumption the values $\sigma_j[\ \bar{x}\ ]$ cannot be constant arbitrarily long without increasing.

1° is clear, but 2° needs a proof. Consider some intermediate state σ_j in π for which either $\sigma_j = \sigma_0$ or $\sigma_{j-1}[\ \bar{x}\ ] \subset \sigma_j[\ \bar{x}\ ]$ holds. Then, $I = \{1, \cdots, n\}$ can be partitioned into $K_1 \bigcup K_2$ (depending on σ_j), s.t. $\bar{x} = F_k[\ \bar{x}\ ]$ for $k \in K_1$, while $\bar{x} \subset F_l[\ \bar{x}\ ]$ for $l \in K_2$, both hold at σ_j. Note that $K_2 \neq \varnothing$ since σ_j is intermediate in π (not final, where $\bar{x} = F(\ \bar{x}\ )$ already holds).

Thus, as long as K_1-moves are taken, the computation proceeds as

$$\sigma_j = \sigma_{j+1} = \sigma_{j+2} = \cdots .$$

On the other hand, as soon as K_2-move is taken in state σ_m, $m \geqslant j$, then $\sigma_m(\ \bar{x}\ ) \subset \sigma_{m+1}(\ \bar{x}\ )$, the *next* increase. Here the unconditional fairness assumption is used (the formal proof resembles that of the *symmetric-termination* example proved earlier).

Step 2) With this informal discussion in mind we are now prepared for the formal fair termination proof of *FIX* with proof rule **UFAIR**. As the well-founded structure we choose $(L^n \times N, \leqslant)$ where $\leqslant$ is the lexicographic order defined by

$$<\bar{x}_1, n_1> \; > \; <\bar{x}_2, n_2> \text{ if } \bar{x}_1 \subset \bar{x}_2 \vee (\ \bar{x}_1 = \bar{x}_2 \wedge n_1 > n_2\ ).$$

Since L^n has the finite chain property, $>$ is clearly well-founded. The components $\bar{x}$ and n of pairs $<\bar{x}, n> \in L^n \times N$ correspond to the facts 1° and 2° about the termination of *FIX* mentioned above. The invariant is

$$pi(\alpha, z_1, \cdots, z_n) \equiv \bigwedge_{i=1,n}(\perp \subseteq \bar{x} \subseteq F_i[\ \bar{x}\ ] \subseteq \mu F)$$

$$\wedge (B \rightarrow \alpha = <\bar{x}, n + \min\{z_l \mid 1 \leqslant l \leqslant n \wedge \bar{x} \subset F_l[\ \bar{x}\ ]\}>).$$

Note that the set over which the minimum is taken is not empty due to B holding.

Clearly, $pi(\alpha, z_1, \cdots, z_n)$ satisfies the first three premises of the proof rule **UFAIR**. To check premise (DEC) assume that $pi^{in}(\alpha, z_1, \cdots, z_n) \wedge B \wedge turn = i$ holds in some state σ, and let the state σ' result from σ by execution of FIX_i. If $\sigma[\ \bar{x}\ ] \subset \sigma'[\ \bar{x}\ ]$ holds, α gets decreased by the first component. Otherwise $\sigma[\ \bar{x}\ ] = \sigma'[\ \bar{x}\ ]$ is true. Since B holds before the execution of FIX_i, there exist indices $l \in \{1, \cdots, n\}$ s.t. $\bar{x} \subset F_l[\ \bar{x}\ ]$. In fact, $l = i$ holds, since $\bar{x} = F_i[\ \bar{x}\ ]$. The following β is independent of z_i.

$$\beta = <\bar{x}, n+\min\{z_l - 1 \mid 1 \leqslant l \leqslant n \wedge \bar{x} \subset F_l[\ \bar{x}\ ]\}>.$$

Clearly, $\beta < \alpha$, and $pi^{in}(\beta, z_1 - 1, \cdots, z_{i-1} - 1, z_i, \cdots, z_n - 1)$ holds again after the execution of FIX_i for every $z_i \geqslant 0$.

Finally, observe that for this example it is very convenient to have arbitrary well-founded structures as our disposal. If we were restricted to their standard representation as ordinals we would have run into difficulties when dealing with the not further analyzed structure of L^n.

3.2 Weak and Strong Fairness: n Guards

We now develop proof rules dealing with weak and strong fairness for general repetition statements $S \in GC$. We start with *weak fairness.* First we look for a transformation of S which realizes exactly all and only weakly-fair computations of S. As in the transformation T_u of Section 3.1 we associate a (new) priority variable z_i with every direction i. But now these variables will be manipulated individually depending on whether the corresponding guard B_i is true or false. Also when determining which of the directions is to be executed next we have to make sure that only those priority variables z_i are considered for which the guard B_i is true. These remarks lead to the transformation $T_w(S)$(see Figure 3.8).

$$
\begin{array}{l}
T_w(S)::\ \text{for } all\ i \in I\ do\ z_i := ?;\\
\qquad *[\ \underset{i \in I}{[\,]} B_i \wedge turn = i \rightarrow S_i;\ z_i := ?;\\
\qquad\qquad \text{for } all\ j \in I - \{i\}\ do\\
\qquad\qquad [B_j \rightarrow z_j := z_j - 1\\
\qquad\qquad [\,]\\
\qquad\qquad \neg B_j \rightarrow z_j := ?\\
\qquad\qquad]\\
\qquad].
\end{array}
$$

Figure 3.8 Transformation $T_w(S)$.

Here $turn = i$ is an abbreviation defined by

$$turn = i \equiv (i = \min_{k \in I}\{j \mid z_j = \min\{z_k \mid B_k\}\})$$

which holds if i is the smallest index such that z_i has the minimal value among all those z_j for which B_j is true. The priority variables z_j are reset to an arbitrary value as soon as B_j is false. This formalizes exactly the weak- fairness assumption, by which a direction j is certain to be executed only if the guard B_j is continuously true from some moment on. Note that for $B_1 = \cdots = B_n$ the program $T_w(S)$ reduces to $T_u(S)$ of Section 3.1. Note also that the built-in scheduler is deterministic in that in $T_w(S)$ only one guard is enabled. A similar transformation appears in [PA 81] (described in Section 3.2.2) where the built-in scheduler is left nondeterministic. This is achieved by replacing the condition $turn = i$ with the weaker one

$$turn(i) \equiv \forall j \in I: B_j \rightarrow z_j \geqslant z_i .$$

The following lemma proves the correctness of T_w (and hence also of T_u) by showing that the transformation is *faithful* in the sense of Section 3.1.

Lemma: (faithfulness of T_w)

(i) If π is a weakly-fair computation sequence of S then there exists an extension π' of π to the (new) variables $z_1, \ldots, z_n$ such that π' is a computation sequence of $T_w(S)$.

(ii) Conversely, if π' is a computation sequence of $T_w(S)$ then its restriction π to the variables of S is a weakly-fair computation sequence of S.

Proof: (i) Consider a weakly-fair computation sequence

$$\pi = \sigma_0 \rightarrow_{i_0} \cdots \sigma_j \rightarrow_{i_j} \cdots$$

of S with $i_j \in I$. We show how to extend π to a sequence $\pi' = \sigma'_0 \rightarrow_{i_0} \cdots \sigma'_j \rightarrow_{i_j} \cdots$ by assuming new values to the variables $z_1, \ldots, z_n$. Define for $l \in I$

$$\sigma'_j[z_l] = \begin{cases} \min\{k-j \mid k \geqslant j \wedge i_k = l\} & \text{if } \exists k \geqslant l: i_k = l \\ 1+\min\{k-j \mid k \geqslant j \wedge \sigma_k \models \neg B_l\} & \text{otherwise.} \end{cases}$$

We claim that $\sigma'[z_l] \in N$ holds for all j and l. To see this we have to show that in both cases the minimum of a non-empty subset of N is taken. By definition this is true for the case $\exists k \geqslant j: i_k = l$. So, assume $\forall k \geqslant j: i_k \neq l$, i.e. from σ_j onwards, the l-th direction is never scheduled for execution again. Since π is weakly-fair, this can only be the case if there exist infinitely many k, $k \geqslant j$: $\sigma_k \models \neg B_l$ holds. This implies of course $\exists k \geqslant j$: $\sigma_k \models \neg B_l$ which guarantees that the minimum of a non-empty set is taken.

Note that in every state σ'_j exactly one variable z_l has the value 0 - namely z_{i_j}. So the scheduler built into the program $T_w(S)$ will indeed choose the direction i_j in the state σ'_j. Also it is easy to check that the values of the variables $z_1, \ldots, z_n$ in the states σ'_j are defined consistently with the corresponding assignments in $T_w(S)$. Thus π' is indeed a computation sequence of $T_w(S)$.

(ii) Conversely, let π' be a computation of $T_w(S)$ and π be its restriction to the variables of S. Clearly, π is a computation sequence of S, but we have to show that it is weakly fair. Suppose this is not the case. Then π is infinite and one direction of S, say i, is from a certain state σ_j onwards never scheduled for execution though $\sigma_k \models B_i$ holds for all $k \geqslant j$. By definition of $T_w(S)$ the value of the variable z_i gets smaller than $-n+1$ in some state σ'_k with $k \geqslant j$. But this is impossible because the assertion

$$INV \equiv \left(\bigwedge_{i=1,n} |\{k \mid z_k \leqslant -i\}| \leqslant n-i \right) \wedge \left(\bigwedge_{i=1,n} z_i < 0 \rightarrow B_i \right)$$

holds in every state σ'_j of π'. We prove this by induction on $j \geqslant 0$. In σ'_0 all $z_1, \ldots, z_n \geqslant 0$ so that INV is vacuously true. Assume now that INV holds in σ'_{j-1}. We show that INV is also true in σ'_j:

1) Suppose there is some $i \in \{1, \ldots, n\}$ such that there are at least $n-i+1$ indiccs k for which $z_k \leqslant -i$ holds in σ'_j. Let K be the set of all these indices. By the construction of $T_w(S)$ the inequality $z_k \leqslant -i+1$ holds for all $k \in K$ in the state σ'_{j-1}. By the induction hypothesis $|K| \leqslant n-i+1$ holds, so that indeed $|K| = n-i+1$. Again by induction the hypothesis B_k is true in σ'_{i-1} for all $k \in K$. Hence there is also some $k \in K$ with $i_{j-1} = k$, by definition of $T_w(S)$. But this implies that $z_k \geqslant 0$ holds in σ'_j, contradicting the definition of K. Thus, $\bigwedge_{i=1,n} |\{k \mid z_k \leqslant -i\}| \leqslant n-i$ holds in σ'_j.
2) The second conjunct follows immediately from the definition of $T_w(S)$.

This finishes the induction step and establishes the invariance of INV. [ ]

Corollary: Let p be an assertion without $z_1, \ldots, z_n$ as free variables. Then

$$\overset{w}{\models} \ll p \gg S \ll true \gg \textit{ iff } \models < p > T_w(S) < true >.$$

Thus, an application of the rule **NDT** and the random assignment axiom yields the rule **WFAIR** in Figure 3.9.

The only difference between **UFAIR** and **WFAIR** is in the definition of $\tilde{z}_k$, $k \neq i$, which are decremented only if the corresponding direction was enabled before S_i was executed, and reset to an arbitrary value otherwise.

Next, a transformation T_s, realizing strongly-fair scheduling, is presented in Figure 3.10, and a corresponding proof rule is derived. In case of $\neg B_j$, the priority variable z_j is *not* reset to a random number, thus realizing strong fairness. Again we can state:

Proposition: Let p be an assertion without $z_1, \ldots, z_n$ as free variables. Then

$$\models \overset{s}{\ll} p \gg S \ll true \gg iff \models <p>\ T_s(S) < true >.$$

To prove $\overset{w}{\ll} p \gg S \ll true \gg$:

Find a *parametrized invariant pi*: $\mathbf{ord} \times \Sigma_{T_w(S)} \rightarrow \{true, false\}$, satisfying:

i. INIT, CONT, TERM-like in **UFAIR** (with $\bigvee_{i \in I} B_i$ instead of B).

ii. (DEC)

$$\overset{u}{\ll} pi^{in}(\alpha, z_1, \cdots, z_n) \wedge B_i \wedge turn = i \gg$$

$$S_i$$

$$\ll \forall z_1, \cdots, z_n \exists \beta: \beta < \alpha \wedge pi^{in}(\beta, \tilde{z}_1, \cdots, \tilde{z}_n) \gg, \qquad i \in I$$

where the $\tilde{z}_j$'s are new variables defined by

$$\tilde{z}_k = \begin{cases} \tilde{z}_k & k = i \vee k \neq i \wedge \neg B_k \quad (i.e.\ an\ arbitrary\ value) \\ & k \neq i \wedge B_k \end{cases}$$

Figure 3.9 Rule **WFAIR** (weakly-fair termination).

$$
\begin{aligned}
T_s(S) \equiv\ & \text{for } all\ i \in I\ do\ z_i := ?; \\
& *[\ \underset{i \in I}{[\,]}\ B_i \wedge turn = i \rightarrow S_i;\ z_i := ?; \\
& \qquad \text{for } all\ j \in I - \{i\}\ do \\
& \qquad [B_j \rightarrow z_j := z_j - 1 \\
& \qquad [\,] \\
& \qquad \neg B_j \rightarrow skip] \\
&].
\end{aligned}
$$

Figure 3.10 Transformation T_s.

This proposition relies on a lemma analogous to the previous lemma. The main change in the previous proof to carry over for strong fairness instead of weak fairness is the definition of the new values $\sigma'_j[z_l]$ of the variables $z_l, l = 1, \cdots, n$ in the extended computation sequence π' of π considered in part (i). This definition now reads

$$\sigma'_j[z_l] = \begin{cases} \mid \{m \mid j < m \leqslant k_0 \wedge \sigma_m \models B_l\} \mid & \text{if } \exists k \geqslant j\colon i_k = l \\ 1 + \mid \{m \mid j \leqslant m \wedge \sigma_m \models B_l\} \mid & \text{otherwise} \end{cases}$$

where $k_0 = \min\{k \geqslant j \wedge i_k = l\}$. Again it is not difficult to see that these values are well-defined if π is strongly fair and consistent with the transformation T_s. Part (i) of the proof remains virtually unchanged.

ii. Consider some $i \in \{1, \cdots, n-1\}$ such that $\mid K \mid = n-i$ holds for $K = \{k \mid z_k \leqslant -i\}$ in σ'_j. We have to show that B_k is true in σ'_j for some $k \in K$. As in i. we conclude that $z_k \leqslant -i$ holds already in σ'_{j-1} for all $k \in K$, otherwise B_k would be true for some $k \in K$ in σ'_{j-1} by the induction hypothesis. Thus, by the construction of $T_s(S)$ there would be some $k \in K$ with $i_{j-1} = k$ and $z_k \geqslant 0$ in σ'_j, contradicting the definition of K. Hence, there exist some $k \in K$ with $z_k = -i+1$ in σ'_{j-1}. But then, the value of z_k decreased so B_k is indeed true for this k in σ'_j by the definition of $T_s(S)$. This proposition gives rise to the rule **SFAIR** in Figure 3.11.

For the bidirectional repetition statement it is again possible to formulate an easier to apply, simplified rule **SIM-SFAIR**$_2$, (see Figure 3.12), based on the notion of a *round* similarly to the unconditional case .

To prove $\overset{s}{\ll} p \gg S \ll \mathit{true} \gg$:

Find a *parametrized invariant pi*: **ord** $\times \Sigma_{T_s(S)} \rightarrow \{\mathit{true}, \mathit{false}\}$, satisfying:

i. INIT, CONT, TERM–same as in **WFAIR**.

ii. (DEC)

$$\overset{w}{\ll} pi^{in}(\alpha, z_1, \cdots, z_n) \wedge B_i \wedge turn = i \gg$$

$$S_i$$

$$\ll \forall z_1, \cdots, z_n \exists \beta\colon \beta < \alpha \wedge pi^{in}(\beta, \tilde{z}_1, \cdots, \tilde{z}_n) \gg, i \in I$$

where

$$\tilde{z}_k = \begin{cases} z_k & k = i \vee k \neq i \wedge \neg B_k \ (\textit{no resetting!}) \\ z_k - 1 & k \neq i \wedge B_k. \end{cases}$$

Figure 3.11 Rule **SFAIR** (strongly-fair termination).

To prove $\overset{s}{\ll} p \gg S \ll true \gg$:

Find a *parametrized invariant* pi^*: $\mathbf{ord} \times \Sigma_S^* \rightarrow \{true, false\}$, satisfying:

1. (INIT) $p \rightarrow \forall turn \exists \alpha: pi^*(\alpha, turn)$.
2. (CONT) $(pi^*(\alpha, turn) \wedge \alpha > 0) \rightarrow (B_1 \vee B_2)$.
3. (TERM) $pi^*(0, turn) \rightarrow \neg (B_1 \vee B_2)$.
4. (DEC)

$$\overset{s}{\ll} pi^*(\alpha, i) \wedge B_i \gg$$

$$S_i; *[B_i \wedge \neg B_{3-i} \rightarrow S_i]$$

$$\ll \exists \beta: \beta < \alpha \wedge pi^*(\beta, 3-i) \gg.$$

Figure 3.12 Rule **SIM-SFAIR$_2$**.

The soundness of this rule can be established by a similar factoring of the original α, as was the case in **UFAIR**. Note the extra loop in each direction, as long as the other one is disabled, making the application of the rule easier, and allowing the interpretation of α as counting rounds.

3.2.1 Examples for strong fairness

Next, we apply the simplified proof rule **SIM-SFAIR$_2$** for strong fairness to prove the correctness of programs which terminate under strong but not under weak fairness assumptions. These programs are closely related to those studied in Section 3.1.

Example:

$$\vdash_{\mathbf{SIM\text{-}FAIR_2}} \overset{s}{\ll} true \gg S_1 \ll true \gg$$

where S_1 is as in Figure 3.13. The number β of rounds is uniformly bounded and independent of the initial state. We choose as well-founded structure $(\{0,1,2\}, \leqslant)$ and as the parametrized invariant

$$\begin{aligned} pi^*(\alpha, turn) \equiv & (\neg a \wedge \neg b \longleftrightarrow \alpha = 0) \\ & \wedge (a \wedge turn = 1 \rightarrow \alpha = 2) \\ & \wedge (b \wedge turn = 2 \rightarrow \alpha = 1). \end{aligned}$$

```
S1:: *[a → b:= ¬b
       []
       b → a:=false; b:=false
      ].
```

Figure 3.13 Program S_1.

$$
\begin{aligned}
S_2{::}\ *[\,&1{:}\ x > 0 \wedge c \rightarrow a{:=}true;\ d{:=} \neg d\\
&[\,]\\
&2{:}\ x > 0 \wedge d \rightarrow [a \rightarrow x{:=}x-1;\ a{:=}false\\
&\qquad\qquad\qquad [\,]\\
&\qquad\qquad\qquad \neg a \rightarrow skip\\
&\qquad\qquad\qquad];\\
&\qquad\qquad\qquad c{:=} \neg c\ ].
\end{aligned}
$$

Figure 3.14 Program S_2.

It turns out that $pi^*(\alpha, turn)$ satisfies the premises of the rule **SIM-SFAIR$_2$**. Note that the loops to be considered in (DEC) are simply

$$*[a \wedge \neg b \rightarrow b{:=} \neg b]$$

and

$$*[b \wedge \neg a \rightarrow a{:=}false;\ b{:=}false],$$

which terminate after at most one iteration.

Example:

$$\overset{s}{\vdash}_{\mathbf{SIM\text{-}SFAIR_2}} \ll true \gg\ S_2\ \ll true \gg$$

where S_2 is given in Figure 3.14.

This is a refined version of the previous example. Thus, thc observations about the number of rounds remain valid. This can also be seen from the invariant

$$
\begin{aligned}
pi^*(\alpha, turn) \equiv\ & (x \leqslant 0 \vee (\neg c \wedge \neg d) \longleftrightarrow \alpha = 0)\\
& \wedge (x > 0 \wedge c \wedge turn = 1 \rightarrow \alpha = 2x)\\
& \wedge (x > 0 \wedge d \wedge turn = 2 \wedge a \rightarrow \alpha = 2x-1)\\
& \wedge (x > 0 \wedge d \wedge turn = 2 \wedge \neg a \rightarrow \alpha = 2x+1)
\end{aligned}
$$

where the underlying well-founded structure is $(N, \leqslant)$.

3.2.2 Alternative transformations

Related, but somewhat different, transformations for realizing weak and strong fairness in *GC* programs were suggested by Park [PA 81] (see Fig-

Weak fairness: (i-th direction)

$$\bigvee_{j\in I}B_j \wedge \bigwedge_{j\in I}(z_i \leqslant z_j)\rightarrow[B_i\rightarrow S_i \;[\,]\; \neg B_i\rightarrow skip];$$
$$z_i:=z_i+1+?$$

Strong fairness: (i-th direction)

$$B_i \wedge \bigwedge_{j\in I}(B_j\rightarrow z_i \leqslant z_j)\rightarrow S_i;$$
$$z_i:=z_i+1+?$$

Figure 3.15 Park's alternative transformations.

i-th direction:

$$\bigwedge_{j\in I}(\,(B_j\wedge b_j)\rightarrow z_i \leqslant z_j\,)\wedge \bigvee_{j\in I}B_j\rightarrow[B_i\rightarrow S_i;\; z_i:=z_i+1;\; b_i:=false$$
$$[\,]$$
$$\neg B_i\rightarrow b_i:=true\;]$$

where, initially, $b_i:=false,\; z_i:=0$.

Figure 3.16 Transformation realizing strong fairness by weak fairness.

ure 3.15). Similar faithfulness theorems are satisfied by these transformations. The main difference w.r.t. the previously described ones is in using "?" in arithmetic, obtaining unboundedly-growing priority variables. Intuitively, after a direction has been taken, it is "thrown" towards the end of a virtual queue by arbitrarily increasing the corresponding priority variable. Eventually, it reaches the end of this queue, causing preference of other directions.

Another transformation suggested in [PA 81] realizes strong fairness by means of weak fairness (see Figure 3.16). Again a kind of queue is simulated by the z_i variables, however this queue consists only of members for which b_i is *true*.

3.3 All-Levels Fairness

In this section we present a variant of the "explicit scheduler" method, that deals with *fairness of all levels,* not necessarily at the top level of a repetition statement. The presentation basically follows [APS 84]. To stress the fact that fairness is shifted to tests at any level, we slightly modify the language so that nondeterminism is confined to selection statements *only*, while repetition statements are *while*—like, having a *single* guard. Thus, a typical repetition statement has the syntactic form of

$$S::\ *[B \rightarrow S'],$$

while a typical selection statement has the form

$$S::\ [\ \underset{i \in I}{[]}\ i\!:\ B_i \rightarrow S_i].$$

Denote the resulting language by GC_{DI} (for Deterministic Iteration). No change is needed in the definition of the semantics.

The approach involves random assignments again, so $GC_{DI,R}$ denotes the language obtained by the addition of random assignments, as in previous sections in this chapter. The main difference is that priorities are valid uniformly, *across iterations.* We present only the strong-fairness version, the treatment of the unconditional and weak-fairness being similarly developed. The same notation as before is used, this time meaning strong fairness with regards to selections at any level. We again start by presenting a transformation T_s^{DI}: $GC_{DI} \rightarrow GC_{DI,R}$, that reduces *SFT* of $S \in GC_{DI}$ to *NDT* of $T_s^{DI}(S) \in GC_{DI,R}$:

1. For each typical selection substatement in S, select a *unique* set of new variables z_i, initialized by $z_i:=?, i \in I$.
2. Replace the selection substatement S by:

$$\text{for } j \in I \textit{ do } \text{if } B_j \textit{ then } z_j:=z_j-1;$$

$$[\ \underset{i \in I}{[]}\ B_i \wedge z_i = 0 \wedge \bigwedge_{j \in I} z_j \geqslant 0 \rightarrow z_i:=?;\ S_i].$$

The unique variables play the role as in the previous sections of this chapter, assigning priorities to directions according to the strong- fairness policy. We again derive

Lemma: (faithfulness of T_s^{DI})

i. If π is a strongly-fair computation sequence of $S \in GC_{DI}$, then there exists an extension π' of π (to the variables z_i, $i \in I$ for *every* typical selection substatement), which is a computation sequence of $T_s^{DI}(S)$.
ii. Conversely, for (a non-failing) computation sequence $\pi' \in T_s^{DI}(S)$, its restriction π to variables of S is a strongly-fair computation sequence of S.

Proof: Omitted (similar to proofs of previous faithfulness lemmas). Note, however, that "accidentally" failing computations are excluded. For example, if initially $\bigwedge_{i \in I} z_i = 0 \wedge \bigwedge_{i \in I} B_i$ holds, then the z_i's become negative and the computation fails for reasons not relevant to the transformation. []

Again, we are mainly interested in the following corollary of the faithfulness of T_s^{DI}.

Corollary: For a typical selection statement $S \in GC_{DI}$, if none of the delay variables introduced by T_s^{DI} occurs free in p, then

$$\overset{s}{\models} \ll p \gg S \ll true \gg \textit{ iff } \models < p > T_s^{DI}(S) <true>,$$

(provided S does not fail due to no-guard enabledness).

We again know that the r.h.s. can be proved using **NDT** and the random assignment axiom. We now present a proof rule **FAIR-IF** for ***SFT*** in Figure 3.17 of the original program $S \in GC_{DI}$ by absorbing the transformation into the rule, as before. Note that this time the rule does not refer to the whole target program; rather it is applied separately to each occurrence of a selection statement, by working "backwards" through all assignments to the delay variables.

Note that this is a partial-correctness rule; however, p might be parametrized by a well-founded ranking due to **NDT**, which embodies the explicit well-foundedness argument. Denote by **ALSF** (all-levels strong fairness) the resulting proof system.

Figure 3.18 is an example of the application of **ALSF** by proving all-level, strongly-fair termination of a variant of Katz's example L mentioned in Chapter 2. In the annotation, the z's in curly brackets are the ones associated with the corresponding selection statement.

$$\frac{\begin{array}{l} p \rightarrow \bigvee_{i \in I} B_i \\ \{ \bigwedge_{k \in I} z_k \geqslant 0 \wedge B_i \wedge (p)[\tilde{z}_j / z_j,\ j \in I] \}\ S_i\ \{q\},\ i \in I \end{array}}{\{p\} [\ \underset{i \in I}{[]} B_i \rightarrow S_i] \{q\}}$$

where:

$$\tilde{z}_j = \begin{cases} 1 & j = i \\ z_j & \neg B_j \wedge j \neq i \\ z_j + 1 & B_j \wedge j \neq i. \end{cases}$$

Figure 3.17 Rule **FAIR-IF.**

```
L:: *[x > 0 →
          [1: {z1}true → [1.1: {z3}b → x:=x−1
                               []
                               1.2: {z4} b → b:=false
                               []
                               1.3: {z5} ¬b → skip]
          []
          2: {z2} true → b:=true
          ]
    ].
```

Figure 3.18 Program L: all-levels fair termination.

We want to show

$$\overset{s}{\vdash}_{\mathbf{ALSF}} \ll true \gg L \ll true \gg \qquad (1)$$

i.e. that L always all-levels, strongly-fair terminates.

The well-founded set chosen is N^4 under lexicographic ordering. The ranking which underlies the formal proof is given by

$$\rho(x,\ b,\ \bar{z}) \overset{def.}{=} (x,\ z_3,\ 1-b,\ (b \to z_1,\ z_2)).$$

In the expression $1-b$, *true* is interpreted as 1, *false* as 0.

The crucial fact upon which the proof depends is that in an all-level, strongly-fair execution the value of ρ decreases on each iteration of the loop. We first demonstrate this fact informally, delaying the formal proof. An iteration of the loop can be characterized by the selected direction, shortened by the associated delay variable.

Consider first the z_1,z_3 path. Here x is decremented so that ρ certainly decreases. Along the z_1,z_4 path, the z_3 guard was enabled since b must have been true for z_4 to be selected. Consequently, z_3 is decremented, being an enabled but unselected guard. Since x remains the same ρ again decreases. Along the z_1,z_5 path, b must have been false so that the fourth component of ρ is z_2 which is decremented when its guard is not selected. In the z_2 path we have to distinguish between the case that b is initially false, in which case $1-b$ drops from 1 to 0, and the case that b is initially true, in which case, z_1, the last component of ρ is decremented, since z_2 is selected.

We now present the formal proof. Since this system has a less stressed separation between partial and total correctness , we give also the partial correctness reasoning involved. Let L' be the body of the loop. We have to find an assertion $p(\alpha)$ such that

$$\{p(\alpha) \wedge \alpha > 0 \wedge x > 0\}\ L'\ \{\exists \beta\colon \beta < \alpha \wedge p(\beta)\} \qquad (2)$$

and

$$\exists\alpha: p(\alpha). \tag{3}$$

We define

$$p(\alpha) \stackrel{def.}{\equiv} x \geqslant 0 \wedge \bigwedge_{i=1,5} z_i \geqslant 0 \wedge \alpha = \rho(x, b, z_1, \cdots, z_5).$$

It this clear that (3) holds. To prove (2) we have to apply the **FAIR-IF** rule so we have first to prove the premises

$$\{(p(\alpha) \wedge \alpha > 0 \wedge x > 0)[z_2 + 1/z_2][1/z_1] \wedge z_1, z_2 \geqslant 0\} \tag{4}$$

$$L_1$$

$$\{\exists\beta: \beta < \alpha \wedge p(\beta)\}$$

and

$$\{(p(\alpha) \wedge \alpha > 0 \wedge x > 0)\ [z_1 + 1/z_1][1/z_2] \wedge z_1, z_2 \geqslant 0\} \tag{5}$$

$$b := true$$

$$\{\exists\beta: \beta < \alpha \wedge p(\beta)\}$$

as the first premise of the **FAIR-IF** rule is obviously satisfied. We use square brackets for substitutions, as well as conditional expressions of the form $B \rightarrow E_1, E_2$ with their usual interpretation. Here L_1 is as in the Figure 3.19.

To prove (4) we once again wish to apply the **FAIR-IF** rule. The premises to prove are

$$\{p_1[b \rightarrow z_4 + 1, z_4/z_4][\neg b \rightarrow z_5 + 1, z_5/z_5][1/z_3] \wedge b \wedge z_3, z_4, z_5 \geqslant 0\} \tag{6}$$

$$x := x - 1$$

$$\{\exists\beta: \beta < \alpha \wedge p(\beta)\}$$

$$\{p_1[b \rightarrow z_3 + 1, z_3/z_3][\neg b \rightarrow z_5 + 1, z_5/z_5][1/z_4] \wedge b \wedge z_3, z_4, z_5 \geqslant 0\} \tag{7}$$

$$b := false$$

$$\{\exists\beta: \beta < \alpha \wedge p(\beta)\}$$

$$
\begin{aligned}
L_1 :: [&b \rightarrow x{:=}x-1 \\
&[\,] \\
&b \rightarrow b{:=}\mathit{false} \\
&[\,] \\
&\neg b \rightarrow \mathit{skip} \\
&].
\end{aligned}
$$

Figure 3.19 Program section L_1.

and

$$\{p_1[\, b \rightarrow z_i + 1, z_i/z_i\,]_{i=3,4}[1/z_5] \wedge \neg b \wedge z_3, z_4, z_5 \geqslant 0\}\ \mathit{skip}\ \{\exists \beta\colon \beta < \alpha \wedge p(\beta)\} \tag{8}$$

where $p_1 \equiv (p(\alpha) \wedge \alpha > 0 \wedge x > 0)[z_2 + 1/z_2][1/z_1] \wedge z_1, z_2 \geqslant 0.$

We have by the assignment axiom

$$\{\rho(x,1,0,1) = \alpha \wedge b \wedge x > 0 \wedge \textstyle\bigwedge_{i=1,5} z_i \geqslant 0\}$$

$$x{:=}x-1$$

$$\{\rho(x+1,1,0,1) = \alpha \wedge b \wedge x \geqslant 0 \wedge \textstyle\bigwedge_{i=1,5} z_i \geqslant 0\}$$

which implies (6) by the consequence rule as the necessary implication clearly holds.

To prove (7) we note that by the assignment axiom and the consequence rule

$$\{\rho(x,z_3,0,1) = \alpha \wedge b \wedge x > 0 \wedge \textstyle\bigwedge_{i=1,5} z_i \geqslant 0\}$$

$$b{:=}\mathit{false}$$

$$\{\rho(x,z_3,1,z_2) = \alpha \wedge \neg b \wedge x > 0 \wedge \textstyle\bigwedge_{i=1,5} z_i \geqslant 0\}$$

so (7) holds by the consequence rule.

Finally, to prove (8) we note that

$$p_1[\, b \rightarrow z_i + 1,\ z_i/z_i\,]_{i=3,4}[1/z_5] \wedge \neg b \wedge z_3, z_4, z_5 \geqslant 0 \quad \text{implies}$$

$$\rho(x, z_3, 1, z_2+1) = \alpha \wedge \neg b \wedge \textstyle\bigwedge_{i=1,5} z_i \geqslant 0 \wedge x > 0$$

which in turn implies

$$\exists \beta\colon \beta < \alpha \wedge \rho(\beta).$$

Hence (8) holds by the *skip* axiom.

Thus, from (6)–(8) we get (4) by the **FAIR-IF** rule.

To prove (5) we note that by the assignment axiom and the consequence rule

$$\{\rho(x,z_3,1-b,(b \rightarrow z_1 + 1,1)) = \alpha \wedge x \geqslant 0 \wedge \bigwedge\nolimits_{i=1,5} z_i \geqslant 0\}$$

$$b{:=}\mathit{true}$$

$$\{\rho(x,z_3,0,z_1 + 1) = \alpha \wedge b \wedge x > 0 \wedge \bigwedge\nolimits_{i=1,5} z_i \geqslant 0\}$$

so (5) follows by the consequence rule.

We now have proved both (4) and (5) and we get (2) by the **FAIR-IF** rule. Finally, (2) and (3) imply by the *while*-rule $<\mathit{true}>\ S\ <\mathit{true}>$, which concludes the proof.

The soundness and completeness of **ALSF** follow from the corresponding theorems about GC_R.

Finally, we note that a less-syntactic version of the all-level fairness can be obtained if we try to use the *same* delay variables whenever logically equivalent guards are used in different syntactic location in the program. Thus, if the test $x > 0$ appears in many unrelated selection statements, we might wish to have a fairness-concept roughly meaning: "if infinitely often $x > 0$, then . . .", independently of any syntactic location where it is tested. This kind of fairness has not been explicitly treated in the existing literature.

3.4 Comparing Explicit Scheduler with Helpful Directions

As already mentioned, the two methods are based on different intuitions. Both are complete, so again the reasonable comparison is the interreducibility among proofs in both approaches. To date, a solution has been formulated (based on an idea due to A. Pnueli) only for one direction of the problem: reducing a helpful-directions proof to an explicit-scheduler proof. The state-directed choice of helpful direction is used.

Theorem: (reduction of helpful directions to explicit scheduler) For a typical repetition statement $S \in GC$:

every proof of $\overset{s}{\ll} p \gg S \ll \mathit{true} \gg$ using rule **F**, can be converted to a proof using rule **SFAIR**.

Proof: Suppose $(W^1, \leqslant)$, ρ^1, Q_i^1, $i \in I$ are given, satisfying all clauses of the rule **F**. We want to derive $(W', \leqslant)$ and

$$pi\colon W' \times \Sigma_{T_s(S)} \rightarrow \{true,\ false\}$$

that satisfies all clauses of rule **SFAIR**.

Let $h\colon \Sigma_S \rightarrow I$ be the function identifying the helpful direction for each $\xi \in \Sigma_S$. This is a function, as the completeness proof of **F** shows that the Q_i, $i \in I$, may be taken to be disjoint, as each ξ satisfies at most one Q_i; let that i be $h(\xi)$. Since the proof may apply up to r recursive applications of itself, with $r \leqslant |I|$, denote by $(W^j, \rho^j, Q_i^j, h^j)$, $1 \leqslant j \leqslant r$, the corresponding constructs at the j-th level subproof. The main observation is that at any level l, ρ^j, h^j, $1 \leqslant j \leqslant l$, remain constant.

We now take the tuples $(\rho^1, z_{h^1}, \rho^2, z_{h^2}, \cdots, \rho^r, z_{h^r})$, lexicographically ordered, as the variant for **SFAIR**.

Thus, let $W' = \Pi_{1 \leqslant j \leqslant r}(W^j \times N)$.

The W'-parametrized invariant is defined by

$$pi((w_1, n_1, \cdots, w_r, n_r), \xi, z_1, \cdots, z_n) \stackrel{def.}{\equiv}$$

$$\exists j\colon 1 \leqslant j \leqslant r \wedge \forall l\colon 1 \leqslant l \leqslant j \rightarrow (\rho^l(\xi) = w_l \wedge z_{h^l(\xi)} = n_l).$$

We now show that all clauses of **SFAIR** are satisfied.

INIT: Let ξ_0 be the initial state and take $j = 1$; by clause F1 of rule **F**, $Q(\xi)$ holds, and hence for some $i \in I$ $Q_i(\xi)$ holds. Take $w_1 = \rho^1(\xi_0)$ and $n_1 = z_{h^1(\xi_0)}$, which satisfies pi.

CONT, TERM: Immediate from clause F1 of rule **F**.

DEC: Suppose $pi^{in}((w_1, n_1, w_2, n_2, \cdots, w_r, n_r), \xi, z_1, \ldots, z_n) \wedge B_i(\xi) \wedge turn = i$ holds, for some $i \in I$. Let ξ' be the state resulting by executing S_i on ξ. Let $i^* = \min_{j \in I} \xi \models B_j$; obviously, $i^* \leqslant i$. Consider two cases:

1. $i^* < i$: In this case $\tilde{z}_{i^*} = z_{i^*} - 1 < z_{i^*}$, while $\tilde{z}_k = z_k$ for $1 \leqslant k < i^*$. By clauses F2, F3 of rule **F**, $h^k(\xi') = h^k(\xi)$, and $\rho^k(\xi') \leqslant \rho(\xi)$ for $1 \leqslant k < i^*$, so that pi is satisfied at ξ', $\tilde{z}$ by the lexicographically smaller r-tuple

$$(\rho^1(\xi'), n_1, \cdots, \rho^{i^*-1}(\xi'), n_{h^{i^*-1}(\xi')}, \rho^{i^*}(\xi'), \tilde{z}_{i^*}, \cdots, w_r, n_r).$$

2. $i^* = i$: In this case $\tilde{z}_{i^*}$ is reset arbitrarily, and $\tilde{z}_k = z_k$ for $k < i^*$. By clause F4, however, we have that $\rho^{i^*}(\xi') < \rho^{i^*}(\xi)$, and by clause F2 $\rho^k(\xi') \leqslant \rho^k(\xi)$ for $1 \leqslant k \leqslant i^*$, so again pi is satisfied at ξ', $\tilde{z}$ with a lexicographically smaller r-tuple.

Finally, to show that INV holds for $\tilde{z}$, we use the fact that $turn = i$ was the case. []

A similar proof, with (ρ, z_h) as the variant, may be used for reducing proofs of weakly-fair termination. As we mentioned, the reducibility of the "explicit scheduler" proofs to "helpful directions" proofs is still an open question. For the sake of comparison, the ordinal-directed helpful-direction **UFT** proof for the symmetric-termination problem, would use

$W = \{0,1\}^n$ with

$$(i_1, \cdots, i_n) < (i'_1, \cdots i'_n) \longleftrightarrow \bigwedge_{k=1,n} i_k \leqslant i'_k \wedge \bigvee_{k=1,n} i_k < i'_k$$

$$pi(<i_1, \cdots, i_n>, a_1, \cdots, a_n) \overset{def.}{\equiv} \bigwedge_{k=1,n}(i_k = 1 \equiv \neg a_k),$$

$$D_{<i_1, \cdots, i_n>} = \{j \mid 1 \leqslant j \leqslant n,\ i_j = 1\}.$$

This proof seems easier than the one using **UFAIR** presented before.

3.5 More on Fairness and Random Assignments

In previous sections of this chapter we used random assignments to "implement" fairness. This section is devoted to the other direction: the "implementation" of various random assignments by means of (strongly) fair iterations.

The basic observation is that Dijkstra's fairly terminating (natural) random number generator can be used to implement every single random assignment with its usual semantics.

We present here some other variants of random assignments, with a variety of termination requirements, and discuss their implementability by *FT GC* programs. The presentation follows unpublished notes by Francez, Katz and Makowsky (1982).

Let b be an atomic formula (Boolean expression) with y a free variable in b. We define the *relativized random assignment* $x{:=}\rho y{:}\ b(y)$ (where ρ is a variable binding operator, used also in [BA 83]). The meaning of the relativized random assignment is to pick an arbitrary element satisfying the relativizing condition b and assign it to x. In case b is *true* we just write $x{:=}\rho$ (instead of $x{:=}?$ of the previous sections, for emphasis) and call it the *unrelativized random assignment.* Note that b does not contain quantifiers.

We consider two ways of assigning meaning to the relativized random assignment. As we wish to compare different programming languages using the same syntax but different (though related) semantics, we need to capture this distinction explicitly. A programming language *PL* is an ordered pair (L, M) comprised of a set L of formal program expressions and a meaning function M. As before we assume an unspecified, implicit interpretation **I** with carrier **A**. We assume that **A** is an *arithmetic* structure, though the results may be formulated in terms of arbitrary *countable reachable structures*, i.e. structures generated by some $a_0 \in \mathbf{A}$ and an acyclic successor function. For *finite reachable* structures all the languages considered can easily seen to be equivalent.

For simplicity, we consider the random assignment to be the *only* source of nondeterminism in the otherwise deterministic language augmented by it. Recall that GC_D is the deterministic sublanguage of GC. Let GC_D^{rd} be GC_D augmented by the relativized random assignments. We now define two meaning functions for programs in GC_D^{rd}. If S is $x:=\rho y: b(y)$ we put

$$M_{con} [\![S]\!] (\sigma) \stackrel{def.}{=} \begin{cases} \{\sigma[a/x] \mid a \in \mathbf{A} \wedge \sigma \models b(a)\} & \text{if} \exists y: \sigma \models b(y) \text{ holds,} \\ \{fail\} & \text{otherwise} \end{cases}$$

i.e. if there is an element in $\mathbf{A}$ satisfying b when the values in σ are used.

$M_{div} [\![S]\!] (\sigma)$ is defined similarly, replacing *fail* by $\perp$. Thus, the two functions differ only in that the first terminates and explicitly fails in case there is no element in $\mathbf{A}$ satisfying the condition b, while the second does not terminate in that case.

We abbreviate by *RDD, RDC* the programming languages (GC_D^{rd}, M_{div}), (GC_D^{rd}, M_{con}), respectively.

To stress the fact that we consider here GC with its (strongly) fair termination meaning function, we denote it by *GCF*, in contrast to *GCU*, the non fair version. We also show, while passing, the relationship between *GCU* and *GCF*.

Definition: A programming language $PL_1 = (L_1, M_1)$ *implements* $PL_2 = (L_2, M_2)$ iff for every program $S \in L_2$ there is a program $S' \in L_1$ such that for every state σ, $M_2 [\![S]\!] (\sigma) = M_1 [\![S']\!] (\sigma)$. We also say that S implements S' (assuming similarity in states). We denote this relation between programming languages by $PL_1 > PL_2$.

Definition: Two programming languages PL_1 and PL_2 are *equivalent* if $PL_1 > PL_2$ and $PL_2 > PL_1$. This relation is denoted by $PL_1 \equiv PL_2$.

Note that this notion of implementation not only demands that the input-output relations are the same, but also that the failures and loops are faithfully implemented. E.g., $x:=\rho y: b$ in *RDC* fails to implement the program $x:=\rho y: b$ in *RDD*, but $x:=\rho y: b$; if $x=fail$ *then* $*[true \rightarrow skip]$ does. Thus, the implementability requirement corresponds to the faithfulness in the previous sections.

On several occasions, only $M_1 [\![S]\!] (\sigma) \subseteq M_2 [\![S']\!] (\sigma)$ is required, i.e. language 1 will only have results which language 2 could also have. For example, in [BA 83] a random assignment is "masking" a possibly deterministic but unknown procedure implementing it, which may never produce some of the permitted results.

The definition of *GCU* using weakest precondition semantics [DIJ 75] implies this weaker requirement. As noted in [F 77] the stronger notion of implementability requires either quantification over post-conditions in the *wp* semantics, or using a *forward* predicate transformer instead. In [FK 81] the stronger definition is imposed on *GCU*, and in [HA 79] the stronger requirement is also used for the random assignment. The two basic requirements of [HA 79] for a random assignment, adapted to our notation are:

$$\text{(a)} \qquad (\forall y\colon p(y) \rightarrow q_y^x) \equiv [x{:=}\rho y\colon p]q$$

and

$$\text{(b)} \qquad (\exists y\colon p(y) \wedge q_y^x) \equiv \langle x{:=}\rho y\colon p\rangle q.$$

Here [ ] and <> are the Dynamic Logic *box* and *diamond* operators, respectively [HA 79]. Requirement (a) corresponds to

$$M[\![x{:=}\rho y\colon p]\!](\sigma) \subseteq \{\sigma[a/x] \mid p(a)\}$$

and means that every result of the random assignment is an element satisfying p. Requirement (b) implies that $\{\sigma[a/x] \mid p(a)\} \subseteq M[\![x{:=}\rho y\colon p]\!](\sigma)$, i.e. every element satisfying p is the result of at least one of the possible computations of the random assignment operator, and corresponds to our strong implementability requirement. Some relations among the implementability definitions are true for any domain **A**, and help to clarify the definitions.

Theorem: (arbitrary domain implementability) For any domain:

$$\text{(i) } RDC > RDD, \quad \text{(ii) } GCF > GCU.$$

Proof: (i) follows immediately from the example given above of an implementation in *RDC* of the random assignment $x{:=}\rho y\colon b(y)$ from *RDD*, i.e. $x{:=}\rho y\colon b(y)$; if $x{=}fail$ *then* $*[true \rightarrow skip]$.

In order to show (ii), i.e. that there is a program in *GCF* which computes the same results as a given $S \in GCU$, consider a repetition statement S in *GCU*.

The same syntactic S in *GCF* (i.e. executing fairly) does not implement the S of *GCU* only if there are a state σ and a non-terminating computation π of $M_{GCU}[\![S]\!](\sigma)$ which cannot occur in $M_{GCF}[\![S]\!](\sigma)$. In such a case, the possibility of a non-terminating computation must be added to the fair execution, without affecting any of the other possible results, including the possibility for termination.

The program S' of GCF in Figure 3.20 is used to implement S of GCU. A Boolean variable c is used to allow doing nothing for a particular selection of a guard. However, because of the fairness assumption, the Boolean variable will eventually be changed to force one of the statements of the original program to be executed. If there is a nonterminating computation in the (unfair) execution of S, there is also one in the fair execution of the program S', and if S terminates, so does S', with the same possible values. Note that the selection statement involving c and $\neg c$ is completely deterministic. The fairness assumption guarantees that the last guard of the outer loop must be eventually chosen, changing c to *false*, and thus ensuring that a computation step of the original program must be executed on the subsequent pass through the loop. In this way, even though choosing guards fairly, sequences of S_i's which correspond to unfair computations of S can be obtained (interspersed with *skip* statements). All of the terminating computations of the original program will also terminate in this program, again with interspersed *skip* statements. [ ]

Remaining still is the question whether or not $GCU > GCF$ (the inverse directions of ii), and the relations among GCU, the random assignment languages, and GCF. We first show that the various languages do not collapse into one equivalence class as occurred for finite structure. This is clear from the following theorem of Dijkstra [DIJ 76].

Theorem: (implementability in countable reachable structures) For a arithmetic domain **A** $\neg\, GCU > RDD$.

Proof: By definition $x{:=}\rho$ in RDD (our notation for $x{:=}\rho y$: *true*), has a countably infinite number of resulting states for any initial state σ, but does not have $\perp$ as a resulting state, since the predicate *true* is always satisfied. Assume that some $S \in GCU$ implements the program $x{:=}\rho$ of RDD. By the definition of implementation, $M_{GCU}[\![S]\!](\sigma)$ has the same set of resulting states, and in particular does not include $\perp$.

However, as we know, the computation sequences of S, can be described as a finitely branching infinite tree $T_S(\sigma)$ and the tree must

S':: $c{:=}true$;
$*[\ \underset{i=0,n-1}{[\,]}\ b_i \rightarrow [c \rightarrow skip\,[\,]\ \ c \rightarrow S_i;\ c{:=}true]$
$\quad [\,]$
$\quad (\bigvee_{i=0,n-1} b_i) \wedge c \rightarrow c{:=}false].$

Figure 3.20 Program S': fair simulation of unfair computations.

have an infinite number of leaves in order to properly implement $x{:=}\rho$. Therefore, by Koenig's lemma, the tree has some infinite path π and, by definition, $\perp \in M_{GCU}[\![S]\!](\sigma)$, a contradiction. [ ]

The main result which is true for arithmetic **A**, links fair execution and random assignment, and shows, along with the above, that both are stronger than unfairly executing *GC*.

Theorem: (equivalence of fairness and random assignment on arithmetic domains) For an arithmetic domain **A**, $RDD \equiv GCF$.

Proof: First we show that $GCF > RDD$.

The "obvious" candidate for implementing $x{:=}\rho$ of *RDD* in *GCF* is *CHOOSE* (see Figure 3.21), the random (natural) number generator from Chapter 2.

Recall that this program does not terminate in *GCU*, (i.e. $\perp \in M_{GCU}[\![CHOOSE]\!](\sigma)$), since there is a computation in which the second alternative of the loop need never be taken. On the other hand, the only infinite computation is clearly unfair, and thus $\perp \notin M_{GCF}[\![CHOOSE]\!](\sigma)$, and the requirements of $x{:=}\rho$ are easily shown to be met by this program.

In order to generalize this program to obtain an implementation in *GCF* for $x{:=}\rho y{:}\ p(y)$ for any predicate p, some care must be taken. The simplest candidate from *GC*F might be *p-CHOOSE* (see Figure 3.22).

However, this is only a solution if p is true for infinitely many values of **A**. In that case, by the fairness assumption, the required alternative must indeed be chosen eventually. Clearly, whenever the program halts $p(x)$ holds, and every possible value of x satisfying p is a potential result. However, if $p(x)$ is only true for a finite number of values $a \in \mathbf{A}$, even in

```
CHOOSE:: x:=0; b:=true;
         *[ b → x:=x+1
            []
            b → b:=false].
```

Figure 3.21 *CHOOSE*: implementing random assignment by fairness.

```
p−CHOOSE:: x:=0; b:=true;
           *[ b → x:=x+1
              []
              b ∧ p(x) → b:=false].
```

Figure 3.22 *p-CHOOSE*: wrong implementation of restricted random assignment by fairness.

GCF, there is a legal computation which does not choose the second guard. In order to implement $x:=\rho y\colon p(y)$ in full generality, we choose a random "starting point" and conduct a *bidirectional search* until "the closest" element a satisfying $p(a)$ is found. The program diverges if no such element exists, as required by *RDD*. The randomized "starting point" guarantees that every a satisfying $p(a)$ is a potential result of the implementation. The use of subtraction is only for convenience, and we could instead start at 0 and use addition, and remember the last value satisfying $p(a)$ before the 'starting point' is reached. The program *any-p-CHOOSE* is shown in Figure 3.23.

Note that the fairness assumption is only used to guarantee that finding the starting point will terminate. The program will diverge only if there is no value a such that $p(a)$ is true. Whenever it does terminate $p(x)$ holds, and every a for which $p(a)$ holds is a possible final value of x in this program.

Thus, $GCF > RDD$ as required. Finally, $RDD > GCF$ follows from the explicit scheduler construction in the previous sections. [ ]

Finally, we mention that there is another level of comparison between programming languages, namely, the level of logics of programs built on top of them. Usually, such logics induce a coarser equivalence relation in terms of expressiveness power. In particular, it can be shown that for a naturally chosen logic of programs, all the variants of fairness and random assignments discussed collapse into one equivalence class. The non-implementability relation among languages yields to the expressibility in the logic. A further elaboration of this subject is beyond the scope of the current treatment.

```
any-p-CHOOSE:: z:=0; b:=true;
*[ b → z:=z+1[ ]b → b:=false];
b:=true; y:=z;
*[b ∧ ¬p(y) ∧ ¬p(z) →
                          [y≠0 → y:=y−1[ ]y=0 → skip];
                          z:=z+1
  [ ]
  b ∧ p(y) → x:=y; b:=false
  [ ]
  b ∧ p(z) → x:=z; b:=false
 ].
```

Figure 3.23 Program *any-p-CHOOSE*: implementing restricted random assignments using fairness.

CHAPTER 4
Extension and Generalizations of Fairness

4.0 Overview

The aim of this chapter is to introduce extensions and generalizations of the previously studied concepts of fairness, in order to understand better both the scope of applicability and limitations of the proof methods for fair termination introduced. For these extensions and generalizations it is assumed that states may be augmented by *auxiliary variables* (and auxiliary assignments to them), by means of which it is possible to express properties of any *prefix* of the computation up to any given intermediate state occurrence.

We first study the property of *equifair termination,* a strengthening of fair termination imposing stronger restrictions on infinite computations, requiring infinitely many *equalizations* among sets of directions along infinite computations. In particular, we present proof rules for equifair termination for *GC* and prove their soundness and semantic completeness with respect to the semantics of computation trees. This is an attempt towards understanding properties of programs executed under a variety of restrictions on infinite behavior, a variety richer than the previously discussed fairness assumption, by means of a representative concept. The material in these sections is based on [GF 82] and [GFK 83]. Then we introduce the abstract notion of *generalized fairness,* relative to an arbitrary finite set of pairs of state conditions, and study termination under it, thereby generalizing both fairness and equifairness, as well of a whole family of related concepts. All these concepts have in common the property that they require similar proof methods for proving termination, and share a similar construction for completeness proofs. This section is based on [FK 83].

Then, we introduce the concept of *extreme fairness,* which requires yet stronger properties of the scheduler. Its main merit is its constituting a better approximation to *probabilistic termination* (termination with probability 1 when selection probabilities are attributed to directions). We present a proof rule for Extremely Fair Termination; however, it is not known whether this rule is complete for the strong version. The exposition is an adaptation of [PN 83] to our context and terminology.

Finally, we consider another modification of the fairness concept, whereby the focus is shifted from fair selection of directions to *fair reachability* of predicates, following [QS 83].

4.1 Equifairness

Recall that a fair execution of an iterative statement with n directions means that every direction which is infinitely often enabled is also infinitely often taken, and the corresponding command executed. However, there is no further commitment (by the fair scheduler) as to relative scheduling of the enabled guards, e.g. as far as the *number of times* they are being chosen for execution.

In this section we are interested in a more committed scheduler–one that tries to give *an equally fair chance to each guard in a group of jointly enabled guards.* In its strongest form, the scheduler guarantees that if such a group of guards is infinitely often enabled along an infinite computation, then there exist infinitely many time instants where all these guards are *equalized,* namely have been *(all)* chosen the *same* number of times. We call such an execution a *strongly equifair* execution and the corresponding scheduler a strongly *equifair scheduler. Weak equifairness* and *unconditional equifairness* are also correspondingly defined.

One possible interpretation of these concepts is in terms of a situation in which n processors, roughly of the same speed, execute a program. They may over take each other locally, but in the long run are equal. Another interpretation, is an abstraction of a specific kind of probabilistic execution thereby disregarding details in reasoning about the program.

To give the flavor of the concept, we note that in an equifair behavior of an unbounded buffer, the buffer becomes empty infinitely often, whenever the 'read' and 'write' operations have been equalized. At such instants, "buffer maintenance" may take place. A typical simple program *UE* to exemplify the concept of unconditionally equifair termination is shown in the Figure 4.1 (where x is integer valued).

```
UE:: *[1: x > 0 → x:=x + 1
       []
       2: x > 0 → x:=x − 2
      ].
```

Figure 4.1 Program *UE*.

```
SE:: *[1: z > 0            → x := x+1
      []
      2: z > 0            → y := y+1
      []
      3: z > 0 ∧ x=y      → z := z-1
     ].
```

Figure 4.2 Program *SE*.

This program is not fairly terminating, as the infinite fair sequence $(112)^\omega$ shows. However, it is unconditionally-equifair terminating; whenever the two guards are equalized, say after $2k > 0$ times since the previous equalization, the new value of x is $x_0 + k - 2k = x_0 - k < x_0$ (where x_0 is the old value at the previous equalization state). Thus, an infinite sequence containing infinitely many equalized states would cause an eventual dropping of x below 0–a contradiction. This phenomenon will be the basis of our proof rule.

A typical simple program *SE* to demonstrate the concept of strong equifairness is shown in the Figure 4.2, where x, y and z range over natural numbers.

This program is not ***SFT*** in an initial state satisfying $x = y \wedge z > 0$, as is evident from the infinite, strongly fair computation $1(12)^\omega$. However, it is strongly-equifair terminating in that state: whenever the set of jointly enabled directions $\{1,2\}$ is equalized, $x = y$ holds again and direction 3 becomes enabled and must be eventually taken, thereby decrementing z. Thus, $z = 0$ will eventually hold and the program terminates. We omit the treatment of weak equifairness.

In the following two subsections we convert this intuitive reasoning into properly stated proof rules. It is rather surprising that a cone construction, similar to that of fairness, is useful for the completeness proofs. This similarity gives rise to the generalization presented at the next subsection.

What is not surprising is that countable ordinals are again needed for termination proofs and countable nondeterminism is again present, as in the case of fair termination.

Since, in general, the equifairness criteria need not be definable in terms of the proper state of the program, we have to add auxiliary variables to this end, called *direction counters* and assignments to these variables. These variables count the number of times the various directions are taken. Hence, we defer the formal definitions to after the introduction of these auxiliary elements.

4.1.1 Unconditional equifairness

In order to be able to express the property of unconditional equifairness, we augment each *GC* iterative *S* with *direction counters* $c_1, \cdots, c_n$, which are (new) auxiliary variables, needed only for the sake of the proof. Thus, the form of a typical repetition statement becomes the following:

$$S' :: c_1 := c_2 := \ldots := c_n := 0;$$

$$*[\ \underset{i \in I}{[]}\ i\colon B_i \rightarrow S_i;\ c_i := c_i + 1].$$

We denote by S_i' the augmented body of the i-th direction. Obviously, S and S' have the same computations modulo the original states, since the added counters do not have any effect on the flow of the computation.

The introduction of the c_i's can be avoided in case their value can be determined as a function of the state. We do not bother with this issue here. We use the abbreviation $E(\xi)$ for an augmented state ξ, to mean that ξ is an *equalized* state, i.e., $c_1 = \cdots = c_n$ holds in ξ.

Again, without loss of generality, we further assume that $B_1 = \cdots = B_n$ is an invariant of the program. In other words, all directions are simultaneously enabled or disabled, and we may take them all as the *same* guard, B.

Definition: For a typical repetition statement $S \in GC$ and a computation path $\pi \in T_S(\xi)$ (for an initial state ξ),

1. π is *unconditionally equifair* (*UEF*) iff it is finite, or infinite and contains infinitely many equalized states.
2. S is *unconditionally-equifair terminating* (UEFT), iff all its unconditionally-equifair execution sequences are finite.

Thus, in an unconditionally-equifair terminating program S, every infinite execution sequence contains only finitely many equalized states. In other words, from some point onwards, all states are non-equalized. We refer to such a tail as an *equalization-avoiding* path.

We use the notation $\overset{u}{[}\ p\ \underline{]}\ S\ \underline{[}\ q\ \underline{]}$ to denote the fact that, given a precondition p, S is *UEFT* with a postcondition q holding upon termination. Again, we restrict the attention to proving termination only, always taking $q = \textit{true}$ at the top level, using partial correctness reasoning to establish q at intermediate levels.

Obviously, every unconditionally-fair terminating *GC* program is also unconditionally-equifair terminating, since an unconditionally-equifair computation is also unconditionally fair.

In case an unconditionally-equifair terminating program is executed by an unconditionally-equifair scheduler, it will always terminate.

A simple "implementation" of a scheduler which guarantees unconditional equifairness uses a random (natural) number generator. It keeps a table of n (the number of guards) entries, initially all equal to zero. Whenever it discovers that all entries are equal to zero, it draws a random natural number, say k, and initializes all the table entries to k. Whenever

To prove $\overset{u}{[}\ p\ ]\ S'\ [true]$:
Find: a well-founded, partially-ordered, set $(W, \leqslant)$, a *parametrized invariant* pi: $\Sigma_{S'}^{*} \times W \rightarrow \{true, false\}$, satisfying:
1. (INIT) $p \rightarrow \exists w: pi(w)$
2. (CONT) $(pi(w) \wedge w > 0) \rightarrow \bigvee_{i \in I} B_i$
3. (TERM) $pi(0) \rightarrow (\neg \bigvee_{i \in I} B_i)$
4. (NOINC) $\overset{u}{[} pi(w) \wedge B_i]\ S_i'\ [\neg E \rightarrow \exists v: v \leqslant w \wedge pi(v)]$, for $i \in I$ and $w > 0$.
5. (DEC) $\overset{u}{[} pi(w) \wedge B_i]\ S_i'\ [E \rightarrow \exists v: v < w \wedge pi(v)]$, for $i \in I$ and $w > 0$.

Figure 4.3 Rule **UEFT** (unconditionally-equifair termination).

the direction i, $1 \leqslant i \leqslant n$ is selected for execution, the corresponding entry is decremented by 1. A direction will not be taken if its corresponding entry is equal to 0, even though it is enabled at that stage.

We next proceed to introduce our proof rule **UEFT** (see Figure 4.3) for proving unconditionally-equifair termination. The basic intuition behind the suggested rule is to find a well-founded variant *which decreases whenever the state becomes equalized* and does not increase between successive equalized states. Thus, an infinite decreasing sequence would occur in the presence of infinitely many equalized states, in contradiction to well-foundedness. As the completeness proof shows, we again can always consider an initial sequence of the countable ordinals as the required well-founded partially ordered set.

Let $\Sigma_{S'}^{*}$ denote the domain of states of the augmented *GC* repetition statement S'. The meaning of the proof rule is as follows:

Find a well-founded ordering $(W, \leqslant)$ and a parametrized invariant $pi(w)$, which is initially established (by (INIT)), is preserved with a non-increasing parameter v after the execution of any enabled direction (NOINC), and is preserved with a strictly smaller parameter v whenever the result of following an enabled direction is an equalized state (DEC); finally, $pi(0)$ implies termination. We did leave in the rule the distinction of different guards B_i though, by assumption, B suffices. This is because later versions, having additional clauses, refer to different guards.

A notable difference between this rule for equifairness and previous rules for fairness is that a rank decrease is not attributed any more to a specific direction: rather, it is attributed to an event during computation, namely, direction equalization.

Following are examples of the application of the rule **UEFT**.

Example: Consider again the program *UE* mentioned above, augmented with direction counters (see Figure 4.4). This time we add an additional

UE':: c_1:=c_2:=0; c:=0;

    $*[1$: $x > 0 \rightarrow x$:=$x+1$; c_1:=$c_1 + 1$; $[c_1=c_2 \rightarrow c$:=$c_1 [] c_1 \neq c_2 \rightarrow skip]$

    $[]$

    2: $x > 0 \rightarrow x$:=$x-2$; c_2:=$c_2 + 1$ $[c_1=c_2 \rightarrow c$:=$c_1 [] c_1 \neq c_2 \rightarrow skip]$

    $]$.

Figure 4.4   Augmented program UE'.

auxiliary variable c in order to record the common value of the counters at equalization states. We want to prove $[x > 0]$ UE' $[true]$.

We take W as N, the natural numbers, with their usual ordering. As the parametrized invariant we choose

$$pi(x, c_1, c_2, c, n) \overset{def.}{\equiv} [(n=0 \wedge x \leqslant 0) \vee$$

$$(n > 0 \wedge x > 0) \wedge n = x - (c_1 - c) + 2(c_2 - c)]$$

$$\wedge c \geqslant 0 \wedge c_1 \geqslant c \wedge c_2 \geqslant c.$$

The intuitive meaning of the invariant is that the parameter n is equal to the value of x at the most recent equalized (augmented) state. In particular, at equalization states $c_1 = c_2 = c$ and $n = x$. We show next that the clauses of the proof rule **UEFT** hold.

(INIT)–trivial.   Take $n = $ if $x \leqslant 0$ then 0 else x.   (Recall   that $c = c_1 = c_2 = 0$ holds, by the augmented program construction).

(CONT), (TERM)–trivial.

(NOINC) for $i = 1$ we have to show, after substituting the effect of UE'_1:

$$pi(x, c_1, c_2, c, n) \wedge x > 0 \wedge c_1 + 1 \neq c_2 \rightarrow$$

$$\exists m: m \leqslant n \wedge pi(x + 1, c_1 + 1, c_2, c, m).$$

Clearly, we may choose $m = n$, since

$$x - (c_1 - c) + 2(c_2 - c) = x + 1 - ((c_1 + 1) - c) + 2(c_2 - c)$$

For $i = 2$, we have to show:

$$pi(x, c_1, c_2, c, n) \wedge x > 0 \wedge c_2 + 1 \neq c_1 \rightarrow$$

$$\exists m: m \leqslant n \wedge pi(x-2, c_1, c_2 + 1, c, m).$$

Again, we may choose $m = n$.

(DEC) For $i = 1$, we have to show

$$pi(x, c_1, c_2, c, n) \wedge x > 0 \wedge c_1 + 1 = c_2 \rightarrow$$
$$\exists m{:}\, m < n \wedge pi(x + 1, c_1 + 1, c_2, c, m).$$

The antecedent implies $n = x - (c_1 - c) + 2(c_2 - c) > x + 1$, and we may choose $m = x+1$ for the consequent.

For $i=2$, we have to show

$$pi(x, c_1, c_2, c, n) \wedge x > 0 \wedge c_2 + 1 = c_1 \rightarrow$$
$$\exists m{:}\, m < n \wedge pi(x-2, c_1, c_2 + 1, c, m).$$

It is easy to verify that $m =$ if $x \leqslant 2$ *then* 0 *else* $x-2$ does the job.

Theorem: (soundness of UEFT) For a typical repetition statement $S \in GC$:

$$\text{if } \vdash_{\text{UEFT}} \overset{u}{\underline{[}}\ p\ \underline{]}\ S\ \underline{[}\,true\,\underline{]}, \text{ then } \models \overset{u}{\underline{[}}\ p\ \underline{]}\ S\ \underline{[}\,true\,\underline{]}.$$

Proof: Similar to previous contradictions to well-foundedness. [ ]

Theorem: (semantic completeness of UEFT) For a typical repetition statement $S \in GC$:

$$\text{if } \models \overset{u}{\underline{[}}\ p\ \underline{]}\ S\ \underline{[}\,true\,\underline{]}, \text{ then } \vdash_{\text{UEFT}} \overset{u}{\underline{[}}\ p\ \underline{]}\ S\ \underline{[}\,true\,\underline{]}.$$

The proof is along similar lines to that for the semantic completeness of **UFT**, the idea again being to take an infinite, not well-founded tree $T_{S'}(\xi_0)$ the infinite paths of which are unconditionally equifair and contract it to another infinite tree $T^*_{S'}(\xi_0)$ which is well-founded (but, of course *not* necessarily finitely branching as $T_{S'}(\xi_0)$ is). We present only the essential differences from the fairness case.

Proof: Consider any initial state ξ_0 satisfying p, and the tree $T_{S'}(\xi_0)$.

Definition: For a state occurrence $\xi \in T_{S'}(\xi_0)$, we let $CONE(\xi)$ be the set of all state occurrences residing on *equalization-avoiding* infinite paths of $T_{S'}(\xi_0)$ originating at ξ. The state ξ is the *root.*

Again, such a cone will be contracted to a node in $T^*_{S'}(\xi_0)$.

Lemma: (cone-exit) A computation path leaves a cone $CONE(\xi)$, iff it is either finite or contains an equalized state (see Figure 4.5).

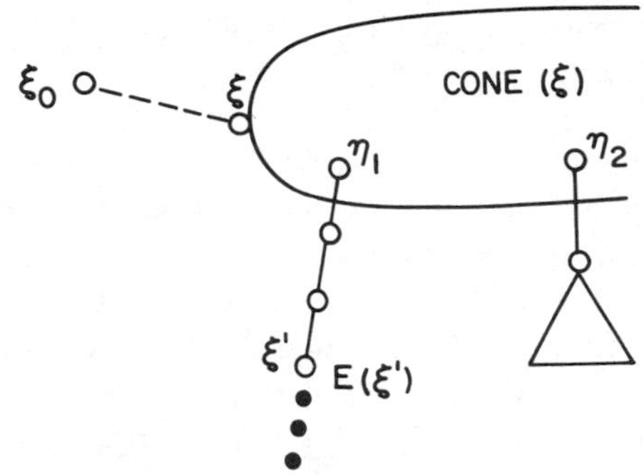

Figure 4.5 Cone exits.

We proceed with an inductive definition of a hierarchy of families of states, covering all the states occurring on infinite paths of $T_{S'}(\xi_0)$.

Induction Basis: We distinguish between two cases:

a. The root ξ_0 is the origin of an equalization-avoiding path. In this case, define

$$A_0 = CONE(\xi_0).$$

b. Otherwise, take $A_0 = \{\xi_0\}$.

In both cases, we say that A_0 is at level 0 with root ξ_0.

Induction Step: Assume that $A_{i-1} = CONE(\xi_{i-1})$ is constructed at level $i-1$ at an equalized root ξ_{i-1}. If no infinite path leaves $CONE(\xi_{i-1})$, A_{i-1} has no descendant cones. Otherwise, consider such an infinite path leaving the cone. By the cone-exit lemma, it contains an occurrence of an equalized state. For any such path construct $CONE(\xi_i')$ at level i for ξ'_i the nearest equalized state along the path (see Figure 4.6). Finally, if $A_{i-1} = \{\xi_{i-1}\}$, treat it like ξ_0 in the basis step.

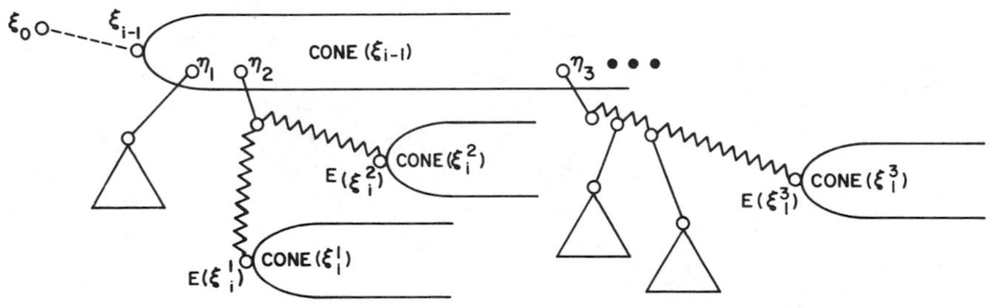

Figure 4.6 Descendant cones.

Lemma: (cone-chain) There does not exist an infinite chain of descendant cones $CONE(\xi_i)$, $i = 0,1,\ldots,$ whose roots ξ_i, $i=0,1\cdots$ reside on a computation sequence of $T_{S'}(\xi_0)$.

Proof: Assume the contrary, i.e. the existence of an infinite chain of descendant cones whose roots reside on a computation sequence of $T_{S'}(\xi_0)$ (as shown Figure 4.7). By the construction, the roots labels ξ_i, $i \geqslant 0$, are all equalized states. Hence, this existing infinite path has infinitely many nodes labeled with equalized states, and, hence, is an infinite unconditionally equifair path. This contradicts the assumption that the given program S' (whose execution tree is $T_{S'}(\xi_0)$) unconditionally-equifair terminates for all initial states satisfying the precondition. Hence, such an infinite chain cannot exist. []

As before, we now have everything needed for the construction of $T^*_{S'}(\xi_0)$ out of the cones. We omit the details.

Using a similar ranking ρ we are now able again to construct the required parametrized invariant. We define:

$$pi(\xi, w) \overset{def.}{\equiv} \exists \xi' : \xi \in CONE(\xi') \wedge \rho(CONE(\xi')) = w$$

$$\vee$$

$$\neg \exists \xi' : \xi \in CONE(\xi') \wedge \rho(\xi) = w.$$

We now have to show that the invariant pi as defined above satisfies all the clauses of the proof rule. The reasoning is similar to the strong fairness case and is omitted.

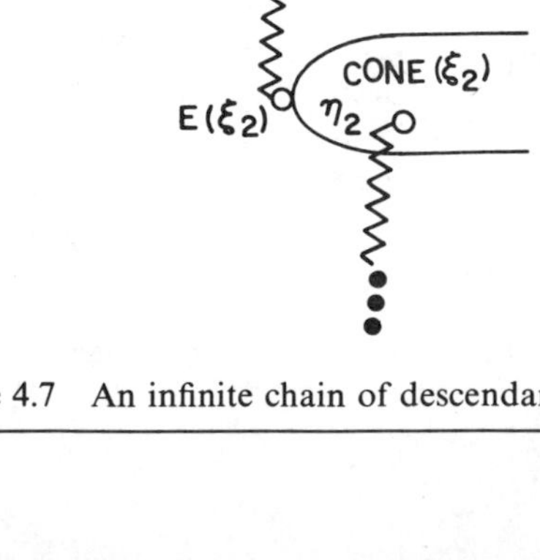

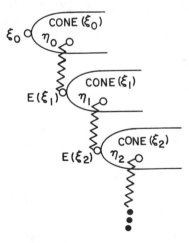

Figure 4.7 An infinite chain of descendant cones.

Remark: Note that the phenomenon of the same state ξ having more than one rank, which caused a rank-shift, is of no concern here, since descending in rank is not attributed to a specific direction (for a given $w > 0$).

4.1.2 Strong equifairness

In this section we present a proof rule for strongly-equifair termination, apply it to examples and show its soundness and semantic completeness. We again assume a typical repetition statement $S \in GC$ of the form: $S:: *[\underset{i \in I}{[]} i: B_i \rightarrow S_i]$, with arbitrary Boolean guards, B_i, $i \in I$. The presentation follows [GFK 83].

Definition: A set of directions $A \subseteq I$ is *jointly enabled* in a state σ if $\sigma \models B_A \overset{def.}{=} \bigwedge_{i \in A} B_i$.

In order to be able to express strong equifairness, we augment each n-directional GC program with $n \times 2^{n-1}$ *direction counters,* which again are auxiliary variables, needed only for the sake of the proof. For each $i \in I$ let A_i^j, $1 \leqslant j \leqslant 2^{n-1}$, be some fixed enumeration of the subsets of I containing i. The counter c_i^j counts the number of times the direction i was executed when the set of directions A_i^j was jointly enabled. The form of an augmented repetition statement is shown in Figure 4.8. In the sequel, we occasionally refer to the augmented program as if it is the given one, using the same name and omitting the quote superscript.

The auxiliary section increases the counters c_i^j of direction i by one (when S_i is executed) for every jointly enabled set of directions A_i^j containing i. Also, S'_i denotes the augmented body of direction i in S'. Note that the counters were not initialized to zero, but may have any initial values satisfying a given precondition. At the top level of a proof we

$$
\begin{array}{ll}
S':: *[\underset{i=1,n}{[]} i: B_i \rightarrow & [B_{A_i^1} \rightarrow c_i^1 := c_i^1 + 1 \\
 & [] \\
 & \neg B_{A_i^1} \rightarrow skip \\
 &]; \; \cdots \\
 & [B_{A_i^{2^{n-1}}} \rightarrow c_i^{2^{n-1}} := c_i^{2^{n-1}} + 1 \\
 & [] \\
 & \neg B_{A_i^{2^{n-1}}} \rightarrow skip \\
 &]; \\
 & S_i \\
 ]. &
\end{array}
$$

Figure 4.8 Augmented program for strong equifairness

assume initial values all equal to 0. In the examples, we augment the programs only with these counters that participate in the proof, and omit reference to all others. Obviously, S and S' have the same computation modulo the original states, since the added counters do not have any effect on the flow of the computation. Once again, the introduction of the c_i^j,s can be avoided in case their value can be determined from the state. We do not bother with this issue here. We use the abbreviation $E_A(\xi)$, for augmented state ξ, to mean that ξ is an *A-equalized* state, i.e. $\xi \models c_{i_1}^{j_1} = \cdots = c_{i_k}^{j_k}$, for $A = \{i_1, \ldots, i_k\} = A_{i_1}^{j_1} = \cdots = A_{i_k}^{j_k}, k \geqslant 1$. Thus, the initial values of the counters are taken into account also. Note that for $|A| = 1$, *every* state is A-equalized.

Definition: For a typical repetition statement $S \in GC$, and computation path $\pi \in T_S(\xi_0)$:

(1) π is *strongly equifair* iff it is finite, or infinite and contains infinitely many A-equalized states for every $A \subseteq I$ that is infinitely-often jointly-enabled along π.
(2) A program S is *strongly-equifair terminating* (abbreviated *SEFT*) iff all its strongly equifair execution sequences are finite. We use the notation $\overset{s}{[}\; p \;]\; S\; [\; true\;]$.

Thus, in a strongly-equifair terminating program S, every infinite execution sequence contains only finitely many A-equalized states for some infinitely-often jointly-enabled set of directions $A \subseteq I$. In other words, from some point onwards, all states are non-A-equalized. We refer to such a tail as *A-equalization avoiding*.

Obviously, every *SFT GC* program is also *SEFT* since a strongly equifair computation sequence is also strongly fair.

If a *SEFT* program is executed by a strongly-equifair scheduler, it will always terminate, since infinite strongly-equifair sequences are not generated by such a scheduler, by its definition.

A simple "implementation" of a scheduler, which guarantees strong equifairness, uses a random (natural) number generator. It keeps a table $T(A, i)$, $\emptyset \neq A \subseteq I$, $i \in A$, initially with all entries equal to zero. Whenever it discovers that all the entries corresponding to some A are equal to zero, it draws a random natural number, say k, and reinitializes all these entries to k. Whenever the guard B_i, $i \in I$, is selected for execution, the entries corresponding to all sets containing i which are jointly-enabled at that stage are decremented by 1. A direction will not be selected for execution if there is an entry corresponding to a set of jointly-enabled guards containing it and equal to 0, even though it is enabled at that stage.

Actually, for technical reasons, we consider a slight variation, where the table has some arbitrary initial values (this becomes clear when the recursive application of the intended rule is discussed).

Figure 4.9 shows another (less obvious) example of a strongly-equifair terminating program Q.

By $\{1,2\}$ equalization, $x = y$ is infinitely often the case. Then, by $\{2,3\}$ equalization, $a = b$ will infinitely often be the case, and hence direction 4 is infinitely often enabled, and z decremented, whereby Q strongly-equifair terminates. A formal *SEFT* proof follows after the introduction of the proof rule.

We next proceed to introduce the proof rule **SEFT** (see Figure 4.10) for strongly equifair termination. The basic intuition behind the suggested rule is to find a well-founded, partially-ordered set, and a variant function of the state, *which decreases whenever the state becomes A-equalized for some "helpful" set of directions A* and does not increase between consecutive A-equalized states. The "helpful" sets vary as the computation proceeds. Thus, an infinite decreasing sequence would occur in the presence of infinitely many A-equalized states, in contradiction to well-foundedness. As the completeness proof shows, we can always consider an initial sequence of the countable ordinals to the required well-founded partially-ordered set. Here we pursue only the ordinal directed choice of helpful direction sets. The state predicate method has not been applied to equifairness until now. The meaning of the proof rule is as follows: INIT, CONT and TERM are as for **UEFT**. As for DEC, only D_w-equalization has to cause decrease in rank.

Again, we show that each decreasing set is infinitely-often jointly-enabled, by proving the strongly-equifair termination of the *derived program* (IOJE). The derived program conjoins to each guard the negation of joint-enabledness of the directions in the decreasing set, and terminates once they do become jointly enabled (or the whole original program terminates). Note that the precondition $pi(w)$ may imply initial values of the counters of the derived program.

```
Q:: {x = y ∧ a = b ∧ z ≥ 0}
*[1: z > 0 → x:=x + 1
  []
  2: z > 0 → [ x = y → a:=a + 1
               []
               x≠y → skip
               ]; y:=y + 1
  []
  3: z > 0 ∧ x=y → b:=b + 1
  []
  4: z > 0 ∧ a=b → z:=z − 1
].
```

Figure 4.9 Program Q.

To prove $\underset{-}{[}\ p\ \overset{s}{\underset{-}{]}}\ S\ \underset{-}{[}\mathit{true}\ \underset{-}{]}$:

Find: a well-founded, partially-ordered, set $(W, \leqslant)$, a *parametrized invariant*

$$pi\colon \Sigma_S^* \times W \rightarrow \{true, false\},$$

and, for each $0 < w \in W$, a set $\varnothing \neq D_w \subseteq I$ (*decreasing set*), all satisfying:

1. (INIT) $p \rightarrow \exists w\colon pi(w)$,
2. (CONT) $pi(w) \wedge w > 0 \rightarrow \bigvee_{i=1,n} B_i$
3. (TERM) $pi(0) \rightarrow \neg \bigvee_{i=1,n} B_i$
4. (DEC) $\overset{s}{\underset{-}{[}} pi(w) \wedge w > 0 \wedge B_i \underset{-}{]}\ \ S_i\ \underset{-}{[} E_{D_w} \rightarrow \exists v{:}v < w \wedge pi(v) \underset{-}{]}$, $i \in D_w$
5. (NOINC) $\overset{s}{\underset{-}{[}} pi(w) \wedge w > 0 \wedge B_i \underset{-}{]}\ \ S'_i\ \underset{-}{[} \neg E_{D_w} \rightarrow \exists v\colon v \leqslant w \wedge pi(v) \underset{-}{]}$, $i \in I$
6. (IOJE) $\overset{s}{\underset{-}{[}} pi(w) \wedge w > 0 \underset{-}{]}\ \bar{S}_w{::}{*}[\ \underset{i \in I}{[]} i\colon B_i \wedge \neg B_{D_w} \rightarrow S_i]\ \underset{-}{[} true \underset{-}{]}$

Figure 4.10 Rule **SEFT** (strongly equifair termination).

Example: Consider again the program *SE* augmented with appropriate counters (see Figure 4.11). Since the first two guards are identical, we omit the test of joint-enabledness before incrementing the counters.

We prove $\overset{s}{\underset{-}{[}}\ x = y \wedge z \geqslant 0 \wedge c_1^{1,2} = c_2^{1,2} = 0 \underset{-}{]}\ SE\ \underset{-}{[} true \underset{-}{]}$.

As the well-founded set we choose the natural numbers *N*, under the usual ordering. The parametrized invariant is

$$pi(x, y, z, c_1^{1,2}, c_2^{1,2}, n) \overset{def.}{\equiv} (z = n \geqslant 0 \wedge c_1^{1,2} - c_2^{1,2} = x - y)$$

to be abbreviated as $pi(n)$.

The decreasing sets are taken as $D_n = \{3\}$, $n > 0$. We now show that the clauses of the proof rule are satisfied.

INIT, CONT, TERM: To initially establish $pi(n)$, we take $n = z$, the initial value of z. $pi(n) \wedge n > 0$ implies $z > 0$, and hence the first two guards are enabled. Also, $pi(0)$ implies $z = 0$, and hence, no guard is enabled.

$$
\begin{array}{l}
SE{::}\ \{x = y \wedge z \geqslant 0 \wedge c_1^{1,2} = c_2^{1,2} = 0\} \\
\quad {*}[1\colon z > 0 \rightarrow x{:=}x + 1;\ c_1^{1,2}{:=}c_1^{1,2} + 1 \\
\quad\ \ [] \\
\quad\ \ 2\colon z > 0 \rightarrow y{:=}y + 1;\ c_2^{1,2}{:=}c_2^{1,2} + 1 \\
\quad\ \ [] \\
\quad\ \ 3\colon z > 0 \wedge x = y \rightarrow z{:=}z - 1 \\
\quad\ ].
\end{array}
$$

Figure 4.11 Program *SE*.

DEC: Since $|D_n| = 1$ for all $n \geqslant 1$, every state satisfies E_{D_n}, and we have to show

$$\underset{\sim}{[}\ pi(n) \wedge n > 0 \wedge z > 0 \wedge x = y \underset{\sim}{]}\ z:=z-1\ \underset{\sim}{[}\ \exists m: m < n \wedge pi(m)\ \underset{\sim}{]}$$

which holds for $m = n-1$.

NOINC: Immediate with the same n, since the first two directions do not modify z.

IOJE: After some trivial simplification, the derived program, for every $n > 0$, is as in the program $\overline{SE}_n$ in Figure 4.12. The initial values of the counters are determined by the precondition $pi(n)$.

In order to prove strongly-equifair termination of $\overline{SE}_n$, we choose $W = \{0,1\}$, with $0 < 1$. The invariant is

$$pi'(x, y, z, c_1^{1,2}, c_2^{1,2}, w) \overset{def.}{\equiv} (z > 0 \wedge c_1^{1,2} - c_2^{1,2} = x - y)$$
$$\wedge (w=1 \rightarrow x \neq y) \wedge (w=0 \rightarrow x=y).$$

The decreasing set is $D_1 = \{1,2\}$. We now check that all the clauses of the rule are satisfied.

INIT, CONT, TERM: To establish pi', take

$$w = \begin{cases} 1 & x \neq y \\ 0 & x = y \end{cases}$$

$pi'(w) \wedge w > 0$ implies $w=1$ and hence $x \neq y$, so both guards are enabled.

$pi'(0)$ implies $x=y$, so both guards are disabled and $\overline{SE}_n$ terminates.

DEC: The condition $E_{\{1,2\}}$, i.e. $c_1^{1,2} = c_2^{1,2}$, implies $x=y$, hence also $pi'(0)$, which means a decrease.

NOINC: Trivial; take same w=1.

IOJE: The derived program is empty, and hence terminates.

```
SE_n:: {z = n > 0 ∧ c1^{1,2} − c2^{1,2} = x − y}
       *[1: z > 0 ∧ x ≠ y → x:=x+1; c1^{1,2}:=c1^{1,2} + 1
        []
        2: z > 0 ∧ x ≠ y → y:=y + 1; c2^{1,2}:=c2^{1,2} + 1
       ].
```

Figure 4.12 Program $\overline{SE}_n$.

This completes the proof of *SEFT* of $\overline{SE}_n$, and hence of the original program.

Example: Consider again the program Q from the beginning of this section, augmented with the appropriate counters. We insert the counter incrementation to locations in the program where the implied test for joint-enabledness would succeed (see Figure 4.13).

We prove $\overset{s}{[\ p\ ]}\ Q\ [\mathit{true}]$, with p the precondition above. We again choose $W = N$ and use the parametrized invariant

$$pi(x, y, z, a, b, c_1^{1,2}, c_2^{1,2}, c_2^{2,3}, c_3^{2,3}, n) \overset{def.}{\equiv} z = n \geqslant 0 \wedge$$
$$c_1^{1,2} - c_2^{2,3} = x - y \wedge$$
$$c_2^{2,3} - c_3^{2,3} = a - b$$

Finally, we take $D_n = \{4\}$, $n \geqslant 0$. We omit the verification of all clauses except (IOJE). The derived program obtained is $\overline{Q}_n$ (see Figure 4.14). We take $W = \{0,1\}$ and $D_1 = \{2, 3\}$.

$$
\begin{array}{l}
Q\!::\ \{x = y \wedge a = b \wedge z \geqslant 0 \wedge c_1^{1,2} = c_2^{1,2} = c_2^{2,3} = c_3^{2,3} = 0\} \\
\quad *[\,1\!: z > 0 \rightarrow x\!:=x+1;\ c_1^{1,2}\!:=c_1^{1,2} + 1 \\
\quad\ [\,] \\
\quad\ 2\!: z > 0 \rightarrow [x=y \rightarrow a\!:=a+1;\ c_2^{2,3}\!:=c_2^{2,3} + 1 \\
\qquad\qquad [\,] \\
\qquad\qquad x \neq y \rightarrow \mathit{skip}];\ y\!:=y + 1;\ c_2^{1,2}\!:=c_2^{1,2} + 1 \\
\quad\ [\,] \\
\quad\ 3\!: z > 0 \wedge x=y \rightarrow b\!:=b+1;\ c_3^{2,3}\!:=c_3^{2,3} + 1 \\
\quad\ [\,] \\
\quad\ 4\!: z > 0 \wedge a=b \rightarrow z\!:=z-1 \\
\quad\ ].
\end{array}
$$

Figure 4.13 Augmented program Q.

$$
\begin{array}{l}
\overline{Q}_n\!::*[\,1\!: z > 0 \wedge a \neq b \rightarrow x\!:=x+1;\ c_1^{1,2}\!:=c_1^{1,2} + 1 \\
\quad\ [\,] \\
\quad\ 2\!: z > 0 \wedge a \neq b \rightarrow [x=y \rightarrow a\!:=a+1;\ c_2^{2,3}\!:=c_2^{2,3} + 1 \\
\qquad\qquad [\,] \\
\qquad\qquad x \neq y \rightarrow \mathit{skip}];\ y\!:=y + 1;\ c_2^{1,2}\!:=c_2^{1,2} + 1 \\
\quad\ [\,] \\
\quad\ 3\!: z > 0 \wedge a \neq b \wedge x=y \rightarrow b\!:=b+1;\ c_3^{2,3}\!:=c_3^{2,3} + 1 \\
\quad\ [\,] \\
\quad\ ].
\end{array}
$$

Figure 4.14 Augmented program $\overline{Q}_n$.

The invariant is

$$pi'(x, y, z, a, b, c_1^{1,2}, c_2^{1,2}, c_2^{2,3}, c_3^{2,3}, w) \overset{def.}{\equiv} (pi(z) \wedge (w=1 \rightarrow a \neq b) \wedge (w=0 \rightarrow a=b)).$$

We leave it for the reader to verify the first five clauses. As for (IOJE), we obtain the derived program $\overline{Q}_{n,1}$ (see Figure 4.15). We again may choose $V = \{0,1\}$, $D_1 = \{1,2\}$ and the invariant

$$pi''(\ \cdots\ , v) \overset{def.}{\equiv} (pi(v) \wedge (v = 1 \rightarrow x \neq y) \wedge (v = 0 \rightarrow x = y)),$$

and the verification is now immediate.

Theorem: (soundness of SEFT) For a typical repetition statement $S \in GC$:

$$\text{if } \vdash_{\text{SEFT}} \overset{s}{[}\ p\ ]\ S\ [\ true\ ],\ \text{then} \models\ \overset{s}{[}\ p\ ]\ S\ [\ true\ ].$$

Proof: Omitted. []

Theorem: (semantic completeness of SEFT) For a typical repetition statement $S \in GC$:

$$\text{if } \models\ \overset{s}{[}p]\ S\ [true],\ \text{then} \vdash_{\text{SEFT}} \overset{s}{[}\ p\ ]\ S\ [true].$$

Proof: The proof is along similar lines to those in Section 4.1.1, the idea being to take an infinite, not well-founded tree $T_S(\xi_0)$ which is strongly equifair and contract it to another infinite tree $T_S^*(\xi_0)$ which is well-founded (but, of course, *not* necessarily finitely branching as $T_S(\xi_0)$ is). Again, like in the case of fairness, the main difference is in the inductive definition of the hierarchy cones, which now takes into account joint enabledness. The equalizing set is again refered to as the cone's directive.

The two lemmata, the cone-exit and the cone chain, hold again with a similar inductive definition of a hierarchy of cones (see Figures 4.16–4.18).

```
Q̄n,1 :: {pi'(w) ∧ w = 1}
     *[ 1: z > 0 ∧ x≠y ∧ a≠b → x:=x + 1; c1^{1,2}:=c1^{1,2} + 1
      []
      2: z > 0 ∧ x≠y ∧ a≠b → y:=y + 1; c2^{1,2}:=c2^{1,2} + 1; [...].
     ].
```

Figure 4.15 Program $\overline{Q}_{n,1}$.

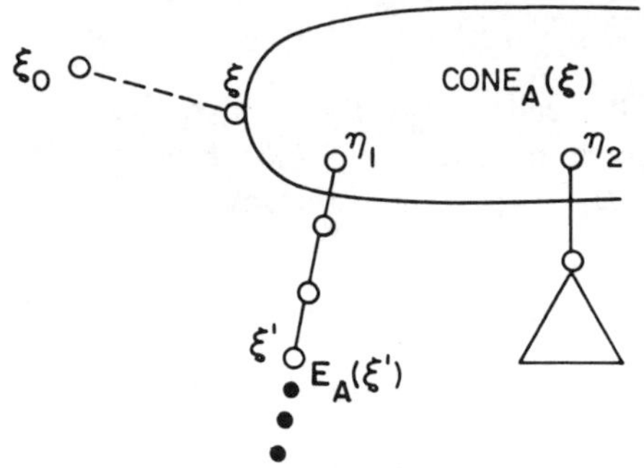

Figure 4.16 Cone exits.

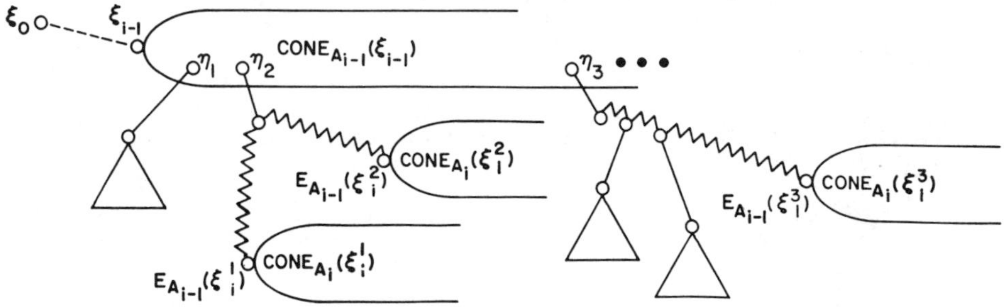

Figure 4.17 Descendant cones.

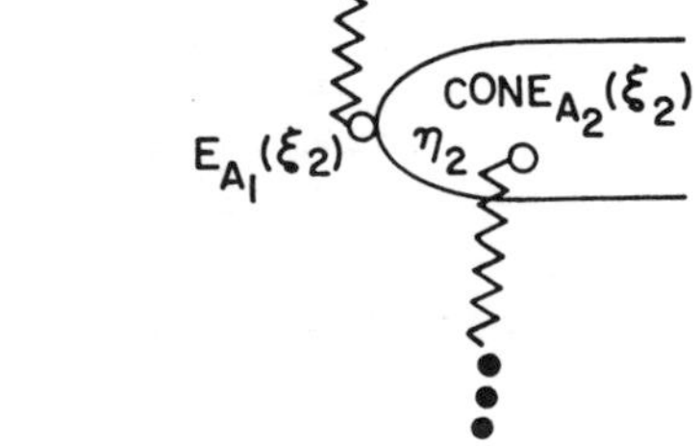

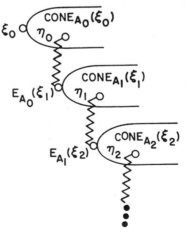

Figure 4.18 An infinite chain of descendant cones.

Lemma: (cone exit) An infinite computation path along which A is infinitely-often jointly-enabled leaves a cone $CONE_A(\xi)$ iff it contains an A-equalized state (see Figure 4.16).

Lemma: (cone-chain) There does not exist an infinite chain of descendant cones $CONE_{A_i}(\xi_i)$, whose roots reside on a computation sequence of $T_S(\xi_0)$.

Again we have all that is needed for the construction of $T_S^*(\xi_0)$.

Claim: $T_S^*(\xi_0)$ is well-founded. Follows immediately from the cone-chain lemma.

We once again rank each node on $T_S^*(\xi_0)$ with countable ordinals. Denote this ranking function by ρ^*, over which a rank-shift is performed to obtain ρ, as for strong fairness. Using the ranking ρ we are now able to construct the required parametrized invariant and decreasing sets. We define:

$$pi(\xi, w) \overset{def.}{\equiv} \exists \xi', A': [\xi \in CONE_{A'}(\xi') \wedge \rho(CONE_{A'}(\xi')) = w]$$

$$\vee$$

$$\neg \exists \xi', A': [\xi \in CONE_{A'}(\xi')] \wedge \rho(\xi) = w.$$

As for the choice of decreasing set D_w, $w > 0$ we have again the two possibilities, depending whether w is a rank of cone or of a "simple" node.

$$D_w = \begin{cases} A & \text{there is a cone } CONE_A(\xi) \text{ whose rank is } w \\ \{1, \ldots, n\} & \text{otherwise} \end{cases}$$

We now have to show that the invariant pi and the descending sets as defined above satisfy all the clauses of the proof rule.

INIT, CONT, TERM: As for **UEFT**.

DEC: Suppose $pi(w) \wedge w > 0 \wedge B_i$ holds for some ξ, where $i \in D_w$. We distinguish between two cases:

a. $\xi \in CONE_A(\xi') \wedge \rho(CONE_A(\xi')) = w$. In this case, applying direction i in a way that causes E_A to hold in the resulting state means that the move left the cone and hence the resulting state has a lower rank.
b. ξ is ranked w and does not reside within a cone. By the construction, it either has a finite subtree, or another cone descendant, and *all* its descendants have a lower rank.

NOINC: Similar. A move either stays within a cone, resulting in state with the same rank, or leaves a cone, resulting in a state with a smaller rank.

IOJE: (Equifair termination of the derived program). First, we note that any execution path of $\bar{S}_w$ is also (a tail of) an execution path of the original program S. Assume that given $pi(w) \wedge w > 0$, $\bar{S}_w$ does not strongly equifair terminate. Hence, it contains an infinite strongly equifair execution path, starting at the root of cone (otherwise it would not be infinite) ranked w. Let A be the cone directive. Since there does not exist an infinite chain of descendant cones, eventually a tail of this path must remain within a cone, which is impossible for an infinite strongly-equifair execution path.

This shows that semantically the derived program equifairly terminates. We now apply an inductive hypothesis to derive provability by **SEFT**. The induction is on the number of directions. Applying recursion again and again, the guards have the form

$$B_i \wedge \neg \bigwedge_{j \in D_{w_1}} B_j \wedge \neg \bigwedge_{j \in D_{w_2}} B_j \cdots .$$

This can go on at most until all subsets are exhausted. Thus, at some stage we reach a level of proof where in the cone construction $T_S^* = T_S$, and the original tree is finite, at which stage we appeal to **NDT**, *without* further recursive calls.

4.2 Generalized Fairness

One cannot fail to notice that in the previous discussion of equifairness, nothing actually depends on the fact that *equality* among counters is tested. Naturally, it is possible to generalize both the proof rules and the completeness proofs to arbitrary (augmented) state properties. This generalization is carried out in this subsection. It unifies the notions of fairness, equifairness and a whole family of similar notions. The completeness proof of the proof rules for proving *generalized fair termination* exploits the similarity in the constructions used in proving completeness of the corresponding rules for fairness and equifairness.

Definition: A (generalized) fairness condition **F** is a finite, nonempty set of pairs of (possibly augmented) *state properties,*

$$\mathbf{F} = \{(\phi_j, \psi_j) \mid 1 \leqslant j \leqslant M\}.$$

Definition: For a typical repetition statement $S \in GC$, an infinite computation sequence π of S and (fixed) fairness condition **F**:

i. π is *unconditionally* **F**-*fair* iff for each j, $1 \leqslant j \leqslant M$, ψ_j occurs infinitely often along π.

ii. π is *weakly* **F**-*fair* iff for each j, $1 \leqslant j \leqslant M$: if ϕ_j holds *continuously* (i.e. almost everywhere) along π, then ψ_j occurs infinitely often along π.

iii. π is *strongly* **F**-*fair* iff for each j, $1 \leqslant j \leqslant M$: if ϕ_j occurs *infinitely often* along π, so does ψ_j.

A finite sequence π is always unconditionally, weakly and strongly **F**-*fair.*

It might be helpful to state the negation of the various **F**-fairness conditions:

i. An infinite computation sequence π is *unconditionally* **F**-*unfair* iff there exists a j, $1 \leqslant j \leqslant M$, such that ψ_j occurs finitely often only along π. As a result, π contains an infinite tail along which ψ_j does not occur *at all.* We refer to such a π as ψ_j-unfair, and to the infinite tail as ψ_j-*avoiding.*

ii. Similarly, π as above is *weakly* **F**-*unfair* iff there exists a j, $1 \leqslant j \leqslant M$, such that ϕ_j holds continuously along π, but ψ_j holds finitely often only.

iii. Finally, π as above is *strongly* **F**-*unfair* iff there exists a j, $1 \leqslant j \leqslant M$, such that ϕ_j holds infinitely often along π while ψ_j holds finitely often only.

In order to see that **F**-fairness generalizes the notions of fairness mentioned above, we consider the following:

a. Augment each state of a typical repetition statement S with a two-state flag f_i, for each direction $i \in I$. Augment each direction subprogram with a setting of f_i and a resetting of f_j, $j \neq i$. Then define, for $i \in I$:

$$\phi_i \equiv B_i, \text{ the guard of the i-th direction}$$

$$\psi_i \equiv (f_i \text{ is set}).$$

By this definition, **F**-fairness, in all three levels, coincides with the three levels of usual fairness.

b. By taking $M = 2^{|I|-1}$, and augmenting the state of S with counters c_i^A for every $\phi \neq A \subseteq I$ such that $i \in A$ (enumerated in some fixed way); incrementing all c_i^A whenever direction i is taken and $\bigwedge_{j \in A} B_j$ holds, and taking

$$\phi_j = \bigwedge_{k \in A_j} B_k, \qquad j = 1, \cdots, M$$

and

$$\psi_j = (c_{i_1}^A = c_{i_2}^A = \cdots = c_{i_{|A|}}^A), \qquad \text{for } A = \{i_1, \cdots, i_{|A|}\},$$

F-fairness coincides with equifairness.

By considering different augmentations of the proper state and appropriate **F**, a variety of generalized fairness conditions are definable.

Definition: A typical repetition statement $S \in GC$ is:

i. *Unconditionally* **F**-*fairly terminating* (abbreviated **F**-*UFT*), iff all its unconditionally **F**-fair sequences are finite.
ii. *Weakly* **F**-*fairly terminating* (**F**-*WFT*), iff all its weakly **F**-fair sequences are finite.
iii. *Strongly* **F**-*fairly terminating* (**F**-*SFT*), iff all its strongly **F**-fair sequences are finite.

We use $\underset{\mathbf{F}}{\ll} p \gg S \ll q \gg$ as a generic notation for generalized fair termination, and

$$\underset{\mathbf{F}}{\overset{\mathbf{u}}{\ll}} p \gg S \ll q \gg,$$

$$\underset{\mathbf{F}}{\overset{\mathbf{w}}{\ll}} p \gg S \ll q \gg$$

and

$$\underset{\mathbf{F}}{\overset{\mathbf{s}}{\ll}} p \gg S \ll q \gg$$

for the more distinctive termination assertions.

Lemma:

$$\models \underset{\mathbf{F}}{\ll} p \gg S \ll q \gg \quad \longleftrightarrow \quad \models \underset{\mathbf{F}}{\ll} p \gg S \ll \mathit{true} \gg \wedge \{p\}\ S\ \{q\}.$$

As before, this is obvious from the definition. Thus, we focus our attention on **F**- fair termination claims only.

Let S:: $*[\ \underset{i \in I}{[\,]}\ i\colon B_i \rightarrow S_i]$ be a typical GC repetition statement. Figure 4.19 is a rule **F-UFT** for proving unconditionally **F**-fair termination. termination.

Explanation: The intuition behind the rule is similar to its special cases already discussed. The components of **F** are partitioned at each intermediate stage into helpful ones (D_w), which cause a decrease in the parameter of *pi*, and the rest (S_w), which do not cause increase. Whenever a helpful ψ_j for $j \in D_w$, occurs, clause (DEC) shows the decrease. Since along unconditionally **F**-fair infinite computations every ψ_j occurs infinitely often, some ψ_j for $j \in D_w$ will eventually occur, causing a decrease in the parameter of *pi*. and by well-foundedness of $(W, \leqslant)$ prevents diverging.

To prove $\underset{\mathbf{F}}{\overset{\mathbf{u}}{\ll}} p \gg S \ll \mathit{true} \gg$:

Find: a well-founded, partially-ordered, set $(W, \leqslant)$, a *parametrized invariant* pi: $\Sigma_S \times W \rightarrow \{\mathit{true, false}\}$, a *partition* of $\{1, \ldots, M\}$ into $\varnothing \neq D_w \bigcup S_w$, for $0 < w \in W$, satisfying:

1. (INIT) $p \rightarrow \exists w\colon pi(w)$.
2. (CONT) $(pi(w) \wedge w > 0) \rightarrow \bigvee_{i \in I} B_i.$
3. (TERM) $pi(0) \rightarrow \neg \bigvee_{i \in I} B_i.$
4. (DEC)

$$\underset{\mathbf{F}}{\overset{\mathbf{u}}{\ll}} pi(w) \wedge w > 0 \wedge B_i \gg$$

$$S_i$$

$$\ll \bigwedge_{j \in D_w} (\psi_j \rightarrow \exists v\colon v < w \wedge pi(v)) \gg,\ i \in I.$$

5. (NOINC) $\underset{\mathbf{F}}{\overset{\mathbf{u}}{\ll}} pi(w) \wedge w > 0 \wedge B_i \gg S_i \ll \exists v\colon v \leqslant w \wedge pi(v) \gg,\ i \in I.$

Figure 4.19 Rule **F-UFT** (unconditionally **F**-fair termination).

Theorem: (soundness of F-UFT) For a typical repetition statement $S \in GC$:

$$\text{if } \vdash_{\textbf{F-UFT}} \underset{\mathbf{F}}{\overset{\mathbf{u}}{\ll}} p \gg S \ll \mathit{true} \gg, \text{ then } \models \underset{\mathbf{F}}{\overset{\mathbf{u}}{\ll}} p \gg S \ll \mathit{true} \gg.$$

Proof: Omitted. []

Theorem: (semantic completeness of F-UFT) For a typical repetition statement $S \in GC$:

$$\text{if } \models \underset{\mathbf{F}}{\overset{\mathbf{u}}{\ll}} p \gg S \ll \mathit{true} \gg, \text{ then } \vdash_{\textbf{F-UFT}} \underset{\mathbf{F}}{\overset{\mathbf{u}}{\ll}} p \gg S \ll \mathit{true} \gg.$$

Proof: Assume $\models \underset{\mathbf{F}}{\overset{\mathbf{u}}{\ll}} p \gg S \ll \mathit{true} \gg$ holds, and consider any computation tree of S, $T_S(\xi_0)$, such that $\xi_0 \models p$. The general idea is once again to contract every such tree to another one, $T_S^*(\xi_0)$, which has finite paths only, rank $T_S^*(\xi_0)$ with countable ordinals, and use this ranking to define the invariant and partitions. We repeat only the basic definition in its generalized context.

Definition: For a state occurrence $\xi \in T_S(\xi_0)$ and $1 \leqslant j \leqslant M$, let

$\textbf{F-}\mathit{CONE}_{\psi_j}(\xi) \overset{def.}{=} \{\eta \mid \eta$ *is a state-occurrence on an infinite* ψ_j*-avoiding path originating at* $\xi\}$.

To prove $\underset{\mathbf{F}}{\overset{\mathbf{w}}{\ll}} p \gg S \ll true \gg$:

i. Prove clauses (1)–(5) of rule **F-UFT** with **w** replacing **u**.
ii. (CE) prove ($pi(w) \wedge w > 0 \rightarrow \phi_j$), for some $j \in D_w$.

Figure 4.20 Rule **F-WFT** (weakly **F**-fair termination)

The state-occurrence ξ is the *root* of the cone, and ψ_j is its *directive*.

Under this definition, it is again possible to carry the cone-chain construction and obtain the partitions and invariant similarly to the way obtained for unconditional fairness and equifairness. We omit the details. []

We now extend the rule to deal with the weak and strong version of **F**-fair termination. In both cases, an extra clause is added, taking into account the extra condition guaranteeing infinite occurrence. The extra clause (CE) in the rule **F-WFT** (see Figure 4.20) calls for showing continuous enabledness of a helpful direction, as encountered before.

Theorem: (soundness of F-WFT) For a typical repetition statement $S \in GC$:

$$\text{if } \vdash_{\mathbf{F\text{-}WFT}} \underset{\mathbf{F}}{\overset{\mathbf{w}}{\ll}} p \gg S \ll true \gg, \text{ then } \models \underset{\mathbf{F}}{\overset{\mathbf{w}}{\ll}} p \gg S \ll true \gg.$$

Proof: Omitted. []

Theorem: (semantic completeness of F-WFT) For a typical repetition statement $S \in GC$:

$$\text{if } \models \underset{\mathbf{F}}{\overset{\mathbf{w}}{\ll}} p \gg S \ll true \gg, \text{ then } \vdash_{\mathbf{F\text{-}WFT}} \underset{\mathbf{F}}{\overset{\mathbf{w}}{\ll}} p \gg S \ll true \gg.$$

Proof: similar to the completeness proof of **F-UFT**, the difference being in the definition of a cone-chain, taking into account continuous enabledness of the directives. []

For the strong case (see Figure 4.21), once again the extra clause (IO) guarantees infinite occurrence of a helpful ϕ_j, which will force ψ_j to occur eventually and cause decrease. Note that the eventual occurrence $\bigvee_{j \in D_w} \phi_j$ is reduced to the strong **F**-fair termination of a *derived program* $\bar{S}_w$, which terminates as soon as any ϕ_j, $j \in D_w$, holds.

Theorem: (soundness of F-SFT) For a typical repetition statement $S \in GC$:

To prove $\underset{\mathbf{F}}{\overset{\mathbf{s}}{\ll}} p \gg S \ll true \gg$:

i. Prove clauses (1)–(5) of rule **F-UFT** with **s** replacing **u**.

ii. (IO) prove $\underset{\mathbf{F}}{\overset{\mathbf{s}}{\ll}} pi(w) \gg \bar{S}_w \ll true \gg$, $w > 0$, where

$$\bar{S}_w :: *[\underset{i \in I}{[\,]} (B_i \wedge \neg \bigvee_{j \in D_w} \phi_j) \rightarrow S_i].$$

Figure 4.21 Rule **F-SFT** (strongly **F**-fair termination).

$$\text{if } \vdash_{\text{F-SFT}} \underset{\mathbf{F}}{\overset{\mathbf{s}}{\ll}} p \gg S \ll true \gg, \text{ then } \models \underset{\mathbf{F}}{\overset{\mathbf{s}}{\ll}} p \gg S \ll true \gg.$$

Proof: Omitted. [ ]

Theorem: (semantic completeness of F-SFT) For a typical repetition statement $S \in GC$:

$$\text{if } \models \underset{\mathbf{F}}{\overset{\mathbf{s}}{\ll}} p \gg S \ll true \gg, \text{ then } \vdash_{\text{F-SFT}} \underset{\mathbf{F}}{\overset{\mathbf{s}}{\ll}} p \gg S \ll true \gg.$$

Proof: Again, all we need is to modify the definition of a cone-chain and take into account infinite enabledness of the directives. We again omit the details. Note, however, the syntactic induction on the number of non-negated ϕ_i's in the guards of the derived programs, preventing infinite recursive applications of the rule. [ ]

The generalizations discussed in this section rely on the fact that the state conditions can serve as guards, in order to allow for the construction of derived programs. This again is a property of the underlying programming language.

In [HA 84], Harel discusses related issues in a programming language independent context. He introduces a specification language by means of which one can specify various *marking patterns* in infinite trees. He then shows the existence of a recursive bijection between infinite paths having a specified marking pattern in some finitely branching tree, and arbitrary infinite paths in another, possibly countably branching, tree. As a consequence, the absence of infinite properly marked paths in the first tree is equivalent to the absence of any infinite paths in the second tree. This gives a method of specifying large famillies of fairness-like properties. It turns out that most of these properties can be described by Π_1^1-formulae of arithmetic. The *tree-theorem* (of recursion-theory [SH 67]) guarantees the existence of semantically complete proof rules for proving termination under the expressed (Π_1^1 definable) properties. Rules obtained by this general method need not be natural or intuitively appealing. Thus, as admitted by Harel [HA 84], the exploration of programming language oriented proof rules should be pursued independently, as more applicable tools for program verification. Work relating Harel's general results both with helpful directions and with explicit scheduling is still going on.

4.3 Extreme Fairness

4.3.0 Overview

We start by relating our notions of fairness to probabilistic executions of *GC* programs. Suppose we have an extension GC_P of *GC*, with *probabilities* attached to its directions. Thus, a typical repetition statement might be given as

$$S:: *[\ \underset{i \in I}{[\,]} p_i\colon B_i \rightarrow S_i], \qquad 0 \leqslant p_i \leqslant 1,\ \sum_i p_i = 1.$$

We do not develop a formal semantics for GC_P (one general such attempt is [KO 81]). Rather, we interpret p_i intuitively as the probability of selecting direction i when enabled.

Consider now the program *PP* (see Figure 4.22), taken from [PN 83]. Since the probability of following the execution sequence $(1)^\omega$ is $\lim_{k \to \infty} 2^{-k} = 0$, this program halts with probability 1. This could be formally proven in several recent extension of logics of programs [FH 83], [HSP 82], [KO 83], [LS 83], [RE 80], [TM 83]. However, one can easily see that the corresponding *GC* program *P*, *without probability assignments* to directions, fairly terminates! Thus, as stated before, for some programs, fair termination can be taken as an approximation to *probabilistic termination* (abbreviated *PT*) with probability 1. This is the main qualitative property of interest for probabilistic programs.

Consider, however, the probabilistic program *PQ* (see Figure 4.23). By assigning the corresponding probabilities to the arcs of the computation tree, we get the tree for the main loop shown in Figure 4.24.

$$
\begin{aligned}
PP::\ & b:=0;\\
& *[\tfrac{1}{2} : b = 0 \rightarrow skip\\
& [\,]\\
& \tfrac{1}{2} : b = 0 \rightarrow b:=1\\
&].
\end{aligned}
$$

Figure 4.22 Probabilistic program *PP*.

$$PQ::\ b:=0;$$
$$*[\frac{1}{2} : b \leqslant 1 \rightarrow b:=0$$
$$[\,]$$
$$\frac{1}{2} : b \leqslant 1 \rightarrow b:=b+1$$
$$].$$

Figure 4.23 Probabilistic program *PQ*.

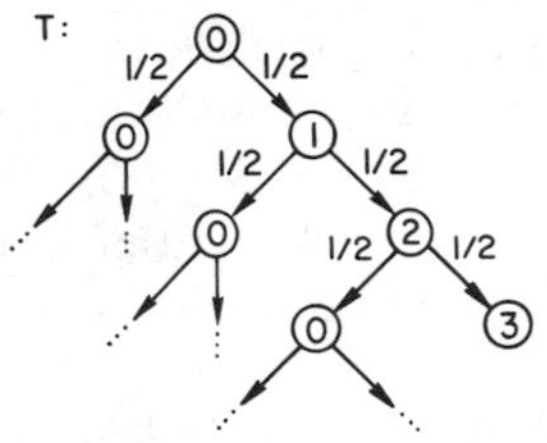

Figure 4.24 Probabilistic computation-tree for *PQ*.

Analyzing this tree, one sees that from a state in which $b = 0$ holds, there is a probability of ¼ to reach a state satisfying $b = 2$, in which the program *PQ* terminates. Thus, the probability of *not* terminating *PQ* is $\lim_{k \to \infty}(3/4)^k = 0$, and hence *PQ* is also *PT* with probability 1.

Now, consider again the corresponding program *Q* (see Figure 4.25), without probability assignment to directions.

The program *Q* is *not* fairly terminating under *any* of the fairness conditions discussed so far! Clearly, the sequence

$$\pi: b = 0 \overset{2}{\rightarrow} b = 1 \overset{1}{\rightarrow} b = 0 \overset{2}{\rightarrow} \cdots$$

is (unconditionally!) fair .

$$Q::\ b:=0;$$
$$*[1: b \leqslant 1 \rightarrow b:=0$$
$$[\,]$$
$$2: b \leqslant 1 \rightarrow b:=b+1$$
$$].$$

Figure 4.25 Program *Q*.

Thus, fair-termination, under any of the fairness conditions discussed so far, cannot serve always as a good approximation to *PT* with probability 1.

A closer analysis of π reveals the reason for the inadequacy of fair-termination for some probabilistic programs. The probabilities assigned to the enabled directions are *state independent,* while π displays a *perfect correlation* between states and directions: direction 2 is infinitely often chosen, but taken *only* in states satisfying $b = 0$! Had it been chosen in a state satisfying $b = 1$, that computation would (immediately) terminate.

Thus, what is needed in order to capture the qualitative behaviour of probabilistic programs is a strengthening of fairness that will prevent such state-dependent correlations. This is the purpose of *extreme-fairness* [PN 83]. The way to eliminate these correlations is by *relativizing* the fairness requirements to (arbitrary) subsets (predicates) of states occurring at the point of the nondeterministic choice (see [PN 83] for an explanation why single states relativization is not sufficient). Again, states are assumed to be augmented by auxiliary variables to enable the expression of properties of prefixes of computations.

For the general definition, we wish to keep the restricting subsets as a parameter in some standard way.

Let $\Gamma = \{\phi^0, \phi^1, \phi^2, \cdots\}$ be any countable collection of state properties, enumerated in some fixed way. Pnueli's original definition considered Γ as the collection of all first order definable predicates over Σ_S.

In general, we consider membership in Γ modulo logical equivalence, not distinguishing between a predicate and the set of states satisfying it.

Definition: For a typical repetition statement $S \in GC$, and an infinite computation path $\pi \in T_S(\xi)$ (for any initial state ξ), π is:

i. *Unconditionally* Γ*-extremely-fair* (abbreviated Γ-***UXF***) iff for every $\phi \in \Gamma$ and direction $i \in I$, i is infinitely often chosen in states satisfying ϕ.

ii. *Weakly* Γ*-extremely-fair* (Γ-***WXF***) iff for every $\phi \in \Gamma$ and direction $i \in I$: if i is continuously enabled in states satisfying ϕ, then i is infinitely often chosen in states satisfying ϕ.

iii. *Strongly* Γ*-extremely-fair* (Γ-***SXF***) iff for every $\phi \in \Gamma$ and direction $i \in I$: if i is infinitely-often enabled in states satisfying ϕ, then i is infinitely often chosen in states satisfying ϕ.

A finite π is always unconditionally, and hence also weakly and strongly, Γ-extremely-fair.

By choosing $\Gamma = \{true\}$, the identically-true predicate, one obtains the usual fairness notions as special cases of extreme fairness.

It is again instructive to consider the negations of these properties: an infinite π is weakly Γ-extremely-unfair iff there exist a $\phi_0 \in \Gamma$ and direction $i_0 \in I$, such that i_0 is continuously enabled along π in states satisfying ϕ_0 but only finitely often chosen in such states. We refer to such a π as (ϕ_0, i_0)-extremely-unfair. We say that (ϕ_0, i_0) is a *witness* to π's unfairness. Such a π has an infinite tail, along which direction i_0 is *never* taken, while every state in the tail satisfies ϕ_0. We refer to such a tail as (ϕ_0, i_0) *-avoiding*. A similar terminology is used for strong extreme-unfairness, and for the unconditional version.

Definition: A typical repetition statement $S \in GC$ is:

1. *Unconditionally* Γ*-extremely-fair terminating* (abbreviated Γ-***UXFT***) iff all its Γ-***UXF*** computation sequences are finite.
2. *Weakly* Γ*-extremely-fair terminating* (Γ-***WXFT***) iff all its Γ-***WXF*** computation sequences are finite.
3. *Strongly* Γ*-extremely-fair terminating* (Γ-***SXFT***) iff all its Γ-***SXF*** computation sequences are finite.

We use the notation $\underset{\Gamma}{\ll} p \gg S \ll q \gg$ as generic for extremely-fair termination (***XFT***) with postcondition q, under precondition p. For distinguishing the specific extreme-fairness meant, we use $\overset{u}{\underset{\Gamma}{\ll}} p \gg S \ll q \gg$, $\overset{w}{\underset{\Gamma}{\ll}} p \gg S \ll q \gg$ and $\overset{s}{\underset{\Gamma}{\ll}} p \gg S \ll q \gg$.

We once again concentrate only in termination assertions of the form $\underset{\Gamma}{\ll} p \gg S \ll \mathit{true} \gg$.

In [PN 83], temporal-logic is used to reason about extreme fairness and its consequences. Here, we are interested in proof rules that appeal directly to well-foundedness arguments. In particular, we show how to apply the ordinal-directed choice of helpful directions under a natural assumption about Γ.

In [LPZ 85], the case of finite state programs has been shown to equate ***PT*** and ***XFT*** under the assumption of properly augmented states, assumed here anyhow. They refer to it as α-fairness.

4.3.1 Proof rules for extremely-fair termination

In this section we extend the ideas of the "helpful direction" methods for proving fair termination to handle also unconditional extremely-fair termination. We remark that by itself the unconditional version is not interesting; however, the rule extends to the weak and strong versions and serves as a basis, and is therefore presented. The basic intuition is the following: in addition of identifying helpful directions at each intermediate stage of the computation, we require also finding a *helpful condition*

$\phi \in \Gamma$, so that the helpful direction will cause a decrease in a well-founded variant only and *whenever it is taken in a state satisfying the helpful condition.* Since unconditional extreme fairness guarantees the activation of every direction infinitely often in states satisfying *every* $\phi \in \Gamma$, in particular this will happen also with the helpful ϕ, and an infinite *UXF* computation would contradict well-foundedness. The choice of the *helpful condition* will also be directed by the ordinal measuring the abstract "distance" from termination. This is formalized in the rule **Γ-UXFT** in Figure 4.26. Let Γ be given, and S be a typical repetition *GC* statement, with all guards being the same Boolean expression, B.

Note that $\phi_{w,j}$ is not an invariant, and does not have to be preserved. It only identifies the circumstances under which direction $j \in D_w$ is helpful, i.e. causes a decrease in w. This is the extension over the corresponding proof rule for fair terminations, the helpful direction need not be helpful *whenever* taken. Again it is assumed that all members of Γ can serve as guards in *GC*.

Following is an example of the application of rule **Γ-UXFT**.

Example: Consider again the program Q discussed above.

We prove that its main loop, denoted *QL*, is Γ-***UXFT*** under the precondition $p \equiv (b = 0)$ for every Γ containing $\phi \equiv (b = 1)$.

We use the following:

$$W = \{0,\ 1\} \quad \text{with } 0 < 1,$$

$$D_1 = \{2\}, \quad S_1 = \{1\},$$

$$\phi_{1,2} \equiv (b{=}1),$$

$$pi(b,\ w) \equiv b \geqslant 0 \wedge (b \geqslant 2 \rightarrow w = 0) \wedge (b \leqslant 1 \rightarrow w = 1).$$

We now show the satisfaction of all clauses of **Γ-UXFT**.

INIT: $b = 0$ implies $pi(1)$.

CONT: $pi(1)$ implies $b \leqslant 1$, i.e. continuation of *QL*.

TERM: $pi(0)$ implies $b \geqslant 2$, i.e. termination of *QL*.

DEC: Suppose $pi(1) \wedge b = 1$ holds. Executing S_2 (since 2 is the only direction in D_1), causes $b = 2$ to hold, and hence $pi(0)$, a decrease in rank.

NOINC: Suppose $pi(1)$ holds, and hence $b \leqslant 1$. Executing $S_1 :: b{:=}0$ causes $b = 0$, hence $pi(1)$ still holds. Executing $S_2 :: b{:=}b{+}1$ either leaves $b \leqslant 1$ true, and hence $pi(1)$, or causes $b = 2$ to hold, hence establishing $pi(0)$, a decrease.

Thus, we proved $\vdash_{\Gamma\text{-UXFT}} \overset{u}{\underset{\Gamma}{\ll}} b{=}0 \gg QL \ll true \gg$ as required. [ ]

To prove $\overset{u}{\underset{\Gamma}{\ll}} p \gg S \ll true \gg$:

Find : a well-founded, partially-ordered, set $(W, \leqslant)$, a parametrized invariant $pi: \Sigma_S \times W \rightarrow \{true, false\}$, a partition of I into $S_w \cup D_w \neq \varnothing$, for $0 < w \in W$, a *helpful condition* $\phi_{w,j}$ for $j \in D_w$, $0 < w \in W$, satisfying:

1. (INIT) $p \rightarrow \exists w\colon pi(w)$,
2. (CONT) $pi(w) \wedge w > 0 \rightarrow B$,
3. (TERM) $pi(0) \rightarrow \neg B$,
4. (DEC) $\overset{u}{\underset{\Gamma}{\ll}} pi(w) \wedge w > 0 \wedge \phi_{w,j} \gg S_j \ll \exists v\colon v < w \wedge pi(v) \gg$, $j \in D_w$, $w \in W$,
5. (NOINC) $\overset{u}{\underset{\Gamma}{\ll}} pi(w) \wedge w > 0 \gg S_i \ll \exists v\colon v \leqslant w \wedge pi(v) \gg$, $w \in W, i \in I$.

Figure 4.26 Rule **Γ-UXFT** (unconditional Γ-extremely-fair termination).

Theorem: (soundness of Γ-UXFT) For a typical repetition statement $S \in GC$ (with identical guards):

$$\text{if} \vdash_{\Gamma\text{-UXFT}} \overset{u}{\underset{\Gamma}{\ll}} p \gg S \ll true \gg, \text{ then} \models \overset{u}{\underset{\Gamma}{\ll}} p \gg S \ll true \gg.$$

Proof: Omitted. [ ]

Theorem: (semantic completeness of Γ-UXFT) For a typical repetition statement $S \in GC$ (with identical guards):

$$\text{if} \models \overset{u}{\underset{\Gamma}{\ll}} p \gg S \ll true \gg, \text{ then} \vdash_{\Gamma\text{-UXFT}} \overset{u}{\underset{\Gamma}{\ll}} p \gg S \ll true \gg.$$

Proof: Suppose $\overset{u}{\underset{\Gamma}{\ll}} p \gg S \ll true \gg$ holds. We have to show the existence of $(W, \leqslant)$, pi, (D_w, S_w) and $\phi_{w,j}$, $j \in D_w$ satisfying the rule. The proof again expands the ideas of completeness proofs for fair-termination proof-rules, by contracting the execution tree $T_S(\xi_0)$ to a well-founded tree $T_S^*(\xi_0)$ used to define an initial sequence of the countable ordinals as the well-founded set. We present only its essentials. Let ξ_0 be an initial state satisfying p, and suppose $T_S(\xi_0)$ is infinite (otherwise there is nothing to prove). By assumption, every infinite computation sequence $\pi \in T_S(\xi_0)$ is not Γ-*UXF*.

Definition: For a state occurrence $\xi \in T_S(\xi_0)$, condition $\phi \in \Gamma$ and direction $i \in I$ let

$$CONE_{\phi,i}(\xi) = \{\eta \mid \eta \textit{ is a state occurrence on some infinite } \pi \textit{ starting in } \xi, \textit{ the tail of which is } (\phi, i)\textit{-avoiding}\}.$$

ξ is the *root* of the cone, and (ϕ,i) its *directive*.

Lemma: (cone-exit) An infinite computation sequence π leaves a cone $CONE_{\phi,i}(\xi)$ iff it contains an activation of direction i in a state satisfying ϕ.

Proof: Omitted.

We next construct again the covering hierarchy of cones. The only essential difference from the fairness case is in the choice of directives to ensure *maximal variation.* We use the following sequence of elements of Γ (under the fixed enumeration): ϕ^0, ϕ^0,ϕ^1, ϕ^0, ϕ^1, ϕ^2, ϕ^0, ϕ^1, ϕ^2, ϕ^3 $\cdots$. As for the directions d, we form a round-robin: for each ϕ^k, the first time it takes part as a cone-directive, choose $d=1$, the next time $d=2$, etc. Whenever ξ_i does not avoid (ϕ, d) thus chosen, take $A_i = \{\xi_i\}$

Under these definitions we again obtain that the cone-chain lemma holds, and the construction of the parametrized invariant, decreasing directions and helpful conditions resembles the one in the fairness case.

[]

Similarly to the previous cases of fair termination, the rules for the weak and strong version are obtained from the rule for the unconditional version by adding an extra clause, taking care of the condition of choosing a direction. Here we relax the assumption of identical guards and consider a typical repetition statement S:: $[* \underset{i \in I}{[]} i\text{: } B_i \rightarrow S_i]$.

We restrict our attention to the case of *strong extreme fairness* only. We assume again that it is possible to use elements of Γ as guards in auxiliary programs. Thus, we make the assumption that this is possible, for example taking Γ as all quantifier-free first order definable predicates. Otherwise, the relativized version can be employed once again.

The rule T-**SXFT** is shown in Figure 4.27.

Once again, the role of the extra clause is to guarantee that a helpful direction is infinitely-often enabled in states satisfying the helpful condition. It does so by proving Γ-**SXF** termination of an auxiliary program, terminating under the precondition $pi(w)$, as soon as helpful direction is enabled with a helpful condition satisfied.

To prove $\underset{\Gamma}{\overset{\mathbf{s}}{\ll}} p \gg S \ll true \gg$:

i. Prove clauses (1)–(5) of rule Γ-**UXFT** with **s** replacing **u**.

ii. (IOE) prove $\underset{\Gamma}{\overset{\mathbf{s}}{\ll}} pi(w) \wedge w > 0 \gg \bar{S}_w \ll true \gg$, where

$$\bar{S}_w\text{:: } [* \underset{i \in I}{[]} (B_i \wedge \neg \bigvee_{j \in D_w} (B_j \wedge \phi_{w,j})) \rightarrow S_i].$$

Figure 4.27 Rule Γ-**SXFT** (Strong Γ-extremely-fair-termination).

Example: Consider the program E (see Figure 4.28). This program is not fairly terminating under the precondition $\neg(even(x))$, as is manifested by the infinite fair sequence $(2,2,1)^\omega$. This sequence is not ***SXF***, since direction 1 is taken only when x is odd, never when x is even. The program is also not equifairly terminating (under same preconditions), as is manifested by the infinite equifair sequence $(1,2,2,1)^\omega$.

We now show that

$$\vdash_{\Gamma\text{-SXFT}} \overset{s}{\underset{\Gamma}{\ll}} x \geqslant 0 \wedge y \geqslant 0 \gg E \ll true \gg$$

where $even(x) \in \Gamma$.

As $(W, \leqslant)$ we choose $(N, \leqslant)$. For every $n \in N$, we take $D_n = \{1\}$, and $\phi_{n,1} \equiv (even(x))$.

The parametrized invariant is:

$$pi(x, y, n) \overset{def.}{\equiv} x \geqslant 0 \wedge y = n \geqslant 0.$$

INIT, CONT, TERM–Immediate. NOINC–Direction 2 is trivially non increasing, not modifying y at all. Direction 1 with $odd(x)$ does not modify y either.

DEC–When direction 1 is taken in a state satisfying the helpful condition $even(x)$, y decreases, so a smaller n satisfies pi.

IOE–The derived program $\bar{E}_1$ is as in Figure 4.29 after simplification.

```
E:: *[1: y > 0 → [even(x) → y:=y−1
                  []
                  ¬even(x) → skip
                  ]
      []
      2: y > 0 → x:=x+1
     ].
```

Figure 4.28 Program E.

```
Ē1:: *[y > 0 ∧ ¬even(x) → [even(x) → y:=y−1
                           []
                           ¬even(x) → skip
                           ]
       []
       y > 0 ∧ ¬even(x) → x:=x+1
      ].
```

Figure 4.29 Derived program $\bar{E}_1$.

For the subproof, take $W = \{0,1\}$ with $D_1 = \{2\}$, $\phi_{1,2} \equiv true$, (i.e. "simple" fairness is sufficient),

$$\pi'(x, y, w) \equiv (x \geqslant 0 \wedge (even(x) \rightarrow w = 0) \wedge (\neg even(x) \rightarrow w = 1))$$

which again satisfy all clauses. For IOE we obtain an empty derived program.

Theorem: (soundness of Γ-SXFT) For a typical repetition statement $S \in GC$:

$$\text{if } \vdash_{\Gamma\text{-SXFT}} \overset{s}{\underset{\Gamma}{\ll}} p \gg S \ll true \gg, \text{ then } \models \overset{s}{\underset{\Gamma}{\ll}} p \gg S \ll true \gg.$$

Proof: Omitted. [ ]

In contrast to previously discussed rules, the semantic completeness of Γ-**SXFT** is not known (except for some simple Γ's, e.g. *finite* Γ's). The main problem is in establishing that the chain of recursive applications terminates. The structure of the derived program does not induce any obvious syntactic simplification.

4.4 An Analysis of Predicate-Reachability Fairness

One natural interpretation of fairness (in all its versions) is in terms of execution of enabled transitions (directions). We refer to such fairness as *τ-fairness* and it encompasses all the fairness notions (and their generalizations) discussed so far.

One of the less attractive features of this transition-oriented approach to defining fairness is its syntactic flavor, where it strongly depends on the syntactic form of specifying directions of choice at a given point. Consider the two programs S and S' (see Figure 4.30). The program S' results from S by merging the two directions {2, 3} into one. Clearly, they have the same computation sequences as far as states are concerned. The

S:: x:=0;	S':: x=0;
*[1: x=0 → x:=x−1	*[1: x=0 → x:=x−1
[ ]	[ ]
2: x<0 → x:=x+1	2: $x \leqslant 0$ → x:=x+1
[ ]	].
3: x=0 → x:=x+1	
].	

Figure 4.30 Syntactically different similar programs S and S'.

infinite computation $\pi = (1,2)^{\omega}$ is fair in S' but unfair in S. Thus, a distinction is made only according to the form of a program, which may be too fine at certain circumstances. Furthermore, the unfairness of π in S can be viewed as resulting from the fact that the state $x=0$ occurs infinitely often along it, but only one of it's successor states, namely $x=-1$, occurs infinitely often. Its other successor state $x=1$ does not.

We recall another example program Q from Section 4.3.0, which had an infinite (τ-) fair computation, in which a transition is *never* executed in some state in which it is infinitely-often enabled. That example triggered the definition of extreme fairness. However, one can define differently the notion of fairness, arriving at the concept of *state-reachability fairness* (σ-*fairness*). We present only the strong version. This notion is best presented in terms of arbitrary transition systems, where transition is a relevant direction. We do not further specify at this stage the structure of transition systems (see Chapter 7). All we need to know about them here is that each transition τ has an enabling condition p_{τ} and an associated state transformation f_{τ}. We use $\tau\tau$ for the collection of all transitions in a given system. In the examples we present such systems as *GC* programs. The presentation follows essentially [QS 83].

Definition: An infinite execution sequence π is σ-*fair* iff for every state σ occurring infinitely often along π, and for every transition τ enabled in σ, τ is taken infinitely often along π in σ.

Again, taking the negation, one obtains that an infinite sequence π if σ-*unfair* iff there exist a state σ occurring infinitely often along π and a transition τ enabled on σ s.t. τ is taken only finitely often along π in σ. This notion guarantees that any state σ' *reachable* from σ (by *some* τ) will appear infinitely often in any infinite sequence in which σ appears infinitely often. We refer to the fair termination properties induced as τ-*fair* termination (τ-*FT*) and σ-*fair* termination (σ-*FT*).

Clearly, the program Q from section 4.3.0 is σ-*fairly* terminating, as an infinite computation is σ-*unfair* w.r.t. to a state $\sigma \models b = 1$ and the second transition (direction). However, under this definition, the program P (see Figure 4.31) is *not* σ-*fairly* terminating, *as no state is infinitely-often visited,* while *P is* τ-*fairly* terminating.

```
P:: x:=0;
          *[ 1: x ⩾ 0 → x:=x+1
               []
             2: even(x) → x:=−1
          ].
```

Figure 4.31 A program τ-**FT** but not σ-**FT**.

Thus, these two fairness notions are incomparable in terms of their induced classes of fairly terminating programs. One might think that the incompatibility suggests that the "real" fairness should be the conjunction of both. The example program R (see Figure 4.32) does not fairly terminate even w.r.t. to the conjunction of *τ-fairness* and *σ-fairness*. Consider the computation of R (see Figure 4.33). The infinite sequence $(1;2)^w$ is clearly *τ-fair* as both directions are taken infinitely often; it is also *σ-fair* due to the "independent" y, causing again no state to ever repeat itself.

The fact that the example program R is not *FT* arises from two of its properties:

1. Reaching a terminating state is possible infinitely often but from *different* states each time.
2. All these states behave the same w.r.t. to x but differ in an "independent" variable y.

Thus, we would like to have a *weakening* of σ-fairness, where subsets of states replace the role of a specific state in the definition. While doing this we consider reachability in its full power, in contrast to example R where a terminating state was always immediately reachable (i.e. by a single transition).

Definition: An infinite computation sequence π is *ϕ-fair*, for a state predicate ϕ, iff π contains infinitely many state occurrences satisfying ϕ whenever it contains infinitely many states from which a ϕ-state is reachable.

Again, if we consider *ϕ-unfairness*, it holds on an infinite computation π iff π has infinitely many state occurrences σ_{i_j}, $j = 0, 1, \cdots$ and there exist infinitely many states σ_{i_j}', $j = 0, 1, \cdots$ such that $\sigma_{i_j}' \models \phi$ and $\sigma_{i_j} \overset{*}{\rightarrow} \sigma_{i_j}'$, but only finitely many σ_{i_j}' occur on π.

It is easy to see that the example program R is not ϕ-fair for $\phi(x, y) \overset{def.}{=} x = 1 \wedge odd(y)$, the collection of reachable terminal states.

Definition: An infinite computation sequence π of a program S is *ρ-fair* (reachably-fair), iff it is ϕ-fair for every $\phi \subseteq \Sigma_S$.

```
R:: x:=0; y:=0;
        *[ 1: x=0 → x:=x−1; y:=y+1
           []
           2: x ⩽ 0 → x:=x+1; y:=y+1
        ].
```

Figure 4.32 A non-σ, τ terminating program.

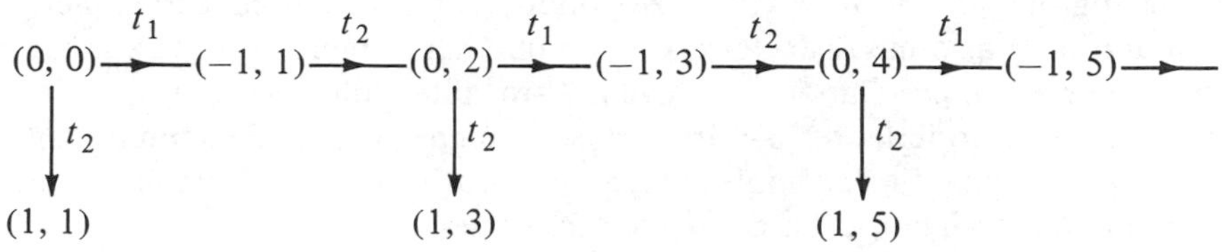

Figure 4.33 A computation of *R*.

We still could relativize this definition w.r.t. to some collection of predicates Γ, instead of all them, as we did for extreme fairness. Note once again the difference between extreme fairness and ρ-fairness, as the role played by the predicates ϕ is different. ϕ characterizes source states in extreme fairness, while characterizing (reachable) target states for ρ-fairness.

Still, ρ-fairness does not cover τ-fairness or σ-fairness, as can be realized from the example *SR* in Figure 4.34.

In this example, states are reachable in *different ways.* The infinite execution sequence $\pi = (1;\ 2;\ 1;\ 2)^\omega$ is σ-unfair, as the state $\sigma \models x{=}0 \wedge y{=}0$ occurs infinitely often along it, but the subsequence (σ, σ'), where $\sigma' \models x{=}1 \wedge y{=}0$, does not occur infinitely often. The transition 2 is never taken from σ. However, π is clearly ρ-fair, as *each* state occurs infinitely often along it, and hence, also every ϕ.

By similarly ignoring transition identities that lead to a state, we can construct an example of a program *TF* (see Figure 4.35) which has a π that is ρ-fair but not τ-fair. Let π be the sequence $(1)^\omega$.

```
SR:: x:=0; y:=0;
*[ 1: true → x:=(x+1) mod 2
   []
   2: true → y:=(y+1) mod 2
 ].
```

Figure 4.34 Program *SR*.

```
TF:: x:=0;
   *[ 1: true→x:=x+1 mod 2
      []
      2: true→x:=0
    ].
```

Figure 4.35 Program *TF*.

Taking the *intersection* of all three notions of fairness discussed, namely τ, σ and ρ, is also unsatisfactory. On the one hand, there is no guarantee that different interpretations of "event" are not applicable at some circumstances. Furthermore, ρ-fairness itself might be too demanding on various occasions. For example, there is no obvious way of simulating it with random-assignment based explicit schedulers.

However, the importance of ρ-fairness is in that other fairness notions in a program P can be expressed as ρ-fairness in a *derived* transition system (program) $\delta(P)$. The states of the derived system $\delta(P)$ consist of all single steps in the given system P. Thus, such a state is $\xi = (\sigma, \tau, \sigma')$, so that σ, σ' are states in the given system, $\tau \in \tau\tau_P$ and $\sigma \models p_\tau$, $\sigma' = f_\tau(\sigma)$. The underlying labeled graph of $\delta(P)$ is the same as that of P. The transitions of the derived system $\tau\tau_{\delta(P)}$ are defined by $\bar{\tau} = (\bar{p}_\tau, \bar{f}_\tau)$, where $\xi = (\sigma, \tau', \sigma') \models \bar{p}_\tau$ iff

$$\sigma \models p_\tau \wedge \exists \tau'' \in \tau\tau\colon \sigma' \models p_{\tau''},$$

and

$$\bar{f}_{\tau''}((\sigma, \tau', \sigma')) = (\sigma', \bar{\tau}, f_\tau(\sigma')).$$

The derived system $\delta(P)$ is, by its definition, closely related to the given P. It "memorizes" in its state the immediate past in any given computation. Any computation of $\delta(P)$ starting in a state $\xi = (\sigma, \tau, \sigma')$ gives rise to a computation of P starting in σ' and vice versa. Such a state is "equivalent" to σ' with the difference that its predecessor states are states of the form $\xi' = (-, -, \sigma)$, i.e. states "equivalent" to σ. All transitions leading to ξ are τ-transitions. Consequently, if a state ξ as above is *reached* in a computation of $\delta(P)$, then σ' is reached in P by τ executed on σ. This establishes the following two propositions.

Proposition: If an infinite computation sequence π (of a program P) is τ-unfair, then there exists a transition $t \in \tau\tau_P$ such that every execution sequence π' in $\delta(P)$ corresponding to π is ρ-unfair w.r.t.

$$\phi = after(\tau) \overset{def.}{=} \{(\sigma, t, \sigma')\}.$$

Proposition: If an infinite computation sequence π (of a program P) is σ-unfair, there exist states σ, σ' of P, such that every execution sequence π' in $\delta(P)$ corresponding to π is ρ -unfair w.r.t.

$$\phi = between(\sigma, \sigma') \overset{def.}{=} \{(\sigma, \tau, \sigma') \mid \tau \in \tau\tau_P\}.$$

Note that the reduction technique employed here is nothing but the familiar addition of auxiliary variables to the state, and are a special case of the same technique applied before to obtain the *generalized fairness,* where auxiliary variables were not restricted to "memorize" the immediate past only.

Indeed, arbitrary ρ-unfairness in $\delta(P)$ need not correspond to (a combination of) τ-unfairness and σ-unfairness in P. It would correspond to some generalized unfairness property in P, however.

As shown in [QS 83], ρ-fairness fits well for being expressed by a special logic, as discussed in Chapter 7.

CHAPTER 5
Fair Termination of Concurrent Processes

5.1 Overview

Though the main interest and motivation for the consideration of fair termination stems from concurrency, almost all of the recent results are formulated in terms of nondeterministic programs, as discussed in previous chapters. The main reason for this is the elegance of formalisms for structured nondeterminism, such as *Guarded Commands.* In this chapter, we present extensions of the methods to concurrency, trying to preserve as much as possible the structured approach.

The method of the helpful direction is applied to a language in which concurrency takes place among disjoint processes communicating by means of *message passing*. As mentioned before, the *relativized* version of the method is applied, as the language considered does not have the closure properties needed to reduce eventual occurrence of a condition to (fair) termination of a derived program. The main interesting new phenomena discussed are the impacts of *simultaneity* (in terms of *joint enabledness*) and overlapping computations due to concurrency, on fair termination. As a consequence, one can now formalize arguments which characterize behaviours such as the ability of a process to communicate a finite unbounded number of times and yet always terminate. The presentation basically follows [GFK 84].

The method of explicit schedulers is applied to a language in which concurrent processes communicate using *shared variables*. Such a language emphasizes *mutual exclusion* and not simultaneity. The main aspect treated is that of the transformations realizing fairness, taken from [OA 84].

The application of a particular method to a particular programming language is immaterial and both methods may be successfully applied to both languages. We decided to follow existing presentations. The reader should be able at this stage to figure out the details.

In both cases, it is found convenient to model concurrent executions of communicating processes by interleaving their atomic actions. Once fairness assumptions are included, the interleaving model is somewhat more satisfactory than in the case of arbitrary interleaving. Still, attempts are made also to capture a more "truly concurrent" model. Obviously, this distinction collapses if one is interested only in the state-transformation semantics of concurrent programs. Due to the possibility of using nondeterministic interleaving to model concurrency it became possible to use the successful tools for proving fair termination in a larger context.

5.2 Fairness and Communicating Processes

In this section we first introduce a model programming language which allows for the expression of concurrent programs consisting of *disjoint* processes communicating via synchronized message passing (known also as *handshaking*). After a general discussion of fairness in this context, a proof rule is introduced, implementing the helpful-directions method for a *serialized semantics* of that language. Then, conditions are formulated under which a proof of fair-termination in the restrictive semantics is valid also under a more "liberal" semantics, in which concurrent subcomputations can overlap instead of being purely interleaved. The programming language chosen is basically a sublanguage of CSP [HO 78], where the simplifications assumed ease the notational burden.

5.2.1 The CSP sublanguage for communicating processes

We start by presenting the syntactic structure of the language, strongly influenced by that of *GC*.

1) A *program* consists of $n > 1$ communicating processes, P:: $[P_1 \,||\, \cdots \,||\, P_n]$, disjoint in their state spaces (i.e. no shared variables are considered). For notational convenience we subscribe each variable with the subscript of the process to the state of which it belongs.
2) A *process* has the following *iterative* form:

$$P_i :: *[\underset{k=1,n_i}{[]} B_k^i ; \alpha_k^i \rightarrow S_k^i],$$

where

B_k^i is a Boolean expression over the local state of P_i;

α_k^i is a communication command naming some target process P_j, $j \neq i$, $1 \leqslant j \leqslant n$ (called P_i's *partner*), either for *input* ($P_j?x$, x being the variable receiving the message), or for *output* ($P_j!y$, the contents of y being sent).

S_k^i is some loop-free and communication-free statement. As mentioned already, these restrictions are imposed only for simplifying the notation and the presentation of the intended rule, and can be easily eliminated. By transformations due to Apt and Clermont [AC 85], every CSP program is equivalent to one in this form.

Remark: The distributed termination convention is not treated in the rule given here. This is again a technical point which can be incorporated into the rule at the expense of some extra notation. Moreover, in view of [AF 84] its exclusion does not affect the expressive power of the language.

Before treating in detail the two semantics mentioned above, we first delineate on an intuitive level an operational description of executing such programs, so that we can make some general observations regarding fairness in the context of communicating processes.

Each process is executing its own local instructions in parallel and independently of other processes. As processes are disjoint and do not share any variables, their local actions do not interfere. Whenever a process is at the "top level" of an iteration, it is willing to communicate with any of the partners specified in its communication guards. In order to determine the collection of eligible partners for communication, the *open* alternatives are determined. These are all the alternatives the Boolean part of which evaluates to *true* and the partners of which are also at their top level, attempting communication. Again, due to disjointness, the evaluation of Boolean conditions is local to a process and is not influenced by possible local actions of some other process.

Whenever two processes contain two *matching* open alternatives, namely two communication commands one of which is *input* and the other is *output* and each names the other as its partner, these two processes may *communicate*. The effect of a communication is the same as that of an assignment of the output value to the variable designated in the input command. Once a communication takes place, both its participants "pass the arrow" and execute the local action guarded by that communication command.

As we shall see in the sequel, the exact determination of when to choose matching communication distinguishes different semantics. However, the following general observations can be made on the basis of the informal description presented.

In a programming language for nondeterministic programs such as *GC* the candidates for the application of fair selection are *directions,* which have to be (in the strong case) infinitely-often taken along an infinite execution on which they are infinitely-often *enabled.*

When passing to a CSP-like language [HO 78], which has a much richer structure, two new aspects of fairness emerge:

A) Choice-Levels. There are more candidates for the application of fair selection. Following [KR 82], [FR 80], one can distinguish between several levels of fairness. We indicate here the main three. For each of them, one can consider the orthogonal subdivision into the unconditional, weak and strong versions. For explanatory reasons, we formulate everything in terms of the strong subcase in this section.

(1) *Process-fairness*–at this level, the requirement is that in an infinite execution each process which is infinitely often enabled (i.e. capable of advance) will do so. In the CSP case, this means that each process will infinitely often communicate (without imposing restrictions on its partners for communication) if it is infinitely often willing to communicate.
(2) *Channel-fairness*–at this level, the requirement is that *each pair* of processes which infinitely often are *mutually willing* to communicate with each other will infinitely often do so.
(3) *Communication fariness*–similar to (2) but regarding two *specific* communication requests within two processes.

We explicitly treat (3) only. The treatment of (1) and (2), though different in details, is similar in essence.

Following are some example programs examplifying intuitively the notions of fair termination of communicating processes on the various levels mentioned.

Example: (unbounded chattering) A very simple program is a generalization of the random number generator discussed in Chapter 2 (see Figure 5.1). In this program P_1 and P_2 may communicate for any number of times. Once the communication between P_2 and P_3 occurs the value of *go_on* is set to *false* and all processes terminate.

Thus, termination here depends on P_3 eventually getting its chance to communicate. Hence, process-fairness suffices to terminate this program. Note that P_3 is loop-free and communicates once only before terminating.

$$P:: [P_1 \,||\, P_2 \,||\, P_3]$$

where

P_1:: $b := true$;
$*[1{:}\ b;\ P_2?b \rightarrow skip]$

P_2:: $go\_on := true;\ c := true$;
$*[1{:}\ c;\ P_1!go\_on \rightarrow [go\_on \rightarrow skip\ [\,]\ \neg go\_on \rightarrow c := false]$
  [ ]
  $2{:}\ c;\ P_3?go\_on \rightarrow skip]$

P_3:: $P_2!false$

Figure 5.1 Communicating processes–unbounded chattering.

Example: (neglected channel) Figure 5.2 is another example program which does not terminate under the assumption of process fairness but does terminate under the channel-fairness assumption. In this example, P_1 is willing to communicate indefinitely both with P_2 and with P_3. Once, however, the communication between P_2 and P_3 occurs, both *go_on* variables become false and the program terminates eventually. Thus, channel fairness is needed to prevent neglecting indefinitely the channel (P_2, P_3).

Finally, we present an example program the termination of which is not guaranteed even by channel fairness and communication fairness is needed.

Example: (neglected communication) This time, two processes suffice to illustrate the problem (see Figure 5.3). As there are only two processes (one channel) both process fairness and channel fairness are guaranteed. However, P_1 and P_2 may communicate indefinitely along P_2's first direction. As soon as the second direction is chosen the program terminates.

$$P{::}\ [P_1 \ || \ P_2 \ || \ P_3]$$

where

```
P1:: a2:=true; a3:=true;
*[1: a2; P2?a2→skip
  []
  2: a3; P3?a3→skip]

P2:: b:=true; go_on_2:=true; x:=0;
*[1: b; P1!go_on_2→[¬go_on_2→b:=false [] go_on_2→skip]
  []
  2: b; P3!x→go_on_2:=false]

P3:: c:=true; go_on_3:=true;y:=0;
*[1: c; P1!y→[¬go_on_3→c:=false [] go_on_3→skip]
  []
  2: c; P2?y→go_on_3:=false]
```

Figure 5.2 Communicating processes–neglected channel.

$$P{::}\ [P_1 \ || \ P_2]$$

where

```
P1:: *[1: b; P2?b→skip]

P2:: *[1: c; P1!true→skip
       []
       2: c; P1!false→c:=false]
```

Figure 5.3 Communicating processes–neglected communication.

Thus, the various fairness levels form a hierarchy. A similar hierarchy can be observed in the context of more general communication primitives, involving more than two processes in a single communication. For example, see the discussion of *joint actions* in [BKS 83], [BKS 84].

B) Simultaneity. An extra element of *simultaneity* must be considered. As processes execute asynchronously, and are synchronized in our model only when actually communicating, enabledness should mean some kind of *joint enabledness.* Moreover, when a process is busy in one communication, it, of course, is not available to participate in others, even if their Boolean guards could be evaluated to true at that moment. If the definitions are not sensitive enough to this aspect, almost every infinite computation might be "fair", and very few such programs will fairly terminate. Complexity analysis of implementations of fairness that consider the aspect of joint enabledness may be found in [SI 83].

5.2.2 Serialized semantics and overlapping semantics

We now pass to a more rigorous definition of the semantics of the programming language and introduce some notation. A pair of communication commands $(\alpha_k^i, \alpha_{k'}^{i'})$ is called *matching* iff one of them is an input command, the other is an output command and they name each other as partners, e.g. $\alpha_k^i = P_{i'}?x$, $\alpha_{k'}^{i'} = P_i!y$. We use the abbreviation $B_{k,k'}^{i,i'}$ for $B_k^i \wedge B_{k'}^{i'}$ and the abbreviation $(<i,k>,<i',k'>)$ for the matching pair itself.

Let Σ_i denote the local state space of P_i (taken as a mapping from P_i's variables to some value domain) and Σ be the *global* state corresponding to a tuple of local states. A process P_i is *available* in a state if control of P_i resides at the top level of its loop (where the guards are chosen) at that state.

A pair of matching communication commands $(\alpha_k^i, \alpha_{k'}^{i'})$ is *jointly enabled* in a state $\sigma \in \Sigma$ iff $\sigma \models B_{k,k'}^{i,i'}$ and P_i and P_i' are both available.

Definitions:

1. An infinite execution π of P is *strongly communication-fair* (henceforth abbreviated to *fair)* iff every matching pair of communication commands which is infinitely-often jointly-enabled is infinitely-often executed. A finite execution of P is always fair.
2. P is *fairly terminating* iff all its fair executions are finite.

Two semantic definitions for the language will be considered, both using sequences of (global) states. According to both, a transition between two consecutive states in a computation, referred to as a *move,* occurs when two processes with jointly enabled matching communif ation commands communicate, and execute the corresponding sections guarded by the selected communication commands. It is sufficient to consider only those states and transitions for which a move is either beginning or ending. In the *serialized* semantics, intuitively, all processes synchronize at their loop's top level, and then exactly one matching pair of communication commands is selected for execution, advancing the execution to the next state, where again all processes are at their top level. Thus, only the two processes executing the current move are active, while all the rest are idle, until the next choice. Note that, in the serialized semantics, there is no need to record process availability in the state, since all processes are available at every state. The collection of all serialized computations of a program P starting from an initial state σ_0 can be viewed once again as a tree, similarly to the nondeterministic case. This tree is again the basis of the construction establishing semantic completeness of the rule presented in the next section.

In the *overlapping* semantics, concurrent execution of moves is captured by not requiring all processes to be available (at their top level) in every state. A move is *enabled* when the corresponding pair of matching communication commands are jointly enabled (implying that the processes involved are available). If the move is chosen for execution, in subsequent states the two processes are *not* available for selection, until the conclusion of the move, a "commit" state which changes all the relevant variables according to the instructions following the communication, and indicates that the processes are again on their top levels. In this case, recording availability within the state *is* important. If an arc is drawn from the state initiating a move to the one concluding it, we obtain a pictorial display of a computation (see Figure 5.4). For the overlapping computations no simple tree representation applies. The overlapping semantics is, of course, closer to the nature of CSP as originally defined, differing only in that the right-hand sides following the guards are assumed to end at the same time after a communication in the guards. It is most likely that truly-concurrent implementations of the language will adhere to some form of overlapping semantics. On the other hand, the serialized semantics is handier to reason about, reflecting interleavings of communications (and their associated local actions).

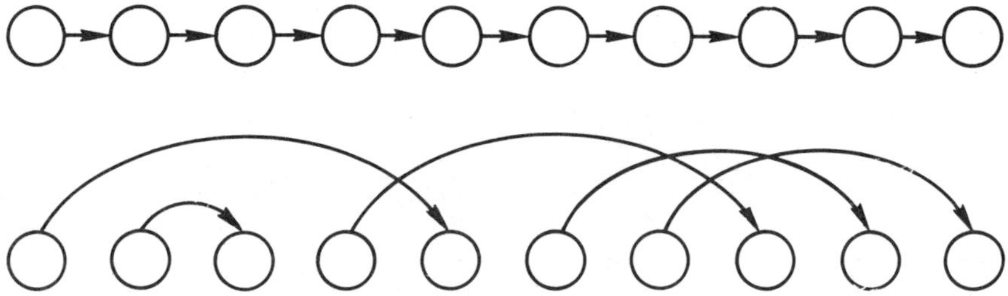

Figure 5.4 Serialized and overlapping concurrent computations [GFK 84]

The difference between the fair termination properties induced by the two semantics stems from the possibility of "*conspiracy*" against some move, in the overlapping semantics. By this we mean that, though both the two Boolean guards involved are infinitely often true, it is almost everywhere the case that one of the processes involved is not available, being engaged in some other move. Thus, along an infinite computation, such a "conspired-against" move is not infinitely often enabled, and the computation is fair, hence the program is *not* fairly terminating. On the other hand, the serialized semantics prevents "conspiracies" by forcing top-level synchronization of all processes. In the corresponding serialized computations, that communication is infinitely-often enabled and only finitely-often taken, thus causing the computation to be unfair, and the program is fairly terminating serially. Figure 5.5 is an example showing the difference between the fair termination properties induced by the two semantics. In this program, communications between processes are in a cyclic pattern. Every process P_i may communicate with its right neighbour P_{i+1} and with its left neighbour P_{i-1} (all additions/subtractions are *mod n*). Sending left is unconditional while sending right is possible only following reception from left. Sending right causes termination of the process. Following is an informal argument showing the claimed fair termination properties. Both the serialized and overlapping computations to be described start from an initial state, in which

$$r{::}\ \bigwedge_{i=1,n} b_i \bigwedge xgo_1 \wedge \bigwedge_{i=2,n} \neg\, xgo_i$$

holds.

(a) *Fair termination of the serialized computations*: In these computations, by fairness, eventually P_i will send right and terminate immediately thereafter. This enables the sending right by P_{i+1}, etc., until P_n is the only "surviver" and terminates due to the "Distributed Termination Convention" of CSP. This convention is appealed to only for simplifying the examples and is not assumed in the proof-rule suggested below.

$$
\begin{aligned}
&P{::}\ [P_1 \,||\, \cdots \,||\, P_n],\quad \textit{where}\\
&P_i{::}\ *[b_i;\ P_{i-1}?x_i \rightarrow xgo_i := \textit{true}\\
&\qquad [\,]\\
&\qquad b_i;\ P_{i+1}?y_i \rightarrow \textit{skip}\\
&\qquad [\,]\\
&\qquad xgo_i \wedge b_i;\ P_{i+1}!x_i \rightarrow b_i := \textit{false}\\
&\qquad [\,]\\
&\qquad b_i;\ P_{i-1}!y_i \rightarrow \textit{skip}\,].
\end{aligned}
$$

Figure 5.5 The effect of conspiracies [GFK 84] ©1984, Association for Computing Machinery, Inc., reprinted by permission.

(b) *Non-fair-termination of the overlapping computations*: We have to point to *one* infinite fair computation in order to substantiate the claim.

Consider a computation in which a conspiracy takes place against the move in which P_1 and P_2 participate. This is done by alternating repeatedly the communications between P_1 (sending left) and P_n and the communication between P_3 (sending left) and P_2. The execution is such that the second move starts *before* the first one ends. The non-selection of the move being conspired against does not contradict fairness, as that move is not infinitely often enabled.

Next we present another example (see Figures 5.6 and 5.7) similar to the previous one, except that conspiracies are impossible; its serialized fair termination therefore implies its overlapping fair termination. We will apply the proof rules presented below to this example. In Figure 5.7, the enabling condition appears above an arc, while the resulting state (marked by (*)) appears underneath the arc.

Again, the common initial state is given by:

$$r:: \bigwedge_{i=1,n} b_i \wedge xgo_1 \wedge ygo_1 \wedge \bigwedge_{i=2,n} (\neg xgo_i \wedge \neg ygo_i).$$

Conspiracy is impossible, since sending left must follow receiving from the right.

We first show (in Section 5.2.3) how to prove fair termination assuming the serialized semantics. Then (in Section 5.2.4), we present a sufficient condition for this proof to apply to the overlapping executions. The sufficient conditions suggested imply the absence of conspiracies. A similar approach, but in a different context, is taken in [BKS 84] and also in [R 84]. They, however, do not deal with proof rules at all.

5.2.3 Relativized fair termination in the serialized semantics

In this section we extend the helpful-directions method to apply to communicating processes under the serialized semantics. In applying this method to

---

$$
\begin{aligned}
&Q::[Q_1 \parallel \cdots \parallel Q_n], \quad \textit{where}\\
&Q_i:: *[b_i;\ Q_{i-1}?x_i \rightarrow xgo_i := \textit{true}\\
&\qquad [\,]\\
&\qquad b_i;\ Q_{i+1}?y_i \rightarrow ygo_i := \textit{true}\\
&\qquad [\,]\\
&\qquad xgo_i \wedge b_i;\ Q_{i+1}!x_i \rightarrow b_i := \textit{false}\\
&\qquad [\,]\\
&\qquad b_i \wedge ygo_i;\ Q_{i-1}!y_i \rightarrow ygo_i := \textit{false}].
\end{aligned}
$$

Figure 5.6 Absence of conspiracies [GFK 84] © 1984, Association for Computing Machinery, Inc., reprinted by permission.

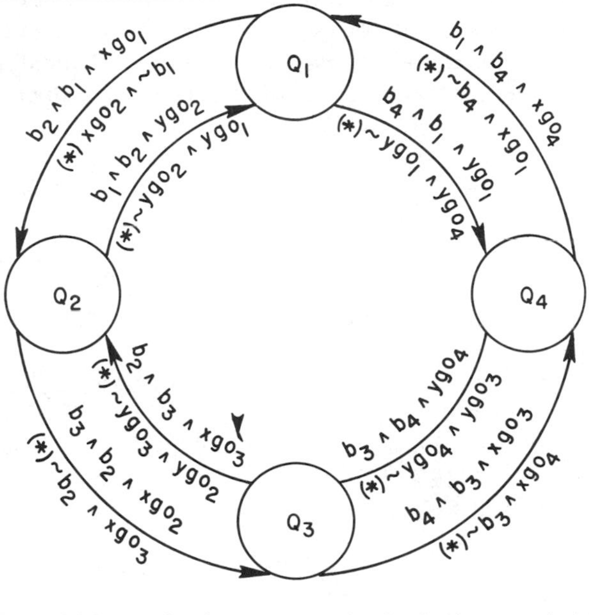

Figure 5.7 A fairly terminating program (under both semantics) [GFK 84]

nondeterministic (GC) programs the eventual enabledness of a helpful direction is expressed by means of a subproof establishing fair termination of a derived program the guards of which were augmented with the negation of the guard (the enabledness condition) of the decreasing direction. Essentially, the same approach is taken by [LPS 81].

This approach to establishing infinite enabledness is only possible if the programming language has some closure properties allowing the expression of the derived program. As it turns out, CSP does not have the required closure property. Since enabledness depends on the simultaneous holding of two guards, taken from two different processes, the negation of such a conjunction cannot be added to *any* of the involved processes without violating the basic property of state disjointness of different processes. Therefore, the other variant of the approach, appealing to relativizing invariants, which avoids the closure problem, is applied in the case of CSP. Let I be a predicate over σ the (global) state, called the *relativizing invariant.*

Definition: A concurrent program P is *I-fairly terminating* iff all its infinite (serialized) executions are either unfair or contain a state σ s.t. $\sigma \models \neg I$.

We recall that this kind of fair termination is denoted by I: $\ll p \gg P \ll q \gg$, where p and q are the pre- and post-conditions, respectively, which here refer to the global state. Note, that the rule establishes the *absence of infinite computations*. Thus, a *deadlock* (a situation where each process waits for communication to occur but no matching communication command are present) counts as termination as far as this rule is concerned. Absence of deadlocks, a safety property, is shown by the usual partial correctness rules (see for example [AFR 80]). The possibility of deadlocks is yet another difference between the concurrent and sequential contexts. The rule, called **I-CFAIR** (for Communication Fairness), is given in Figure 5.8.

Thus, infinite enabledness is established by considering (recursively) the *same* program, but with a different relativizing invariant I. Basically, the negation of the (joint) enabledness condition of the decreasing move is added to the previous invariant.

For the invariance part of the reasoning, one can use any of the partial correctness proof systems for CSP, e.g. [AFR 80] or [LG 81]. Obviously, for top-level proofs one takes I :: *true* (the identically true predicate).

Theorem: (soundness of I-CFAIR)

$$\text{If } \vdash_{\textbf{I-CFAIR}} I\text{: } \ll p \gg P \ll \mathit{true} \gg \text{ then } \models I\text{: } \ll p \gg P \ll \mathit{true} \gg .$$

Proof: Similar to the nondeterministic case. [ ]

Theorem: (semantic completeness of I−CFAIR)

$$\text{If } \models I\text{: } \ll p \gg P \ll \mathit{true} \gg \textit{ then } \vdash_{\textbf{I-CFAIR}} I\text{: } \ll p \gg P \ll \mathit{true} \gg .$$

To prove I: $\ll p \gg P \ll \mathit{true} \gg$:

Choose a well-founded, partially-ordered, set $(W, \leqslant)$, and a parametrized invariant $pi: \Sigma_P \times W \rightarrow \{\mathit{true}, \mathit{false}\}$; also for each $w \in W$, w not minimal, choose a *decreasing* matching pair of directions $d_w = (<i_w,k_w>, <i'_w,k'_w>)$, satisfying

(DEC)

$$\ll pi(w) \wedge B_{k_w,k'_w}^{i_w,i'_w} \wedge w > 0 \gg \alpha_{k_w}^{i_w} \rightarrow S_{k_w}^{i_w} \,||\, \alpha_{k'_w}^{i'_w} \rightarrow S_{k'_w}^{i'_w} \ll \exists v{:}v < w \wedge pi(v) \gg .$$

(NOINC) $\ll pi(w) \wedge B_{k,k'}^{i,i'} \wedge w > 0 \gg \alpha_k^i \rightarrow S_k^i \,||\, \alpha_{k'}^{i'} \rightarrow S_{k'}^{i'} \ll \exists v{:}v \leqslant w \wedge pi(v) \gg$ for every matching pair $(<i,k>, <i',k'>)$.

(CONT) $pi(w) \wedge w > 0 \rightarrow \bigvee_{(<i,k>,<i',k'>)} B_{k,k'}^{i,i'}$. (Again for matching pairs.)

(TERM) $pi(0) \rightarrow \bigwedge_{(<i,k>,<i',k'>)} \neg (B_{k,k'}^{i,i'}) \vee \neg I$.

(INIT) $p \rightarrow \exists w{:}pi(w)$.

(IOE) I': $\ll pi(w) \wedge w > 0 \gg P \ll \mathit{true} \gg$, for $I' = I \wedge \neg (B_{k_w,k'_w}^{i_w,i'_w})$, for the decreasing pair $(<i_w,k_w>, <i_w',k_w'>)$.

Figure 5.8 The rule **I-CFAIR** (relativized communication fairness) [GFK 84]

Proof: The proof is an adaptation of the tree-transformation construction to the context of communicating processes. The details are omited. [ ]

Example: Fair termination under the serialized semantics is proven for the program Q presented in the previous section, with four processes, and the initial condition p with n=4. The proof depends on the facts that at each moment there is only one left communication which can occur anywhere on the ring, and also only one such right communication. This can be expressed in terms of the program variables by the invariant:

$$IN :: \bigvee_{i=1,4}(ygo_i \wedge \bigwedge_{j\neq i} \neg\, ygo_j) \wedge$$

$$\bigvee_{i=1,4}(xgo_i \wedge b_i \wedge \bigwedge_{1\leqslant j<i} \neg\, b_j \wedge \bigwedge_{i<j\leqslant 4}(\neg\, xgo_j \wedge b_j))$$

The proof of the invariance is easy and is omited.

In order to prove

$$true\!: \ll p \gg Q \ll true \gg$$

we choose $W=\{0,1,2,3\}$ and

$$pi(w)\!:: IN \wedge xgo_{4-w} \wedge b_{4-w}\,.$$

For each w>0, the decreasing move is $(<4-w,3>,<5-w,1>)$, and we prove:

$(TERM)$ $\quad pi(0) \rightarrow xgo_4 \wedge b_4$

which, in turn, implies, using IN,

$$\neg\, b_1 \wedge \neg\, b_2 \wedge \neg\, b_3$$

so that no move is possible.

$(INIT)$ $\quad p \rightarrow pi(3)$.

For each $w>0$, we will define $k=4-w$, so that the decreasing move is $(<k,3>,<k+1,1>)$, and then prove

(DEC) $\quad \ll pi(w) \wedge xgo_k \wedge b_k \wedge b_{k+1} \gg$

$$Q_{k+1}!x_k \rightarrow b_k\!:=\!false \;||\; Q_k?x_{k+1} \rightarrow xgo_{k+1}\!:=\!true$$

$\ll pi(w-1) \gg$.

$(NOINC)$ holds for every enabled non-decreasing move because no b_i changes its value.

$(CONT)$ $\quad pi(w) \wedge IN \rightarrow xgo_k \wedge b_k \wedge b_{k+1}$.

(IOE) we have to show

$$I': \ll pi(w) \gg P \ll true \gg,$$

where

$$I':: \neg (b_k \wedge b_{k+1} \wedge xgo_k).$$

We now choose $W' = \{0\}$, and the proof is immediate.

Thus, we have proved the fair termination of Q under the serialized semantics.

5.2.4 Proofs for the overlapping semantics

In this subsection the relevance is considered of fair termination of P under the serialized semantics for fair termination under the overlapping semantics. We formulate a theorem expressing sufficient conditions for the applicability of a fair termination proof in the serialized semantics to the overlapping semantics. Since we know how to prove properties that hold under the serialized semantics, we would like to formulate the conditions in terms of this semantics. To this end, we describe a *similarity* relation between serialized computations and overlapping ones.

Definitions:

1. The sequence of *occurrences* of P_i along a computation π is the sequence of move occurrences along π in which P_i participates.
2. A serialized computation π_s and an overlapping computation π_o are *similar* if they start from the same initial state (up to availability) and for each process P_i in P, the sequences of occurrences of P_i in both computations are the same.

We denote by $\sigma|_i$ the restriction of the state σ to the variables of process P_i. Similarly, for a move A, $\sigma|_A$ denotes the restriction of σ to the processes participating in A. When the relative position of the *directions* determining A is immaterial, we abbreviate A to (i,j) where P_i, P_j participate in A.

We now describe an injection between occurrences of moves on two similar computations π_s and π_o. For each computation, we enumerate all the move occurrences of each process P_i. Thus, with a move A in which P_i and P_j participate, we associate the corresponding pair of its relative positions in the enumerations (where, for uniqueness, the first element in a pair corresponds to the inputing process). Two move occurrences of A in the two computations will be called *corresponding* in case they receive the same pair.

Lemma: (projection) Let π_s and π_o be similar computations, and let two corresponding move occurrences of a move A start in σ_s and σ_o, respectively, and end in states σ'_s and σ'_o, respectively. Then

$$\sigma_o \mid_A = \sigma_s \mid_A \wedge \sigma'_o \mid_A = \sigma'_s \mid_A .$$

In other words, corresponding move occurrences have identical effects on the variables involved.

Proof: By induction on the relative position of the move occurrence. [ ]

Definition: A serialized computation π_e is the *ending-ordered* (EO) of an overlapping computation π_o if they start in the same initial state and move occurrences on π_e occur in the order of their final states in π_o.

The importance of this special ordering of overlapping moves stems from the fact that in the way we represented a move, the final effect it has on the appropriate variables takes place "instantly" on the final state of the move. Any other way of attributing this effect would induce its corresponding natural ordering of moves, to satisfy the following lemma.

Lemma: (similarity of end-ordered computations) The EO computation of an overlapping computation π_o is similar to π_o.

Proof: Let π_o be an overlapping computation and let π_e be its EO computation. Consider any two moves A_1, A_2 in which some process P_i participates. As A_1 and A_2 share a participating process, they do not overlap. Thus, the two moves will appear in the same order in both computations, implying the required similarity. [ ]

The main property of the EO computation is that final states of corresponding move occurrences on both computations are identical (up to availability).

Definition: A move A is *unblockable* (in a program P) if whenever A is infinitely often enabled in the EO computation corresponding to an overlapping computation π_o of P, then A is also infinitely often enabled along π_o itself.

We next formulate a theorem, stating a sufficient condition for unblockability. The condition prevents conspiracies against a move whose Boolean guard is infinitely often true, by implying that the potentially "conspiratory processes" are disabled infinitely often at crucial moments. The condition is convenient to verify, as it is formulated in terms of serialized computations only. The condition, however, is not *complete* in that it is not a necessary one. We show an example in which no conspiracy may occur, though this is not captured by the rule. Ways of strengthening the rule to catch more cases of unblockability are still under investigation.

Theorem: (sufficient condition for unblockability) A move (i,j) in P is unblockable if for every *serialized* computation of P: either infinitely often

$$B^{i,j} \bigwedge_{\substack{k \neq l \\ k,l \notin \{i,j\}}} (\neg B^{i,k} \wedge \neg B^{j,l})$$

holds, or, almost always $\neg B^{i,j}$ holds.

Proof: The first condition is denoted by NOBLOCK. Let π_o be an overlapping computation with a corresponding EO computation having (i,j) infinitely often enabled (i.e. $B^{i,j}$ is infinitely often true). We must show that the condition NOBLOCK holding infinitely often, guarantees that (i,j) is also infinitely often enabled on π_o. Since NOBLOCK holds infinitely often for all serialized computations, it holds also for EO . Also, since final states of move occurrences are identical in EO and π_o, NOBLOCK also holds infinitely often on π_o. Thus, it remains only to show that the processes i and j are available infinitely often when $B^{i,j}$ is true on π_o .

Assume to the contrary, that either P_i or P_j is not available in almost all states σ for which $B^{i,j}$ is true. Thus, each such σ is between the initial state and the final state of a move (i,k) (or (j,k)), for some $k \neq i,j$. In the initial state $B^{i,k}$ holds and there is no change in the values of variables in P_i and P_k until the final state. Thus $B^{i,k}$ holds also in σ, along with $B^{i,j}$, contradicting the condition which holds for π_o. The case of (j,k) is similar. [ ]

Theorem: (transferability to overlapping semantics) A program P fairly terminates for the overlapping semantics if:

1) it fairly terminates for the serialized semantics, and
2) for all descending moves used in a proof of 1), the moves are unblockable in the overlapping computations of P.

Proof: By way of contradiction, suppose the contrary. Hence, there exists an infinite fair overlapping computation π_o, starting in an initial state satisfying p though 1) and 2) above are satisfied. Let π_e be the EO computation corresponding to π_o. It also is infinite and, hence, unfair due to 1). By the proof of 1) there exists a non-minimal $w \in W$ such that $pi(w)$ holds on π_e from some stage onwards and d_w is infinitely often enabled and never chosen from that stage onwards. Since π_e is similar to π_o, d_w is also not chosen on π_o from some stage onwards. By 2) d_w is unblockable and, hence, is also infinitely often enabled on π_o. Thus, π_o is not fair, contradicting the assumption. [ ]

By using the proof rule and the two above theorems, we obtain a proof for fair termination of programs under the overlapping semantics.

As mentioned, this theorem presents a sufficient condition only, and hence is not semantically complete. We believe it captures many of the natural fairly terminating programs. An approach with the same spirit may be found in [BKS 84].

Below, the condition of the unblockability theorem is applied to an example program Q (see Figures 5.6 and 5.7). By symmetry, it is sufficient to consider the move (<1,3>,<2,1>), whose Boolean condition is denoted by $B^{1,2}$. We show that every infinite (serialized) execution of Q from an initial state satisfying p either infinitely often satisfies *NOBLOCK*, or almost always satisfies $\neg B^{1,2}$. We do this by showing

(1) If $B^{1,2}$ holds, then eventually (without any fairness assumptions) $NOBLOCK \vee \neg B^{1,2}$ holds.
(2) If $\neg B^{1,2}$ ever holds, it continuously remains true thereafter.

To show (1), choose $W = \{0,1\}$ and

$$pi(w) :: IN \wedge (w = 0 \equiv NOBLOCK \vee \neg B^{1,2})$$
$$\wedge (w = 1 \equiv \neg(NOBLOCK \vee \neg B^{1,2}))$$

where IN is the invariant used in the proof of fair termination of Q under the serialized semantics. Since the proof of (1) does not assume fairness, a decrease must be shown for every possible move, which is left as an exercise for the interested reader. In addition, we must show that $pi(0)$ implies $NOBLOCK \vee \neg B^{1,2}$, which is trivially true.

In order to show (2), we note that IN implies that $\neg B^{1,2}$ will hold if and only if $\neg b_1 \vee \neg b_2$ is true. Since Q has no move which changes the values of b_1 or b_2 from false to true, if $B^{1,2}$ ever becomes true, it will remain so from then on.

We now present an example program (due to Orna Grumberg) where our unblockability theorem fails to detect the freedom from conspiracies. In this case the weakness of the method is due to its inability to identify pairs of disjoint moves which cannot be jointly activated since their enabledness conditions are dependent.

Example: (non-detection of unblockability) Consider the following program P (Figure 5.9) graphically displayed in Figure 5.10. In the graphic description the links represent data communication in the direction of the

$$P::[\ ||_{i=1,3} S_i\ ||\ ||_{j=1,3} R_j]$$

where

$$S_i::*[S_{i-1}?in_i \rightarrow USE(in_i)$$
$$[\,]$$
$$sent_i; S_{i+1}!out_i \rightarrow sent_i := false$$
$$[\,]$$
$$\neg\, sent_i; R_i?order_i \rightarrow USE(order_i);\ sent_i := true$$
$$]$$

and

$$R_j::*[S_j!req_j \rightarrow COMP(req_j)]$$

Figure 5.9 Non-detection of unblockability.

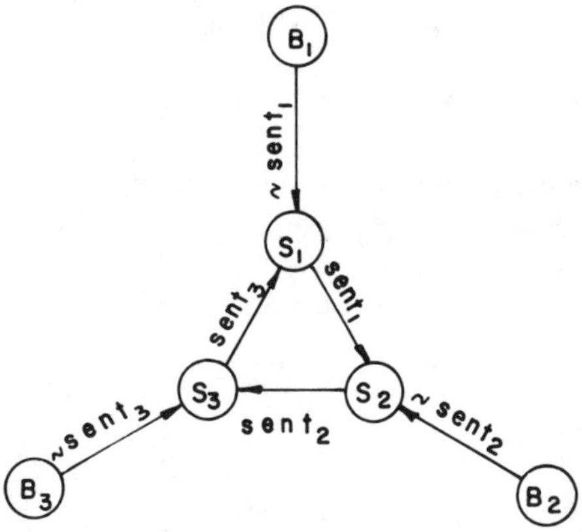

Figure 5.10 Graphic representation of non-detection of unblockability.

arrow. On each link is the enabledness condition for the corresponding move.

We first present an argument to show that the moves in this program are unblockable.

(a) Suppose A is a move in which S_i and R_i participate. Such a move is trivially unblockable since R_i does not participate in *any* other move.
(b) For symmetry reasons it suffices to consider the move A in which S_1 and S_2 participate. The candidates for blocking A are the following three pairs of moves:

1) (R_1,S_1) and (R_2,S_2)
2) (R_1,S_1) and (S_2,S_3)
3) (S_3,S_1) and (R_2,S_2).

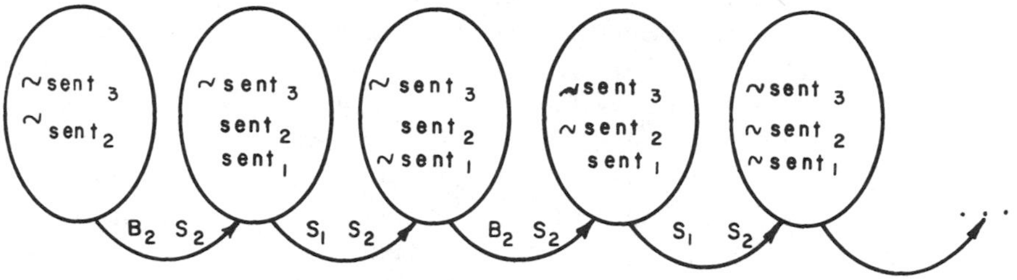

Figure 5.11 An unblockable computation not satisfying the sufficient unblockability conditions.

In every pair S_1 participates in the first move and S_2 participates in the second move. Note that the pair (S_1, S_3) and (S_2, S_3) is not considered, as its moves are not disjoint.

A possible blocking of A would imply that $sent_1$ is true infinitely often. However, once $sent_1$ becomes true it remains true as long as A is not executed. Thus, the move (R_1, S_1) is not enabled and cannot participate in such blocking. Thus, the only pair of moves left to be considered is 3). In order to use this pair of moves to block A, each of them should become enabled before the other terminates. Hence, all the moves which need to be executed in order to reenable each of them must be executed in the overlapping period with the other. But, one of these intermediately-needed moves is (S_2, S_3), which is not disjoint from (S_1, S_3) and, hence, cannot be executed in this overlapping period.

To see that the unblockability theorem does not apply we show the existence of a computation that does not satisfy any of the theorem's conditions. The computation is shown in Figure 5.11. In this computation $sent_1$ holds infinitely often, violating the second condition of the theorem; the first condition is contradictory on this computation for a move in which two S processes participate.

5.3 Fairness in Shared-Variables Concurrency

5.3.0 Overview

In this section we introduce a model programming language for expressing concurrent processes communicating via *shared variables.* While the main stress in the previous section was put on the effect of *simultaneity* on fairness, here we focus on *mutual-exclusion* as the main feature. Such an exclusion is ensured by a special language construct. The structural level of fairness considered, in terms of the previous section, is that of *process fairness.*

Our main concern is the presentation of (faithful) *transformations* realizing fairness, once again, by explicit scheduling using *random assignments.* Once such transformations are obtained, they can be used in proofs of fair termination. We shall see, however, that matters are more complicated here than in chapter 3, due to some properties of known proof systems for shared-variables concurrency. The presentation basically follows [OA 84]. More results about the existence and non-existence of such transformations for various variants of the language considered may be found there.

In designing the transformation an extra-consideration, absent in the treatment of guarded commands, is introduced. The transformations should *preserve the parallelism* in the original programs. Such a preservation excludes solutions like that of [FS 81], where the source program is "folded" into one big nondeterministic loop, executing one atomic step of some process in each iteration. We prefer to leave the nondeterministic interleaving of atomic actions on the level of the semantics of the language, and apply *compositional* methods of verification. The basic approach of *interference-freedom* [OG 76] is used to handle the shared variables.

In showing the faithfulness of the transformations there is also a new aspect, absent in the nondeterministic case, namely, the absence of *deadlock* in the transformed program.

5.3.1 The shared-variables language *SVL*

We again start by describing the syntactic structure of the language *SVL* considered in this section. The general form of an *SVL* program is

$$P{::}\ S;\ [P_1 \ || \ \cdots \ || \ P_n];\ T.$$

Here S is referred to as the *initial part* (of P), T is the *final part* (of P), and P_i, $1 \leqslant i \leqslant n$, are the component *processes,* whose *concurrent composition* forms the main body of P.

Each of S, T and P_i, $i = 1, \cdots, n$, is basically a (deterministic) statement composed of assignments, *if-then-else* branching and *while* loops, which is a syntactic variant of the language GC_D mentioned in chapter 1. Both simple assignments of the form $x{:=}t$ and random assignments of the form $x{:=}?$ are allowed.

In contrast to the language of message-passing considered in the previous section, in which processes were disjoint, here a central property of the language is the *sharing* of variables by the processes P_i, $i = 1, \cdots, n$.

A special statement dealing with the shared variables is the *await* statement, whose form is:

$$\textit{await } B \textit{ then } S \textit{ end}$$

where B is Boolean condition and S is a statement without inner *await* statements. Thus, nesting of *awaits* is excluded here. Such a statement may appear in any of the component processes P_i, $1 \leqslant i \leqslant n$. With the exclusion of random assignments, this is essentially the language studies in [OG 76] for the purposes of proving partial correctness and freedom from deadlock.

Next, we present an informal semantics of SVL. Every program has a (global) state, assigning values to all its variables. In the examples, we consider only *integer* and *Boolean* variables. We use σ, ξ to range over states and use again the notion of a variant state to capture the effect of assignments. An execution of a program P starts by executing its initial part S. If (and when) S terminates, the process P_i, $1 \leqslant i \leqslant n$ are executed concurrently. We again perceive here concurrent execution as *interleaving* of atomic actions. Here the basic atomic actions are taken to be the empty action *skip,* the assignments and the evaluation of Boolean conditions.

The role of the *await* statement is to allow *synchronization* among the processes by means of *delay.* When a statement of the form

$$\textit{await } B \textit{ then } S \textit{ end}$$

is encountered by some process P_i, $1 \leqslant i \leqslant n$, it attempts to evaluate the Boolean condition B. In case B is found to hold (on the current state), the statement S is executed *indivisibly.* If B does not hold the process P_i is *delayed* until B holds (or indefinitely, if this is *never* the case). Thus, the *await* statement also constitutes an *atomic* action, a *compound* one. It is either executed completely, without any other process interfering and modifying the values of the shared variables, or is not executed at all. When executed, S is guaranteed that B holds when its execution starts. If separation of the testing of B and the subsequent execution of S were allowed, another process might "destroy" the values of the shared variables and causing $\neg B$ to hold when execution of S is started, though the testing of B ended positively.

Finally, once the concurrent composition $[\ P_1 \,||\ \cdots\ ||\, P_n\ ]$ has terminated, implying the termination of *each* component process P_i, $1 \leqslant i \leqslant n$, the final part of P, namely T, is executed.

This informal presentation of the semantics of SVL can be formalized in various ways. Following [OA 84], we use here the method of *structural* definition of the transition relation [HP 79, PL 81].

A *configuration* is a pair $<S, \sigma>$ consisting of a program $S \in SVL$ and a state σ. A *transition relation* $\rightarrow$ between configurations is introduced. The notation $<S, \sigma> \rightarrow <S_1, \sigma_1>$ means: executing S one step in σ can lead to σ_1 with S_1 being the remainder of S still to be executed. To express termination we allow the empty program E with $E;S = S;E = S$.

The relation $\rightarrow$ is defined by structural induction on SVL. Typical clauses are:

1) $<z:=?, \sigma> \rightarrow <E, \sigma[d/x]>$ for *every* $0 \leqslant d$.
2) $<while\ B\ do\ S_1, \sigma> \rightarrow <S_1;\ while\ B\ do\ S_1, \sigma>$ if $\sigma \models B$.
3) $<while\ B\ do\ S_1, \sigma> \rightarrow < E, \sigma>$ if $\sigma \models \neg B$.
4) $<await\ B\ then\ S_1\ end, \sigma> \rightarrow <E, \tau>$ if $\sigma \models B$ and $<S_1, \sigma> \overset{*}{\rightarrow} <E, \tau>$ where $\overset{*}{\rightarrow}$ denotes the reflexive, transitive closure of $\rightarrow$.
5) *If* $<S_1, \sigma> \rightarrow <S_2, \tau>$ then

$$<S_1;S, \sigma> \rightarrow <S_2;S, \tau>.$$

6) *If* $<P_i, \sigma> \rightarrow <P_i', \tau>$ then

$$<[P_1 \,||\, \cdots \,||\, P_n], \sigma> \rightarrow <[P_1 \,||\, \cdots \,||\, P_{i-1} \,||\, P_i' \,||\, P_{i+1} \,||\, \cdots \,||\, P_n], \tau>.$$

Based on the transition $\rightarrow$ some further concepts are introduced. A configuration $<S, \sigma>$ is *maximal* if it has no successor w.r.t. $\rightarrow$. A terminal configuration is a maximal configuration $<S, \sigma>$ with $S = [\ E \,||\, \cdots \,||\, E\ ]$. All other maximal configurations are called *deadlocked*. A computation of S (starting in σ) is a finite or infinite sequence

$$\xi: <S, \sigma> \rightarrow <S_1, \sigma_1> \rightarrow \cdots \rightarrow <S_k, \sigma_k> \rightarrow \cdots .$$

A computation of S is called *terminating* (deadlocking) if it is of the form

$$\xi: <S, \sigma> \rightarrow \cdots \rightarrow <T, \tau>$$

where $<T, \tau>$ is terminal (deadlocked). Infinite computations of S are called *diverging*. We say that S can diverge from σ (can deadlock from σ) if there exists a diverging (deadlocking) computation of S starting in σ.

The interleaving semantics of programs $P \in SVL$

$$\mathbf{M}[\![P]\!]: \Sigma \rightarrow P(\Sigma \cup \{\perp, \delta\})$$

is now defined by

$$\mathbf{M}[\![P]\!](\sigma) = \{\tau \mid <P, \sigma> \overset{*}{\rightarrow} <[E \,||\, \cdots \,||\, E], \tau>\}$$

$$\cup\ \{\perp \mid P\ can\ diverge\ from\ \sigma\}$$

$$\cup\ \{\delta \mid P\ can\ deadlock\ from\ \sigma\}$$

where **P** (X) denotes the power-set of the set X.

For simplicity M identifies all infinite computations with $\perp$*(divergence)*. This identification makes sense since we are mainly interested in terminating programs. However, a process semantics which preserves the infinite computations can be also defined [OA 84].

The component process P_i has terminated in $<[P_1 \| \cdots \| P_n], \sigma>$ if $P_i = E$. The component process P_i is *disabled* in $<[P_1 \| \cdots \| P_n], \sigma>$ if either $P_i = E$ or $P_i =$ *await B then S end*; T with $\sigma \models \neg B$. The component process P_i is *enabled* if it is not disabled, i.e. if P_i is not terminated and whenever $P_i =$ *await B then S end*; T holds, then $\sigma \models B$. The component process P_i is *active* in the step

$$<[\, S_1 \| \cdots \| S_n \,], \sigma> \rightarrow <T_1 \| \cdots \| T_n, \tau>$$

if $<S_i, \sigma> \rightarrow <T_i, \tau>$. A program P is deadlock-free if $\delta \notin M[\![P]\!]$.

As a very simple example of a program in SVL (which is even synchronization free), a concurrent variant of Dijkstra's random (natural) number generator, consider the following program R.

Example: (concurrent random number generator)

$$R{::}\ x{:=}0;\ b{:=}true;\ [R_1{::}\ \textit{while}\ \mathrm{b}\ \textit{do}\ x{:=}x+1 \ \|\ R_2{::}\ b{:=}false].$$

Under the interleaving semantics described above it is possible to choose always transitions of the first process and thus never terminate. Once the (unique) transition of the second process takes place the program terminates. Clearly, the (unique) infinite computation of R is, intuitively, unfair towards the second process which is continuously enabled but its transition is never chosen.

As is clear from this example, the phenomenon of *countable* (*unbounded*) *nondeterminism* is again present, indicating the need for countable ordinals higher then ω for termination proofs.

As another example, consider the following:

Example: (parallel zero searching) Suppose we are given a function f mapping integers to integers and we wish to search for some zero w of f. A program P_{zero} for this task should satisfy the following specification:

$$\{\exists u{:}f(u) = 0\}\ P_{zero}\{f(w) = 0\}$$

i.e. provided f possesses a zero, the variable w will contain such a zero upon termination.

A natural solution for P_{zero} is to run two processes in parallel, say P_x and P_y. The process P_x searches for the zero of f by continuously decrementing a test value x and the process P_y by continuously incrementing a test value y. This idea is expressed by the following program:

$$P_{zero} :: x:=0;\quad y:=0;$$

$$[P_x:: \textit{while } f(x) \neq 0 \wedge f(y) \neq 0 \ \textit{ do } x:=x-1$$

$$||$$

$$P_y:: \textit{while } f(x) \neq 0 \wedge f(y) \neq 0 \ \textit{ do } y:=y+1$$

$$];$$

$$\text{if } f(x) = 0 \ \textit{then } w:=x \ \textit{else } w:=y$$

It is easy to see that the interleaving model is not sufficient to guarantee successful termination. For example, P_{zero} might exclusively activate the component P_x while only P_y could find a zero. What is needed is a fair concurrent execution of both P_x and P_y.

5.3.2 Explicit scheduling of shared-variables concurrent programs

In this section several transformations are considered, whose effect is to enforce the various fairness conditions by means of the addition of new variables and random assignments to them, in analogy to the explicit scheduling of *GC* programs discussed in Chapter 3. As mentioned before, we want all the transformations considered to preserve the concurrent structure of the source program. This syntactic property is captured by the following definition.

Definition: A transformation T: $SVL \rightarrow SVL$ is *concurrency preserving* (CP) if

$$T([\ P_1 \ || \ \cdots \ || \ P_n\ ]) = [\ T_1^n(P_1)\ || \ \cdots \ || \ T_n^n(P_n)\ ]$$

where T_i^n is a sub-transformation acting on an i-th component (out of n) of a concurrent program.

As is clear from this definition, the sub-transformation may use only the number of processes n and the index i, and not any other structural properties of the source program.

5.3.2.1 Unconditional fairness for synchronization-free programs

We start the discussion by introducing a transformation realizing unconditional fairness. Before formally defining the concept we would like to make the following remark. In the case of unconditional fairness for *GC* programs we could assume that all the directions have the same (or, actually, invariantly equivalent) enabling conditions, as the enabling condition is syntactically present in the program in the form of a guard. Consequently, either *all* directions are enabled or *no* direction is enabled.

In the case of synchronization free *SVL* programs, enabled means just *not yet terminated.* Hence, in a concurrent composition where some process has terminated while the other processes did not (yet) terminate, the enabling situation is different. We modify the definition of unconditional fairness to adjust to this difference. The difficulty was already noted in [LPS 81] where impartiality is discussed. They were led, however, to consider (our equivalent of) weak fairness as their next stage.

For this reason, we restrict the discussion of unconditional fairness to synchronization-free programs (i.e. programs that contain no *await* statements). The presence of such statements affects the enabledness conditions in such a way that no simple modification of the definition is natural as for the distinction between terminating/nonterminating component processes mentioned above. Indeed, for such programs only weak and strong fairness, as discussed in the next section, are meaningful. In [OA 84] this observation is formulated as a negative result, stating the nonexistence of a certain faithful transformation.

Definition: An infinite computation π of a (synchronization free) *SVL* program P on an initial state σ,

$$\pi{:}<P, \sigma> \;=\; <T_1, \sigma_1> \;\rightarrow\; \cdots \;\rightarrow\; <T_j, \sigma_j> \;\rightarrow\; \cdots$$

is *unconditionally fair* iff for every $i \in \{1, \cdots, n\}$: either the i-th component process P_i *terminated* at some $<T_j, \sigma_j>$, or there are infinitely many j's such that the component process P_i is active in the step $<T_j, \sigma_j> \rightarrow <T_{j+1}, \sigma_{j+1}>$ of π. Also, every finite computation is unconditionally fair.

On the semantic level, we may obtain the unconditionally-fair version of $\mathbf{M}$, called $\mathbf{M}_u$, by modifying the condition under which the diverging value is introduced; namely, only in the presence of an infinite unconditionally-fair computation.

We now present a transformation T_u (using the same names as for the *GC* case should cause no confusion) which realizes unconditional fairness in *SVL*. In its description we make use of another auxiliary concept, defined below.

Definition: An *immediate atomic statement* of a loop

while B do S

is an atomic statement which occurs in S but outside any further while-loop nested within S. For example; in

$$\textit{while } B \textit{ do } [\textit{while } C \textit{ do } x{:}=1]$$

the assignment x: = 1 is an immediate atomic statement of

$$\textit{while } C \textit{ do } x{:}=1$$

but not of

$$\textit{while } B \textit{ do} \ldots$$

Thus some while-loops do not have an immediate atomic statement. But every such a loop in a parallel program P, say

$$\textit{while } B \textit{ do } S$$

can be replaced by

$$\textit{while } B \textit{ do } [\textit{skip};S].$$

Such a change obviously does not alter the meaning of the program P with respect to any semantics of concern here. More generally, the following lemma holds whose proof we omit.

Lemma: (padding) Consider a program $P \in SVL$. Let P^* result from P by replacing an occurrence of a substatement S in P by *skip*; S. Then

$$M[\![P]\!] = M[\![P^*]\!]$$

and

$$M_u[\![P]\!] = M_u[\![P^*]\!]$$

Due to the padding lemma we can implicitly assume in the sequel that every while-loop has an immediate atomic statement. Given a program $P \in SVL$, $T_u(P)$ is obtained by performing the following steps.

(1) Prefixing P with an initialization part

$$INIT{::}\ z_1{:}=?;\ldots;z_n{:}=?;\ end_1{:}=\mathit{false};\ldots;\ end_n{:}=\mathit{false}$$

(2) Replacing in every loop

$$\textit{while } B \textit{ do } S$$

of a component process P_i the first immediate atomic statement A in S by

$$TEST_i(A){::}\ \textit{await turn} \bigvee \bar{z} \geqslant 1 \textit{ then}$$

$$z_i{:=}?;\ \text{for } j{\neq}i \textit{ do}$$

$$\text{if} \neg\ end_j \textit{ then } z_j{:=}z_j-1;$$

$$A$$

$$\textit{end}$$

(for $i = 1, \cdots, n$).

(3) Suffixing every component process P_i by

$$END_i{::}\ end_i{:=}true$$

(for $i{=}1, \cdots, n$).

The z_i's and end_i's are new variables not present in P. As an additional abbreviation we use

$$turn = \min\{j \mid z_j = \min\{z_k \mid \textit{where} \neg\ end_k\}\}.$$

Due to (3) all component processes of the transformed program $T = T_u(P)$ have terminated when all variables end_i are true. Thus the expression *turn* is properly defined whenever a test $TEST_i(A)$ is executed in T.

We use also the following obvious abbreviations:

$$\bar{z} \geqslant 1 \equiv z_1 \geqslant 1 \wedge \cdots \wedge z_n \geqslant 1,$$

$$\text{for } j{\neq}i \textit{ do } z_j{:=}z_j-1 =$$

$$z_1{:=}z_1-1;\ \cdots\ ;\ z_{i-1}{:=}z_{i-1}-1;\ z_{i+1}-1;\ \cdots\ ;z_n{:=}z_n-1.$$

In this transformation, the role of the z_i variables is to control priorities, ensuring unconditional fairness in a similar way to their role for *GC* programs (Chapter 3). The role of the end_i variable is to account for component processes that have already terminated. Clearly, this transformation is concurrency preserving, as required.

We next state and prove a theorem that expresses the *faithfulness* of the transformation, justifying formally its intuitive meaning of realizing unconditional fairness.

The formulation of faithfulness differs somewhat from the one in chapter 3, as infinite computations contribute a diverging element to the **M** semantics. However, the same formulation, by means of extension/restriction of (finite or infinite) computation sequences may be used as well. One could also refine the state transformation semantics (both for **M** and for M_u) so as to distinguish between states in which some component processes diverge while others converge. We shall not deal with such partial states here.

Theorem: (faithfulness of T_u) For every program $P \in SVL$ and $T = T_u(P)$:

$$M_u \llbracket P \rrbracket = M \llbracket T \rrbracket \ mod\ A$$

where A is the set of auxiliary variables z_i and end_i in T.

Proof: Let P and T as above be given. For a subsequent simplification, we may assume that the initialization $INIT$ introduced by T_u is indivisible, i.e. is of the form

$$await\ true\ then\ z_1 := ?;\ \cdots\ ,\ z_n := ?;\ \cdots\ end_n := false\ end$$

as such an assumption does not affect M_u.

For programs U with possible occurrences of $INIT$, $TEST_i(A)$ and END_i let U^* denote the result of replacing in U every occurrence of $INIT$ and END_i by $skip$ and every occurrence of the form $TEST_i(A)$ by A itself. Thus, T^* results from P by replacing several substatements S' by $skip$; S'. Hence, it suffices to prove

$$M \llbracket T \rrbracket = M_u \llbracket T^* \rrbracket \ mod\ A$$

l.h.s → *r.h.s*: Every finite or infinite computation

$$\pi: <T, \sigma> \to \cdots \to <T_j, \sigma_j> \to \cdots$$

of T can be transformed into a computation π^* of T^* by replacing pointwise every intermediate configuration $<T_j, \sigma_j>$ in π by $<T_j^*, \sigma_j^*>$ where σ_j^* is given by $\sigma_j^* = \sigma_j[\ \sigma(z_1,\ \cdots\ , end_n)/z_1,\ \cdots\ , end_n\ ]$:

$$\pi^*: <T^*, \sigma> \to \cdots \to <T_j^*, \sigma_j^*> \to \cdots .$$

Of course, $\tau \in M \llbracket T \rrbracket (\sigma)$ implies $\tau^* \in M_u \llbracket T^* \rrbracket (\sigma)$.

Next, we show that T does not deadlock, i.e. $\delta \notin M \llbracket T \rrbracket (\sigma)$. Suppose the contrary. Recall that the source program P is synchronization free and cannot deadlock by definition. Hence, any deadlock configuration of T is up to a permutation of the component processes of the form

$$<[\ E\ ||\ \cdots\ ||\ E\ ||\ TEST_j(A_j); R_j\ ||\ \cdots\ ||\ TEST_n(A_n); R_n\ ], \tau>$$

with $1 \leqslant j \leqslant n$, $\bar{z} \geqslant 0$ and $turn \neq i$ for all $i \in \{j,\ \cdots\ , n\}$. But by its definition $turn$ is well defined and $turn = i$ for some $i \in \{j,\ \cdots\ , n\}$. Contradiction.

Finally, consider $\perp \in M[\![T]\!](\sigma)$. Then there is an infinite computation

$$\pi: \langle T, \sigma \rangle = \langle T_1, \sigma_1 \rangle \to \cdots \to \langle T_j, \sigma_j \rangle \to \cdots$$

of T. To prove $\perp \in M_u[\![T^*]\!](\sigma)$ it suffices to show that π is unconditionally fair.

Suppose π is not unconditionally fair. Then there are $i \in \{1, \cdots, n\}$ and $j \geqslant 1$ such that the i-th component process of T is neither terminated nor active in any of the steps $\langle T_k, \sigma_k \rangle \to \langle T_{k+1}, \sigma_{k+1} \rangle$ for $k \geqslant j$. By the construction of T the variable z_i gets arbitrarily small values. In particular, z_i becomes $\leqslant -n$ in some state σ_k with $k \geqslant j$. But this is impossible because the assertion

$$INV = \bigwedge_{k=1}^{n} |\{i \mid z_i \leqslant -k\}| \leqslant n-k$$

holds in every state σ_j of π.

We prove this invariant by induction on $j \geqslant 1$ using an argument similar to that in chapter 3, where a similar invariant has been established in the case of GC. In σ_1 we have $z_1, \cdots, z_n \geqslant 0$ so that INV is trivially satisfied. Assume now that INV holds in σ_{j-1}. We show that INV holds also in σ_j.

Suppose INV is false in σ_j. Then there is some $k \in \{1, \cdots, n\}$ such that there are at least $n-k+1$ indices i for which $z_i \leqslant -k$ holds in σ_j. Let I be the set of all these indices. Thus, $|I| \geqslant n-k+1$. The definition of T implies that $z_i \leqslant -k+1$ holds for all $i \in I$ in σ_{j-1}. By the induction hypothesis $|I| \leqslant n-k+1$. So, actually $|I| = n-k+1$ and

(*) $\quad I = \{i \mid z_i \leqslant -k+1 \text{ holds in } \sigma_{j-1}\}.$

At least one z_{i_0} with $i_0 \in I$ got decremented in the step

(**) $\quad \langle T_{j-1}, \sigma_{j-1} \rangle \to \langle T_j, \sigma_j \rangle.$

Otherwise, for all z_i with $i \in I$ we would have $z_i \leqslant -k$ in σ_{j-1}, so

$$|\{i \mid z_i \leqslant -k\}| \geqslant |I| = n-k+1$$

in σ_{j-1}. But by the induction hypothesis $|\{i \mid z_i \leqslant -k\}| \leqslant n-k$ in σ_{j-1}, a contradiction.

So step (**) must be of the form

$$\langle [\cdots \| TEST_i(A); R \| \cdots], \sigma_{j-1} \rangle \to \langle [\cdots R \| \cdots], \sigma_j \rangle$$

for some i. Thus

$$turn = i \vee \bar{z} \geqslant 0$$

holds in σ_{j-1}. If $\bar{z} \geqslant 0$ is true in σ_{j-1} then $k = 1$ and $I = \{1, \cdots, n\}$ follows from (*). Otherwise, we must have $turn = i$ in σ_{j-1}. Thus $end_i = false$ in σ_{j-1}. Since also $end_{i_0} = false$ in σ_{j-1} (otherwise z_{i_0} could not be decremented), we have $z_i \leqslant z_{i_0}$ in σ_{j-1}. Also $i_0 \in I$ implies by (*) that $z_{i_o} \leqslant -k+1$ holds in σ_{j-1}. So also $z_i \leqslant -k+1$ holds in σ_{j-1}. Thus, in both cases $i \in I$, i.e. by the definition of I we have $z_i \leqslant -k$ in σ_j. This is a contradiction because $TEST_i(A)$ executes $z_i{:=}?$ so that $z_i \geqslant 0$ holds in σ_j. Thus INV remains true in σ_j.

r.h.s → *l.h.s*: We show that for every finite or infinite unconditionally fair computation

$$\pi^*: <T^*, \sigma> = <T_1', \sigma_1'> \rightarrow \cdots <T_k', \sigma_k'> \rightarrow \cdots$$

of T^* there is a corresponding computation

$$\pi: <T, \sigma> = <T_1, \sigma_1> \rightarrow \cdots \rightarrow <T_k, \sigma_k> \rightarrow \cdots$$

of T such that π^* results from π by defining pointwise

$$<T_k', \sigma_k'> = <T_k^*, \sigma_k^*>.$$

To obtain π the values of the auxiliary variables $z_1, \cdots, z_n, end_1, \cdots, end_n$ have to be defined in every state σ_k of π consistently with T. This is trivial for $end_1, \cdots, end_n$. For z_i with $i \in \{1, \cdots, n\}$ we put

$$\sigma_k(z_i) = 1 + |\{l \mid k \leqslant l \leqslant m_i \wedge \exists j \neq i \exists A \exists R:$$

$$T_l = [\cdots \| TEST_j(A); R \| \cdots] \text{ and } T_{l+1} = [\cdots \| R \| \cdots]\}|$$

where

$$m_i = min\{m \mid k \leqslant m \wedge (T_m = E \vee \exists A \exists R:$$

$$T_m = [\cdots \| TEST_i(A); R \| \cdots] \, and \, T_{m+1} = [\cdots \| R \| \cdots])\}.$$

The values $m_i \in \mathbf{N}$ are well-defined because π^* is unconditionally fair. The z_i's are always $\geqslant 1$ and their definition agrees with the construction of T.

Informally, m_i is the index of the first possibility after $<T_k, \sigma_k>$ to reset z_i to a new non-negative value via a random assignments $z_i{:=}?$ inside some $TEST_i$. Then $\sigma_k(z_i)$ is the number of times $TEST_j$ with $j \neq i$ will be executed before the next execution of $TEST_i$. In all these tests the value of z_i will be decremented by 1. Thus till $<T_{m_i}, \sigma_{m_i}>$ is reached the value of z_i will always be $\geqslant 1$. This again avoids deadlocks in T. Moreover, in every step $<T_l, \sigma_l> \rightarrow <T_{l+1}, \sigma_{l+1}>$ with $T_l = [\ \cdots\ \| \ TEST_i(A);\ R\ \|\ \cdots\ ]$ and $T_{l+1} = [\ \cdots\ \|\ R\ \|\ \cdots\ ]$ exactly one of the variables $z_1, \cdots, z_n$ has the value 1, namely z_i. Again, these values of z_i can be achieved by the assignments to z_i within T. []

Recall that in the definition of T_u we insisted on transforming the first immediate atomic statement A of every while-loop. But from this proof it is clear that T_u remains correct if we just transform some immediate A in every while-loop. Similar observations apply to the transformations developed later.

This faithfulness theorem states that the transformation T_u precisely models the input-output behaviour of parallel programs S under the assumption of unconditional fairness. But in fact we proved more: a one-one correspondence between *UF* computation of P and arbitrary computations of $T = T_u(P)$. To express this close relationship between P and $T_u(P)$, we need a process semantics which preserves the infinite computations. Therefore we can view T_u as an abstract specification of schedulers which enforce unconditional fairness in parallel programs $P \in SVL$. Such a scheduler should at certain "critical" moments determine which component of a parallel program is to be executed next. In particular, a deterministic scheduler regards every moment as a critical one and thus completely fixes the computation of the program ([FP 83]). "Abstract specification" now means that all schedulers for unconditional fairness can be implemented by just reducing the inherent nondeterminism in $T_u(P)$, i.e. by implementing the random assignments $z:=?$ by deterministic assignments $z:=t$ where the expression t yields non-negative values. This concept of implementation for specifications exhibiting unbounded nondeterminism was first described in [PA 79]. Moreover, the faithfulness theorem guarantees that all these implemented schedulers are deadlock-free and hence never require any rescuing or backtracking from deadlocked configurations [HO 78a]. This viewpoint naturally extends to the transformations of the other fairness notions introduced in the sequel.

5.3.2.2 Explicit scheduling for weak and strong fairness in shared-variables programs

In this section we extend the ideas presented in the previous section to present a faithful transformation that realizes weak fairness.

Definition: A computation π: $<P, \sigma> = <T_1, \sigma_1> \rightarrow \cdots \rightarrow <T_j, \sigma_j> \rightarrow \cdots$ of an *SVL* program P is *weakly fair* iff π is finite or the following holds for every $i \in \{1, \cdots, n\}$: if for all but finitely many j the component process P_i is enabled in $<T_j, \sigma_j>$ then there are infinitely many j such that component P_i is active in step $<T_j, \sigma_j> \rightarrow <T_{j+1}, \sigma_{j+1}>$.

Thus in a weakly-fair computation every component which is from some moment on continuously enabled will eventually make progress. This definition induces semantics $\mathbf{M}_w$ analogous to $\mathbf{M}_u$. The transformations simulating weakly fair computations are necessarily more complex than for unconditional fairness because we have to check the enabledness of components in front of every atomic statement, not only at the entrance of loop bodies. This point is illustrated by the following program:

$$P :: [\textit{while } b \textit{ do } [l_1 : c := \neg c \,;\, l_2 : c := \neg c] \,||\, [\textit{ await } c \textit{ then } b := \textit{false end }]].$$

Started in a state σ with $\sigma(b) = \textit{true}$ and $\sigma(c) = \textit{true}$ the program P can diverge. This is true even under the weak fairness assumption because the second component process is never continuously enabled: at l_2 the synchronization condition c is always false. but by testing c only at the loop entrance l_1 we find c always enabled and would conclude wrongly that the second component process should eventually make progress and thus terminate the whole program P.

This additional complexity is reflected in the following transformation T_w being a refinement of the transformation T_u. Given a program P in SVL the transformation T_w employs the following sets of auxiliary variables: z_i, end_i, pc_i, $i = 1, \cdots, n$. The z_i's and end_i's are used as in T_u. The pc_i' s are a restricted form of program counters which indicate when the component process P_i is in front of an *await*-statement and if so in front of which one. To this end, we assign to every occurrence of an *await*-statement in P_i a unique number $l \geqslant 1$ as label. Let L_i denote the set of all these labels for P_i and B_l denote the Boolean guard of the *await*-statement labeled by l. Further on we introduce for P_i the abbreviation

$$enabled_i \;=\; \neg\, end_i \;\wedge\; \bigwedge\nolimits_{l \in L_i} (pc_i = l \;\rightarrow\; B_l).$$

By the following construction of T_w, $enabled_i$ is true iff the component process P_i of P is indeed enabled.

As in the previous section we can assume that every while-loop in S has an immediate atomic statement.

(1) Prefixing P with

$$INIT :: \text{for } i=1, \cdots, n \textit{ do } [\; z_i := ?;\; end_i := \textit{false};\; pc_i := 0 \;].$$

(2) Replacing every substatement *await* B_l *then* S *end* with $l \in L_i$ in P_i by

$$pc_i{:=}l;\ await\ B_l\ then\ S;\ pc_i{:=}k\ end$$

where $k \notin L_i$ holds, e.g. $k = 0$ (for $i=1, \cdots, n$).

(3) Replacing in every loop *while* B *do* S of a component process P_i :

(i) the first immediate atomic statement A in S by

```
TEST_i(A) :: await turn=i ∨ z̄ ≥ 1 then
                 z_i:=?; for j≠i do
                              if enabled_j then z_j:=z_j−1
                                           else z_j:=?;
                 A
                 end
```

(ii) every other immediate atomic statement B in S by

```
RESET_i(B) :: await true then
                   for j ≠ i do if ¬enabled_j then z_j:=?;
                   B
                   end
```

(for $i=1 \cdots, n$). If A or B are already *await*-statements, we "amalgamate" their Boolean expressions with $turn=i \ \vee\ \bar{z} \geqslant 1$ or *true* to avoid nested *awaits*. The expression *turn* is defined as follows:

$$turn = \min\{j \mid z_j = \min\{z_k \mid enabled_k\}\}.$$

(4) Suffixing every component P_i of P with

$$END_i{::}\ end_i{:=}true$$

(for $i=1, \cdots, n$).

Inside $RESET_j(B)$ and $TEST_i(A)$ each of the variables associated with P_j is reset as soon as P_j gets disabled. Thus z_j is continuously decremented by $z_j{:=}z_j - 1$ inside $TEST_i(A)$ only if P_j is continuously enabled. This formalizes the idea of weak fairness where only those components which are continuously enabled are guaranteed to progress eventually. By the following theorem, T_w can be viewed as an abstract specification of all schedulers enforcing weak fairness in parallel programs. These schedulers are all deadlock-free.

Theorem: (faithfulness of T_w) For every program $P \in SVL$ and $T = T_w(P)$:

$$M_w [\![P]\!] = M [\![T]\!]\ mod\ A$$

where A is the set of auxiliary variables z_i, end_i and pc_i in T.

Proof: Take P and T as stated. As in the proof of the faithfulness of T_u theorem let $INIT$ be indivisible and superscript * denote the result of replacing every occurrence of *INIT*, $pc_i := 1$ and END_i by *skip* and replacing every occurrence of the form $TEST_i(A)$ or $RESET_i(B)$ by A or B, respectively. In particular, T^* results from P by replacing several substatements S by *skip*; S. Thus by the padding lemma (now stated for M_w) it suffices to prove

$$M[\![T]\!] = M_w [\![T^*]\!] \ mod \ A.$$

l.h.s → *r.h.s*: The finite computations of T are dealt with analogously to the T_u case. This in particular covers the freedom from deadlock of T, i.e. that $\delta \notin M[\![T^*]\!](\sigma)$ implies $\delta \notin M[\![T]\!](\sigma)$.

Consider the crucial case of divergence: $\perp \in M[\![T]\!](\sigma)$. Then there exists an infinite computation

$$\pi: <T, \sigma> = <T_1, \sigma_1> \rightarrow \cdots \rightarrow <T_j, \sigma_j> \rightarrow \cdots$$

of T. To show $\perp \in M_w[\![T^*]\!](\sigma)$ it suffices to prove that π is weakly fair. The argument is the same as for T_u, using the same invariant to derive a contradiction.

r.h.s → *l.h.s* Consider a weakly fair computation π^* of T^*. Similar to the T_u case we have to define the values of the auxiliary variables z_i, end_i, pc_i to obtain a corresponding computation

$$\pi: <T, \sigma> = <T_1, \sigma_1> \rightarrow \cdots \rightarrow <T_k, \sigma_k> \rightarrow \cdots$$

of T. This definition is obvious for the variables pc_i and end_i. For z_i we define

$$\begin{aligned}\sigma_k(z_i) = 1 + \ |\{l \mid k \leqslant l \leqslant m_i \wedge \exists j \neq i \exists A \exists R:& \\ T_l = [\ \cdots\ \|\ TEST_j(A);\ R\ \|\ \cdots\ ] \ and& \\ T_{l+1} = [\ \cdots\ \|\ R\ \|\ \cdots\ ]\}\ |&\end{aligned}$$

as for T_u but with the following new definition of m_i:

$$\begin{aligned}m_i = \min\{m \mid k \leqslant m \wedge& \\ (\ (1)\ T_m = E& \\ \vee\ (2)\ \exists A \exists R:& \\ T_m = [\ \cdots\ \|\ TEST_i(A);\ R\ \|\ \cdots\ ] \quad and& \\ T_{m+1} = [\ \cdots\ \|\ R\ \|\ \cdots\ ]& \\ \vee\ (3)\ \exists j \neq i \exists B \exists R:\ T_m = [\ \cdots\ \|\ RESET_j(B);\ R\ \|\ \cdots\ ] \quad and& \\ T_{m+1} = [\ \cdots\ \|\ R\ \|\ \cdots\ ]\ ).&\end{aligned}$$

The values $m_i \in \mathbf{N}$ are well-defined because π^* is weakly fair. Indeed, if neither (1) nor (2) above holds for some $m \geqslant k$ then weak fairness of π^* implies that from some moment on the i-th process component of T is in front of an *await* statement, but never active any more because for infinitely many $m \geqslant k$ it is disabled in $<T_m, \sigma_m>$. For sufficiently large m this will be "discovered" by some $RESET_j(B)$ inside a while-loop. The z_i's are always $\geqslant 1$ and their definition agrees with T. [ ]

We turn now to strong fairness. Typical examples requiring strong fairness are mutual exclusion algorithms where one wishes to ensure that no process which is infinitely often capable of entering a critical section will be prevented from doing so. This property is often referred to as "freedom from starvation".

Definition. A computation $\pi: <P, \sigma> = <T_1, \sigma_1> \rightarrow \cdots \rightarrow <T_j, \sigma_j> \rightarrow \cdots$ of an SVL program P is *strongly fair* if π is finite or the following holds for every $i \in \{1, \cdots, n\}$: if for infinitely many j the component process P_i is enabled in $<T_j, \sigma_j>$ then there are infinitely many j such that P_i is active in step $<T_j, \sigma_j> \rightarrow <T_{j+1}, \sigma_{j+1}>$.

Analogously to M_w we define M_s. We present a transformation T_s for strong fairness which is a refinement of the previous transformation T_w. Consider a program P in SVL such that every while-loop in P has an immediate atomic statement. This is possible again since the padding lemma holds for the semantics M_s as well. Then $T_s(P)$ results from P by applying the steps (1) , (2) and (4) of T_w but with the following new step (3):

(3) Replace every immediate atomic statement A occurring in a while-loop of P_i by

$TEST_i(A)$ :: *await* $turn=1 \vee \bar{z} \geqslant 1$ *then*

$z_i:=?$; for $j \neq i$ *do*

if $enabled_j$ *then* $z_j:=z_j-1$;

A

end

(for $i=1, \cdots, n$). Here *turn* is defined and *await* statements A are dealt with as for T_w.

As for weak fairness we have to test the enabledness of the component process P_i of P in front of every atomic statement. But in contrast to T_w the transformed program $T_s(P)$ does not reset the variable z_j for component process P_j when P_j gets disabled. Instead it decrements z_j (and is prepared for switching to another component) whenever P_j is enabled. This change ensures that those P_j which are infinitely often enabled eventually make progress. Indeed, due to the following theorem T_s can be viewed as an abstract specification of deadlock-free schedulers enforcing strong fairness in parallel programs.

Theorem: (faithfulness of T_s) For every program $P \in SVL$ and $T = T_s(P)$:

$$M_s[\![P]\!] = M[\![T]\!] \ mod\ A$$

where A is the set of auxiliary variables z_i and end_i in T.

Proof: Using again the superscript notation and the padding lemma it suffices to show

$$M[\![T]\!] = M_s[\![T^*]\!] \ mod\ A.$$

l.h.s $\rightarrow$ *r.h.s*: similar to the T_w case.

r.h.s $\rightarrow$ *l.h.s*: Every strongly-fair computation π^* of T^* has to be simulated by a corresponding

$$\pi: < T, \sigma > \ = \ < T_1, \sigma_1 > \rightarrow \ \cdots \ \rightarrow < T_k, \sigma_k > \ \cdots$$

of T. The values of z_i are defined as before, but with the following definition of m_i:

$$m_i = min\{m \mid k \leqslant m \wedge ((\forall n: n \geqslant m \rightarrow \text{i-th component of T is disabled in } < T_n, \sigma_n >)$$

$$\vee (\exists A \exists R: T_m = [\ \cdots\ \| TEST_i(A);\ R \|\ \cdots\ ] \ and$$

$$T_{m+1} = [\ \cdots\ \| R \|\ \cdots\ ]))\}$$

The remaining is the same as for T_w. []

5.3.2.3 Proving fair termination of shared-variables programs

The transformations presented can also be used for syntax directed fair-termination proofs of *SVL* programs. This idea is illustrated by the following version *P* of the zero-searching program.

$$P{::}\ [\textit{while } f(x) \neq 0 \wedge f(y) \neq 0 \textit{ do } x{=}{:}x - 1$$

$$\|\ \textit{while } f(x) \neq 0 \wedge f(y) \neq 0 \textit{ do } y{=}{:}y + 1\ ].$$

Let *P* start in a state satisfying the precondition

$$\exists u{:}\ f(u) = 0 \wedge x = y.$$

Under the semantics M_u, *P* is certain to terminate in a state satisfying the postcondition

$$f(x) = 0 \vee f(y) = 0.$$

In other words

$$\overset{u}{\models}\ \ll \exists u{:} f(u) = 0 \wedge x = y \gg P \ll f(x) = 0 \vee f(y) = 0 \gg \qquad *$$

holds. To prove (*) we consider an appropriately transformed version *T* of *P*. In considering the transformation, we allow a somewhat simpler transformation than described above, due to two reasons:

a) The program *P* has the property (called *strong* in [OA 84]) that none of its execution is such that one process component terminates while another diverges (as both *while*-loops have the same termination condition). Thus, testing the termination of a component process is not needed.
b) As we are interested in proving the absence of infinite unconditionally-fair computations, we can relax part of the faithfulness conditions imposed on T_u and allow for the introduction of deadlocks, which count as termination. This would not be the case if fair total correctness had to be proven.

A more comprehensive treatment of such relaxations may be found in [OA 84], where the transformations are of primary concern, rather than the termination proofs.

We end up with the need of proving

$$\models\ <\exists u{:}\ f(u){=}0 \ \wedge\ x{=}y>\ T\ <f(x){=}0\ \vee\ f(y){=}0> \qquad (2)$$

which means proof of non-diverging of an *SVL* program (without any reference to fairness).

To prove (2) we use a simple extension **O** of the proof system of Owicki and Gries [OG 76] which ignores deadlocks but deals with termination in the presence of random assignments $x:=?$. Following [OG 76] proofs in **O** proceed in two steps. First one has to find appropriate correctness proofs for the process components of a parallel program. (Appropriateness will be explained below.) This is done using the proof rules of [OG 76] except for a new *Random assignment axiom*

$$\{p\} \ z:=? \ \{p \wedge z \geqslant 0\}$$

where z is not free in p, and a modified *while-rule*

$$\frac{\{pi(\alpha) \wedge B\} \ S \ \{\exists \beta < \alpha: pi(\beta)\}}{\{\exists \alpha: pi(\alpha)\} \ \textit{while } B \textit{ do } S \ \{\exists \alpha: pi(\alpha) \wedge \neg B\}}$$

where α is a free variable of the parametrized loop invariant $pi(\alpha)$. Intuitively, α counts the number of times the *while* loop is still to be executed before termination. As mentioned already, due to the presence of random assignments it is, however, not sufficient to let α range over natural numbers. Instead, we need countably infinite ordinals.

As a second step one establishes the appropriateness of the correctness proofs for the process components. This is done using the test of *interference freedom.* In the case of our example program it means that a loop invariant of one component cannot be invalidated by the execution of the other component. This test of interference freedom is a premise of the standard proof rule for parallel composition.

To see how this proof system **O** is used let us return to the example of zero searching. The transformed program appearing in claim (2) is:

$$T:: \ [T_1 \ || \ T_2], \ \textit{where}$$

$T_1 :: z_1:=?; \ z_2:=?;$

$\quad [\textit{while } f(x) \neq 0 \wedge f(y) \neq 0 \textit{ do}$

$\qquad \textit{await } z_1, z_2 \geqslant 1 \textit{ then}$

$\qquad\quad z_1:=?; \ z_2:=z_2-1; \ x:=x-1 \textit{ end}]$

and

$T_2 :: [\textit{while } f(x) \neq 0 \wedge f(y) \neq 0 \textit{ do}$

$\qquad \textit{await } z_1, z_2 \geqslant 1 \textit{ then}$

$\qquad\quad z_1:=z_1-1; \ z_2:=?; \ y:=y+1 \textit{ end}].$

To prove

$$\vdash_{\mathrm{o}} <\exists u\colon f(u)=0 \ \wedge\ x=y>\ T\ <f(x)=0\ \vee\ f(y)=0>$$

in this system, we split the precondition into two subcases:

(a) $f(u)\ =\ 0\ \wedge\ u\ \leqslant\ x=y$
(b) $f(u)\ =\ 0\ \wedge\ u\ \geqslant\ x=y$.

In the subcase (a) a zero u can be found by activating the first component process T_1 of T sufficiently often. For (a) we prove

$$\vdash_{\mathrm{o}} <f(u)=0\ \wedge\ u\ \leqslant\ x=y>\ T\ <f(x)=0\ \vee\ f(y)=0>.$$

We have to find interference free loop invariants $pi_1(\alpha_1)$ and $pi_2(\alpha_2)$ for the process components T_1 and T_2 of T. It is clear that T_1 terminates due to the fact that x gets decremented and $f(u)=0\ \wedge\ u\ \leqslant\ x$ holds invariantly. Thus $\alpha_1=x-u$ is an obvious choice for α_1.

Summarizing, we choose

$$pi_1(\alpha_1)\colon\ \alpha_1=x-u\ \wedge\ f(u)=0\ \wedge\ u\ \leqslant\ x.$$

Clearly $pi_1(\alpha_1)$ satisfies the premise of the while-rule applied to T_1, thus yielding

$$\vdash_{\mathrm{o}} <\exists\alpha_1{:}pi_1(\alpha_1)>\ T_1\ <\exists\alpha_1{:}pi_1(\alpha_1)\ \wedge\ (f(x)=0\ \vee f(y)=0)>.$$

Moreover, $pi_1(\alpha_1)$ is interference free w.r.t. the second component T_2 because neither u nor x is changed by T_2.

Things are a bit more complicated with the loop invariant $pi_2(\alpha_2)$ of T_2. If T_2 were executed in isolation, $\alpha_2=z_1\ \wedge\ z_1\ \geqslant 0$ would be an appropriate choice for $pi_2(\alpha_2)$. This condition of T_2 is not interference free w.r.t. T_1: an activation of T_1 can increase z_1 by executing $z_1{:=}?$ and thus invalidate the formula $\alpha_2=z_1$. However, indivisibility coupled with every reset of z_1 by T_1 is a decrease of the variable x by the assignment $x{:=}x-1$. This observation suggests the following parametrized loop invariant.

$$pi_2(\alpha_2)\colon\ \alpha_2=(x-u)\times\omega+z_1\ \wedge\ f(u)=0\ \vee\ u\ \leqslant\ x\ \wedge\ z_1\ \geqslant 0$$

for T_2. Here the first infinite ordinal ω is used, and,

$$(x-u)\ \times\ \omega+z_1$$

corresponds to the lexicographical ordering of pairs $<x-u,\ z_1>$. Now, $pi_2(\alpha_2)$ is indeed interference free w.r.t. T_1 because an increase of z_1 is compensated by a decrease of $x-u$ in $\alpha_2=(x-u)\ \times\ \omega+z_1$. Again it is easy to see that $pi_2(\alpha_2)$ satisfies the premise of the *while*-rule applied to T_2, i.e. we prove

$$\vdash_0 <\exists \alpha_2{:}\ pi_2(\alpha_2)>\ T_2\ <\exists \alpha_2{:}\ pi_2(\alpha_2)\ \wedge\ (f(x)=0\ \vee\ f(y)=0)>.$$

Using (essentially) the rule of parallel composition we arrive at

$$\vdash_0 <f(u)=0\ \wedge\ u \leqslant x=y>\ T\ <f(x)=0\ \vee\ f(y)=0)>.$$

Subcase (b) above is treated analogously. This completes the correctness proof of claim (2) and hence of claim (1). [ ]

We conclude with some comments on the above proof. First, note that the auxiliary variable z_1 in the transformed program T plays the role of a "helpful variable" when formulating the loop invariant $pi_2(\alpha_2)$. Without z_1 we cannot find an appropriate ordinal α_2 which is decremented with every execution of the loop body of T_2.

Second, we stress the fact that for proving claim (1) about P it is sufficient to prove total correctness modulo deadlocks for T in claim (2). Therefore it is sufficient also to use a simple deadlocking transformation. For describing schedulers we are of course advised to use faithful transformation only. This observation may be interpreted as follows: in proofs of program correctness we need not worry about the exact course of a computation but rather more abstractly about its results. This inherent abstraction in program proving allows the employment of transformations that model the program behaviour in an imprecise manner.

Third, note that in the above correctness proof the reasoning was not about the original program P, but about its transformed version T. This should be contrasted with the approach taken in Chapter 3 to reason about fairness in *GC*. There we also started with transformations realizing the fairness assumptions, but in a second step when we developed proof rules dealing with fairness we were able to "absorb" the transformations into the assertions of existing rules. Thus the resulting proof rules for fairness could be applied directly to the original *GC* programs.

For *SVL* the idea of absorption does not work properly. This is because of the test of interference freedom: when applied to the transformed program it has to deal also with all assignments affecting the auxiliary variables z inside the added *await*-statements. So even if these *await* statements were absorbed into the assertions of the standard proof rules for the process components of parallel programs, they would reappear in the final test of interference freedom. Therefore, it is proposed to apply the transformations explicitly as a part of the correctness proofs.

It would be interesting to find transformations that use the auxiliary variables in such a way that the interference freedom with respect to these variables is *guaranteed by construction* for some canonically constructed assertions. Such transformation would once again allow their absorption within appropriate proof rule applied directly to source *SVL* program.

Alternative Transformations

All the transformations test and set auxiliary variables z_i to simulate the fair computations of parallel programs P. For simplicity this was always done as one atomic action. It is interesting to note that one can relax the requirement of atomicity somewhat. For example, in the transformation T_u one can use the shown in definition of $TEST_i(A)$ Figure 5.12.

Such a form of $TEST_i(A)$ allows a more efficient implementation of the scheduling parts because the parallel execution of the components is not suspended for the time needed to reset the variables z_i and execute A. The faithfulness theorem of T_u under the semantics M remains valid with this change. Only the technical argument in its proof gets slightly more complicated as the computations of P and $T_u(P)$ are no longer running step in step. Analogous results hold for the *TEST* and *RESET* parts of the other transformations considered.

An interesting alternative way of maintaining the values of the scheduling variables z_i in T_u is by using the following form of $TEST_i(A)$:

$$TEST_i(A) = \textit{await turn}{=}i \textit{ then } z_i{:=}z_i+1+?;\ A \textit{ end}$$

or even

$$TEST_i(A) = \textit{wait turn}{=}i;\ z_i{:=}z_i + 1 + ?;\ A$$

where ? stands for an arbitrary non-negative integer just as in $z{:=}?$. Again the faithfulness theorems remain valid, and analogous results hold for the other transformations.

This way of updating z_i resembles the construction used in Lamport's "bakery algorithm" for mutual exclusion [LA 74]. It is particularly useful when dealing with so-called *distributed* parallel programs where each variable can be modified by at most one component (but read by arbitrarily many components): then the above forms of the scheduling parts preserve

---

$$\begin{aligned} TEST_i(A) = {} & \textit{wait turn}{=}i \ \vee\ \bar{z} \geqslant 1;\\ & z_i{:=}?;\ \text{for } j{\neq}i \textit{ do } z_j{:=}z_j-1;\\ & A. \end{aligned}$$

where *wait B, B* some Boolean expression, stands for *await B then skip end.*

Figure 5.12 Alternative transformation.

---

this property. On the other hand, an implementation of ? by deterministic values unavoidably leads to unbounded values of the variables z_i in the case of infinite computations. This need not be the case for the original form of $TEST_i(A)$. A similar problem arises in [LA 74].

CHAPTER 6

Syntactic Expressibility

6.0 Overview

In the previous chapters we described a variety of proof rules for proving fair termination. All these rules were described independently of any formal assertion language in which the various predicates needed for the proof might be expressed. In particular, the completeness proofs establish the existence of the sets of states needed without their representation by a formula in a calculus.

In this chapter we deal with the issue of *syntactic expressibility* in a formalized calculus. We introduce an assertion language, which we call $\mathbf{L}_\mu$, based on the (*positive*) μ-*calculus* and show that this language is sufficiently powerful for our needs. This language has already been used in the past to express predicates needed in termination proofs of recursive procedures [HP 73, deB 80].

The main concern is to show that in this calculus it is possible to express formally the *weakest precondition for fair termination* (*fwp*), characterizing the set of all the (initial) states for which no infinite fair computations of a given program exist. The first discussion of such a *predicate transformer* for weak fairness appears in [PA 81]; for unconditional and strong fairness we follow the ideas of [deR 81], and, mainly, of [SdeRG 84].

The version of the μ-calculus used is augmented with (constants denoting) all the recursive ordinals, an odering relation (on ordinals) and the characteristic predicate for the closing ordinal (of a structure). A similar language is used also by [AP 82] in the context of random assignments. A source book for the mathematics of monotone operators and inductivity is [MO 74].

6.1 Fixedpoints of Monotone Transformations

We start by considering a specialization of the basic Knaster–Tarski theorem [TA 55] (mentioned already in an example in Chapter 3).

Definition: A *complete partially ordered set* (*cpo*) is a partially-ordered set $(A, \sqsubseteq)$, such that

(i) A contains a *least* element $\perp$ (i.e. $\forall a \in A$: $\perp \sqsubseteq a$).
(ii) A is closed under *least upper bounds* (*lub's*) of (ascending) *chains* (i.e. if $a_0 \sqsubseteq a_1 \cdots$, then $\bigsqcup_i a_i \in A$).

Traditionally, *cpo's* are used in the denotational semantics approach [deB 80, ST 77] as domains of denotation for programs. The reason for this usage is the ability to take advantage of the existence of *fixedpoints* of various mappings over *cpo's*, as described below.

Let A be (the carrier of) some *cpo*.

Definition: A mapping f: $A \to A$ is *monotone* iff for every $a, b \in A$

$$a \sqsubseteq b \text{ implies } f(a) \sqsubseteq f(b).$$

Thus, monotone functions are order preserving.

Definition: Let f: $A \to A$ be a mapping.

1) An element $a \in A$ is a *fixedpoint* of f iff $f(a)=a$.
2) An element $a \in A$ is a *least fixedpoint* of f iff the following two conditions hold:
   a) $f(a)=a$ (i.e. a is a fixedpoint of f)
   b) for any $b \in A$, if $f(b)=b$ then $a \sqsubseteq b$ (i.e. a is smaller then any other fixedpoint).
3) *Greatest fixedpoints* are defined analogously.

If a mapping f has least fixedpoint it is denoted by μa: $f(a)$ or abbreviated to μf. Similarly, the greatest fixedpoint is denoted by νf. Obviously, existence of extremal fixedpoints implies their uniqueness. The main theorem, in our context, regarding least fixedpoints is the following:

Theorem: (Knaster–Tarski: existence of least fixedpoints) Every monotone mapping f: $A \to A$ over a *cpo* A has a least fixedpoint.

Proof: See [TA 55]. []

There are several ways of regarding μf when it exists. One such way is to observe that

$$\mu f = \sqcap \{a \in A \mid f(a) = a\},$$

i.e. the greatest lower bound of all fixedpoints of f (see, e.g [deB 80]). This characterization does not have much computational significance. A better approach allows obtaining μf by a (transfinite) iteration. For each ordinal λ define the λ*-iterate* f^λ of f as follows:

$$f^0(a) = a$$

$$f^\alpha(a) = \sqcup_{\beta<\alpha} f^\beta(a)$$

for $\alpha > 0$. This *lub* exists, as $\{f^\beta \mid \beta < \alpha\}$ is a chain by the monotonicity of f. Then, it can be shown [MO 74] that $\mu f = f^\lambda(\perp)$, for some ordinal λ.

By a theorem of Kleene (in [K 52]), if f is (ω-)*continuous*, i.e. it preserves least upper bounds of (ω)-chains, then $\lambda \leqslant \omega$, i.e. only *finite approximations* are relevant. This is the main reason for the crucial role played by ω-continuity in denotational semantics, inducing a very appealing computational meaning to the limiting process of obtaining μf.

As noted in the Introduction, the fairness assumptions cause non ω-continuity of the semantic functions, and higher countable ordinals are needed to iteratively reach the fixedpoint.

One special *cpo* of concern here is that of *truth values*

$$T = \{ff, tt\}, \qquad ff \sqsubseteq tt.$$

The collection of all predicates ordered by implication also form a *cpo* with **false** as its least element.

In the sequel, we deal with fixedpoints involving *relations*. We denote by ID the identity relation and by R a typical relation (or relational variable). Recall the use of the relational operators: ";" for composition, " $\cup$ " for union and " $\neg$ " for negation, with composition having a higher priority over union. If not stated otherwise, relations are taken to be binary, for notational convenience.

We now define several relations by means of fixedpoints. This is done both for exemplifying this method of definition and for later use. Let R be a given relation and p a given predicate. Define a predicate $R \to p$ by

$$[R \to p](x) \qquad \textit{iff} \;\; \forall y\colon R(x,y) \to p(y).$$

Thus, $R \to p$ holds for some x iff all its *R-pictures* satisfy p. By considering R as a relation over a state space of some (nondeterministic) program P that corresponds to P's state transformation, $R \to p$ represents all the initial states for which P is partially correct (w.r.t the postcondition p). This predicate is also known as the result of *wlp*, the weakest liberal precondition transformer corresponding to P, applied to p. Note that $R \to$ **true** $\equiv$ **true**.

The *dual* predicate of $R \to p$, denoted by $R \cdot p$, is defined by

$$R \cdot p \quad \textit{iff} \quad \neg (R \to \neg p)$$

which can easily seen to be equivalent to

$$[R \cdot p](x) \quad \textit{iff} \quad \exists y \colon R(x,y) \wedge p(y).$$

When applied to a predicate variable p, both these predicates are predicate transformers, which play an important role in axiomatic semantics. They are also the same as the *box* and *diamond* operators of *dynamic logic* [PR 79, HA 79].

Next, note that $R \to p$ is monotone in p and, therefore, $\mu p \colon [R \to p]$ exists. Similarly for its dual. We characterize this least fixedpoint in terms of well foundedness.

Theorem: $\mu p \colon [R \to p](x)$ holds iff R is well-founded on x (i.e. there does not exist an infinite sequence $(x_i)_{i=0,\,1,\,\cdots}$ with $x_0 = x$ and $R(x_i, x_{i+1}),\ i \geqslant 0$).

Proof: Denote $R \to p$ by $\tau(p)$. Then τ is monotone in p. By the iterative characterization of $\mu p \colon \tau(p)$, there is some ordinal λ s.t

$$\mu p \colon \tau(p) = \tau^{\lambda}(\mathbf{false}).$$

Using transfinite induction on β, we prove that

$$\tau^{\beta}(\mathbf{false})(x) \to \neg \exists \textit{infinite sequence } x_i, \quad i{=}0,1 \ \cdots, \ x_0 = x, \ R(x_i, x_{i+1}).$$

The induction basis for $\beta{=}0$ is trivial.

Assume the implication holds for all $\alpha < \beta$. Then it follows that

$$\tau^{\beta}(\mathbf{false})(x) \longleftrightarrow (R \to \bigsqcup_{\alpha<\beta} \tau^{\alpha}(\mathbf{false}))(x)$$

$$\longleftrightarrow \forall y \colon [R(x,\ y) \to \bigsqcup_{\alpha<\beta} \tau^{\alpha}(\mathbf{false})(y)].$$

So, by the induction hypothesis, $\tau^{\beta}(\mathbf{false})(x)$ implies that for all y s.t. $R(x,y)$ no infinite R-sequence exists, starting in y. Therefore, no such sequence exists starting in x.

To prove the other direction, i.e. to show that the absence of an infinite R-sequence starting in x implies that $\tau^{\lambda}(\mathbf{false})(x)$ holds, assume that the equivalent condition $\neg \mu p \colon [R \to p](x)$ holds. By the fixedpoint property,

$$\neg (R \to \mu p \colon [R \to p])(x)$$

holds too. Thus, there exists some x_1 s.t $R(x_0,x_1)$ and $\neg \mu p \colon [R \to p](x_1)$. This process can be repeated indefinitely, producing an infinite R-

sequence, contrary to the assumption of the non-existence of such a sequence. []

We conclude that

(1) μp: $[R \to p](x)$ holds in case of the absence of an infinite R-sequence starting in x.
(2) $\neg \mu p$: $[R \to p](x)$holds in case such a sequence exists.

In the *cpo* of predicates (which actually is a complete lattice), greatest fixedpoints of monotone mappings also always exist. Moreover, they are closely related to least fixedpoints [cf. deB 80, lemma 8.29]:

$$\nu p: \tau(p) = \neg \mu p: \neg \tau(\neg p).$$

Using this relationship, it immediately follows that

$$\nu p: R \cdot p \equiv \neg (\mu p: \neg (R \cdot \neg p)) \equiv \neg \mu p: [R \to p].$$

Consequently, $[\nu p: R \cdot p](x)$ holds iff there exists an infinite R-chain starting from x.

Let $\tau(X) = R;X \cup ID$ be a relational transformer, where X ranges over relations. It is clear that $\tau(X)$ is monotone in X, so that μX: $\tau(X)$ exists. Informally, this relation is given by the infinite union

$$ID \cup R \cup R^2 \cup \cdots \cup R^n \cdots .$$

We use the familiar notation R^* for this relation, obtained by composing R with itself any (including zero) finite number of times. Also, $R^+ \overset{def.}{=} R;R^* = R^*;R$.

6.2 The Assertion Language $\mathbf{L}_\mu$

In this section we introduce the formal language $\mathbf{L}_\mu$ used for the expression of predicates characterizing fair termination. Let M be a first-order structure. The first-order logic over M is defined as usual. We now extend this logic in a way allowing for the expression of fixedpoints. We introduce variables ranging over predicates and relations: $p,X,Y, \cdots$ Such variables will always appear *free* in formulae and may not be bound by quantifiers. Their use is carrying the fixedpoint definitions.

To ensure existence of extremal fixedpoints we have to ensure monotonicity of the expressible operators. For this purpose, we introduce a weaker sufficient condition, known as *syntactic monotonicity* that has the advantage of being syntactic, i.e. depending only on the form of formulae. Such a condition, therefore, is easier to be checked. In essence, this condition requires that each occurrence of an induction (relational) variable is within the scope of an *even* number of negations. An odd number of negation implies *anti-monotonicity,* i.e. *order-reversal.*

To formalize this condition, we simultaneously define, using mutual recursion, two sets of formulae, denoted by $sm(p)$ and $sa(p)$, respectively, of syntactically-monotone and syntactically anti-monotone formulae (in a variable p) ([deB 80]).

Definition:

1) $\phi \in sm(p)$ if p does not occur free in ϕ.
2) $\neg\phi \in sm(p)$ if $\phi \in sa(p)$.
3) $(\phi_1 \rightarrow \phi_2) \in sm(p)$ if $\phi_1 \in sa(p)$ and $\phi_2 \in sm(p)$.
4) $\forall x\colon \phi, \exists x\colon \phi \in sm(p)$ if $\phi \in sm(p)$.
5) $p \in sm(p)$
6) $\mu p_1\colon \phi,\ \nu p_1\colon \phi \in sm(p)$ if $\phi \in sm(p) \cap sm(p_1)$.
7) 1)–4) with *sm* and *sa* interchanged.
8) $\mu p_1\colon \phi,\ \nu p_1\colon \phi \in sa(p)$ if $\phi \in sa(p) \cap sm(p_1)$.

For example, by substituting the definition of $R \rightarrow p$ and of conjunction (in terms of implication and negation), one can see that

$$\neg \mu p_1\colon [S \rightarrow (p_1 \wedge \neg p_2)]$$

is both in $sm(p_1)$ and in $sm(p_2)$.

Definition: The assertion language $\mathbf{L}_\mu$ (over a structure *M*) is the smallest language such that:

(i) $\phi,\ \mu p\colon \psi(p),\ \nu p\colon \psi(p) \in \mathbf{L}_\mu$, where ϕ, ψ are first-order formulae (over *M*), ϕ does not contain any free predicate variable and $\psi \in sm(p)$.
(ii) if $\phi,\psi \in \mathbf{L}_\mu$ then $\phi \wedge \psi,\ \phi \vee \psi,\ \phi \rightarrow \psi$ and $\neg\phi \in \mathbf{L}_\mu$.

Remark: Strictly according to this definition, no nesting of μ-terms is allowed in $\mathbf{L}_\mu$. However, it is proved in [MO 74] that nested terms are expressible (i.e. equivalent to unnested terms). Thus, we use nested terms unrestrictively.

The semantics of $\mathbf{L}_\mu$ is determined by the definition of *validity.* The validity of μ, ν-free formulas is defined as usual. The only new cases are the formulae involving μ, ν. Their validity is defined by means of formulae expressing the iterates of the operators defined by the bodies of such fixedpoints terms.

Thus, for each $\phi(p)$ and ordinal λ we introduce a predicate I_ϕ^λ by:

$$I^0_\phi(\bar{x}) \stackrel{def.}{=} \mathbf{false}$$

$$I^\beta_\phi(\bar{x}) \stackrel{def.}{=} \phi(\sqcup_{\alpha<\beta} I^\alpha_\phi)(\bar{x})$$

and also we let

$$I_\phi(\bar{x}) \stackrel{def.}{=} \cup_\alpha I^\alpha_\phi(\bar{x}).$$

By the (syntactic) monotonicity of ϕ, using the facts about fixedpoints of monotone operators, we immediately get the following properties of these predicates [MO 74].

Proposition:

1) $\alpha \leqslant \beta \rightarrow (I^\alpha_\phi(\bar{x}) \rightarrow I^\beta_\phi(\bar{x}))$.
2) for some ordinal κ

$$I_\phi = I^\kappa_\phi = \cup_{\lambda<\kappa} I^\kappa_\phi.$$

3) I_ϕ is the least predicate p satisfying

$$p(\bar{x}) = \phi(p)(\bar{x}).$$

Now validity of μp: $\phi(p)$ is defined in terms of I_ϕ.

Definition:

$$\models \mu p\colon \phi(p) \textit{ iff for all } \bar{x}, \models \mu p\colon \phi(p)(\bar{x})$$

and

$$\models \mu p\colon \phi(p)(\bar{x}) \textit{ iff } I_\phi(\bar{x}).$$

The validity of the dual predicate is derived correspoundingly.

Coding and acceptability

As is often the case in representability issues, some assumptions are needed about the ability to code finite sequences as elements of the structure, as well as the inverse operation of decoding, enabling the reconstruction of the coded sequence from the code element. The existence of such representations are well known to computer scientist, who deal daily with data structures. In the current framework, this amounts to the assumption that the structure dealt with contains a "copy" of the natural numbers, denoted by N^M, and that it is equipped with the following functions and predicates:

1) *Coding:* For any $x_1, \cdots, x_n$ in M, we denote by

$$< x_1, \cdots, x_n > \in N^M$$

the code of the corresponding sequence.

2) *Codification:*

$$seq(x) \longleftrightarrow \exists x_1, \cdots x_n: x = < x_1, \cdots, x_n >$$

i.e. $seq(x)$ holds in case x is a code of *some* sequence. Note that $<>$ is also a code (of the empty sequence). The coding function is also assumed to be *one-to-one*.

3) *Length:*

$$lh(x) \stackrel{def.}{=} \begin{cases} 0 & \text{if } \neg\, seq(x) \\ n & \text{if } seq(x) \wedge x = < x_1, \cdots, x_n > \\ & \text{for some } x_1, \cdots, x_n. \end{cases}$$

i.e. $lh(x)$ is the length of the sequence (if any) of which x is the code.

4) *Projection:*

$$(x)_i \stackrel{def.}{=} \begin{cases} x_i & x = < x_1, \cdots, x_n > \text{for some } x_1, \cdots, x_n, \text{and } 1 \leqslant i \leqslant n. \\ 0 & \textit{otherwise} \end{cases}$$

i.e. $(x)_i$ is the i-th element of the sequence of which x is the code.

All these functions and predicates are assumed to be *elementary*, i.e. first-order definable in the given structure. A structure admitting such coding facilities is called *admissible*. We assume that we deal here with admissible structures only and do not bother too much about coding details. A more comprehensive treatment of coding may be found in [MO 74] or in standard textbooks on Mathematical Logic.

Finally, we assume the availability (either primitivie or defined) of constants for the ordinals (up to the closing ordinal of the implicit structure), a (unary) predicate *ord* satisfied by (and only by) these ordinals and a (binary) order relation $<$ between them.

Basic representability

We end this subsection by showing the representability in $\mathbf{L}_\mu$ of some basic relations, before diving into the fairness-related issues.

Lemma: (representability of the relational semantics) For $S \in GC$ the relation $R_S(\sigma_0, \sigma_1)$ (which holds if σ_1 is a possible outcome of the execution of S on σ_0) is representable.

We omit here a full proof of this lemma, which is a standard exercise in relational semantics, using structural induction on *GC*. In order to avoid the annoying difficulties of the relational semantics associated with nonterminating iterative statements, we assume in this chapter that we do not deal with nested iteration. In other words, when "passing the arrow" the r.h.s has a (non-empty) relation associated with it. As a simple example, if

$$S{::}\ *[B_1 \to S_1 [\,] B_2 \to S_2\,]$$

then R_S is defined by

$$R_S(\sigma, \sigma') = \mu X{:}\ [R_1;\ X \vee R_2;\ X \vee \neg(B_1 \vee B_2)](x, y)$$

where $R_i = R_{B_i;\ S_i}$, $i = 1, 2$. Conditions such as B_i are taken as subsets of the identity relation *ID*. The arguments x, y are codes for the states σ and σ', respectively, taken as sequences of the free variables appearing in S. Obviously, R_S does not depend on any other variables.

As a consequence of this lemma, we may consider the language to be augmented with such relations, taken as "primitives" without affecting the theory of the given structure.

Lemma: (basic representability) Let R, R_1, R_2 be given relations. The following constructs are representable in $\mathbf{L}_\mu$:

$R_1;\ R_2,\ R_1 \cup R_2$
$R*$
$\mu p{:}\ [R \to p]$
$r \cdot R$, for a predicate r.

Proof: Composition and union–obvious. As for the reflexive-transitive closure, the defining expression has already been mentioned, namely

$$\mu X{:}\ (R;\ X \cup ID).$$

In order to express $\mu p{:}\ R \to p$, define

$$\phi(x, p) \overset{def.}{=} \forall y{:}\ R(x, y) \to p(y).$$

Then, the defining formula is $\mu p{:}\ \phi(x, p)$. Finally, $[r \cdot R](x) \overset{def.}{=} \exists y{:}\ r(y) \wedge R(y, x)$. This predicate reads as "x is R-reachable from r".[ ]

6.3 The Weakest Precondition for Fair Termination

In this section we present $\mathbf{L}_\mu$ formulae expressing the weakest preconditions for unconditionally–and strongly–fair termination of *GC* programs.

Intuitively, an assertion $p = wp(S, q)$ is the weakest precondition w.r.t a program S and predicate q, iff

$$i) \quad < p > S < q >,$$

and for all predicates r:

$$ii) \quad < r > S < q > \text{ implies } r \rightarrow p.$$

In other words, S always terminates in a state satisfying q, whenever activated in a state satisfying $wp(S, q)$. Thus, wp is a *predicate transformer* associated with S, transforming q into p.

The intention here is to define analogously the predicate transformers

$$p = ufwp(S, q) \quad and \quad p = sfwp(S, q)$$

where in the intuitive explanation unconditionally-fair termination (repectively, strongly-fair termination) replace (ordinary) termination. Thus, the following definition is obtained:

Definition: A predicate $p = ufwp(S, q)$ (respectively, $p = sfwp(S, q)$) is the *unconditionally-fair (respectively, strongly-fair) weakest precondition* w.r.t a *GC program P and predicate q, iff:*

i) $\overset{\mathbf{u}}{\ll} p \gg S \ll q \gg$ (respectively, $\overset{\mathbf{s}}{\ll} p \gg S \ll q \gg$), and

ii) for *all predicates r*:

$\overset{\mathbf{u}}{\ll} r \gg S \ll q \gg$ (respectively, $\overset{\mathbf{s}}{\ll} r \gg S \ll q \gg$) implies $r \rightarrow p$.

In the original formulation of the wp for ordinary termination, the predicate

$$wp(*[\underset{i=1,n}{[\,]} B_i \rightarrow S_i], \textbf{true})$$

was defined iteratively, by taking the least upper bound $\sqcup_i H_i$ of the following ω-chain H_i of approximating predictes:

$$H_0 \equiv \neg \bigvee_{i=1,n} B_i$$

$$H_{i+1} \equiv H_i \vee \bigwedge_{i=1,n} (B_i \rightarrow wp(S_i, H_i)).$$

As was noted later, this direct construction is valid only in the case of *bounded nondeterminism*. Consider the following example due to Park ([PA 81]), showing the failure of this construction in the presence of unbounded nondeterminism, arising due to random assignments. Let

$$S{::}\ *[\ 1{:}\ z < 0 \rightarrow z{:=}?\ [\,]\ 2{:}\ z > 0 \rightarrow z{:=}z - 1].$$

By applying the construction above, the following chain is obtained.

$$H_0 \equiv (z = 0)$$

$$H_{i+1} \equiv H_i \bigvee (\ (\ z < 0 \rightarrow wp(z{:=}?,\ H_i))$$
$$\bigwedge\ (\ z > 0 \rightarrow wp(z{:=}z - 1,\ H_i))\ ).$$

By induction we get that

$$H_i \equiv (\ 0 \leqslant z \leqslant i\ )$$

noting that

1) $wp(\ z{:=}?,\ 0 \leqslant z \leqslant i\ ) \equiv$ **false** (the identically false predicate), and
2) $wp(\ z{:=}z - 1,\ 0 \leqslant z \leqslant i\ ) \equiv 0 < z \leqslant i + 1.$

By taking the least upper bound, the predicate $\sqcup_i H_i \equiv (\ z \geqslant 0\ )$ is obtained. This contradicts the expected result **true** (the identically true predicate), which follows from the semantics of random assignments and *GC*.

Clearly, what went wrong is the number of iterations used to obtain the required fixedpoint, which is one too short in this example. This can be seen by noting that

1) $wp\ (\ z{:=}?,\ z \geqslant 0\ ) =$ **true** and
2) $wp\ (\ z{:=}z - 1,\ z \geqslant 0\ ) = (\ z \geqslant 1\ ).$

As observed by Park in [PA 81], the right solution is obtained if the appropriate predicate transformer is taken as the strongest solution of a recursive equation of the form

$$H = (\ \bigwedge_{i=1,n} \neg B_i\ ) \rightarrow q\ \bigwedge\ \bigwedge_{i=1,n}(\ B_i \rightarrow wp\ (\ S_i,\ H\ )\ ).$$

The correct solution uses the right number of iterations, in particular using higher-order countable ordinals.

Thus, it turns out that $\mathbf{L}_\mu$ is an appropriate formalism for expressing such solutions. We proceed by defining the required predicate transformers. Again, we are in particularly interested in strong fairness. But, as was encountered before, unconditional fairness is an essential component in the definition of strong fairness.

We first show how to represent in $\mathbf{L}_\mu$ the assertion stating that a *GC* program

$$P{::}\ *[\ \underset{i=1,n}{[\,]}\ B \rightarrow S_i\,]$$

is unconditionally-fair terminating in an initial state ξ. We denote the expressing formula by $\neg\, UFAIR(R_1, \cdots, R_n)$, where R_i is the relation associated with B; S_i, $i=1, n$. Thus, the formula $UFAIR(R_1, \cdots, R_n)$ is satisfied in a state ξ in case there exists an infinite unconditionally-fair computation of P starting in ξ.

To illustrate the idea, consider the construction of such a term for the program

$$*[b \rightarrow x:=x+1 \ [\,]\ b \rightarrow b:=false].$$

As we already know, this program is ***UFT*** for any initial state. We use the construct μp: $[R \rightarrow p]$, which, as we also know already, holds in a state ξ iff there is no infinite R-chain starting in ξ. The way that this program terminates in a state in which b has the value tt is by executing b; $b:=false$ after some arbitrary finite number of executing b; $x:=x+1$. Such a sequence may be described as

$$(b;\ x:=x+1)^*;\ b;\ b:=false$$

and so the required predicate expressing fair termination is given by

$$\mu p:\ [(\ (b;\ x:=x+1)^*;\ b;\ b:=false) \ \rightarrow\ p].$$

Note that statements are occasionally used to stand for the relation associated with them. This is a useful abbreviation.

In the sequel we assume that the relations associated with S_i are always defined for states satisfying B. Our intermediate goal is to express the fact that in an infinite execution sequence every R_i, $i=1, n$, appears infinitely often. Consider such an infinite execution. As each R_i appears infinitely often, this sequence can be decomposed into an infinite number of *finite* sections, which we call *full segments* (abbreviated as *fseg*). Every *fseg* satisfies:

(*Fullness*): Each R_i, $i=1, n$ occurs in the *fseg*.
(*Minimality*): The *fseg* is the *smallest* satisfying fullness, i.e. every initial segment of an *fseg* leaves out some R_i.

To define a relation $Fseg(R_1, \cdots, R_n)$, which expresses, for a pair of states ξ, ξ' reachability of ξ' from ξ by means of executing an *fseg* (w.r.t $R_1, \cdots, R_n$), it suffices to consider full segments in which the first occurrences of the directions are in some predescribed order, to which we refer as an *ordered full segment* (abbreviated as *ofseg*). This is so since any *fseg* over $R_1, \cdots, R_n$ is an *ofseg* over some permutation $R_{i_1}, \cdots, R_{i_n}$. The relation $Ofseg(R_1, \cdots, R_n)$ is defined inductively (over n).

For $n=1$ simply take $Ofseg(R_1) \overset{def.}{=} R_1$. Suppose $Ofseg(R_1, \cdots, R_k)$ has been defined. Then, $Ofseg(R_1, \cdots, R_{k+1})$ looks like

$$R_1;\ \cdots\ ;R_i;\ \cdots\ ;R_k;\ \cdots\ ;R_{k+1}$$

where the first occurrences of R_1, R_i, R_k, R_{k+1} are explicitly shown ($i < k < n$). Note that R_{k+1} occurs *once only*, due to the requirement of minimality. Note also that the initial sequence

$$R_1;\ \cdots\ ;R_i;\ \cdots\ ;R_k\,,$$

is an *ofseg* over $R_1, \cdots, R_k$. Furtheremore, the sequence up to (but not including) R_{k+1} is *not* necessarily an *ofseg*, but only has a prefix which is. The remaining part beyond that prefix may contain a finite number of occurrences of R_i, $i < k + 1$. This motivates the following recursive definition.

Definition:

$$Ofseg(R_1) \stackrel{def.}{=} R_1$$

$$Ofseg(R_1, \cdots, R_{n+1}) \stackrel{def.}{=} Ofseg(R_1, \cdots, R_n); (R_1 \cup \cdots \cup R_n)^*; R_{n+1}$$

For example, we have:

$$Ofseg(R_1, R_2) = R_1;\ R_1{}^*;\ R_2$$

and

$$Ofseg(R_1, R_2, R_3) = R_1;\ R_1{}^*;\ R_2;\ (R_1 \cup R_2)^*;\ R_3\,.$$

Definition: For $n > 1$ and $P(n)$ the set of permutations over $1, \cdots, n$:

$$Fseg(R_1, \cdots, R_n) \stackrel{def.}{=} \bigvee_{(i_1, \ldots, i_n) \in P(n)} Ofseg(R_{i_1}, \cdots, R_{i_n}).$$

The existence of an infinite sequence of full segments (i.e. an infinite unconditionally-fair computation), starting in a state ξ, is expressed by satisfaction of the predicate $UFAIR(R_1, \cdots, R_n)$ defined as follows.

Definition:

$$UFAIR(R_1, \cdots, R_n) \stackrel{def.}{=} \nu p\colon [Fseg(R_1, \cdots, R_n)\cdot p].$$

Consequently, $\neg\, UFAIR(R_1, \cdots, R_n)$ denotes the weakest precondition for unconditionally-fair termination of the program

$$S{::}\ *[\ \underset{i=1,n}{[]}\ B \rightarrow S_i\ ],$$

where R_i is the relation associated with $B; S_i$, $i=1, \cdots, n$.

Returning to the example considered at the begining of the section (for which $n = 2$), one can obtain easily the term given there as the correct expression by substituting into the example of *Ofseg* for $n = 2$.

We proceed to define the $\mathbf{L}_\mu$ formula characterizing the states for which a *GC* program of the form $S:: *[\ \underset{i=1,n}{[]}\ B_i \rightarrow S_i]$ strongly-fair terminates. Note once again the difference in form of the program w.r.t the one considered in the unconditional case. Each direction has once again its own enabledness condition, taken into account. We denote by R_i the relation associated with S_i and by D_i the relation associated with $B_i; S_i$. We again assume that B_i implies that R_i is is a total relation. Detaching the guard from the body of the direction turns out to be useful in the sequel.

One possibility of an infinite computation to be strongly fair is by being unconditionally fair. Thus, $Fseg\ (R_1, \cdots, R_n)$ is one component of the defining formula.

Next, suppose that some move $B_n; R_n$ eventually becomes never enabled anymore. Then an infinite strongly fair sequence of $B_1; R_1, \cdots, B_n; R_n$ consists of some finite sequence of these moves followed by an infinite strongly fair sequence of $B_1; R_1, \cdots, B_{n-1}; R_{n-1}$, in which all intermediate states satisfy $\neg B_n$. In case no other move becomes continually disabled afterwards, this is expressed by the predicate

$$(B_1; R_1 \cup \cdots \cup B_n; R_n)^*$$

$$\cdot UFAIR(B_1 \wedge \neg B_n; R_1, \cdots, B_{n-1} \wedge \neg B_n; R_{n-1}).$$

Forming the intermediate $B_i \wedge B_{n-1}$ is the advantage of the split between the guard and its body mentioned before.

The possibility that other directions eventually become continuously disabled too leads to the following definition (due to Peter van Emde–Boas).

Definition: Let $n \geqslant 2$ and consider some permutation $p = (i_1, \cdots, i_n)$ of $1, \cdots, n$. For $1 \leqslant k \leqslant n$, let

$$SFAIR_k^p\ (B_1; R_1, \cdots, B_n; R_n) \overset{def.}{=}$$

$$(\cup_{i=1,n} B_i; R_i)^* \cdot UFAIR(B_{i_1} \wedge \wedge_{j=k+1,n} \neg B_{i_j}; R_{i_1}, \cdots,$$

$$B_{i_k} \wedge \wedge_{j=k+1,n} \neg B_{i_j}; R_{i_k}).$$

The predicate $SFAIR_k^p$ is satisfied whenever there exists an infinite strongly-fair sequence in which the moves $D_{i_{k+1}}, \cdots, D_{i_n}$ are eventually continuously disabled. Note the dependence of the definition on the particular permutation chosen.

We now come to the definition of *SFAIR* itself.

Definition:

$$SFAIR(\ B_1;\ R_1\ ) \overset{def.}{=} UFAIR(\ B_1;\ R_1\ )\ (\ = \nu p\colon [(B_1;\ R_1\ )\cdot p]\ ).$$

$$SFAIR(\ B_1;\ R_1,\ \cdots,\ B_n;\ R_n\ ) \overset{def.}{=}$$

$$UFAIR(\ B_1;\ R_1,\ \cdots,\ B_n;\ R_n\ ) \lor$$

$$\bigvee_{\substack{p \in P(n) \\ 1 \leqslant k < n}} SFAIR_k^p(\ B_1;\ R_1,\ \cdots,\ B_n;\ R_n\ ).$$

In the sequel we once again incorporate the guard's relation in the body's relation and use D_i for B_i; R_i.

Lemma: (U-reduction)

$$\neg\, SFAIR\ (D_1,\ \cdots,\ D_n) \leftrightarrow \neg\, UFAIR\ (D_1,\ \cdots,\ D_n) \land$$

$$\bigwedge_{\substack{P(n) \\ 1 \leqslant k < n}} [\ (\ \cup_{i=1,n} D_i)^* \rightarrow \neg\, UFAIR\,(\ (\ \bigwedge_{j=k+1,n} \neg\, B_{i_j});$$

$$D_{i_1},\ \cdots,\ (\ \bigwedge_{j=k+1,n} \neg\, B_{i_j});\ D_{i_k})\ ].$$

Proof: Follows from the definitions of *SFAIR*, $SFAIR_k^p$ and *UFAIR*. This lemma captures the role of the derived programs in the **SFT** rule in Chapter 2. [ ]

Definition: The *weakest precondition for strongly-fair termination* is defined by

$$sfwp(\ *[\ [\ ]_{i=1,n} B_i \rightarrow S_i\ ],\ q) \overset{def.}{=}$$

$$\neg\, SFAIR(D_1,\ \cdots,\ D_n) \land [(\ (\ \cup_{i=1,n} D_i)^*;\ \neg \bigvee_{i=1,n} B_i) \rightarrow q].$$

To summarize and justify this definition as the intended one according to the intuitive understanding, the following theorem is stated, connecting *sfwp* with strongly-fair termination. Note that *ufwp* can be defined analogously and induce a corresponding theorem.

Theorem: (weakest precondition for strongly-fair termination)

$$\overset{s}{\ll} p \gg *[\ \underset{i=1,n}{[\,]} B_i \rightarrow S_i\ ] \ll q \gg \textit{iff}\ p \rightarrow sfwp(\ *[\ \underset{i=1,n}{[\,]} B_i \rightarrow S_i\ ],\ q\ ).$$

Proof:

l.h.s → *r.h.s*: Suppose that

$$\overset{s}{\ll} p \gg *[\ \underset{i=1,n}{[\,]} B_i \rightarrow S_i] \ll q \gg$$

holds. Choose some state ξ such that $\xi \models p$ holds. By way of contradiction, assume that $SFAIR\ (D_1, \cdots, D_n)(\xi)$ is the case. Then, by the construction of *SFAIR*, a contradiction is immediately derived, as this implies the existence of an infinite strongly fair execution sequence, starting in ξ.

Thus, $\neg SFAIR\ (D_1, \cdots, D_n)$ is the case. We still have to show that

$$((\cup_{i=1,n} D_i)^*; \wedge_{i=1,n} \neg B_i \rightarrow q)(\xi)$$

is also true. To this end, choose some state ξ' such that

$$\xi\ ((\cup_{i=1,n} D_i)^*; \wedge_{i=1,n} \neg B_i)\ \xi'.$$

By the proof of the representability of the relational semantics lemma, also $\xi *[\ \underset{i=1,n}{[\,]} B_i \rightarrow S_i]\ \xi'$, and by hypothesis $\xi' \models q$.

r.h.s → *l.h.s*: Suppose that

$$p \rightarrow (\neg SFAIR(D_1, \cdots, D_n) \wedge [(\cup_{i=1,n} D_i)^*; \wedge_{i=1,n} \neg B_i \rightarrow q].$$

Choose a state ξ s.t. $p \models \xi$. Since, by hypothesis, $\neg SFAIR(D_1, \cdots, D_n)(\xi)$, the repetition always strongly-fair terminates by the construction of *SFAIR*. Establishing q for any final state is also immediate. [ ]

6.4 Syntactic Completeness of the SFT Rule

In this section we return to the *helpful directions* method of proving ***SFT*** and show its syntactic completeness by using $\mathbf{L}_\mu$ as the underlying assertion language. Following [SdeRG 84], the proof presented is inspired by the ordering presented in the semantic completeness proof of [LPS 81] for the state-directed choice of the decreasing directions, modified so as to apply to the ordinal-directed choice in the **SFT** rule.

We fix some acceptable first-order structure M (with the ordinals-augmentation as discussed above), and satisfaction is always considered in this structure. Let $\mathbf{Th(M)}$ denote the *theory* of M, i.e. $\{p \in \mathbf{L}_\mu \mid M \models p\}$, needed for *relative completeness*.

Theorem: (syntactic completeness of SFT w.r.t $\mathbf{L}_\mu$)

$$\text{if } \mathbf{M} \overset{s}{\models} \ll p \gg *[\ \underset{i=1,n}{[\,]} B_i \rightarrow S_i] \ll q \gg$$

$$\text{then } \mathbf{Th(M)} \overset{s}{\vdash}_{\mathbf{SFT}} \ll p \gg *[\ \underset{i=1,n}{[\,]} B_i \rightarrow S_i] \ll q \gg.$$

Proof: Assume that $\overset{s}{\ll} p \gg S \ll q \gg$ holds, for S as in the theorem.

By the weakest precondition for ***SFT*** theorem, it may be also assumed that

$$p \rightarrow \neg SFAIR(\ D_1,\ \cdots\ ,\ D_n\ ) \wedge [(\ \cup_{i=1,n} D_i)^*;\ \wedge_{i=1,n} \neg B_i \rightarrow q\ ].$$

As the first stage, a well-founded set W and parametrized invariant $pi(\ \xi,\ w\ )$ must be defined, ranking every S-reachable state. As S is ***SFT*** it is also ***UFT***.

At any stage, there is at least one decreasing move (otherwise there exists a state in which no move would bring the program closer to termination and this would result in the existence of an infinite ***UF*** sequence, a contradiction). So, if in a successive sequence of iterations, every move has been executed at least once, then certainly the program has come closer to termination. This shows that viewing execution sequences as consisting of *fsegs* (full segments), is a natural one. Unfortunately, counting *fsegs* does not quite work, because *all* states have to be ranked in order for the **SFT** rule to apply.

Consider such an *fseg*. It suffices that the states, reached by executing this *fseg*, are ranked in a way reflecting the "progress" that is made w.r.t. executing this *fseg* itself. A move leads to such a relative progress if it is a new one that is not made in *fseg* as yet. This gives the intuition behind the suggested definitions of W and *pi*.

Since by definition

$$\neg SFAIR(D_1,\ \cdots\ ,\ D_n) \rightarrow \neg UFAIR(D_1,\ \cdots\ ,\ D_n)$$

and by the previous discussion

$$\neg UFAIR(D_1\ , \ldots ,\ D_n)\ \longleftrightarrow$$

$$\neg \nu p\colon [Fseg(D_1,\ \cdots\ ,\ D_n) \cdot p]\ \longleftrightarrow$$

$$\mu p\colon [Fseg(D_1,\ \cdots\ ,\ D_n) \rightarrow p]$$

we obtain that

$$\neg SFAIR(D_1,\ \cdots\ ,\ D_n) \rightarrow \mu p\colon [Fseg(R_1,\ \cdots\ ,\ R_n) \rightarrow p].$$

As least fixedpoints can be obtained by iteration, define τ by

$$\tau(p) = \lambda\xi\text{: } (Fseg(D_1, \cdots, D_n) \rightarrow p)(\xi) \textit{ and}$$

$$\tau^{\bar{0}}(p) = \lambda\xi\text{: } \mathbf{false}$$

$$\tau^{\bar{\lambda}}(p) = \tau(\bigsqcup_{\bar{\beta}<\bar{\lambda}} \tau^{\bar{\beta}}(p)) \textit{ for } \bar{\lambda} \neq \bar{0}.$$

Let $\bar{\alpha}$ denote the least ordinal $\bar{\lambda}$ such that

$$\tau^{\bar{\lambda}}(\mathbf{false}) = \mu p\text{: } [Fseg(D_1, \cdots, D_n) \rightarrow p].$$

If $\bar{\beta} \leqslant \bar{\alpha}$ then $\tau^{\bar{\beta}}(\mathbf{false})(\xi)$ holds for some $\bar{\beta}$ iff ξ is at most $\bar{\beta}$ *fsegs* away from termination. Hence, this gives a way to rank the states related by *fsegs*. Of course, for this to work we need to show that $\tau^{\bar{\beta}}(\mathbf{false})$ is representable by a formula in $\mathbf{L}_\mu$.

Claim: (representability of *fseg* ranking) There exists a formula $\phi(x, y)$ in $\mathbf{L}_\mu$ such that for all ξ and all $\bar{\beta} \leqslant \bar{\alpha}$ $\tau^{\bar{\beta}}(\mathbf{false})(\xi)$ holds iff $\phi(\bar{\beta}, \xi)$.

Proof: Define

$$\phi(x, y) \overset{def.}{=} \mu r\text{: } \exists\, \alpha<\beta\text{: } (Fseg(D_1, \cdots, D_n)(\xi) \rightarrow r(\alpha)(y))].$$

By induction on $\bar{\beta}$, making use of the fixpoint property, we may prove that for all $\bar{\beta} \leqslant \bar{\alpha}$ and all ξ, $\tau^{\bar{\beta}}(\mathbf{false})(\xi)$ holds iff $\phi(\bar{\beta}, \xi)$.

Now, we define the well-founded ordered set W and the ranking predicate *pi*: each non-minimal $w \in W$ consists of two components $(\bar{\lambda}, s)$:

1) $\bar{\lambda}$ counts *fsegs*.
2) s records progress within the last (incomplete) *fseg* and is a sequence of length at most n (the number of directions of the repetition), which records the directions within this *fseg*, that already have been taken. Here we make use of the codification of $Seq_n(s)$, asserting that s is a sequence (of directions) of length n. []

Definition:

$$Seq_n(s) \overset{def.}{=} Seq(s) \wedge (lh(s) \leqslant n) \wedge$$

$$\wedge\, \forall i\text{: } [(1 \leqslant i \leqslant lh(s)) \rightarrow (1 \leqslant (s)_i \leqslant n)] \wedge$$

$$\wedge\, \forall i,j\text{: } [(1 \leqslant i,j \leqslant lh(s) \wedge i \neq j) \rightarrow ((s)_i \neq (s)_j)].$$

Note that only directions are recorded and each direction at most once!

Definition:

$$W_{\bar{\alpha},\, n} \overset{def.}{=} \{(\bar{\lambda}, s) \mid \bar{0} \leqslant \bar{\lambda} \leqslant \bar{\alpha} \wedge seq_n(s)\} \cup \{\bar{0}\}.$$

(A fully formalized definition would use here the characteristic of W.)
The ordering $<$ defined on $W_{\bar{\alpha},\, n}$ is the following :

$\bar{0} < (\bar{\lambda}, s)$ for all $(\bar{\lambda}, s) \in W_{\bar{\alpha},\, n}$, and $(\bar{\lambda}_1, s_1) < (\bar{\lambda}_2, s_2)$ iff

$$(\bar{\lambda}_1 < \bar{\lambda}_2) \vee [\, (\bar{\lambda}_1 = \bar{\lambda}_2) \wedge$$
$$(lh(s_2) < lh(s_1)) \wedge$$
$$\forall\, i{:}\ (\ (1 \leqslant i \leqslant lh(s_2)\ ) \rightarrow ((s_2)_i = (s_1)_i))].$$

Now the parametrized invariant can be defined.

Definition: The predicate $pi(\xi, w)$, $w = (\bar{\lambda}, s)$, is defined by

$$pi(\bar{\lambda}, <>\ ) = \tau^{\bar{\lambda}}(\textbf{false}) \wedge p \cdot (\cup_{i=1,n} D_i)^* \wedge \vee_{i=1,n} B_i,$$

$$pi(\bar{\lambda}, <i_1, \cdots, i_k>) = \tau^{\bar{\lambda}}(\textbf{false}) \cdot Ofseg(D_{i_1}, \cdots, D_{i_k}); (\cup_{j=1,k} D_{i_j})^*)$$
$$\wedge\ p \cdot (\cup_{i=1,n} D_i)^* \wedge \vee_{i=1,n} B_i, \qquad (for\ 1 \leqslant k < n),$$

$$pi(\bar{\lambda}, <i_1, \cdots, i_n>) = \sqcup_{\bar{\beta} < \bar{\lambda}} \tau^{\bar{\beta}}(\textbf{false}) \wedge p \cdot (\cup_{i=1,n} D_i)^* \wedge \vee_{i=1,n} B_i,$$

$$pi(\bar{0}) = \wedge_{i=1,n} \neg B_i.$$

To define S_w and D_w for $w > \bar{0}$ observe that if at the start of an *fseg* (i.e. $w = (\bar{\lambda}, <>\ )$ or $w = (\bar{\lambda}, <i_1, \cdots, i_n>)$ for some $\bar{\lambda} \leqslant \bar{\alpha}$) then every move leads to eventual completion of this *fseg*. Otherwise, $w = (\bar{\lambda}, <i_1, \cdots, i_k>)$ for some $\bar{\lambda}$, $1 \leqslant k < n$, and only moves different from $R_{i_1}, \cdots, R_{i_k}$ lead to eventual completion of this *fseg*.

All the intermediate assertions derived in providing the lematta denote valid statements (in the underlying structure). The '$\models$' sign is omitted occassionally for brevity.

Definition: Let $w \in W_{\bar{\alpha},\, n}$, $w = (\bar{\lambda}, s)$.
If $lh(s) = 0$ or $lh(s) = n$ then $D_w = \{1, \cdots, n\}$ and $S_w = \varnothing$.
If $0 < lh(s) < n$ then

$$D_w = \{i \mid 1 \leqslant i \leqslant n \wedge \forall\, j \leqslant lh(s){:}\ [(s)_j \neq i]\},$$

$$S_w = \{1, \cdots, n\} - D_w.$$

Note that for all $w \in W_{\bar{\alpha}, n}$ and $w > \bar{0}$

$$D_w \cap S_w = \emptyset, \text{ and } D_w \cup S_w = \{1, \ldots, n\}.$$

The satisfaction of the **SFT** clauses is expressed in a sequence of lematta. Recall the assumption p implies $(\neg SFAIR(D_1, \cdots, D_n) \wedge ((\cup_{i=1,n} D_i)^*; \wedge_{i=1,n} \neg B_i \rightarrow q))$.

Lemma: (DEC) Suppose that $\models \overset{s}{\ll} p \gg S \ll q \gg$ holds. Let $w \in W_{\bar{\alpha}, n}$ and $j \in D_w$. Then

$$\mathbf{Th(M)} \vdash \overset{s}{\ll} pi(w) \wedge w > \bar{0} \gg S_j \ll \exists v < w\text{: } pi(v) \gg.$$

Proof: We have to show that for all states ξ, ξ' such that $\xi D_j \xi'$, $(pi(w) \wedge w > \bar{0})(\xi) \rightarrow \exists\, v < w\text{: } pi(v)(\xi')$. Choose states ξ, ξ' satisfying $\xi D_j \xi'$, and suppose that $pi(w, \xi) \wedge w > \bar{0}$ holds.

We distinguish two cases:

$$(a)\quad \wedge_{i=1}^{n} \neg B_i(\xi') \quad \text{(trivial)}.$$

$$(b)\quad \vee_{i=1}^{n} B_i(\xi').$$

Since $pi(w, \xi)$ holds, $p \cdot (\cup_{i=1,n} D_i)^*(\xi)$ holds, too. In other words,

$$\exists \xi''\text{: } [p(\xi'') \wedge \xi''(\cup_{i=1,n} D_i)^* \xi]. \tag{ii}$$

Now,

$$(\cup_{i=1,n} D_i)^*; D_j \subset (\cup_{i=1,n} D_i)^*.$$

So it follows from $\xi D_j \xi'$ and (ii) that

$$\exists \xi''\text{: } [p(\xi'') \wedge \xi''(\cup_{i=1,n} D_i)^* \xi'], \tag{iii}$$

i.e.

$$p \cdot (\cup_{i=1,n} D_i)^*(\xi').$$

Let $w = (\bar{\lambda}, s)$. To prove $\models \exists v < w\text{: } pi(v, \xi')$, We distinguish three cases:

(1) $lh(s) = 0$, so $s = <>$.
Since $\models pi(w, \xi)$, $\tau^{\lambda}(\mathbf{false})(\xi)$ holds. Consequently, it follows that $\exists \xi''\text{: } [\tau^{\lambda}(\mathbf{false})(\xi'') \wedge \xi'' R_j \xi']$. Hence, from $R_j \subset R_j^+$ we know $\exists \xi''\text{: } [\tau^{\lambda}(\mathbf{false})(\xi'') \wedge \xi'' R_j^+ \xi']$ holds, i.e. $(\tau^{\lambda}(\mathbf{false}) \cdot R_j^+)(\xi')$. Together with (i) and (iii) $pi((\bar{\lambda}, <j>), \xi')$ follows and hence $\exists v < w\text{: } pi(v, \xi')$.

(2) $1 \leqslant lh(s) < n$, so $s = <i_1, \cdots, i_k>$ for some $i_1, \cdots, i_k$, such that $\{i_1, \cdots, i_k\} \subset \{1, \cdots, n\}$ and $1 \leqslant k < n$.

From $pi(w, \xi)$, we derive

$$({}_{T}\bar{\lambda}(\mathbf{false})\cdot Ofseg(D_{i_1}, \cdots, D_{i_k}); (\cup_{t=1}^{k} D_{i_t})^*)(\xi).$$

Since

$$Ofseg(D_{i_1}, \cdots, D_{i_k}); (\cup_{t=1}^{k} D_{i_t})^*; D_j = Ofseg(D_{i_1}, \cdots, D_{i_k}, {}_D\, j)$$

(by its definition and $j \neq i_1, \cdots, i_k$ *for* $j \in D_w$).

$$\subseteq Ofseg(D_{i_1}, \cdots, D_{i_k}, D_j); (\cup_{t=1}^{k} D_{i_t} \cup D_j)^*.$$

This together with (i) and (iii) implies $pi((\bar{\lambda}, <i_1, \cdots, i_k, j>), \xi')$. Again, $\exists v < w$: $pi(v, \xi')$ follows.

(3) $lh(s) = n$.
From $pi((\bar{\lambda}, s), \xi)$ and definition of pi, the existence of a $\bar{\beta} \leqslant \bar{\lambda}$ such that $pi((\bar{\beta}, <>), \xi)$ follows.
As in case (1), $\exists v < (\bar{\beta}, <>)$: $pi(v, \xi')$, and so

$$\exists v < (\bar{\lambda}, <>): pi(v, \xi'). \qquad [\,]$$

The proof of this lemma shows how the same ideas used in a semantic completeness proof may be cast to their defining expression in $\mathbf{L}_\mu$. The same holds also for the lematta taking care of the other clauses.

Lemma: (NOINC) Suppose that $\models \ll p \gg \overset{s}{S} \ll q \gg$ holds. Let $w \in W_{\bar{\alpha}, n}$ and $j \in S_w$. Then

$$\mathbf{Th(M)} \vdash \ll pi(w) \wedge w > \bar{0} \wedge B_j \gg \overset{s}{S_j} \ll \exists v \leqslant w: pi(v) \gg.$$

Proof: We have to show that for all ξ, ξ' such that $\xi D_j \xi'$, $(pi(w, \xi) \wedge w > \bar{0}) \rightarrow \exists v \leqslant w: pi(v, \xi')$.

Choose such ξ, ξ' and suppose that $(pi(w, \xi) \wedge w > \bar{0})$ holds. Let $w = (\bar{\lambda}, s)$. Again, there are two cases.

(a) $\models \bigwedge_{i=1}^{n} \neg B_i(\xi)$.
Trivial.

(b) $\models \bigvee_{i=1}^{n} B_i(\xi)$.

We have to prove $\exists v \leqslant w: pi(v, \xi')$. Note that $lh(s) \neq 0$ and $lh(s) \neq n$, because $lh(s) = 0$ or $lh(s) = n$ implies that $St_w = \varnothing$. So let

$$w = (\bar{\lambda}, <i_1, \cdots, i_k>), \qquad 1 \leqslant k < n, \{i_1, \cdots, i_k\} \subset \{1, \ldots, n\}.$$

Since $j \in St_w$, $j = i_s$ for some s, $1 \leqslant s \leqslant k$. Now $pi(w, \xi)$, so

$$\tau^{\bar{\lambda}}(\mathbf{false}) \cdot Ofseg\ (D_{i_1}, \cdots, D_{i_k});(\ \cup_{t=1,k} D_{i_t})^*(\xi),$$

i.e.

$$\exists \xi''(\tau^{\bar{\lambda}}(\mathbf{false})(\xi'') \ \wedge \xi''\ Ofseg\ (D_{i_1}, \cdots, D_{i_k});(\ \cup_{t=1,k} D_{i_t})^*\xi). \quad \text{(ii)}$$

Since

$$(\ \cup_{t=1,k} D_{i_t})^*;\ D_j \subseteq (\ \cup_{t=1,k} D_{i_t})^*$$

we obtain that

$$Ofseg(D_{i_1}, \cdots, D_{i_k});(\ \cup_{t=1,k} D_{i_t})^*; D_j \subseteq Ofseg(D_{i_1}, \cdots, D_{i_k})\ (\ \cup_{t=1,k} D_{i_t})^*.$$

From (ii) it then follows that:

$$\exists \xi'': (\tau^{\bar{\lambda}}(\mathbf{false})(\xi'') \wedge \xi'' Ofseg(D_{i_1}, \cdots, D_{i_k});\ (\ \cup_{t=1,k} D_{i_t})^*\xi'),$$

i.e.

$$(\tau^{\bar{\lambda}}(\mathbf{false}) \cdot Ofseg(D_{i_1}, \cdots, D_{i_k});\ (\ \cup_{t=1,k} D_{i_t})^*)(\xi'). \quad \text{(iii)}$$

Moreover, as in the proof of the lemma for DEC, we see that

$$p \cdot (\ \cup_{i=1,n} R_i)^*(\xi'). \quad \text{(iv)}$$

Now, (i), (iii) and (iv) imply

$$\models\ pi(\bar{\lambda}, <i_1, \cdots, i_k>, \xi'),$$

whence

$$\models\ \exists\, v \leqslant w\colon pi(v, \xi').$$

[]

Lemma: (IOE) Suppose that $\models\ \overset{s}{\ll} p \gg S \ll q \gg$ holds. Then

$$\mathbf{Th(M)} \vdash\ \overset{s}{\ll} pi(w) \wedge w > \bar{0} \gg *[\ \underset{i \in St_w}{[\,]}\ B_i \wedge\ \wedge_{j \in D_w} \neg B_j \rightarrow S_i] \ll \mathbf{true} \gg.$$

Proof: Observe that for all $w \in W_{\bar{\alpha}, n}$, $w > \bar{0}$, $D_w \neq \varnothing$. So, $S_w \subset \{1, \cdots, n\}$. It follows that the program

$$S' :: *[\underset{i \in St_w}{[\,]} B_i \wedge \bigwedge_{j \in D_w} \neg B_j \to S_i]$$

contains less directions than the original program S, so the induction hypothesis may be applied. If $S_w = \varnothing$ then by convention $S' \equiv skip$, in which case the lemma is trivial. So assume $S_w \neq \varnothing$.

After a possible renumbering, we may assume, too, that $S_w = \{1, \cdots, k\}$, $1 \leqslant k < n$. So $D_w = \{k+1, \cdots, n\}$. Let B' denote $\bigwedge_{j \in D_w} \neg B_j = \bigwedge_{j=k+1,n} \neg B_j$, and let $D_i' = B'; D_i$. By the induction assumption and $swfp$-lemma

$$\mathbf{Th(M)} \overset{s}{\vdash} \ll pi(w) \wedge w > \bar{0} \gg *([\underset{i=1,k}{[\,]} B_i \wedge \bigwedge_{j=k+1,n} \neg B_j \to S_i]) \ll \mathbf{true} \gg.$$

iff

$$(pi(w) \wedge w > \bar{0}) \to \neg SFAIR(D_1', \cdots, D_k').$$

So to prove the lemma, it suffices to show the latter. This follows from the next two claims:

Claim 1: Under the aformentioned assumptions

$$(pi(w) \wedge w > \bar{0} \to \neg UFAIR(D_1', \cdots, D_k').$$

Proof: (of Claim 1) Suppose that $pi(w, \xi) \wedge w > \bar{0}$.

Then $p \cdot (\cup_{i=1,n} D_i)^*(\xi)$ holds. Since $p \to \neg SFAIR(D_1, \cdots, D_n)$, it follows that

$$\exists \xi'': [\neg SFAIR(D_1, \cdots, D_n)(\xi'') \wedge \xi''(\cup_{i=1,n} D_i)^* \xi]$$

holds too. Thus,

$$\exists \xi'': [(\cup_{i=1,n} D_i)^* rrows \neg UFAIR(\bigwedge_{i=k+1,n} \neg B_i; D_1, \cdots, \bigwedge_{i=k+1,n} \neg B_i; D_k)(\xi'') \wedge \xi''(\cup_{i=1,n} D_i)^* \xi] \quad (\textit{U-reduction} \text{ lemma}).$$

Consequently,

$$\exists \xi'': [((\cup_{i=1,n} D_i)^* \to \neg UFAIR(D_1', \cdots, D_n'))\xi'' \wedge \xi''(\cup_{i=1,n} D_i)^* \xi],$$

from which $\neg\, UFAIR(D_1', \cdots, D_k')(\xi)$ follows by the definition of $R \rightarrow p$). This ends the proof of Claim 1.

Now, if $k=1$, the lemma follows immediately from claim 1 and the definition of $SFAIR$. So assume that $k \geqslant 2$.

Claim 2: Under the aformentioned assumptions,

$$(pi(w) \wedge w > \bar{0}) \rightarrow \bigwedge_{\substack{p \in P(n) \\ 1 \leqslant k < n}} \neg\, SFAIR_k^p(D_1, \cdots, D_n) \text{ holds.}$$

Proof: (of Claim 2) For simplicity we consider only the permutation $p = (1, \cdots, n)$. Other permutations are treated similarly. Let $1 \leqslant l < k$. By definition of $SFAIR_k^p$, we must show that $pi(w) \wedge w > \bar{0}$ implies

$$[\,(\cup_{i=1,n} D_i')^* \rightarrow \neg\, UFAIR(\neg B' \vee \wedge_{i=l+1,n} \neg B_i; D_1', \cdots,$$
$$\neg B' \vee \wedge_{i=l+1,n} \neg B_i; D_l').$$

This is a consequence of the previous definitions. The details are skipped. []

Lemma: (INIT, FIN) Suppose that $\models^{s} \ll p \gg S \ll q \gg$ holds. Then

(i) $\mathbf{Th(M)} \vdash p \rightarrow \exists v{:}\ pi(v)$.
Let a state ξ satisfy $\models p(\xi)$. If $\wedge_{i=1,n} \neg B_i(\xi)$, then we are done, because $pi(\bar{0}, \xi)$ holds. Hence, let $\vee_{i=1,n} B_i(\xi)$. That $p \cdot (\cup_{i=1,n} D_i)^*(\xi)$ holds, follows immediately. Since $p(\xi)$, also $\neg\, SFAIR\ (D_1, \ldots, D_n)(\xi)$, and consequently $\neg\, UFAIR\ (D_1, \cdots, D_n)\ (\xi)$. It follows that $pi((\bar{\alpha}, <>, \xi)$ holds.

(ii) $\mathbf{Th(M)} \vdash pi(\bar{0}) \rightarrow (\wedge_{i=1,n} \neg B_i \wedge q)$
Note that we actually showed that if

$$p \rightarrow (\neg\, SFAIR(D_1, \cdots, D_n) \wedge (\cup_{i=1,n} D_i)^*; \wedge_{i=1,n} \neg B_i \rightarrow q)$$

then

$$\mathbf{Th(M)} \vdash^{s} \ll p \gg *[\ \mathop{[]}_{i=1,n} B_i \rightarrow S_i] \ll pi(\bar{0}) \gg . \qquad (*)$$

$\mathbf{Th(M)} \vdash pi(\bar{0}) \rightarrow \wedge_{i=1}^{n} \neg B_i$ follows immediately from the definition of pi. As a consequence of the hypothesis

$$p \rightarrow ((\cup_{i=1,n} D_i)^*; \wedge_{i=1,n} \neg B_i \rightarrow q).$$

So, by (*) $\models pi(\bar{0}) \rightarrow q$. Now, $\mathbf{Th(M)} \vdash pi(\bar{0}) \rightarrow q$ follows.

These lematta conclude the completeness proof, as all clauses of the rule have been shown to apply.

6.5 The Ordinal Size for Fair-Termination Proofs

In this subsection we deal with the following question: how complicated are the well-founded sets needed in order to prove fair termination? In other words, what is the size of the corresponding ordinals parametrizing *pi*.

Though the issue is *not* of syntactic nature, it is dealt with in this chapter because the connection with coding and arithmetical structures, and the heavy use $\mathbf{L}_\mu$ makes of ordinals.

For a typical repetition statement $S \in GC$, let α_S be the *least* ordinal for which there exist *w* and *pi* enabling a proof of fair termination, say using one variant of the helpful directions method. So, our problem is to bound α_S. To this end, we first assume that *S* computes over an arithmetical structure, and the coding mechanisms mentioned in the first section are available.

The fully detailed discussion of the issue involves a lot of *recursion-theoretic* machinery, that may be found, for example, in [RO 67]. We outline the main result at a rather intuitive level, avoiding the formalities of *notations* for ordinals. A somewhat more technical presentation, relying on the reduction of fairness to random assignments, appears in [AP 82].

In order to make the connection with effectiveness as treated in recursion theory, we use the following definition of a *tree.*

Definition:

1. A *tree* is a set of finite sequence of natural number which is prefix closed and partially ordered by the *extension* relation.
2. A tree is *recursive* iff the set of *codes* of its elements is recursive.

In other words, for a recursive tree there is an algorithm that can determine, for an arbitrary natural number *n*, whether *n* is the code of an element of the tree (i.e. a finite sequence).

Definition: A tree is well-founded if it does not contain an infinite descending sequence of elements (i.e. an infinite sequence of finite sequences, each extending its predecessor).

The reader should be able to connect these definitions to the way execution trees and paths were described before, and the coding techniques mentioned in this chapter.

As manifested in previous (semantic) completeness proofs, there is a standard natural way of ranking a well-founded tree with ordinals. Each leaf (i.e. maximal element under extension) is ranked with 0, and by transfinite induction, each nonleaf element is ranked by the *least* ordinal greater than the ranks of its immediate descendants. The ordinal ranking the root (the minimal element under extension) is called the *height* of the tree.

Definition: An ordinal is *recursive* iff it is the height of a recursive tree.

Another recursion-theoretic notion needed is the code (or *index)* of a partial recursive function. As is well known, the set of partial recursive functions is *enumerable* (in any of a variety of ways, which are immaterial in this context). Denote by $\{x\}$ the partial recursive function with code x, $x \in N$. Thus $\{x\}y$ means applying the function with code x to the argument y. We can regard $\{x\}$ also as a code of a tree by identifying it with its characteristic function. The main theorem identifies the recursive ordinals with fair ordinals of *GC* programs.

Theorem: (recursive fair ordinals)

i. For every $S \in GC$, α_S is a recursive ordinal.
ii. If α is a recursive ordinal, then there exists a *GC* program S (over an arithmetic structure), s.t. $\alpha < \alpha_S$ (actually, $\alpha_S \leqslant \omega\alpha$).

Proof:

i. An exact proof would need a formal definition of the operational semantics of *GC*, yielding execution trees. By again applying standard coding it should be clear that the execution tree T_S is recursive, and therefore α_S is also recursive.
ii. To show this part, we produce, for each recursive α, a *GC* program S, s.t. $\alpha < \alpha_S$. Intuitively, S systematically *searches* through a given recursive tree. The program presented here (see Figure 6.1) is a variant on a similar program in [AP 82], due to Rob Gerth.

To understand how S operates note first, that $\{x\}y$ represents a *divergent* computation if the partial function with code x is *undefined* on y.

While S is in is first stage (i.e. *stage*$=0$), it attempts to repeatedly extend an (initially empty) finite sequence u, with a random element v, as long as u is in $\{x\}$. Once a u is found outside the tree $\{x\}$, S passes to its second stage, where a random w is tested for membership in the tree $\{x\}$. Thus, well foundedness is tested in the first stage and totalness–in the second stage. We can now show

Claim: S fairly terminates iff x is the code of a recursive well-founded tree, say of height α.

```
S:: u:=<>, b:=false; stage:=0;
*[stage=0 ∧ ¬b→z:={x}u;
        [z=0 → stage:=1; w:=0
        []
        z=1 → b:=true; v:=0
        ]
[]
stage=0 ∧ b    → v:=v+1
[]
stage=0 ∧ b    → b:=false; u:=u conc v
[]
stage=1        → w:=w+1
[]
stage=1        → w:={x}w; stage:=2
].
```

Figure 6.1 A program searching a recursive tree.

First, let x be such a code. Then, as $\{x\}$ is well-founded, the first stage can be repeated finitely often only. In the second stage, the test $\{x\}w$ terminates, since $\{x\}$ is recursive. For the other direction, assume S does not fairly terminate. There are two cases:

Case 1: The first stage is repeated infinitely often. This means that $\{x\}$ is not a well-founded tree.

Case 2: $\{x\}w$ fails to terminate. This means that $\{x\}$ is not *total.*

In both cases $\{x\}$ is not a recursive well-founded tree, establishing the claim.

A further analysis of the computations of S establishes the ω-blowup in the associated ordinal, finishing the proof. [ ]

Clearly, the program S "takes advantage" of the coding ability avaialble in computing over arithmetic structures. So, it is interesting to see how complicated can α_S become for "natural" programs S, not using any explicit codings. The following examples, taken from [AO 83], show that all ordinals α, $\alpha < \omega \cdot \omega^\omega$ are necessary. For each natural number n, a program S_n is presented, such that $\beta = \omega^n$ is its number of rounds (see Chapter 3). Thus, $\omega \cdot \omega^\omega$ is needed for counting rounds in the family $\mathbf{S} = \{S_n \mid n > 0\}$, establishing the requirement.

The idea of the construction is to force a behaviour of n nested, unbounded, loops.

For S_1 (see Figure 6.2), the following behaviour is induced.

```
S1:: *[x1>0 ∧ 1≤q≤3 → [q=1 → x1:=x1+1
                       []
                       q=2 → skip
                       []
                       q=3 → q:=2
                       ]
     []
      x1>0 ∧ 1≤q≤3 → [q=1 → q:=3
                       []
                       q=2 → x1:=x1-1; q:=3
                       []
                       q=3 → skip
                       ]
                      ]
```

Figure 6.2 S_1: ω^1 *rounds.*

The effect of executing the first stage with $q = 1$ is choosing a random x_1. Then, in the second stage, x_1 is decremented by 1 once in every two rounds.

Suppose, inductively, that S_{n-1} has been constructed, using variables $x_1, \cdots, x_{n-1}$ and q. Assume also it has a similar two-stages structure, with the guard

$$x_1 > 0 \wedge x_2 \geqslant 0 \wedge \cdots \wedge x_{n-1} \geqslant 0 \wedge 1 \leqslant q \leqslant 2(n-1) + 1.$$

Finally, assume that each stage is a choice between branches for every value of q.

The following changes are made to obtain S_n from S_{n-1} as above.

(1) The top level guards are replaced by

$$x_1 > 0 \wedge x_2 \geqslant \wedge \cdots \wedge x_{n-1} \geqslant 0 \wedge x_n \geqslant 0 \wedge 1 \leqslant q \leqslant 2n+1.$$

(2) The part

$$[\,]\, q = 2(n-1) + 1 \rightarrow q{:=}2(n-1)$$

is replaced by

$$\begin{array}{ll} [\,]\, q=2(n-1)+1 & \rightarrow q{:=}2n+1 \\ [\,]\, q=2n \wedge x_n > 0 & \rightarrow x_n{:=}x_n-1;\ q{:=}2n+1 \\ [\,]\, q=2n \wedge x_n = 0 & \rightarrow q{:=}2(n-1) \\ [\,]\, q=2n+1 & \rightarrow \mathit{skip}. \end{array}$$

(3) The part

$$[\,]\ q=2(n-1)+1 \ \rightarrow\ skip$$

is replaced by

$$[\,]\ q=2(n-1)+1 \ \rightarrow\ x_n:=x_n+1$$

$$[\,]\ q=2n \ \rightarrow\ skip$$

$$[\,]\ q=2n+1 \ \rightarrow\ q:=2n.$$

An inductive argument yields the result that indeed S_n has ω^n rounds, as claimed.

No "natural" more complicated fairly terminating programs have been discussed in the literature. Also, it is an open problem of characterizing the fair ordinals of programs computing an arbitrary structures where coding is impossible.

CHAPTER 7
Fairness in Temporal Logic

7.0 Overview

In this chapter a different pattern of reasoning is introduced, known as *temporal-reasoning.* It uses a notation which is directly interpreted on infinite sequences (or trees) which, in turn, can be used to represent the evolution in time of the program state. An important distinguished characteristic of this approach (as presented here) is its being *endogenous,* i.e. it considers the set of complete computation sequences (or trees) as given, and reasons directly about the behavior of the *whole* program.

Thus, given a program, the reasoning is factored as follows:

a) define the set of all its computation histories,
b) prove any required property in terms of these histories, independently of the program.

This may be contrasted with the *exogenous* approach of the proof rules in previous chapters, where the rules related properties of the whole program to properties of its parts.

One consequence of this distinction is that the temporal approach is more suitable for dealing with programs presented as *transition systems* in contrast to the exogenous systems, that fit nicely in dealing with well-structured programs. Recently several attempts were made to provide temporal semantics in a more structured, compositional way.

Another observation is that the temporal approach is rather more powerful for general *liveness* properties, of which termination is just a special case. Hence, in dealing with fair termination of *GC* programs, one does not take full advantage of the whole power of the system. Consequently, we deviate in this chapter from the previous focuses on *GC* and on fair termination. Instead, we present the theory in terms of unstructured transition systems and the more general liveness properties.

The first application of *temporal reasoning* to establish several *liveness* properties (in a context of cyclic, nonterminating concurrent programs) appears in [F 76] and [FP 78]. There, program properties are described as depending explicitly on *time* which is referred to by quantifying over time variables. A typical description of a property that states "whenever event *A* occurs, event *B* will eventually follow", would be $\forall t \exists t' \geqslant t$: $A(t) \rightarrow B(t')$. Later, Pnueli suggested [PN 77, PN 81] the use of (*linear time*) *temporal logic* (**LTL**)," which has special *temporal operators* hiding the explicit quantification over time and making the expressibility of many program properties concise and compact. The idea of using a *modality* for the description of program properties can be traced back to [BU 74].

Later, another approach appeared, which takes as the interpretation domain trees instead of sequences. It became known as "branching time Temporal Logic (**BTL**)". The issue of the comparative merits of the two approaches has not been finally settled yet.

Recently, [MP 83] gave a general methodology for "cooking a temporal semantics" for an arbitrary programming language. In the next section, we basically follow this methodology and apply it to example languages for parallel programming. According to this methodology, one first presents a "general part" (or the "pure" part) of **LTL**, which is independent of any programming language or data domain. We give an expository description of this part, avoiding the discussion of its deductive system. Then, one adds axioms to characterize the data domains. As in previous chapters, we avoid this stage also, considering on examples dealing with natural numbers and truth values, taken to be known. Finally, one adds axioms and proof rules to capture the restrictions imposed on sequences so as to generate a model consisting of all and only execution sequences of a given program. Similar rules appear also in [MP 84]. A thorough description of this method of reasoning can be found in [MP ??] which contains further references. A closely related method is presented in [OL 82]. The first application of the temporal logic framework to fairness appears in [GPSS 80].

Then, a section is devoted to the **BTL** (Branching Time) treatment of fairness. The two basic works in this area, which our presentation follows, are [QS 83] and [EL 85]. Most of the research in **BTL** deals with its propositional level, attempting to answer classical questions regarding decidability and its complexity, axiomatizability, etc. We discuss only the issues directly connected to expressibility of fairness. In the literature, there are no **BTL**-based proof rules for fair termination directly associated with programs.

7.1 Linear-Time Temporal-Logic (LTL)

In this subsection we introduce the notation and interpretation of the general part of **LTL**, that is independent of any programming language. The basic purpose of this logic is to make assertions about (linear) infinite sequences and prove them. The relative progression within a sequence represents the advance of time, which is taken here to be isomorphic to the natural numbers.

We start with some fixed first-order language L (with equality). The variables of L are partitioned into two disjoint subsets, V_L (local variables) and V_G (global variables). Quantification is permitted only over global variables. We assume an interpretation **I** of L in the usual way; in particular, **I** assigns values (from the appropriate domain) to global variables. As before, we do not consider the details of the data-domain dependencies.

Formation rules for well-formed formulas (wffs):

(1) every wff of L belongs to **LTL**.
(2) if $A \in$ **LTL** so are:

  oA (pronounced *nexttime* A)
  FA (pronounced *eventually* A),
  GA (pronounced *henceforth* A).

(3) if $A, B \in$ **LTL**, so is A**U**B (pronounced A *until* B).

These operators are called *temporal operators.* A formula without temporal operators is referred to also as (anticipating the program-part) a *state formula.*

Semantics of **LTL**:. Assume some fixed interpretation **I** of L, to simplify the discussion. A *structure* for **LTL** is an *infinite* sequence of states $\pi = \sigma_0, \sigma_1, \cdots, \sigma_i, \cdots$ where each state σ assigns values to all *local* variables. Denote by $\pi^{(i)}$ the sequence $\pi^{(i)} = \sigma_i, \sigma_{i+1}, \cdots$ the *i-truncation* of π. A sequence π is a *model* of a formula $A \in$ **LTL**, denoted by $\pi \models A$, whenever the following recursive definition holds:

i. $A \in L$: the usual notion of first-order truth.
ii. $A = oB$: iff $\pi^{(1)} \models B$.
iii. $A = \mathbf{F}B$: iff there exists a $k \geqslant 0$, such that $\pi^{(k)} \models B$.
iv. $A = \mathbf{G}B$: iff for every $k \geqslant 0$, $\pi^{(k)} \models B$.
v. $A = B\,\mathbf{U}C$: iff there exists a $k \geqslant 0$ such that

$$\pi^{(k)} \models C, \quad \text{and for every } j, 0 \leqslant j < k, \quad \pi^{(j)} \models B.$$

Thus, π satisfies **F**B iff some tail of it satisfies B, and π satisfies **G**B iff all its tails satisfy B. For B a state formula, this means eventual-occurrence and invariance, respectively. Also π satisfies A**U**B if it has a tail satisfying B and all previous tails satisfy A. For state formulas, this means that B eventually occurs and A holds in all states up to that moment. A formula $A \in \mathbf{LTL}$ is *valid*, denoted by $\models A$, iff for every π, $\pi \models A$ (actually, one has to vary also all possible interpretations $\mathbf{I}$; we do not bother with this here). For Π a set of structures (sequences), we are also interested in Π-*validity*, denoted by $\Pi \models A$, which holds iff for every π, $\pi \in \Pi$ implies $\pi \models A$.

Following are some examples of valid **LTL** formulas.

1. $\mathbf{G}A \longleftrightarrow \neg \mathbf{F} \neg A, \quad \mathbf{F}A \longleftrightarrow \neg \mathbf{G} \neg A.$
   These two formulas express the *duality* of **G** and **F**, which is a main characteristic of the linearity of **LTL**, distinguishing it from branching line temporal logics. For A a state formula, it means that eventual occurrences of A is the same as the non-invariance of $\neg A$. A detailed discussion of this duality appears in [LA 80].
2. $\mathbf{F}(A \wedge B) \rightarrow \mathbf{F}A \wedge \mathbf{F}B.$
   For state formulas, this means that the eventual conjunctive occurrence implies the eventual occurrence of each conjunct. Note that the converse implication is *not* valid, since each conjunct can occur at a different time with never both conjuncts occurring simultaneously.
3. $\mathbf{G}A \longleftrightarrow A \wedge \mathrm{o}\mathbf{G}A, \quad \mathbf{F}A \longleftrightarrow A \vee \mathrm{o}\mathbf{F}A.$
   These formulas serve as *fixedpoint characterization* of the corresponding temporal operators. The first, interpreted for A a state formula, means that to be invariant is the same as to hold currently and be invariant at the next time. Similarly, the second means that to occur eventually is the same as occurrence at present, or eventual occurrence next time.
4. $A\mathbf{U}B \rightarrow \mathbf{F}B$ – obvious.

Many further examples of valid **LTL** formulas, including ones involving quantification, can be found in [MP ??] and in the extensive literature on temporal logic.

There is a complete deductive system for *provability* of valid **LTL** formulas, the details of which can be found also in [MP ??]. As is usual with formalized proofs, they tend to be very tedious. In the next section, we present several derived high-level proof principles which apply to models originating from programs, and some sample proofs.

Finally, we present some non-valid temporal formulas, that can be regarded as specifications (of the intended models). Again, more of these can be found in [MP ??] or in [PN 81]. The informal meaning is explained in terms of state formulas A, B.

1)	$A \rightarrow \mathbf{F}B$	If A is presently true, B will eventually become true.
2)	$\mathbf{G}(A \rightarrow \mathbf{F}B)$	Whenever A becomes true it will eventually be followed by B becoming true.

3)	$\mathbf{FG}A$	At some future instant A will become continuously true.
4)	$\mathbf{F}(A \wedge \circ \neg A)$	There will be a future instant such that A is true at that instant and false at the next.
5)	$\mathbf{GF}A$	Every future instant is followed by a later one in which A is true; thus A is true *infinitely often.*
6)	$\mathbf{G}(A \rightarrow \mathbf{G}B)$	If A ever becomes true, then B is true at that instant and ever after.
7)	$\mathbf{G}A \vee (A\mathbf{U}B)$	Either A holds continuously or it holds until an occurrence of B. This is the weak form of the *until* operator that states that A will hold continuously until the first occurrence of B if B ever happens, or indefinitely otherwise.
8)	$\mathbf{F}A \rightarrow ((\neg A)\mathbf{U}B)$	If A ever happens, its first occurrence is preceded by (or coincides with) B.

This kind of expressibility is particularly useful for the direct expressibility of fairness in the formalism. Consider:

i. **FG** *enabled*→**GF** *selected* (weak fairness);
ii. **GF** *enabled*→**GF** *selected* (strong fairness).

Here *"enabled"* and *"selected"* are names for some state formulas with the obvious interpretation.

7.1.1 The temporal semantics of programs

In this subsection we consider a *program P* given as a *transition system.* Such a system can be thought of as a directed graph: the nodes are labeled *locations,* $L = \{l_0, \cdots, l_n\}$; the arcs are labeled guarded transitions of the form $\tau = (p_\tau, f_\tau)$, where p_τ is an *enabling condition* and f_τ is the associated *state transformation.* It is convenient to assume that f_τ is deterministic and defined on all states satisfying p_τ. Let $\tau\tau$ be the set of all transitions. The state is considered to have, in addition to the usual program variables, a *location-counter* variable λ with values in L. For τ originating in a node labeled l and ending in a node labeled l' we assume, by convention, that p_τ implies $\lambda = l$ and f_τ maps λ to l'.

A fixed precondition p is assumed, restricting all legal initial states. By convention, p always implies $\lambda = l_0$, i.e., the execution starts in the *entry label.*

Finally, we associate with P two families of sets of transitions $\boldsymbol{W} = \{T_1^w, \cdots, T_{nw}^w\}$, $\boldsymbol{S} = \{T_1^s, \cdots, T_{ns}^s\}$, $nw, ns \geqslant 0$. Elements of $\boldsymbol{W}$ are sets of transition with respect to which weak fairness is assumed, while elements of $\boldsymbol{S}$ are sets of transition with respect to which strong fairness is assumed. Unconditional fairness can be similarly treated and is omitted (its proof rule does not underly that of the others in this context).

A set of transitions T is said to be enabled iff $\bigvee_{\tau \in \tau T} p_\tau$ holds.

Definition: An *initialized computation* π is an infinite sequence $\pi = \sigma_0, \sigma_1, \sigma_2, \cdots$, such that:

1) $\sigma_0 \models p$;
2) for each pair of consecutive states (σ_i, σ_{i+1}) (called a *step* in π) there exists a $\tau \in \tau\tau$ such that $\sigma_i \models p_\tau$ and $\sigma_{i+1} = f_\tau(\sigma_i)$. We say that τ is *taken* at the state;
3) for each $T^w \in \boldsymbol{W}$, either π contains infinitely many states not satisfying $\bigvee_{\tau \in T^w} p_\tau$, or for infinitely many steps some transition $\tau \in T^w$ is taken;
4) for each $T^s \in \boldsymbol{S}$, either from some state onwards $\bigvee_{\tau \in T^s} p_\tau$ does not hold, or for infinitely many steps some transition $\tau \in T^s$ is taken.

An *admissible* computation is the (infinite) tail of an initialized one.

Note that up to this point, no assumption about concurrency is made. One point of discrepancy, enforced by the fact that temporal logic is interpreted in infinite sequences, is the representation of terminating computations. By convention, this is done by indefinitely replicating the last element of the sequence associated with a terminating computation.

Definition: A state σ is *terminal* if $\sigma \models \neg \bigvee_{\tau \in \tau\tau} p_\tau$; we abbreviate $\neg \bigvee_{\tau \in \tau\tau} p_\tau$ to *term*.

Definition: Let $A, B \in$ **LTL** be two (accessible) state formulas. We say that $\tau \in \tau\tau$ *leads from A to B*, iff for every two states σ, σ' such that $\sigma \models p_\tau$ and $\sigma' = f_\tau(\sigma)$: if $\sigma \models A$ then $\sigma' \models B$.

This is another formulation of the *verification-condition* associated with τ.

Denote by A_P the set of all admissible computation sequences associated with a (fixed) program P. We wish to introduce some rules for characterizing validity in A_P.

The rule **INIT** (see Figure 7.1) states that any property that is invariant on states of initialized computations is invariant for all admissible computations. It expresses that **G**A is hereditary from a sequence to all its suffixes (tails).

The rule **TRNS** (see Figure 7.2) summarizes derivation of facts due to a single transition. The first premise covers all "real" transitions by showing that they lead from A to B. The second premise handles the "water treading" nature of terminal states.

$$\frac{p \rightarrow \mathbf{G}A}{\mathbf{G}A}$$

Figure 7.1 Rule **INIT** (initialization).

$$\frac{\begin{array}{l}\forall \tau \in \tau\tau\text{: } \tau \textit{ leads from } A \textit{ to} B\\ (A \wedge term) \rightarrow B\end{array}}{A \rightarrow \mathrm{o}B}$$

Figure 7.2 Rule **TRNS** (transition).

A useful derived rule is **INV** (see Figure 7.3), which can be used to establish partial correctness properties of P.

The rule **INV** captures the essence of invariance in a transition system as a property holding in the initial state and being preserved by every transition. To represent the Floyd-Hoare-like annotation, one would construct A of the form

$$\bigwedge_{l \in L}(\lambda = l \rightarrow A_l)$$

where A_l is the inductive assertion attached to l.

Liveness properties which are independent of fairness are proved by the usual appeal to induction on some well-founded, partially-ordered, set, given as such by the data-domain part. As an example, we introduce the following rule **F-WIND** (see Figure 7.4). Similar rules may be introduced for other special forms of liveness properties. α ranges over elements of a well-founded set, ordered by $<$.

We now turn our attention to further restricting the models to include all and only fair sequences. Before presenting the rules, we would like to draw the reader's attention to the fact that in this model fairness can be treated in a more flexible way than was presented in the previous frameworks. For example, one can have both weak *and* strong fairness in the same program, attributed to different sets of transition families. Also, the fair scheduling is not necessarily among individual transitions (that correspond to individual directions in the framework we had so far); rather, the scheduling is of sets of transitions, with each member equally well representing the whole set. Though these ideas can be incorporated

$$\frac{\begin{array}{l}p \rightarrow A\\ \forall \tau \in \tau\tau\text{: } \tau \textit{ leads from } A \textit{ to } A\end{array}}{\mathbf{G}A}$$

Figure 7.3 Rule **INV** (invariance).

$$\frac{A(\alpha) \rightarrow \mathbf{F}(B \vee \exists \beta\text{: } \beta < \alpha \wedge A(\beta))}{A(\alpha) \rightarrow \mathbf{F}B}$$

Figure 7.4 Rule **F-WIND** (well-founded **F**-induction).

in the structured models, they are less natural in that context, while fitting rather naturally to general transition systems without a syntactically-imposed structure.

The semantic justification of the rule **Temp-WFAIR** (see Figure 7.5) resembles the arguments in the soundness proofs of the *GC* rules. Consider any admissible sequence satisfying $A \wedge \mathbf{G}(\bigvee_{\tau \in T^w} p_\tau)$ but not $A\mathbf{U}B$. By the first premise, once A holds, it may cease to hold for a suffix of π only in case B holds for that suffix. Hence, $A\mathbf{U}B$ may fail to hold only if B never holds, in which case A holds invariantly throughout π. Since by assumption T^w is continuously enabled, and no $\tau \in T^w$ has been been taken (otherwise B could hold by the second premise) π is not weakly fair. Thus, for all weakly fair sequences the consequence holds whenever the premises do.

A similar reasoning yields the rule **Temp-SFAIR** for strong fairness (see Figure 7.6). In both cases, the consequence ensures, in particular, that $\mathbf{F}B$ holds.

We terminate the presentation of the program-dependent rules by a yet higher-level rule, which is the temporal analog of the helpful-directions method.

Definition: For a set of transition $T \subseteq \tau\tau$, T *leads* from A to B iff every $\tau \in T$ leads from A to B. We also abreviate $\bigvee_{\tau \in T}$ to *enabled* (T).

Let $(W, \leqslant)$ be a partially-ordered, well-founded set, and let $A(w)$ be a W-parametrized state formula. Also, let $h_w\colon W \to [1..nw]$, $h_s\colon W \to [1..ns]$ be functions, called the *helpfulness* functions, which identify, for each $0 < w \in W$, helpful weak, and strong, fairness-sets $T^w_{h_w(w)} \in \mathbf{W}$, $T^s_{h_s(w)} \in \mathbf{S}$, respectively, reducing w in A.

for some $T^w \in \mathbf{W}$:

$\forall \tau \in \tau\tau$: τ *leads from* A *to* $A \vee B$

$\forall \tau \in T^w$: τ *leads from* A *to* B

$A \rightarrow [\ B \vee \bigvee_{\tau \in T^w} p_\tau)\ ]$

$A \rightarrow A\mathbf{U}B$

Figure 7.5 Rule **Temp-WFAIR** (temporal weak fairness).

for *some* $T^s \in \mathbf{S}$:

$\forall \tau \in \tau\tau$: τ *leads from* A *to* $A \vee B$

$\forall \tau \in T^s$: τ *leads from* A *to* B

$A \rightarrow \mathbf{F}[\ B \vee \bigvee_{\tau \in T^w} p_\tau)\ ]$

$A \rightarrow A\mathbf{U}B$

Figure 7.6 Rule **Temp-SFAIR** (temporal strong fairness).

The reader may easily recognize the similarity of the rules **Temp-WWell**, **Temp-SWell** (see Figures 7.7 and 7.8) with the previous formulation of the helpful directions method. We adopted here the version where it is not necessary to reach a minimal w in order to reach the required condition B. The recursive nature of the rule for strong fairness is hidden in clause EVENT, which requires the proof of another eventuality. However, it has to be established w.r.t. $\tau\tau - T^s_{h_s(w)}$, namely a syntactically smaller set of transitions, and hence recursive applications of the rule do terminate. The semantic justification of soundness is the usual one, and is omitted.

An interesting difference between **Temp-SWell** and **SFT** is that the temporal version allows intermediate *increase* in the well-founded variant, as long as an *eventual-decrease* is guaranteed.

In the case of finite-state programs, the **Temp-Well** rules may be simplified. Instead of using parametrized invariants $A(w)$, a *finite* sequence of *indexed* assertions A_j, $1 \leqslant j \leqslant r$, may be used. The proof can then be *diagramatically* presented in certain way, referred to as a *chain* (similar to the *proof-lattice* in [OL 82]). We thus obtain the following two **CHAIN** rules (see Figure 7.9 for **W-CHAIN**).

In order to obtain the corresponding **S-CHAIN** rule for strong fairness in finite-state programs, we use $T^s_{k_i}$ instead of $T^w_{k_i}$ and replace the C clause in **W-CHAIN** by

$$A_i \rightarrow \mathbf{F}[(\bigvee_{j<i} A_j) \vee Enabled(T^s_{k_i})].$$

(INIT): $\exists w\colon A(w)$

(NOINC): τ *leads from* $A(w)$ *to* $B \vee (\exists v\colon v \leqslant w \wedge A(v))$, for every $\tau \in \tau\tau$

(DEC): $T^w_{h_w}(w)$ *leads from* $A(w)$ *to* $B \vee (\exists v\colon v < w \wedge A(v))$

(ENABLE): $A(w) \rightarrow [\ B \vee \exists v\colon v < w \wedge A(v) \vee Enabled(T^w_{h_w}(w))\ ]$

$$(\exists v\colon A(v))\mathbf{U}B$$

Figure 7.7 Rule **Temp-WWell** (temporal well-founded weak liveness).

(INIT): $\exists w\colon A(w)$

(NOINC): τ *leads from* $A(w)$ *to* $B \vee (\exists v\colon v \leqslant w \wedge A(v))$, for every $\tau \in \tau\tau$

(DEC): $T^s_{h_s}(w)$ *leads from* $A(w)$ *to* $B \vee (\exists v\colon v < w \wedge A(v))$

(EVENT): $\tau\tau - T^s_{h_s(w)}$: $A(w) \rightarrow \mathbf{F}[B \vee \exists v\colon v < w \wedge A(v) \vee Enabled(T^s_{h_s}(w))\ ]$

$$(\exists v\colon A(v))\mathbf{U}B$$

Figure 7.8 Rule **Temp-SWell** (temporal well-founded strong liveness).

Let $A_0, A_1, \cdots, A_r$ be a sequence of assertions satisfying:

A. For $i = 1, \cdots, r$

$$\tau\tau \text{ leads from } A_i \text{ to } (\bigvee_{j \leqslant i} A_j)$$

B. For $i = 1, \cdots, r$ there exists a k_i, such that:

$$T^w_{k_i} \text{ leads from } A_i \text{ to } (\bigvee_{j<i} A_j)$$

C. For $i = 1, \cdots, r$ and k_i as above:

$$A_i \rightarrow [(\bigvee_{j<i} A_j) \bigvee Enabled(T^w_{k_i})].$$

$$(\bigvee_{i=0,r} A_i) \rightarrow (\bigvee_{i=1,r} A_i) \mathbf{U} A_0$$

Figure 7.9 Rule **W-CHAIN**.

In order to obtain a diagram representation for the application of the **CHAIN** rules, we do the following:

Anticipating the example in the next section, we choose all the fairness-sets as the set of all transistions of some process P_k.

The nodes of the diagram correspond to the assertions $A_1, \cdots, A_n$. For each two accessible states σ_i, (satisfying A_i) and σ_j (satisfying A_j) and a process (fairness-set) P_k such that $\sigma_i \overset{P_k}{\rightarrow} \sigma_j$, we draw an edge $- - - - \rightarrow$ from the node A_i to the node A_j and label it by P_k, the process responsible for the transition: $A_i \overset{P_k}{- - - - \rightarrow} A_j$. All edges corresponding to the *helpful process* P_{k_i} are drawn as $A_i \overset{P_{k_i}}{=====>} A_j$.

In order for a diagram to represent a valid proof by the **W-CHAIN** rule the following conditions must hold:

- Every successor of an accessible A_i-state, for $i > 0$, satisfies some A_j, $j \geqslant 0$.
- For every edge connecting A_i to A_j, we must have $i \geqslant j$.
- For every edge connecting A_i to A_j, and labeled by P_{k_i} we must have $i > j$.
- For every accessible state σ, if $i > 0$ is the lowest index such that σ satisfies A_i, then P_{k_i} must be enabled on σ.

In order to present examples of application of temporal reasoning, we describe two languages for concurrent programming in this framework.

The first one uses *shared variables* and the second one uses *message passing*. For the first one, we prove liveness properties of some sample programs. The second one is brought in order to examplify the flexibility of the temporal formation and the transition-system model in *specifying* more elaborate fairness requirements.

7.1.1.1 Shared variables

A program P in this model is conceived as a *concurrent composition* of some fixed number n of *processes,* P_i, $i = 1, \cdots, n$. Thus, P:: $[P_1 \parallel \cdots \parallel P_n]$. Each process is represented as a transition system. It is assumed that all the program variables $\bar{y} = (y_1, \cdots, y_n)$ are *shared* among all processes. In addition, each process P_i has its own *location-counter* variable λ_i, taking values in $L^i = \{l_0^i, \cdots, l_{n_i}^i\}$, the set of labels in P_i. The L^i's form a partition of L. We consider l_0^i to be the *entry* label of P_i, and $l_{n_i}^i$ its *exit* label, whose reachability means termination of P_i.

The following transition forms are present:

1) τ: $l \overset{c(\bar{y}) \,\to\, \bar{y} := h(\bar{y})}{- - - - \to} l'$

where $c(\bar{y})$ is a Boolean condition (guard) and $h(\bar{y})$ is a function on the program variables. For this transition occurring in P_i,

$$p_\tau(\lambda, \bar{y}) = (\lambda_i = l \wedge c(\bar{y})), \text{ and } f_\tau(\lambda, \bar{y}) = (\lambda_{l'}^{\lambda_i}, h(\bar{y})).$$

2) τ: $l \overset{request(y_j)}{- - - - \to} l'$

This is a *synchronization* transition (semaphore-like). We have:

$$p_\tau(\lambda, \bar{y}) = (\lambda_i = l \wedge y_j > 0), \text{ and } f_\tau(\lambda, \bar{y}) = \left[\lambda_{l'}^{\lambda_i}, \bar{y} \,\big|\, {}^{y_j}_{y_j - 1}\right].$$

We further stipulate that whenever present, a request transition is the *only* edge leaving a node, i.e. has no alternative.

As the weak fairness sets we take $\mathbf{W} = \{P_1, \cdots, P_n\}$. In other words, we assume weak fairness on the process level: whenever some process is continuously enabled, it will eventually make a transition. This reflects the fact that executing P is an *interleaving* of its processes.

As the strong fairness sets we choose $\mathbf{S} = \{\{e_{r_1},\}, \cdots, \{e_{r_{n_r}}\}\}$, the set of *all* singletons corresponding to the request transitions. Thus, each semaphore operation is treated separately strongly-fair. Note that such a model would be harder to represent within the uniform framework imposed by the syntactically-structured approach. A somewhat more general language for shared variables concurrency is defined in a similar way in [MP 84].

Sample proofs

We start by illustrating diagram proofs by two examples. The first demonstrates a complex invariance proof accompanied by a relatively simple liveness proof. The other example demonstrates a more involved liveness proof with a relatively easy invariance proof. The examples are taken from [MP 84].

Example: (mutual exclusion) The program *PF* (see Figure 7.10), due to Peterson-Fischer [PF 77], provides a distributed solution for achieving *mutual exclusion* without semaphores, a central problem in concurrent computations.

The critical sections are segments to which provision of exclusive access is needed. It is assumed that both critical and noncritical sections do not modify the variables y_1, t_1, y_2 and t_2. Also the critical sections always terminate.

The basic idea of the protection mechanism of this program is that when competing for the access rights to the critical sections, P_1 attempts to make $y_1 = y_2$ in statements l_1^1 to l_4^1, while P_2 attempts to make

---

PF:: $(y_1, t_1, y_2, t_2) := (\perp, \perp, \perp, \perp)$; $[P_1 \,||\, P_2]$.

P_1:: l_0^1: *noncritical−section*$_1$

l_1^1: $t_1 :=$ if $y_2 = ff$ *then* ff *else* tt

l_2^1: $y_1 := t_1$

l_3^1: if $y_2 \neq \perp$ *then* $t_1 := y_2$

l_4^1: $y_1 := t_1$

l_5^1: *loop while* $y_1 = y_2$

\- -

l_6^1: *critical−section*$_1$

$(y_1, t_1) := (\perp, \perp)$

\- -

l_7^1: *goto* l_0^1

P_2:: l_0^2: *noncritical−section*$_2$

l_1^2: $t_2 :=$ if $y_1 = true$ *then* ff *else* tt

l_2^2: $y_2 := t_2$

l_3^2: if $y_1 \neq \perp$ *then* $t_2 = \neg\, y_1$

l_4^2: $y_2 := t_2$

l_5^2: *loop while* $\neg\, y_2 = y_1$

\- -

l_6^2: *critical−section*$_2$

$(y_2, t_2) := (\perp, \perp)$

\- -

l_7^2: *goto* l_0^2

Figure 7.10 Mutual exclusion (Peterson-Fischer).

$\neg y_2 = y_1$ in statements l_1^2 to l_4^2. The synchronization variables y_1 and y_2 range over the set $\{\bot, ff, tt\}$, where $\bot$ signifies no interest in entering the critical section. The partial operator $\neg$ is defined by

$$\neg\, tt = ff, \qquad \neg\, ff = tt, \qquad \neg \bot \text{ is undefined.}$$

Hence in writing $\neg y_2 = y_1$ we also imply that $y_1 \neq \bot$. Protection is essentially assured by the fact that when both processes compete on the entry to the critical section, both $y_1 \neq \bot$ and $y_2 \neq \bot$. Under these assumptions, the entry conditions to the critical sections, $y_1 \neq y_2$ and $\neg y_2 \neq y_1$ respectively, cannot both be true at the same time.

When P_1 gets to l_5^1 it waits until $y_1 \neq y_2$ and then enters the critical section. This condition is satisfied either if $y_2 = \bot$ (since $y_1 \neq \bot$ at l_5^1), implying that P_2 is not currently interested in entering the critical section, or if $y_1 = \neg y_2$ (and $y_1 \neq \bot$) which implies that P_2 reached l_5^2 *after* P_1 got to l_5^1. This is because in l_1^1 to l_4^1, P_1 attempts to set $y_1 = y_2$; if now P_1 finds $y_1 = \neg y_2$ at l_5^1, it knows that P_2 changed the value of y_2 *after* P_1 last read this value. This argument is only intuitive since P_2 may have changed y_2 after P_1 last read it and yet arrive at l_5^2 before P_1 arrived at l_5^1. This is why we need a formal proof of both protection and liveness.

Symmetrically, when P_2 arrives as l_5^2 it waits unti $\neg y_2 \neq y_1$. This can occur only if $y_1 = \bot$, implying that P_1 is not currently interested in entering the critical section, or if $y_2 = y_1$ (and $y_1 \neq \bot$) which now implies that P_1 modified the value of y_1 after P_2 last read it. This is because in l_1^2 to l_4^2, P_2 attempts to make $\neg y_2 = y_1$.

An interesting fact about the algorithm is that two groups of instructions, one consisting of $\{l_1^1, l_2^1\}$ and the other consisting of $\{l_3^1, l_4^1\}$, seem to be redundantly trying to achieve the same goal. Both groups try to make $y_1 = y_2$ if $y_2 \neq \bot$, and $y_1 \neq y_2$ otherwise. Why should we have this redundancy? The answer is that if we could perform the assignment

$$y_1 := \text{if } y_2 = ff \textit{ then } ff \textit{ else } tt$$

as one atomic instruction, then only one such instruction would have been necessary. Once we use an interleaving model for concurrency we have to break this monolithic instruction into two atomic instructions such as given in l_1^1 and l_2^1. This faithfully models the possibility that y_2 could change its value before y_1 is assigned the intended value.

Such breaking is required whenever an instruction contains more than a single critical reference to a shared variable, if the interleaving model is to represent all the possible behaviors of real concurrent executions of such instructions. Consequently, we break the instruction into two simpler instructions, the first fetching the value of y_2 and computing in t_1 the intended value, and the second moves t_1 into y_1.

However, now that the other process may change y_2 between these two instructions the algorithm with a single pair of such instructions is no longer correct. That is, there exists a computation that violates mutual exclusion. The critical interference point is between l_1^1 and l_2^1. By duplicating the sequence of l_1^1, l_2^1 at l_3^1, l_4^1 and similarly in P_2, we make it impossible for the other process to repeat its damaging interaction both when P_1 is at l_2^1 and when it is at l_4^1. By essentially duplicating the broken instruction twice, computations that violate mutual exclusion will be shown to be impossible.

By simple application of the initialized invariance rule **INV**, it is possible to derive the following invariants:

$$J_1: \ _1 \neq \bot \ \leftrightarrow \ \lambda_1 \in l_{2..6}^1$$

$$J_2: y_1 \neq \bot \ \leftrightarrow \ \lambda_1 \in l_{3..6}^1$$

$$J_3: t_2 \neq \bot \ \leftrightarrow \ \lambda_2 \in l_{2..6}^2$$

$$J_4: y_2 \neq \bot \ \leftrightarrow \ \lambda_3 \in l_{3..6}^2$$

where $l_{2..6}$ stands for $\{l_2^1, l_3^{1,} \cdots, l_6^1\}$, etc. Note that stating that J_1 is an invariant is the same as stating that $\mathbf{G}[(t_1 \neq \bot) \equiv \lambda_1 \in l_{2..6}^1]$.

In order to derive safety we prove the following sequence of invariants:

$$J_5: y_1 = t_1 \vee \lambda_1 = l_2^1 \vee \lambda_1 = l_4^1$$

$$J_6: y_2 = t_2 \vee \lambda_2 = l_2^2 \vee \lambda_2 = l_4^2$$

$$J_7: \lambda_1 \in l_{4,5}^1 \rightarrow [t_2 = \bot \vee t_1 = t_2 \vee t_1 = y_1]$$

$$J_8: \lambda_2 \in l_{4,5}^2 \rightarrow [t_1 = \bot \vee t_2 = \neg t_1 \vee t_2 = y_2]$$

$$J_9: [\lambda_1 \in l_{4..6}^1 \wedge \lambda_2 = l_6^2] \rightarrow y_2 = t_1$$

$$J_{10}: [\lambda_2 \in l_{4..6}^2 \wedge \lambda_1 = l_6^1] \rightarrow y_1 = \neg t_2.$$

Invariants J_5 and J_6 are easy to verify since the only transitions that may cause y_1 and t_1 to differ are $l_1^1 \rightarrow l_2^1$ and the only transitions that may cause y_2 and t_2 to differ are $l_1^2 \rightarrow l_2^2$ and $l_3^2 \rightarrow l_4^2$.

In order to verify J_7 and J_8 we observe that they hold initially since both $\lambda_1 \in l_{4..5}^1$ and $\lambda_2 \in l_{4..5}^2$ are initially false. Next, assume that they hold at a certain instant and show that both J_7 and J_8 are preserved by each individual transition. We show first that J_7 is preserved. Denote by t'_1, y'_1, t'_2, y'_2 the values of the respective variables *after* a transition. We only consider transitions that affect variables on which J_7 depends. Consider first such transitions that can be made by P_1.

$l_3^1 \to l_4^1$: If $y_2 = \perp$ then t_1 is not changed and hence by J_5, $t'_1 = t_1 = y_1$. Therefore consider the case that $y_2 \neq \perp$ and hence by J_3 and J_4, $t_2 \neq \perp$. We also have $t'_1 = y_2$. The following two cases are considered:

Case 1: $y_2 = t_2$. Then $t'_1 = y_2 = t_2$ satisfying the second disjunct of J_7.

Case 2: $y_2 = \neg t_2$. In view of J_6, the assumption $y_2 \neq \perp$ and J_4, P_2 can only be at l_4^2. From J_8, the fact that P_1 is at l_3^1 (hence $t_1 \neq \perp$), and the assumption $y_2 = \neg t_2$, it follows that $t_2 = \neg t_1$. We thus obtain $t'_1 = y_2 = \neg t_2 = \neg(\neg t_1) = t_1$. Since $t_1 = y_1$ while P_1 is at l_3^1, we obtain $t'_1 = y_1$ satisfying the third disjunct of J_7.

$l_4^1 \to l_5^1$: $y'_1 = t_1$ satisfying the third disjunct of J_7.

Next, we consider transitions of P_2 made while P_1 is at $l_{4..5}^1$ that affect variables appearing in J_7.

$l_1^2 \to l_2^2$: $t'_2 = \neg y_1$ since $y_1 \neq \perp$. If $y_1 = t_1$ then J_7 continues to hold. We may therefore assume that $y_1 = \neg t_1$ which leads to $t'_2 = \neg(\neg t_1) = t_1$, satisfying the second disjunct of J_7.

$l_3^2 \to l_4^2$: Similarly to the case above, since $y_1 \neq \perp$ while P_1 is at $l_{4..5}^1$, this transition assigns $t'_2 = \neg y_1$. By the same argument as above, J_7 must still hold after this transition.

$l_6^2 \to l_7^2$: Sets t_2 to $\perp$ satisfying the first disjunct of J_7.

In a similar way we establish that J_8 is preserved under any transition initiated from a state that satisfies J_7 and J_8. Consequently, both J_7 and J_8 are invariants.

Next, consider J_9 (and symmetrically J_{10}). The only transition of P_1 that could affect J_9 is $l_3^1 \to l_4^1$ while P_2 is at l_6^2. But then $t'_1 = y_2$.

The only transition of P_2 that could affect J_9 is $l_5^2 \to l_6^2$ while P_1 is at $l_{4..6}^1$. The fact that $l_5^2 \to l_6^2$ is possible implies that $\neg(\neg y_2 = y_1)$, i.e. $y_1 = y_2$. By J_7 either $t_1 = y_1$ or $t_1 = t_2$. In the first case we have $t_1 = y_1 = y_2$ and in the second case $t_1 = t_2 = y_2$ is ensured directly. Note that when P_2 is at l_5^2, $t_2 = y_2$. Thus in any case $t_1 = t_2$.

Safety. The safety of this algorithm is expressed by the statement of mutual exclusion. This means that it is never the case that while P_1 is at l_6^1, P_2 is at l_6^2, i.e.

$$\neg(\lambda_1 = l_6^1 \wedge \lambda_2 = l_6^2).$$

To derive safety assume a state in which both $\lambda_1 = l_6^1$ and $\lambda_2 = l_6^2$ is true. By J_9 and J_{10} we have that $y_2 = t_1$ and $y_1 = \neg t_2$ at the same time. By J_5 and J_6 we also have $y_1 = t_1$ and $y_2 = t_2$. This leads to both $y_1 = y_2$ and $y_1 = \neg y_2$ which is contradictory. Hence, mutual exclusion is guaranteed.

Liveness. The liveness property we wish to show for this program is

$$\lambda_1 = l_1^1 \rightarrow \mathbf{F}(\lambda_1 = l_6^1).$$

We present a diagram proof for this property in Figure 7.11. In constructing the diagram we have freely used some of the invariants derived above. Observe for example the node corresponding to the assertion: A_6: $\lambda_1 = l_5^1 \wedge \lambda_2 = l_0^2$. Here the helpful process (indicated by a double

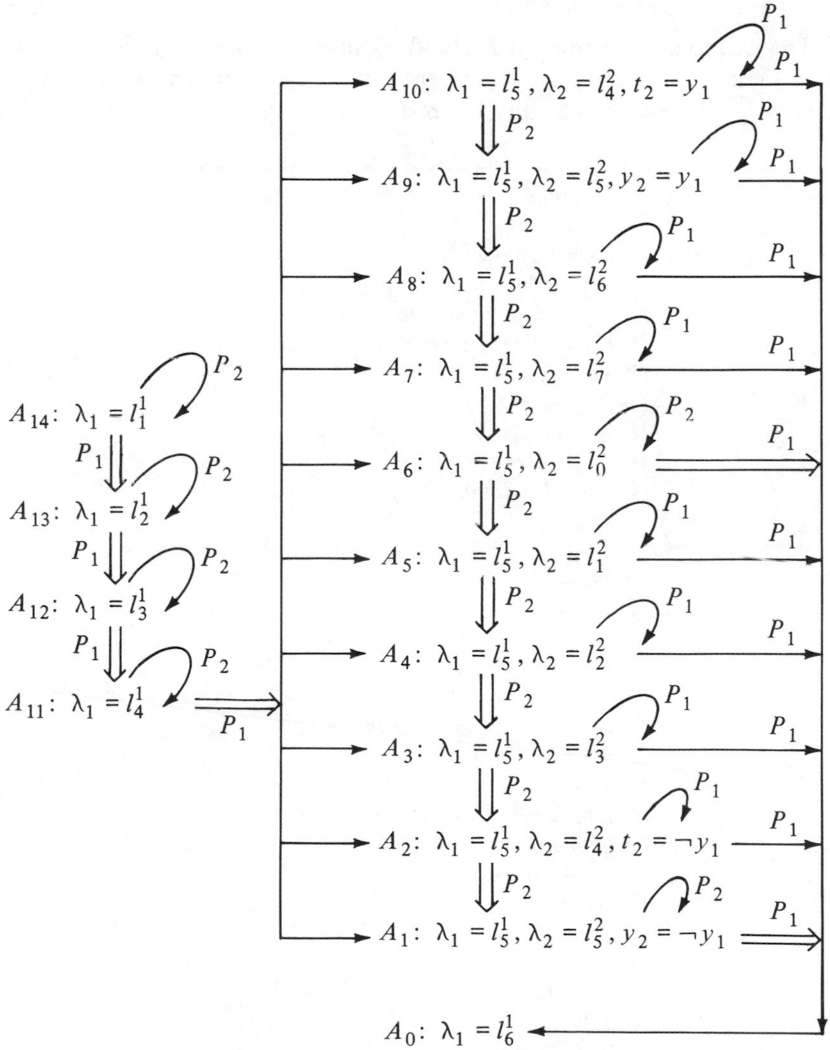

Figure 7.11 **W-CHAIN** diagram for mutual exclusion program *PF*.

arrow $=>$) is P_1 since we know (by J_4) that while P_2 is at l_0^2, $y_2 = \perp$ and while P_1 is at l_5^1 (by J_2) that $y_1 \neq \perp$, hence whenever P_1 is activated at l_5^1 it proceeds immediately to l_6^1, i.e. arrives at a state satisfying A_0. In this diagram we abbreviate at $\lambda_1 = l_5^1 \wedge \lambda_2 = l_0^2$ to (l_5^1, l_0^2).
We leave it to the reader to verify that all clauses of **W-CHAIN** are verifiable according to the figure.

Example: (Dekker's algorithm) The program *DK* in Figure 7.12 provides one of the earliest solutions to the shared-variable mutual exclusion problem without semaphores [DIJ 68], due to Dekker.

The variable y_1 in process P_1 (and y_2 in P_2, respectively) is set to *tt* at l_1^1 to signal the intention of P_1 to enter its critical section at l_7^1. Next, P_1 tests at l_2^1 whether P_2 has any interest in entering its own critical section.

$DK{::}\ (t, y_1, y_2) := (1, ff, ff);\ [P_1 \parallel P_2].$

$P_1{::}$ l_0^1: *noncritical−section*$_1$
l_1^1: $y_1 := tt$
l_2^1: if $y_2 = ff$ *then goto* l_7^1
l_3^1: if $t = 1$ *then goto* l_2^1
l_4^1: $y_1 := ff$
l_5^1: *loop until* $t = 1$
l_6^1: *goto* l_1^1
- -
l_7^1: *critical−section*$_1$
$t := 2$
- -
l_8^1: $y_1 := ff$
l_9^1: *goto* l_0^1

$P_2{::}$ l_0^2: *noncritical−section*$_2$
l_1^2: $y_2 := tt$
l_2^2: if $y_1 = ff$ *then goto* l_7^2
l_3^2: if $t = 2$ *then goto* l_2^2
l_4^2: $y_2 := ff$
l_5^2: *loop until* $t = 2$
l_6^2: *goto* l_1^2
- - - - - - - - - - - - - - - - - - -
l_7^2: *critical−section*$_2$
$t := 1$
- - - - - - - - - - - - - - - - - - -
l_8^2: $y_2 := ff$
l_9^2: *goto* l_0^2

Figure 7.12 Dekker's solution to mutual exclusion.

This is tested by checking if $y_2 = ff$. If $y_2 = ff$, P_1 proceeds immediately to its critical section. If $y_2 = tt$ there is a competition between the two processes on access rights on the critical section. This competition is resolved by using the variable t (*turn*) that has the value 1 if P_1 has the higher priority and the value 2 if P_2 has the higher priority. If P_1 finds that $t=1$ it knows it can insist and so it leaves y_1 on and loops between l_2^1 and l_3^1 waiting for y_2 to drop to ff. If it finds that $t=2$ it realizes it should yield to P_2 and consequently it turns y_1 off and enters a waiting loop at l_5^1, waiting for t to change to 1. As soon as P_2 exits its critical section it will reset t to 1, so P_1 will not be waiting forever. Once t has been detected to be 1, P_1 sets y_1 to *true* and returns to the active competition at l_2^1.

In order to prove safety, i.e. mutual exclusion, for the *DK* program it is sufficient to establish the following invariants:

$$J_1\colon (y_1 = tt) \equiv (\lambda_1 \in l_{2..4}^1 \vee \lambda_1 \in l_{7..8}^1)$$

$$J_2\colon (y_2 = tt) \equiv (\lambda_2 \in l_{2..4}^2 \vee \lambda_2 \in l_{7..8}^2.$$

They can be justified by considering the local transitions in P_1 and P_2 independently. Safety now follows from J_1 and J_2 as an invariant.

$$J_3\colon \neg(\lambda_1 \in l_{7..8}^1) \vee \neg(\lambda_2 \in l_{7..8}^2).$$

The only two transitions that could falsify J_3 are:

$l_2^1 \to l_7^1$ while P_2 is at $l_{7..8}^2$: by J_2, $y_2 = tt$ and the transition $l_2^1 \to l_7^1$ is impossible.

$l_2^2 \to l_7^2$ while P_1 is at $l_{7..8}^1$: similarly impossible by J_1.

The liveness property of program *DK* is given by:

$$\lambda_1 = l_1^1 \to \mathbf{F}(\lambda_1 = l_7^1).$$

We present a diagram proof of this property (see Figure 7.13). In constructing the diagram we are aided by the previously derived invariants J_1, J_2, J_3 and the following two additional invariants:

$$J_4\colon \lambda_2 = l_8^2 \to t=1$$

$$J_5\colon [\lambda_1 \in l_{3..6}^1 \wedge t=2] \to \lambda_2 \in l_{1..7}^2.$$

In particular we use J_5 when constructing the P_1-successors to node A_{23}. In all of these successors P_2 is restricted to the range of locations $l_{1..7}^2$ which is represented by the nodes $A_{16}, \ldots, A_{22}$.

To justify the above invariants, consider first J_4. There are two potentially falsifying transitions that have to be checked:

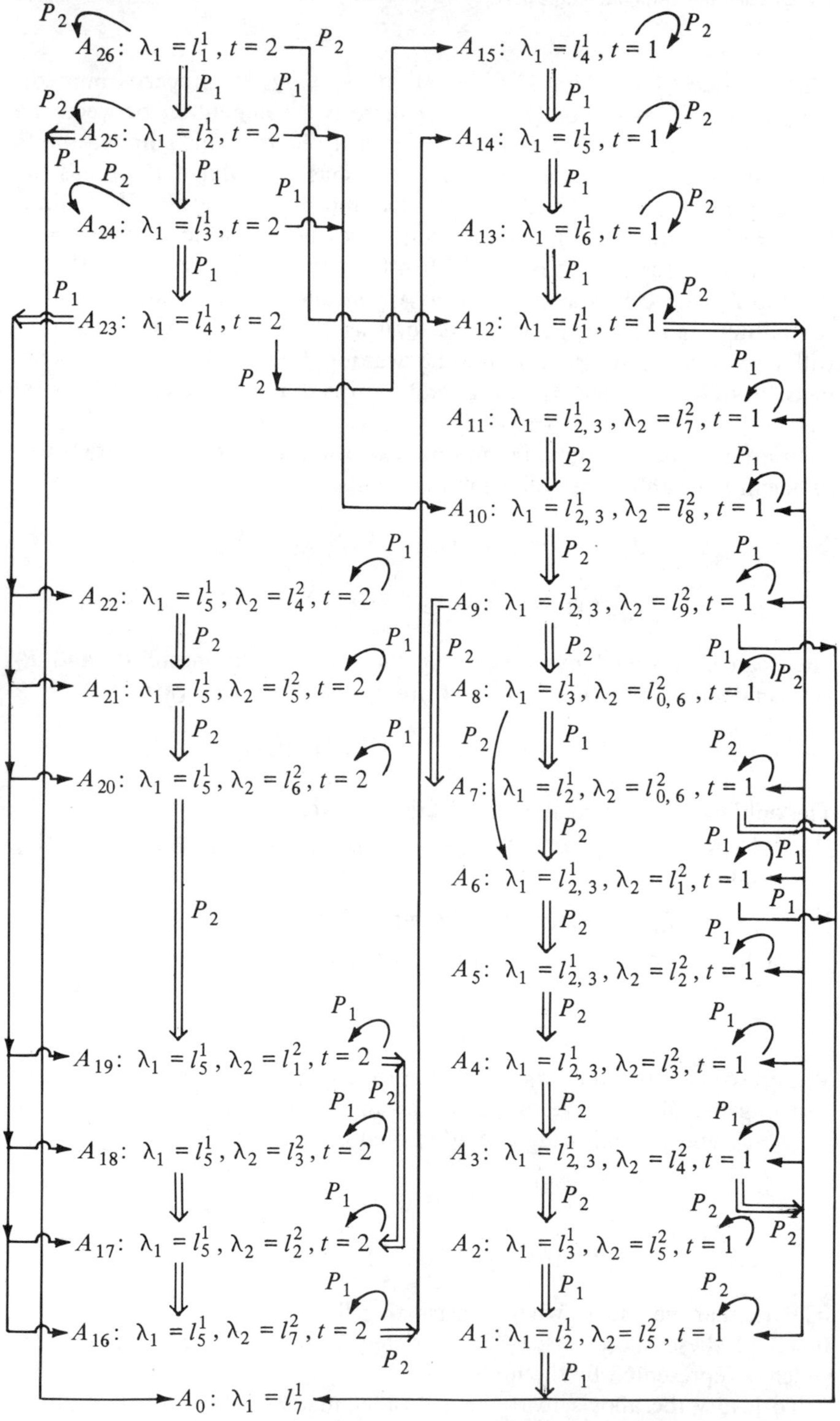

Figure 7.13 Proof diagram for Dekker's algorithm.

$l_7^2 \to l_8^2$: sets t to 1.

$l_7^1 \to l_8^1$ while P_2 is at l_8^2: this transition is impossible since by J_3 while P_2 is at l_8^2, P_1 cannot be at l_7^1.

Consider next J_5. Here the potentially falsifying transitions are:

$l_2^1 \to l_3^1$, while $t=2$: this transition is possible only when $y_2 = tt$ which, due to J_2, implies that P_2 is either in $l_{2..4}^2$ or in $l_{7..8}^2$. In view of J_4, P_2 cannot be at l_8^2 while $t=2$. Hence P_2 is restricted to $l_{2..4}^2$ or l_7^2, which is a subset of $l_{1..7}^2$.

$l_7^2 \to l_8^2$: sets t to 1 and hence makes the antecedent of J_5 false.

We now turn to an example which is *not* a finite-state program and the **W-CHAIN** rule does not suffice for its proof. Rather the parametrized invariants are again needed.

Example: (distributed *gcd*) Consider a program *DGCD* for the distributed computation of the *gcd* function (see Figure 7.14).

We present a proof diagram (see Figure 7.15) of the liveness property:

$$\mathbf{F}[\lambda_1 = l_1^1 \wedge \lambda_2 = \lambda_1^2 \wedge y_1 = y_2]$$

for this program.

In this diagram we mix applications of the **W-CHAIN** rule with an application of the **Temp-WWELL** rule. The **Temp-WWELL** rule ensures that from $A = A_3$ eventually an exit to A_2 or to A_1 occurs, i.e. $B = A_1 \vee A_2$. The well-founded structure used is that of lexicographic pairs (n, k) of which $n \in N$ is a positive integer and $k \in \{1, 2\}$. The second parameter k is determined according to whether $y_1 > y_2$, or $y_1 < y_2$. In turn it determines the helpful process. If $k = 1$, then $y_1 > y_2$ and any transition of P_1 (namely $l_0^1 \to l_0^1$) will decrement $n = y_1 + y_2$, thus decrementing the pair (n, k). On that same state, any transition of P_2 leaves y_1, y_2 and hence n and k invariant. For $k = 2$ the situation is reversed, P_2 being the helpful process.

$DGCD{::}\ (y_1, y_2){:=}(x_1, x_2);\ [P_1 \parallel P_2]$
$P_1{::}\ l_0^1$: *while* $y_1 \neq y_2$ *do*
 if $y_1 > y_2$ *then* $y_1{:=}y_1 - y_2$
l_1^1: *halt*

$P_2{::}\ l_0^2$: *while* $y_1 \neq y_2$ *do*
 if $y_1 < y_2$ *then* $y_2{:=}y_2 - y_1$
l_1^2: *halt*

Figure 7.14 Distributed *GCD*.

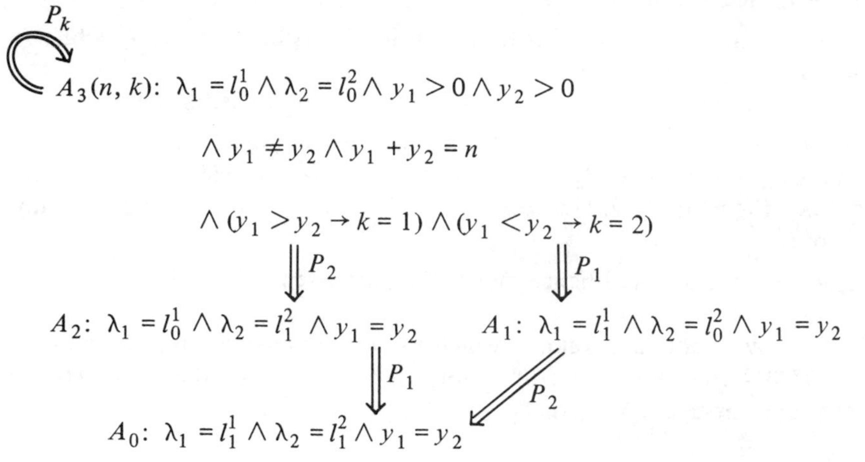
P_k
$A_3(n, k)$: $\lambda_1 = l_0^1 \wedge \lambda_2 = l_0^2 \wedge y_1 > 0 \wedge y_2 > 0$
$\wedge\ y_1 \neq y_2 \wedge y_1 + y_2 = n$
$\wedge\ (y_1 > y_2 \rightarrow k = 1) \wedge (y_1 < y_2 \rightarrow k = 2)$
P_2
P_1
A_2: $\lambda_1 = l_0^1 \wedge \lambda_2 = l_1^2 \wedge y_1 = y_2$
A_1: $\lambda_1 = l_1^1 \wedge \lambda_2 = l_0^2 \wedge y_1 = y_2$
P_1
P_2
A_0: $\lambda_1 = l_1^1 \wedge \lambda_2 = l_1^2 \wedge y_1 = y_2$

Figure 7.15 Diagram proof of the program *DGCD*.

Once at A_2 or A_1 the arrival at A_0 is ensured by the usual application of the **W-CHAIN** rule.

Note that in proof diagrams containing parameterized assertions, we allow edges of the helpful process to lead back to the same node, provided that they always lead to a lower value of the well-founded parameter.

We end the shared-variables examples with two strong fairness examples, the first of which is again a finite-state program.

Example: (producer-consumer) This example (see Figure 7.16) demonstrates the application of the **S-CHAIN** rule for programs with semaphores.

The producer P_1 computes at l_0^1 a value into y_1 without modifying any other shared program variables. It then adds y_1 to the end of the buffer b. The consumer P_2 removes the first element of the buffer into y_2 and then uses this value for its own purposes (at l_7^2) without modifying any other shared program variable. The maximal capacity of the buffer b is $n > 0$.

In order to ensure the correct synchronization between the processes we use three semaphore variables: The variable s ensures that accesses to the buffer are protected and provides exclusion between the critical sections $l_{3..5}^1$ and $l_{2..5}^2$. The variable ce ("count of empties") counts the number of free slots in the buffer b. It protects b from overflowing. The variable cf ("count of fulls") counts how many items the buffer currently holds. It ensures that the consumer does not attempt to remove an item from an empty buffer.

$PC:: (b, s, cf, ce) := (\Lambda, 1, 0, n);\ [P_1 \,||\, P_2].$

$P_1:: l_0^1$: *compute* y_1
l_1^1: *request*(ce)
l_2^1: *request*(s)
l_3^1: $t_1 := b \cdot y_1$
l_4^1: $b := t_1$
l_5^1: $s := s+1$
l_6^1: $cf := cf+1$
l_7^1: *goto* l_0^1

$P_2:: l_0^2$: *request*(cf)
l_1^2: *request*(s)
l_2^2: $y_2 := head(b)$
l_3^2: $t_2 := tail(b)$
l_4^2: $b := t_2$
l_5^2: $s := s-1$
l_6^2: $ce := ce-1$
l_7^2: *compute using* y_2
l_8^2: *goto* l_0^2

Figure 7.16 Producer-consumer.

We wish to show the liveness property

$$\lambda_1 = l_1^1 \rightarrow \mathbf{F}(\lambda_1 = l_3^1).$$

We start by presenting the top-level diagram proof (sec Figure 7.17). This diagram proof is certainly trivial. Everywhere, P_1 is the helpful process and leads immediately to the next step. However, we now have to establish clause C in the **S-CHAIN** rule. This calls for the consideration of fair computations of $P - \{P_1\} = \{P_2\}$. We thus have to construct two subproofs:

$$P_2 \vdash \lambda_1 = l_1^1 \rightarrow \mathbf{F}(ce > 0),$$

$$P_2 \vdash \lambda_1 = l_2^1 \rightarrow \mathbf{F}(s > 0).$$

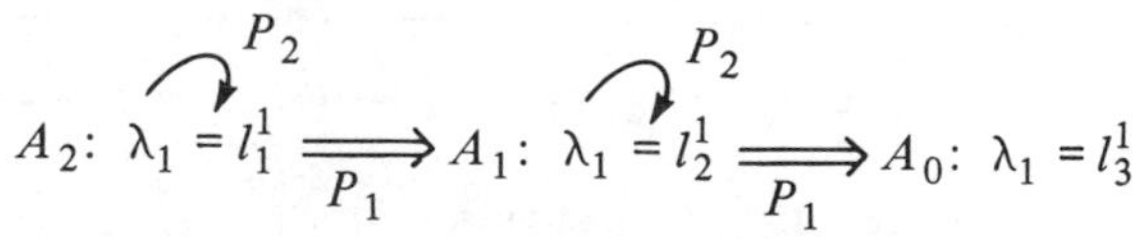

Figure 7.17 Top-level proof diagram.

The first statement ensures that if P_1 is at l_1^1, P_2 will eventually cause ce to become positive which is the enabling condition for P_1 to be activated at l_1^1. Similarly, in the second statement P_2 will eventually cause s to become positive, making P_1 enabled at l_2^1. For both statements we present diagram proofs.

Consider first the diagram proof for the $\lambda_1 = l_1^1$ case (see Figure 7.18). In the construction of this diagram we use some invariants which are easy to derive. The first invariant is:

$$J_1\colon \lambda_1 \in l_{3..5}^1 + \lambda_2 \in l_{2..5}^2 + s = 1 .$$

It has been used in order to derive that being at l_1^1 and l_1^2 implies $s > 0$. In an expression such as the above we arithmetize propositions by interpreting *false* as 0 and *true* as 1. The second invariant is

$$J_2\colon cf + ce + \lambda_1 \in l_{1..6}^2 = n.$$

It is used in order to deduce that being at l_1^1 and at $l_{7,8,0}^2$ implies that either $ce > 0$ or $cf > 0$.

The diagram proof for the $\lambda_1 = l_2^1$ case is even simpler (see Figure 7.19).

Example: (binomial coefficients) The program BC in Figure 7.20 demonstrates the application of the **Temp-SWELL** rule for programs with semaphores.

$$A_9\colon \lambda_2 = l_7^2, cf > 0 \rightarrow A_8\colon \lambda_2 = l_8^2, cf > 0 \rightarrow A_7\colon \lambda_2 = l_0^2, cf > 0$$

$$\downarrow$$

$$A_3\colon \lambda_2 = l_4^2 \leftarrow A_4\colon \lambda_2 = l_3^2 \leftarrow A_5\colon \lambda_2 = l_2^2 \leftarrow A_6\colon \lambda_2 = l_1^2, s > 0$$

$$\downarrow$$

$$A_2\colon \lambda_2 = l_5^2 \rightarrow A_1\colon \lambda_2 = l_6^2 \rightarrow A_0\colon ce > 0$$

Figure 7.18 Proof diagram for $\lambda_1 = l_1^1$.

$$A_4\colon \lambda_2 = l_2^2 \longrightarrow A_3\colon \lambda_2 = l_3^2 \longrightarrow A_2\colon \lambda_2 = l_4^2 \longrightarrow A_1\colon \lambda_2 = l_5^2 \longrightarrow A_0\colon s > 0$$

Figure 7.19 Proof diagram for $\lambda_1 = l_2^1$.

$BC{::}\ (y_1, y_2, y_3, y_4){:=}(n, 0, 1, 1);\ [P_1 \parallel P_2].$

$P_1{::}\ l_0^1$: if $y_1=(n-k)$ *then goto* l_7^1
l_1^1: *request*(y_4)
l_2^1: $t_1{:=}y_3 \cdot y_1$
l_3^1: $y_3{:=}t_1$
l_4^1: $y_4{:=}y_4+1$
l_5^1: $y_1{:=}y_1-1$
l_6^1: *goto* l_0^1
l_7^1: *halt*

$P_2{::}\ l_0^2$: if $y_2=k$ *then goto* l_8^2
l_1^2: $y_2{:=}y_2+1$
l_2^2: *loop until* $y_1+y_2 \leqslant n$
l_3^2: *request*(y_4)
l_4^2: $t_2{:=}y_3/y_2$
l_5^2: $y_3{:=}t_2$
l_6^2: $y_4{:=}y_4+1$
l_7^2: *goto* l_0^2
l_8^2: *halt*

Figure 7.20 Binomial coefficients.

This is a distributed computation of the binomial coefficient $\binom{n}{k}$ for integer n and k such that $0 \leqslant k \leqslant n$. Based on the formula

$$\binom{n}{k} = \frac{n \cdot (n-1) \cdot \ \cdots \ \cdot (n-k+1)}{1 \cdot 2 \cdot \ \cdots \ \cdot k}$$

process P_1 successively multiplies y_3 by n, $(n-1)$, $\cdots$, while P_2 successively divides y_3 by 1,2, $\cdots$. In order for the division at l_4 to come out evenly, we divide y_3 by y_2 only when at least y_2 factors have been multiplied into y_3 by P_1. The waiting loop at l_2^2 ensures this.

Without loss of generality we can relabel the instructions in the program (see Figure 7.21).

The liveness property we wish to prove is:

$$[\lambda_1 = l_7^1 \wedge \lambda_2 = l_3^2 \wedge (y_1, y_2, y_3, y_4) = (n, 0, 1, 1)]$$
$$\rightarrow \mathbf{F}(\ \lambda_1 = l_1^1 \wedge \lambda_2 = l_1^2\ ).$$

We derive first several invariants needed for the liveness proof:

$$J_1{:}\ (\lambda_1 \in l_{3..5}^1 + \lambda_2 \in l_{5..7}^2 + y_4) = 1$$

$$J_2{:}\ ((n-k) + \lambda_1^2 \in l_{2..6}^1) \leqslant y_1 \leqslant n$$

BC^*:: $(y_1, y_2, y_3, y_4) := (n, 0, 1, 1)$; $[P_1 \parallel P_2]$.

P_1:: l_7^1: if $y_1 = (n-k)$ *then goto* l_1^1
l_6^1: *request*(y_4)
l_5^1: $t_1 := y_3 \cdot y_1$
l_4^1: $y_3 := t_1$
l_3^1: $y_4 := y_4 + 1$
l_2^1: $y_1 := y_1 - 1$
l_8^1: *goto* l_7^1
l_1^1: *halt*

P_2:: l_3^2: if $y_2 = k$ *then goto* l_1^2
l_2^2: $y_2 := y_2 + 1$
l_9^2: *loop until* $y_1 + y_2 \leqslant n$
l_8^2: *request*(y_4)
l_7^2: $t_2 := y_3 / y_2$
l_6^2: $y_3 := t_2$
l_5^2: $y_4 := y_4 + 1$
l_4^2: *goto* l_3^2
l_1^2: *halt*

Figure 7.21 Relabeled binomial coefficients program.

$$J_3: 0 \leqslant y_2 \leqslant (k - \lambda_2 \in l_2^2)$$

$$J_4: \lambda_1 = l_1^1 \rightarrow y_1 = n-k.$$

For the well-founded domain we choose:

$$W = (N \times \{0, \ldots, 17\} \times \{0,1\}, >_{lex}),$$

that is, the domain of triples of integers (r, s, t) such that $r \geqslant 0$, $0 \leqslant s \leqslant 17$ and $0 \leqslant t \leqslant 1$. The ordering defined on them is the lexicographic ordering on triples.

The parameterized assertion is:

$$A_0(w, l_i^1, l_j^2, y_1, y_2) = A((r, s, t), l_i^1, l_j^2, y_1, y_2):$$

$$(r = y_1 + k - y_2) \wedge (s = i+j) \wedge (t = \lambda_1 = l_1^1).$$

Thus s is the sum of the indices of the locations of the two processes: also $t=1$ if and only if P_1 is at l_1^1; otherwise $t=0$. The helpfulness function is:

$$h_s(r, s, t) = \begin{cases} P_2 & \text{if } t=1, \\ P_1 & \text{otherwise.} \end{cases}$$

The sequence of labels is designed in such a way that moving to the next instruction will necessarily lead to a lower value of (r, s, t). This is so because the label sequence is always decreasing except for the instructions which decrement y_1 and increment y_2. Changes in the y's have been given the highest priority in the lexicographical ordering. The parameter t has been added in order to make h_s dependent on $w = (r, s, t)$.

There are only two situations to be checked. First, when P_1 is at l_1^1 and P_2 is at l_9^2 we have to show that the next step indeed decrements (r, s, t). This is so because in such a situation we are assured by J_3, J_4 that both $y_2 \leqslant k$ and $y_1 = n-k$ hold, leading to $y_1 + y_2 \leqslant n$, which means that the next step leads to l_8^2. Another point is to show that being at l_6^1 guarantees that eventually y_4 will become positive, by the actions of P_2 alone. This is easily established by the following diagram, supported by invariants J_1 to J_4.

$$A_3\colon l_7^2 \longrightarrow A_2\colon l_6^2 \longrightarrow A_1\colon l_5^1 \longrightarrow A_0\colon y_4 > 0$$

7.1.1.2 Message passing

In this subsection we present another modeling of a language based on *synchronized message passing* (known also as *handshaking*), closely related to *CSP* [HO 78]. We again consider a program to be a concurrent composition of processes, $P\colon\colon [P_1 \,||\, \cdots \,||\, P_n]$, each process being represented as a transition system. The treatment of variables and labels is as in the shared variable model. The transition types, however, are different in this case.

1. $$\textit{test} - \tau\colon\ l \xrightarrow{\ c(\bar{y})\ } l'$$

   where $c(\bar{y})$ is a Boolean expression (guard). For this transition in P_i, $p_\tau(\lambda, \bar{y}) = (\lambda_i = l \wedge c(\bar{y}))$, while f_τ only changes the label component to l'.

2. $$\textit{assignment} - \tau\colon\ l \xrightarrow{\ \bar{y}:=h(\bar{y})\ } l'$$

   as before.

3. $$\textit{input} - \tau\colon\ l \xrightarrow{\ c(\bar{y});\ P_j?y_k\ } l'$$

   This transition can only be executed *jointly* with an output transition in P_j, provided $c(\bar{y})$ holds.

4. $$\textit{output} - \ l \xrightarrow{\ c(\bar{y});\ P_j!h(\bar{y})\ } l'$$

   Similarly, an output transition can only be executed *jointly* with an input transition in P_j, provided $c(\bar{y})$ holds. For a pair of *matching communication transitions,* namely

   $$l^i \xrightarrow{\ c_i(\bar{y});\ P_j?y_k\ } l'^i \text{ in } P_i.$$

   $$l^j \xrightarrow{\ c_j(\bar{y});\ P_i!h(\bar{y})\ } l'^j \text{ in } P_j.$$

We define their *joint* transition τ by

$$p_\tau(\lambda, \bar{y}) = (\lambda_i = l^i \wedge \lambda_j = l^j \wedge c_i(\bar{y}) \wedge c_j(\bar{y})),$$

and

$$f_\tau(\lambda, \bar{y}) = \left[\lambda \mid {}^{\lambda_i,\ \lambda_j}_{l'^i,\ l'^j},\ \bar{y} \mid {}^{y_k}_{h(\bar{y})} \right].$$

In [MP 83] it is shown how to translate *CSP* into this transition-system representation, so that no expressive power is lost. Note that here the process-disjointness is *not* assumed.

We now turn to the selection of weak and strong fairness sets. The original description of the semantics of *CSP* as given by Hoare, no strong fairness requirement is imposed, and the only weak fairness requirement is that as long as at least one process can make a transition (i.e., the program did not terminate), eventually one process will do so. This can be represented by chosing

$$\mathbf{S} = \varnothing, \quad \mathbf{W} = \{\tau\tau\}.$$

Clearly, the levels of process fairness, channel fairness and communication fairness, both in the weak version and in the strong version, mentioned in Chapter 5, can be easily incorporated in this model. Furthermore, once again extra flexibility can be gained (over the structured approach) by using combinations thereof. For example, a combination of weak process fairness together with strong channel (or communication) fairness seems natural.

Yet another natural level, that of *transition fairness* naturally finds its way into the transition-system representation. By this fairness requirement, each single transition (whether local *or* a communication) is treated fairly (either in the weak or in the strong sense). This kind of fairness may be used to enforce fair termination on (the representation by transitions of) the following CSP process

$$P_1 :: \{n > 0\} *[\ 1: n > 0;\ P_2?x \rightarrow skip\ [\,]\ 2: n > 0 \rightarrow n := n-1\ ].$$

In the presence of an "unboundedly chattering" process P_2, P_1 could always participate in a joint transition by taking its first direction. Transition fairness would imply the repeated eventual choice of the second direction in P_1, thus decrementing n and enforcing P_1's eventual termination.

Sample proofs

Example: We show that under the assumption of *process fairness* we can prove that the program *A*1 (see Figure 7.22) satisfies:

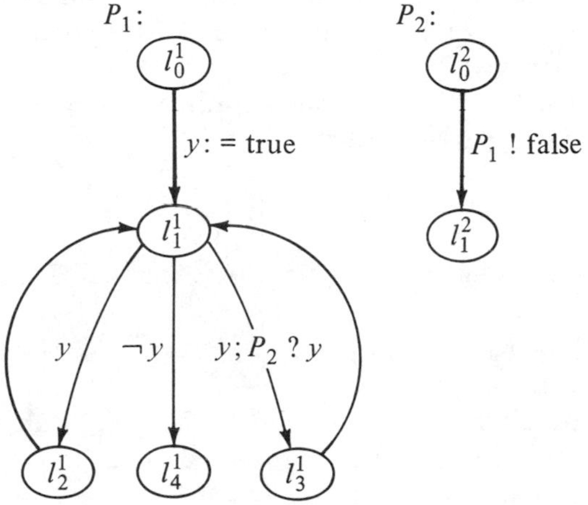

Figure 7.22 Program $A1$ [MP 83] © 1983, Association for Computing Machinery, Inc., reprinted by permission.

$$(\lambda_1 = l_0^1 \wedge \lambda_2 = l_0^2) \rightarrow \mathbf{F}(\lambda_1 = l_1^1 \wedge \lambda_2 = l_1^2).$$

Consider first the **Temp-WFAIR** rule with

$$A: \lambda_1 = l_0^1 \wedge \lambda_2 = l_0^2$$

$$B: \lambda_1 = l_1^1 \wedge \lambda_2 = l_0^2.$$

Obviously the only enabled transition under A is $l_0^1 \rightarrow l_1^1$ which realizes B in one step. Thus the first two premises of the rule are satisfied. It is also clear that A guarantees that P_1 is enabled, i.e. T_1^s is enabled. We conclude:

$$(\lambda_1 = l_0^1 \wedge \lambda_2 = l_0^2) \quad \rightarrow \quad \mathbf{F}(\lambda_1 = l_1^1 \wedge \lambda_2 = l_0^2 \wedge y).$$

Next we apply the **Temp-SFAIR** rule with :

$$A: \lambda_1 \in l_{1,2}^1 \wedge \lambda_2 = l_0^2 \wedge y$$

$$B: \lambda_1 = l_3^1 \wedge \lambda_2 = l_1^2 \wedge y.$$

The relevant fairness set is $T_2^s = \{(l_1^1, l_0^2) \longrightarrow (l_3^1, l_1^2)\}$. To verify the first two premises of the rule, we consider all transitions possible under A:

Clearly $l_1^1 \longrightarrow l_2^1$ and $l_2^1 \longrightarrow l_1^1$ preserve A.

The only other transition possible is the joint communication transition $(l_1^1, l_0^1) \longrightarrow (l_3^1, l_1^2)$. This transition leads from A to B as can be easily checked, and is the only transition in T_2^s. Consequently, every transition leads from A to $A \vee B$ and every transition in T_2^s leads from A to B.

The remaining premise that has to be established states that A implies $F[B \vee Enabled(T_2^s)]$. If P_1 is at l_1^1 then under A the communication transition is certainly enabled.

On the other hand, if P_1 is at l_2^1 we can prove by one more application of the **Temp-WFAIR** rule for P_1 that:

$$(\lambda_1 = l_2^1 \wedge \lambda_2 = l_0^2 \wedge y) \rightarrow \mathbf{F}(\lambda_1 = l_1^1 \wedge \lambda_2 = l_0^2 \wedge y),$$

which leads back to a situation in which P_2 is enabled. Thus we may conclude:

$$(\lambda_1 \in l_{1,2}^1 \wedge \lambda_2 = l_0^2 \wedge y) \rightarrow \mathbf{F}(\lambda_1 = l_3^1 \wedge \lambda_2 = l_1^2 \wedge \neg y).$$

Finally, two applications of the **Temp-WFAIR** rule with respect to P_1 ensure that P_1 proceeds to l_1^1 with $y = false$ then to l_4^1.

Thus, the whole chain of arguments lead to

$$(\lambda_1 = l_0^1 \wedge \lambda_2 = l_0^2) \rightarrow \mathbf{F}(\lambda_1 = l_4^1 \wedge \lambda_2 = l_1^2).$$

We may summarize this proof by the proof diagram in Figure 7.23. In this diagram, which contains only double edges, the fairness set is always immediately enabled except for A_3. For the application of **Temp-SFAIR** to A_3 we need an auxiliary proof which is presented in the following diagram:

$$l_2^1,\ l_0^2,\ y \ \overset{P_1}{=====>}\ l_1^1,\ l_0^2,\ y$$

This diagram proves $A_3 \rightarrow \mathbf{F}[Enabled(P_2)]$.

Example: Consider the program $A2$ (see Figure 7.24), that is guaranteed to terminate under the assumption of channel fairness. Under this assumption we prove its termination.

Using weak fairness it is easy to derive for this program

$$(\lambda_1 = l_0^1 \wedge \lambda_2 = l_0^2) \rightarrow \mathbf{F}(\lambda_1 = l_1^1 \wedge \lambda_2 = l_1^2 \wedge y_1 \wedge y_2).$$

$$A_4\colon\ \lambda_1 = l_0^1,\ \lambda_2 = l_0^2 \ \overset{P_1}{\Longrightarrow}\ A_3\colon\ \lambda_1 = l_{1,2}^1,\ \lambda_2 = l_0^2,\ y \ \overset{P_2}{\Longrightarrow}$$

$$A_2\colon\ \lambda_1 = l_3^1,\ \lambda_2 = l_1^2,\ \neg y \ \overset{P_1}{\Longrightarrow}$$

$$A_1\colon\ \lambda_1 = l_1^1,\ \lambda_2 = l_1^2,\ \neg y \ \overset{P_1}{\Longrightarrow}\ A_0\colon\ \lambda_1 = l_4^1,\ \lambda_2 = l_1^2$$

Figure 7.23 Proof diagram for example $A1$.

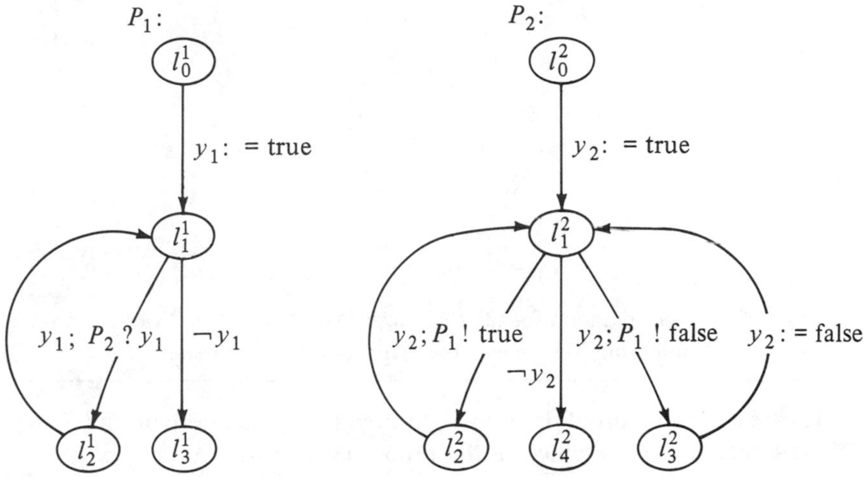

Figure 7.24 Program $A2$ [MP 83] © 1983, Association for Computing Machines, Inc., reprinted by permission.

Consider now channel fairness. Take the channel $C = \{l_1^1, l_1^2) \longrightarrow (l_2^1, l_3^2)\}$ and apply the **Temp-WFAIR** rule relative to C with:

$$A: \lambda_1 \in l^1_{1,2} \wedge \lambda_2 \in l^2_{1,2} \wedge y_1 \wedge y_2$$

$$B: \lambda_1 = l_2^1 \wedge \lambda_2 = l_3^2 \wedge \neg y_1 \wedge y_2.$$

It is not difficult to ascertain that all the transitions possible under A are:

$$(l_1^1, \quad l_1^2) \longrightarrow (l_2^1, \quad l_2^2), l_2^1 \longrightarrow l_1^1, l_2^2 \longrightarrow l_1^2$$

which preserves A and

$$(l_1^1, l_1^2) \longrightarrow (l_2^1, l_3^2)$$

which acnieves B.

Thus, the first two premises of the **Temp-WFAIR** rule are satisfied with respect to

$$T^s = C = \{(l_1^1, l_1^2) \rightarrow (l_2^1, l_3^2)\}.$$

We next have to verify the third premise which has the form: $A \rightarrow \mathbf{F}(\ Enabled(C)\ )$. Certainly when P_1 is at l_1^1 and P_2 is at l_1^2 and A holds then C is enabled. We apply the **Temp-WFAIR** rule several times in order to ensure that under A we always get to this situation. This can be summarized by the proof diagram in Figure 7.25.
Consequently we are ensured that

$$A \rightarrow \mathbf{F}(\lambda_1 = l_2^1 \wedge \lambda_2 = l_3^2 \wedge \neg y_1 \wedge y_2).$$

$$\lambda_1 = l_2^1, \lambda_2 = l_2^1, y_1, y_2$$

$$P_1 \qquad\qquad P_2$$

$$\lambda_1 = l_1^1, \lambda_2 = l_2^1, y_1, y_2 \qquad \lambda_1 = l_2^1, \lambda_2 = l_1^2, y_1, y_2$$

$$P_2 \qquad\qquad P_1$$

$$\lambda_1 = l_1^1, \lambda_2 = l_1^2, y_1, y_2$$

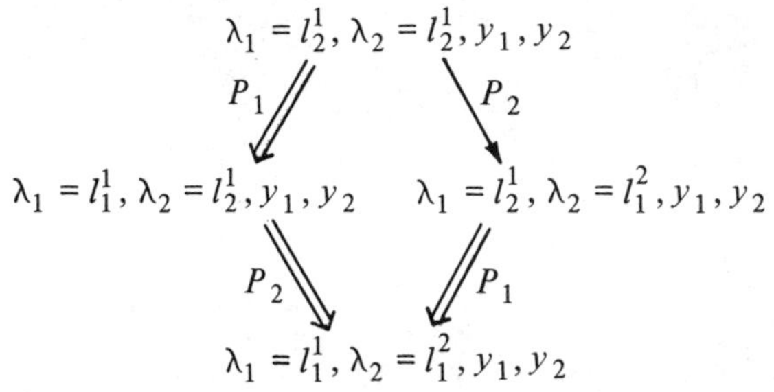

Figure 7.25   Proof diagram for third premise [MP 83] © 1983, Association for Computing Machinery, Inc., reprinted by permission.

The rest of the proof is a straightforward application of the **Temp-WFAIR** rule and is presented in the proof diagram in Figure 7.26.

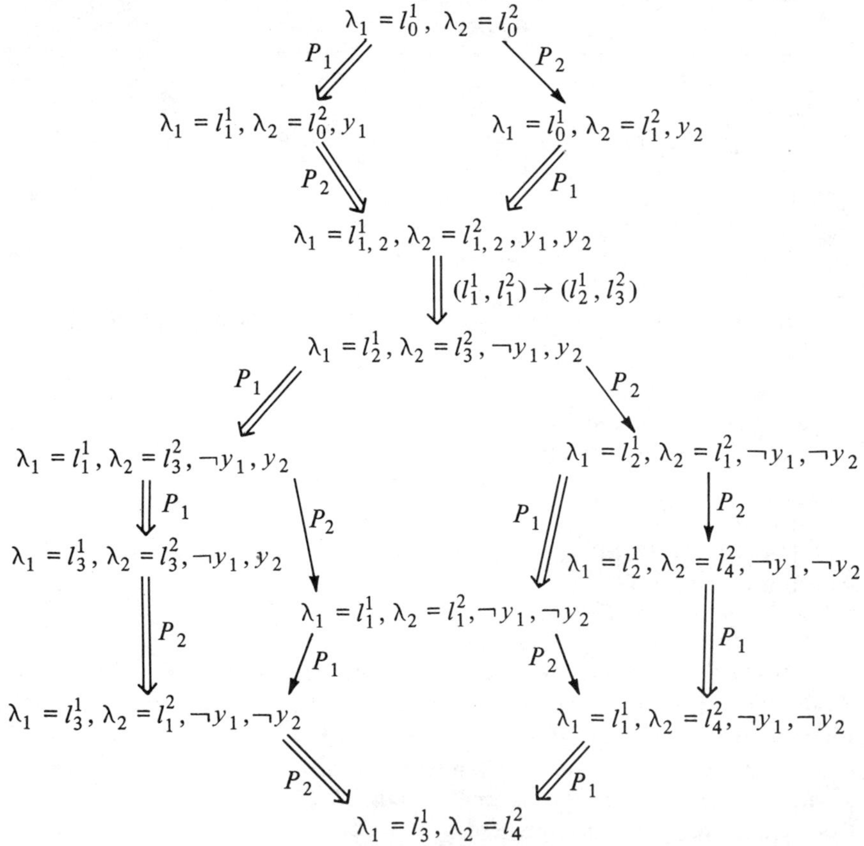

Figure 7.26   Proof diagram for **Temp-WFAIR** (rest of proof) [MP 83] © 1983, Association for Computing, Inc., reprinted by permission.

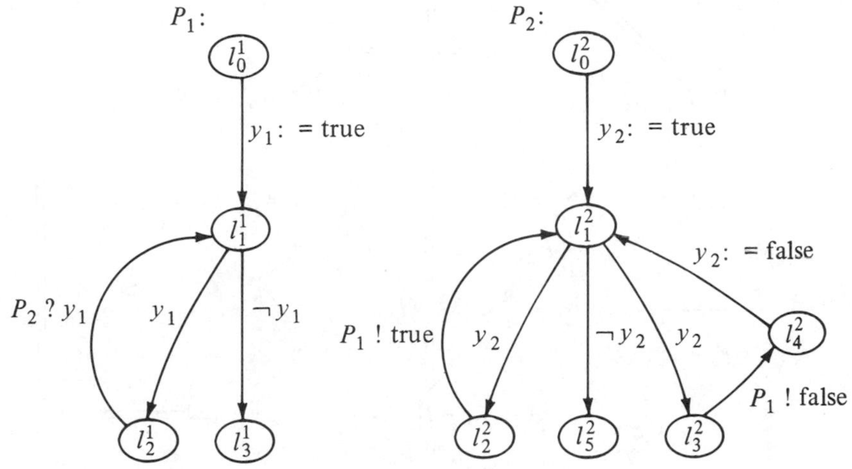

Figure 7.27 Program $A3$ [MP 83] © 1983, Association for Computing Machinery, Inc., reprinted by permission.

Example: Let us prove termination of the program $A3$ (see Figure 7.27) under the assumption of individual transition fairness.

The difference between program $A3$ and the previous program $A2$ is that the nondeterministic choice between the alternatives at l_1^2 is now *local.* Hence, channel fairness does not ensure a fair choice between the alternatives. Only individual transition fairness ensure that eventually the $l_1^2 \rightarrow l_2^2$ transition is taken, which results in termination. The diagram in Figure 7.28 represents the proof of termination of program $A3$.

The only part that is not strictly based on weak fairness is the exit out of A_8 either to A_7 or to A_6. This exit is guaranteed by the **Temp-SFAIR** rule exercising individual transition fairness for the transition $l_1^2 \longrightarrow l_3^2$. The only premise needing further justification is that A_8: $\lambda_1 \in l_{1,2}^1 \wedge \lambda_2 \in l_{1,2}^2 \wedge y_1 \wedge y_2$ guarantees that eventually the transition $l_1^2 \rightarrow l_3^2$ is enabled, i.e., P_2 will be at l_1^2 and $y_1 = true$. This again is proved using weak fairness via the diagram in Figure 7.29.

7.2 Branching-Time Temporal-Logics (BTL)

7.2.0 Overview

In this section we consider another family of temporal logics, in which the branching nature of the computations of nondeterministic and concurrent programs is more explicit. While linear-time temporal-logic formulae are interpreted over sequences, the interpretation of branching-time temporal-logics is over tree-like structures, with explicit quantification

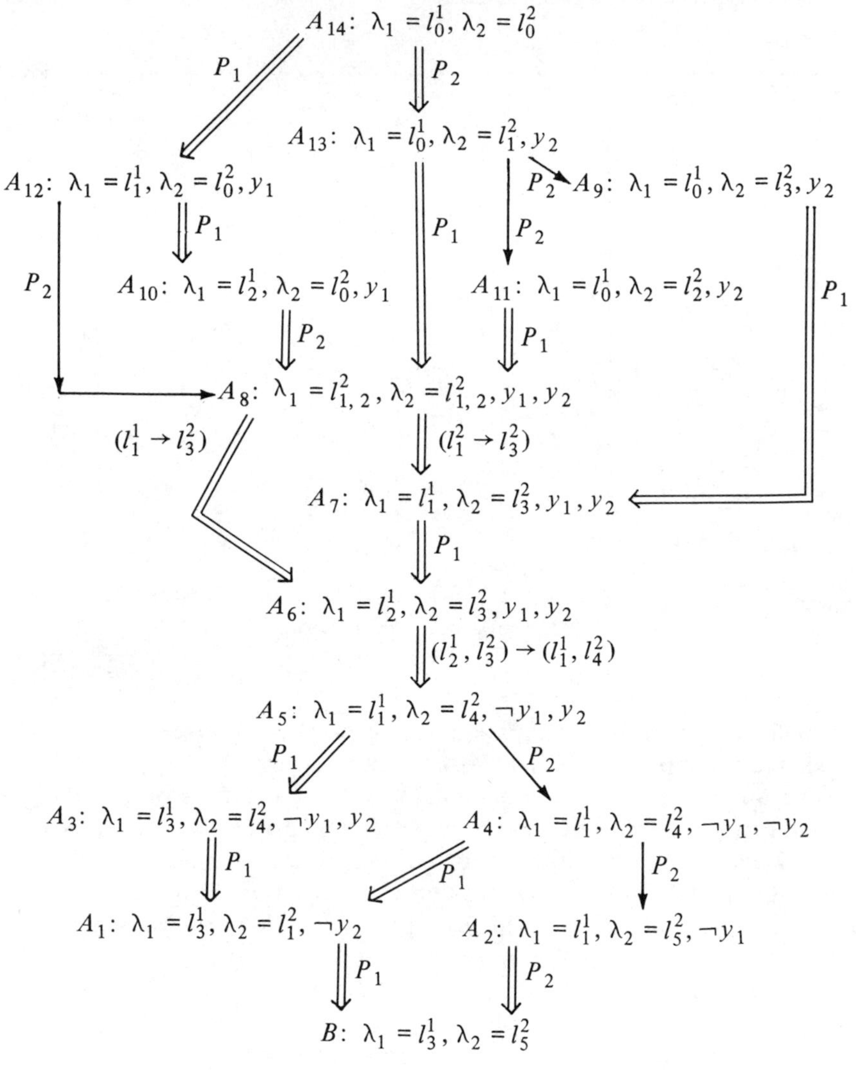

Figure 7.28 Proof diagram for program *A*3.

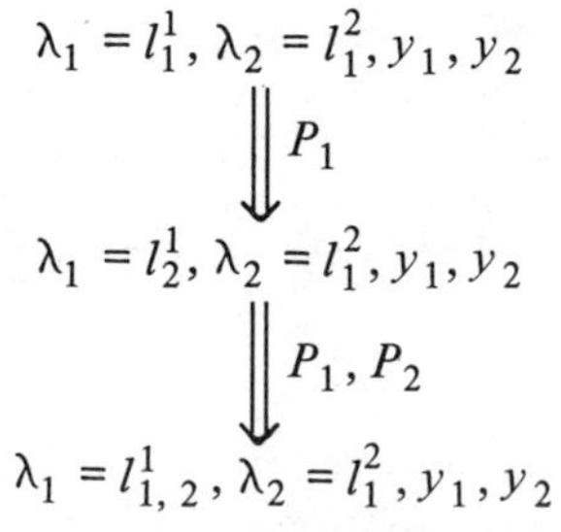

Figure 7.29 Proof diagram for subproof of program *A*3 [MP 83] © 1983, Association for Computing Machinery, Inc., reprinted by permission.

over paths. Alternatively, they can be thought of as interpreted over states (the roots of such trees). Thus, immediate comparison between **LTL**s and **BTL**s is impossible. We return to the issue of comparison later. Several variants of such logics appeared in the literature [AB 79], [BMP 81], [EC 80], [LA 80], [QS 83], [EH 83], [EL 85]. The current presentation follows [EL 85] and [QS 83], which are directly concerned with expressing fairness assumptions.

7.2.1 Two branching-time temporal logics

In this subsection we introduce the notation and interpretation of one variant of *Branching-Time Temporal-Logic.* As mentioned already, the basic modalities of such a logic include an *explicit quantification* over possible future, both existential and universal. This is in contrast to the implicit universal quantification over possible futures underlying the definition of validity in **LTL**. These modalities are **A** (for all futures) and **E** (for some future), followed by an arbitrary **LTL** formula, and arbitrary nesting of such combinations. Thus, time is regarded as having a tree-like branching structure and futures are paths in this tree, the nodes of which are (present) states. Therefore, Branching-Time formulas are naturally interpreted over states, the futures of which should satisfy the interpreted formulas.

This difference in the domain of interpretation causes a problem in comparing the expressive power of **LTL**s and **BTL**s. In a first attempt for such a comparison, Lamport, in [LA80], used a different approach. He used the same syntax for **LTL** and **BTL**, distinguishing them only in the semantics levels. He then lifted the notion of validity to the level of structures, "forgetting" behaviors of specific states or specific paths. On that level he was able to prove the incompatibility of the two interpretations. He then drew some conclusion concerning the suitability of *TL* for expressing properties of programs. His main conclusion, that **LTL** is better suited for specifying properties of concurrent programs, while **BTL** suits better nondeterministic programs. A major cause of this conclusion is the inability of a proper treatment fairness in the **BTL** interpretation as used by him.

Both Lamport's formulation of the distinction between **LTL** and **BTL** and the conclusion based on it were later criticized, and alternatives suggested ([EH 83], [EH 84]). In particular, the ability of handling fairness in **BTL** is shown in [EL 85].

Intuitively, the added expressive power of the two new modalities is due to the ability of reasoning about (and specifying) possibilities in behaviors of programs. The importance of this ability is not universally accepted, which adds another factor to this ongoing controversy. We note that we needed (in Chapter 3) this ability in order to properly specify the properties of random assignments. Compare also the issue of the forward predicate transformer [F 77] mentioned there.

In the conclusion of [EH 84] several more examples of *required possibilities* are given, taken from the specification of the classical synchronization problem of *mutual exclusion.* It is also related to *automatic program synthesis.* Their conclusion is that it is better to have a more expressive language and "tune" it to the level of complexity needed for specific applications. Note, however, that this *does not* contradict the validity of Lamport's observations about incomprability of linear-time to branching-time, as he had in mind a *simpler* branching-time logic.

We now turn to a more detailed description of the **BTL** known as **CTL*** ([EH 83], [CES 82], [EL 85]) and its treatment of fairness. Again, a basic first-order language **L** is assumed, over which a **BTL** extension is constructed.

Formation rule for **CTL***: We inductively define a class of state formulae (true or false of states) which intuitively correspond to branching-time logic, and a class of path formulas (true or false of paths) which intuitively correspond to linear time logic:

S1. Any $A \in \mathbf{L}$ is a state formula.
S2. If A, B are state formulae then so are $A \wedge B$, $\neg A$.
S3. If A is a path formula then $\mathbf{E}A$ is a state formula.
P1. Any state formula A is a path formula.
P2. If A, B are path formulae then so are $A \wedge B$, $\neg A$.
P3. If A, B are path formulae then so are oA, $A\mathbf{U}B$.

We use the abbreviations $\mathbf{F}^{\infty}A$ for $\mathbf{GF}A$ and $\mathbf{G}^{\infty}A$ for $\neg \mathbf{F}^{\infty} \neg A$ (i.e. $\mathbf{FG}A$).

Semantics of **CTL***

We define the semantics of a formula with respect to a structure $M = (\Sigma, R, \mathbf{I})$ where

Σ is a nonempty *set of states* (and $\Sigma = \Sigma_S$ when states of a program S are considered);
R is a nonempty, total *binary relation* on Σ, and
$\mathbf{I}$ is an interpretation of **L** (again left implicit in the sequel).

A *fullpath* $\pi = (\sigma_1, \sigma_2, \sigma_3, \cdots)$ is an infinite sequence of states such that $(\sigma_i, \sigma_{i+1}) \in R$ for all i. We write $M, \sigma \models A$ ($M, \pi \models A$) to mean that state formula A (path formula A) is true in structure M at state σ (of path π, respectively). When M is understood, we write $\sigma \models p$ ($\pi \models p$). We define $\models$ inductively.

S1. $\sigma \models A$ iff $\mathbf{I}, \sigma \models A$ for $A \in \mathbf{L}$.
S2. $\sigma \models A \wedge B$ iff $\sigma \models A$ and $\sigma \models B$,
$\sigma \models \neg A$ iff $\neg(\sigma \models A)$.
S3. $\sigma \models \mathbf{E}A$ iff for some fullpath π starting at σ, $\pi \models A$.

P1. $\pi \models A$ iff $\pi(1) \models A$ for any state formula A.
P2. $\pi \models A \wedge B$ iff $\pi \models A$ and $\pi \models B$,
$\pi \models \neg A$ iff $\neg(\pi \models A)$.
P3. $\pi \models \circ A$ iff $\pi^{(1)} \models A$,
$\pi \models (A\mathbf{U}B)$ iff for some $i \geqslant 1, \pi^{(i)} \models A$ and for all $j \geqslant 1\ [j \leqslant i \rightarrow \pi^{(j)} \models A]$.

We say that state formula A is *valid,* and write $\models A$, if for every structure M and every state σ in M, $M, \sigma \models A$. We say that state formula A is *satisfiable* if for some structure M and some state σ in M, $M, \sigma \models A$. In this case we also say that M defines a *model* of A. We define validity and satisfiability similarly for path (i.e. linear time) formulas, in accordance to the **LTL** definition in Section 7.1.

The set of path formulae generated by rules S1, P1, P2 and P3 forms the **LTL** language of linear time logic. The set of state formulae generated by all the above rules forms the language **CTL***. The language **CTL** is the subset of **CTL*** where only a single linear time operator (**F**, **G**, o, **U**) can follow a path quantifier (**A**, **E**), and was introduced in [CE 81], [CES 83], and also in **MPL** ([AB 79]).

As an example of specification of program properties using **CTL***, consider the famous problem of *readers-writers*, with more elaborate exclusion requirement than present in the simple mutual exclusion problem discussed before. The example is due to Emerson.

Example: (readers-writers specification) Let P_1 be a reader, P_2 a writer process, and suppose that P_2 has priority over P_1 in a solution to the 2 process readers-writers problem.

Absence of starvation for P_1 provided P_2 remains in its noncritical region: $\mathbf{AG}(TRY_1 \rightarrow \mathbf{AF}(CS_1 \vee \neg NCS_2))$.

Absence of starvation for P_2: $\mathbf{AG}(TRY_2 \rightarrow \mathbf{AF}CS_2)$.

Priority of P_2 over P_1 for outstanding requests to enter the critical region: $\mathbf{AG}((TRY_1 \wedge TRY_2) \rightarrow \mathbf{A}[TRY_1 \mathbf{U} CS_2])$.

In this specification, *CS, NCS* and *TRY* are abbreviation for state formulas with the obvious meaning.

The comparison in expressive power between **LTL**s and **BTL**s suggested in [EH 84] uses another level of universal quantification. For an **LTL** language **L**, let $\mathbf{B(L)} \overset{def.}{=} \{\mathbf{A}\phi \mid \phi \in \mathbf{L}\}$. By doing this $\mathbf{B(L)}$ is now interpreted similarly to any **BTL** language. It is shown in [EH 84] that **CTL*** subsumes both interpretations of Lamport, as well as a hierarchy among different *TLs*, all subsumed by **CTL***. As we are not interested in the logics as such, we do not enter into details. We also skip the treatment of the complexity of the decision problem in the finite-state case, another factor in the controversy. This is discussed in [EL 85]. Rather, we turn to the treatment of fairness in **CTL***.

FCTL (fair **CTL**) is defined as follows: An **FCTL** specification (A_0, Φ_0) consists of a functional assertion A_0, which is a state formula, and an underlying fairness assumption Φ_0, which is path formula. The functional assertion A_0 is expressed in essentially **CTL** syntax with basic modalities of the form either $\mathbf{A}_\Phi$ (for all *fair* paths) or $\mathbf{E}_\Phi$ (for some *fair* path) followed by one of the linear time operators **F**, **G**, **o**, **U**. We subscript the path quantifiers with the *symbol* Φ to emphasize that they range over paths meeting the fairness constraint Φ_0, and to syntactically distinguish **FCTL** from **CTL**. A fairness constraint Φ_0 is a Boolean combination of the infinitary linear time operators $\mathbf{F}^\infty A$ (infinitely often A) and $\mathbf{G}^\infty A$ (almost always A), applied to state formulae (only propositional in [EL 85]).

We now define the semantics of an **FCTL** specification (A_0, Φ_0). Φ_0 is a path formula, in a restricted syntax specialized to describing fairness properties, so by expanding the abbreviations $M, \pi \models \Phi_0$ is defined by the rules S1, P1, P2, P3. We can then view a subformula such as $\mathbf{A}_\Phi \mathbf{F} A$ of functional assertion A_0 as an abbreviation for the **CTL*** formula $\mathbf{A}[\Phi_0 \rightarrow \mathbf{F}A]$. Similarly, $\mathbf{E}_\Phi \mathbf{G} A$ abbreviates $\mathbf{E}[\Phi_0 \wedge \mathbf{G}A]$. Note that all path quantification in the functional assertion is relativized to the same Φ_0, and if we were to expand the abbreviations for $\mathbf{E}_\Phi$ and $\mathbf{A}_\Phi$ in a functional assertion, the resulting **CTL*** formula might be rather unwieldy due to the need to repeatedly write down multiple copies of the actual fairness formula Φ_0.

We can succinctly express the following fairness notions using **CTL***:

1. *Unconditional fairness* (*impartiality*):

$$\bigwedge_{i=1,n} \mathbf{F}^\infty \ executed_i,$$

   where $executed_i$ is a state formula which asserts that process i is being executed.
2. *Weak fairness* (*justice*):

$$\bigwedge_{i=1,n} (\mathbf{G}^\infty enabled_i \rightarrow \mathbf{F}^\infty executed_i)$$

$$\equiv \bigwedge_{i=1,n} (\mathbf{F}^\infty(\neg \ enabled_i) \vee \mathbf{F}^\infty executed_i)$$

$$\equiv \bigwedge_{i=1,n} (\mathbf{F}^\infty(\neg enabled_i \ \vee \ executed_i))$$

3. *Strong fairness*:

$$\bigwedge_{i=1,n} (\mathbf{F}^\infty enabled_i \rightarrow \mathbf{F}^\infty executed_i)$$

$$\equiv \bigwedge_{i=1,n} (\mathbf{G}^\infty \neg enabled_i \ \vee \ \mathbf{F}^\infty executed_i).$$

4. *Generalized Fairness*: Note that as we did in Chapter 4, we can replace the predicates $executed_i$ and $enabled_i$ by any arbitrary (augmented)

state formulae so that we can reason not only about, say, strong fairness w.r.t. process enabling and execution but also strong fairness w.r.t. the occurrence of any such properties.

Let $\mathbf{F} = ((P_1, Q_1), (P_2, Q_2), \cdots, (P_k, Q_k))$ be a finite list of pairs of state formulas. Then, we can express that a computation is *unconditionally* $\mathbf{F}$-fair by $\bigwedge_{i=1,k} \mathbf{F}^{\infty} Q_i$, *weakly* $\mathbf{F}$-fair by $\bigwedge_{i=1,k} (\mathbf{G}^{\infty} P_i \rightarrow \mathbf{F}^{\infty} Q_i)$, and *strongly* $\mathbf{F}$-fair by $\bigwedge_{i=1,k} (\mathbf{F}^{\infty} P_i \rightarrow \mathbf{F}^{\infty} Q_i)$.

5. *Fair reachability of a predicate*: This is formulated as $\mathbf{F}^{\infty}\mathbf{EF}p \rightarrow \mathbf{F}^{\infty}p$.

This is an example of usage of the nesting capability of modalities in **CTL***.

A normal form is introduced in [EL 85] for **FCTL** formula, for which a faster model checking procedure exists in the finite-state case. The normal form is $\Phi_0 = \bigvee_{i=1,n} \bigwedge_{j=1,n_i} (\mathbf{G}^{\infty} A_{ij} \vee \mathbf{F}^{\infty} B_{ij})$, where A_{ij}, B_{ij} are independent of temporal modalities. In the general case, passing to this normal form may involve an exponential blowup.

A similar approach to **BTL** is presented in [QS 83], where two binary temporal modalities are taken as primitives in a logic called **CL**:

POT$[A](B)$, read as B is *potentially* reachable under condition A, and
INEV$[A](B)$, read as B is *inevitably* reachable under condition A.

When interpreted in a structure as before (taken as a transition system in [QS 83]), they can be seen to be equivalent to $\mathbf{E}(A\mathbf{U}B)$ and $\mathbf{A}(A\mathbf{U}B)$, respectively. Their dual modalities are

ALL$[A](B)$: for every path π, B holds along it *as long as* A holds.
SOME$[A](B)$: there is a path π such that B holds along it as long as A does.

These modalities refer to reachability of their second arguments under arbitrary paths (executions in the underlying transition system). The next step is to define the fair variant **FCL** of **CL**. Fairness is taken as ρ-fairness relativized to some countable set Γ of subsets of states. The primitive modalities are taken to be $\mathbf{F}_{\Gamma}\mathbf{POT}[A](B)$ and $\mathbf{F}_{\Gamma}\mathbf{INEV}[A](B)$, implying reachability of their second argument under (ρ-) fair path (w.r.t. Γ), provided these second arguments are members of Γ.

Finally, a procedure is described, that for any $A \in$ **FCL** produces a formula $B \in$ **CL** expressing the same reachability property under the fairness assumption.

We have pointed out the use of special *fairness-oriented* logics since we focus on fairness and its influence in general. There is another reason for using such logics instead of full **CTL***, due to the latter's less efficient decision procedure. We do not deal with such complexity issues here.

CHAPTER 8
The Functional Approach

8.0 Overview

In this chapter we examine the fairness notions arising in the context of *functional* (or *applicative*) languages. As a representative language we have chosen Milner's *CCS* (calculus for communicating processes) [M 80]. A similar formalism, with more primitive operators, which is also concerned with fairness, is that of Bergstra and Klop *process algebra* [BK 85]. There, the stress is more on the *algebraic* treatment.

Some new aspects of fairness are treated in the literature in the context of *CCS*. One notable difference from the assumptions in previous chapters is that *dynamic networks* are considered (i.e., with a changing number of processes and interconnections). This issue arises due to presence of *recursion over concurrency,* in contrast to using iteration (tail recursion) in the previously discussed languages.

Another new aspect arises due to the presence of a *restriction* (or *hiding*) operator, which forms a natural ground for distinguishing between *structural fairness,* based on the structure of the processes, and that of *observable fairness,* which restricts attention to observable communications only.

Though the issues raised in Chapter 5 regarding *conspiracies* (or their absence) apply to *CCS* as well, they were not explicitly treated in the literature in this context.

The presentation follows closely the main work on fairness in *CCS*, namely [CS 85].

We mention here also that termination is not a central issue in *CCS*, hence the discussion is not focused on fair termination. Rather, the central issue is *rules* for fair behaviour. Thus, this chapter is concerned with *generating* fairness rather then with the consequences of *assuming* it. In this way, a *metric* characterization of fair *CCS* sequences is also discussed, closely following [C 85]. Finally, *CCS* turns to be a convenient tool for discussing (briefly) one other notion, that of *finite delay* as a primitive operator, which was mentioned in the introduction chapter as a fairness-like concept.

8.1 *CCS*

Milner's *CCS* is a calculus whose *closed expressions* stand for processes. The meaning of a process is given in terms of its *behaviour,* which is determined by the rules of the calculus. Let $Act = \Delta \cup \overline{\Delta}$ be a set of *atomic actions,* where $\overline{\Delta}$ is a set of *co-actions* disjoint from Δ and in bijection with it. The bijection is $-$: $\bar{a} \in \overline{\Delta}$ stands for the co-action of $a \in \Delta$. Using $\bar{a}$ for the inverse means that a is also the co-action of $\bar{a}$. The calculus allows *synchronization* of co-action which is represented by τ, a *silent* (or internal) action. Let $Move = Act \cup \{\tau\}$ and let a,b,c range over Act, m,n over $Move$ and let X, Y, Z be process variables. The syntax of (a subset of) *CCS* (without value passing and renaming) is:

$$E::=X \mid NIL \mid mE \mid E+E \mid fix\ X{\cdot}E \mid E\backslash a \mid E \mid E.$$

NIL is the nullary process which does nothing. $+$ represents nondeterministic choice; $\mid$ concurrency; *fix* recursion; and $\backslash a$ represents restriction (prevention) of a and $\bar{a}$ actions. A restriction on the language is that in the expression $fix\ X.E$ *X is guarded in E:* that is, every free occurrence of X in E is within a subexpression mF of E. An occurrence of X is free if it is not within the scope of $fix\ X$. The ambiguous use of $\mid$ also as the BNF-separator should cause no confusion.

The behaviour of a process E is determined by the rules in Figure 8.1 where $E \overset{m}{--\rightarrow} F$ means process E *becomes* F by performing the move m. They constitute an *operational semantics* for *CCS*. For a detailed discussion of full *CCS*, the reader may consult [M 80].

Three points are worth mentioning. First, situations arise where the $+$ rules do not allow choice: $(aE + bF)\backslash b$ can only become E by performing a because the restriction $\backslash b$ prevents the subprocess bF acting. Secondly, the $\mid$ rules do not, in general, compel synchronization: $a\,E \mid \bar{a}\,F$ can perform a or can perform $\bar{a}$ as well as τ. On the other hand, $(aE \mid \bar{a}F)\backslash a$ can only perform τ because of the restriction. Thirdly, the number of concurrent subprocesses may increase as moves are performed: the process $E = fix\ X.(aX \mid bX)$ becomes $E \mid bE$ after performing a.

Definition:

(1) A *derivation* is any finite or infinite sequence of the form $E_0 \overset{m_0}{--\rightarrow} E_1 \overset{m_1}{--\rightarrow} \cdots$.

Move	$mE \xrightarrow{m} E$			
$+R$	$\dfrac{E \xrightarrow{m} E'}{E+F \xrightarrow{m} E'}$		$+L$	$\dfrac{F \xrightarrow{m} F'}{E+F \xrightarrow{m} F'}$
fix	$\dfrac{E[\mathit{fix}\ X.E/X] \xrightarrow{m} E'}{\mathit{fix}\ X.E \xrightarrow{m} E'}$	where $[\cdot/\cdot]$ denotes substitution		
Res	$\dfrac{E \xrightarrow{m} E'}{E\backslash a \xrightarrow{m} E'\backslash a}$	$m \notin \{a,\bar{a}\}$		
$\mid R$	$\dfrac{E \xrightarrow{m} E'}{E \mid F \xrightarrow{m} E' \mid F}$		$\mid L$	$\dfrac{F \xrightarrow{m} F'}{E \mid F \xrightarrow{m} E \mid F'}$
$\mid Syn$	$\dfrac{E \xrightarrow{a} E' \quad F \xrightarrow{\bar{a}} F'}{E \mid F \xrightarrow{\tau} E' \mid F'}$			

Figure 8.1 Rules for *CCS*.

(2) An *execution sequence* is a maximal derivation: if it is finite its last term is unable to make a move.

We let h, k range over finite nonempty sequences of moves. If $E_0 \xrightarrow{m_0} E_1 \xrightarrow{m_1} \cdots \xrightarrow{m_n} E_{n+1}$ we use $E_0 \xrightarrow{h} E_{n+1}$, where $h = m_0 m_1 \cdots m_n$, as an abbreviation.

Example: Two examples of derivations are:

i. $(aNIL + \bar{b}\tau NIL) \mid b(a\ NIL)\backslash a \xrightarrow{\tau} \tau NIL \mid (aNIL)\backslash a \xrightarrow{\tau}$ $NIL \mid (aNIL)\backslash a$.

ii. $(\mathit{fix}\ X.aX) \mid b\ NIL \xrightarrow{a} (\mathit{fix}\ X.aX) \mid bNIL \xrightarrow{b} (\mathit{fix}\ X.aX) \mid NIL$ $\xrightarrow{a} (\mathit{fix}\ X.aX) \mid NIL$.

The first of these is also an execution sequence.

We have described *CCS* without value passing and renaming. These features are omitted merely for convenience because the main concern is with the issue of fairness in *CCS*: they can be dealt with within the framework presented. Note, however, that a full discussion of conspiracies can be carried out only with value passing.

8.2 Fairness and *CCS*

To see, intuitively, the intended interpretation of fairness in *CCS*, consider, for instance, the process $E \mid F$ where $E = \mathit{fix}\ X.aX$ and

$F = fix\ Y.bY$. The fairness constraints preclude the following *CCS* execution sequence:

$$E \mid F \xrightarrow{a} E \mid F \xrightarrow{a} \cdots \xrightarrow{a} E \mid F \xrightarrow{a} \cdots$$

The subcomponent F is always able to contribute a move to the overall behaviour but never does. On the other hand,

$$G \xrightarrow{a} G \xrightarrow{a} \cdots \xrightarrow{a} G \xrightarrow{a} \cdots,$$

where $G = fix\ X.(aX + bX)$ is admissible because G has no concurrent subcomponents. More generally, any execution sequence from $E \mid F$ involving only a finite number of b moves or a moves is inadmissible: hence, the sequence of actions in any admissible sequence belongs to the fair merge of a^ω and b^ω. Thus, in terms of the terminology of Chapter 5, *process fairness* is considered. As before, fairness constraints, by ruling out execution sequences, affect liveness properties. The process

$$((fix\ X.(aX + bNIL)) \mid \bar{b}NIL) \backslash b$$

always eventually terminates (becomes $(NIL \mid NIL) \backslash b$) when fairness is assumed, because its sole infinitary behaviour is inadmissible: the subcomponent $\bar{b}NIL$ must eventually proceed since it is always enabled to a synchronization and in so doing forces termination of the other subprocess $fix\ X.(aX + bNIL)$.

Occurrence of the restriction operator may prevent concurrent subprocesses from proceeding autonomously. Instead, like $\bar{b}NIL$ above, they may only proceed by synchronizing. This means that different notions of fairness are distinguishable. The subcomponent $\bar{b}NIL$ in $E = (F \mid \bar{b}NIL) \backslash b$ where $F = fix\ X.a(cX + bNIL)$ has no partner to synchronize with and so is *blocked*. The blocking is, however, only temporary: once E performs a move a partner is available since $E \xrightarrow{a} G$ where $G = ((cF + NIL) \mid \bar{b}NIL) \backslash b$. The question arises as to whether the following execution sequence is admissible:

$$E \xrightarrow{a} G \xrightarrow{c} E \xrightarrow{a} \cdots \xrightarrow{c} E \xrightarrow{a} G \xrightarrow{c} \cdots$$

This is the familiar distinction between weak and strong fairness. The sequence above is admissible under the weak but not the strong constraint.

Informally, we regard fairness as an issue to do with concurrent subcomponents. An alternative is to view it in terms of possible events. A natural notion of possible event for *CCS* is an immediately possible atomic action instance: an atomic action instance is autonomously possible in the process E if E can immediately perform it autonomously or within a synchronization. An infinite execution sequence can then be said to be admissible under weak (strong) fairness just in case no possible event remains almost always (infinitely often) possible. This is, in effect, the definition offered in [CS 84] for *CCS* without restriction. However, when restriction is in the language this definition of weak fairness is different from the definition in terms of concurrent subcomponents. (The two definitions of strong fairness coincide.) Consider the following example execution sequence where $E = fix\ X.(c(cX + \bar{a}NIL) + \bar{b}NIL)$ and $F = aNIL + bNIL$:

$$(E \mid F)\backslash a\backslash b \xrightarrow{c} ((cE + \bar{a}NIL) \mid F)\backslash a\backslash b \xrightarrow{c} (E \mid F)\backslash a\backslash b \xrightarrow{c} \cdots$$

F can always contribute to the overall behaviour by synchronizing but never does. In contrast, no event in *F* remains almost always possible. Initially the event *b* is possible whereas *a* is not. But, once *c* is performed, *b* loses its possibility and *a* becomes possible. This swapping of possibilities continues throughout the execution sequence. With respect to subprocesses, but not events, this sequence is inadmissible. A reconciliation could be possible if a more complex notion of possible event is definable. Instead, we define fairness in terms of subprocesses (and therefore count the above sequence as inadmissible).

Following is a formal definition of weak and strong fairness in *CCS* in terms of admissible execution sequences. As a means to this end we make use of a *labelled CCS* syntax. This allows us to use labels to represent concurrent subprocesses. A further reason for labelling is exemplified by the following execution sequence where $E = fix\ X.bX$:

$$E \mid E \xrightarrow{b} E \mid E \xrightarrow{b} \cdots .$$

This representation of an execution sequence does not indicate which subcomponent performs each *b* move. Consequently, we cannot determine the admissibility of this sequence. A solution is to include the proof of each single length derivation in the definition of an execution sequence: which *E* subprocess is actor any point depends upon whether the $\mid R$ or $\mid L$ *CCS* rule is used in the proof of $E \mid E \xrightarrow{b} E \mid E$. It is, however, less cumbersome to use labels instead to disambiguate. This is similar to the introduction of auxiliary state variable to capture the identity of the directions taken.

The precise details of the labelled *CCS* syntax are omitted here and can be found in [CS 85]. Here we point out the features essential for the current subject. The exact details of the labelling method are immaterial.

i. Labels are strings in $LAB = \{1,2\}^*$. They are assigned systematically following the structure of *CCS* expressions. Due to recursion the labelling is in part dynamic: the rule for *fix* generates new labels. We use $u, v, w, \cdots$ to denote labels with ϵ as the empty label.

ii. All the *CCS* operators and variables are labelled in such a way that no label occurs more than once in an expression. We call this property *unicity* of labels. For example

$$(fix\ X)_1.(a_{111}X_{1111} +_{11} b_{112}X_{1121}) |_\epsilon (\bar{a}_{21}b_{211}NIL_{2111})(\backslash b)_2 .$$

We assume here that the *fix X* binds both X_{1111} and X_{1121}, that the restriction $\backslash b$ "binds" b_{111} and that $\bar{a}_{111}$ and $\bar{a}_{21}$ are co-actions.

iii. We assume that the moves performed by labelled processes are not labelled. Hence, the *Move* rule becomes

$$m_u E \ -\overset{m}{-}\rightarrow\ E.$$

The labels on restriction unaffect its powers of prevention: the *Res* rule therefore becomes

$$\frac{E \ -\overset{m}{-}\rightarrow\ F}{E(\backslash a)_u \ -\overset{m}{-}\rightarrow\ F(\backslash a)_u} \qquad m \notin \{a, \bar{a}\}.$$

In the *fix* rule standard substitution $[\cdot/\cdot]$ is replaced by a substitution operation which also changes the labels of the substituted expression: they are prefixed with the label of the variable occurrence they replace. For example, under the labelling *fix X.aX* is "equivalent" to an infinite expression $a_{u_1}a_{u_2}\ \cdots\ a_{u_i}\ \cdots$ where each label u_i occurs only once.

Example: Following are two derivations on labelled *CCS*, where $2 < n \leqslant 5$ represents $\overbrace{11...1}^{n \text{ times}}$:

$$(fix\ X)_1.b_{11}X_3 |_\epsilon (fix\ X)_2.b_{21}X_{211} \ -\overset{b}{-}\rightarrow\ (fix\ X)_3.b_4X_5 |_\epsilon (fix\ X)_2.b_{21}X_{211}$$

$$((a_3E +_{11} b_{112}F) |_1 (a_{121}G +_{12} b_{122}H))(\backslash b)_\epsilon \ -\overset{a}{-}\rightarrow$$

$$(E |_1 (a_{121}G +_{12} b_{122}H))(\backslash b)_\epsilon.$$

As these examples illustrate, if $E' \ -\overset{m}{-}\rightarrow\ F'$, then the labels in F' are determined by those in E' and unicity of labels is preserved. Central to the labelling is the persistence and disappearance of labels under derivation. If a label in E' recurs in F' then it is either attached to the same symbol or to a variable X on E' and a *fix X* in F'. Once a label disappears it can never reappear. These features allow us to recognize when a subcomponent contributes to the performance of a move. In the second example above the disappearance of the label 3 (on a) shows that the left subcomponent contributes a move while the persistence of 12 shows that the right component remains inert. Similar remarks apply to the first example.

Clearly, if R corresponds to the operation of removing labels then if $E \xrightarrow{m} F$ then $R(E) \xrightarrow{m} R(F)$ in unlabelled CCS. Conversely, if $E' \xrightarrow{m} F'$ in unlabelled CCS and $R(E) = E'$ then, for some F where $R(F) = F'$, $E \xrightarrow{m} F$.

Throughout the rest of the discussion the labelled calculus is assumed. However, whenever possible, labels are left implicit to keep the notation simple.

To capture the admissible execution sequences under fairness constraints we need to define the concurrent subprocesses. We also need to know when a subprocess has terminated or is blocked. A concurrent subprocess is *live* if it can currently contribute to the performance of a move. Using labels we define below the set of *live concurrent subprocesses* of a process. We define first the set of concurrent subprocesses, $P(E)$, of a process E, irrespective of liveness. This is done inductively using labels (see Figure 8.2).

The concurrent processes in $E \mid F$ consist of those in E together with those in F. Note that a subprocess is identified by the label of its main combinator, except in the case of $\backslash a$ (restriction) and $fix\ X$. Hence $P(((F \mid G) +_{u1} bH) \mid a_{u2}NIL) = \{u1, u2\}$; that is, $(F \mid G) + bH$ is a single subprocess despite the presence of the parallel operator, $|$, in it, because $+$ is its main combinator. Notice also that we have a dynamic notion of subcomponent: if $E = a_u a_{u1} NIL$ and E performs a then the resulting subcomponents do not include u. A simpler, static, notion of subprocess is inadequate here because the number of subcomponents may grow without a finite bound under derivation. Consider, for instance, the behaviour of $fix\ X.(aX \mid bX)$.

We are interested in a subset of $P(E)$, the set of live concurrent subprocesses in E. For instance, both subprocesses in $(aNIL \mid \bar{a}NIL)\backslash a$ are

$$P(X_u) = \varnothing$$
$$P(NIL_u) = \{u\}$$
$$P(m_u E) = \{u\}$$
$$P(E +_u F) = \begin{cases} \{u\} & \text{if } P(E) \cup P(F) \neq \varnothing \\ \varnothing & \text{otherwise} \end{cases}$$
$$P(E \mid F) = P(E) \cup P(F)$$
$$P(fix\ X.E) = P(E\backslash a) = P(E)$$

Figure 8.2 Concurrent subprocesses.

live because they can both contribute to a synchronization. On the other hand, there is only one live subcomponent, u, in $(a_u\bar{b}_v NIL \mid b_y NIL)\backslash b$, where u,v,y are appropriate labels, because of the restriction $\backslash b$ which prevents y from contributing a move. However, note that y *may become* live: once the action a is performed y can synchronize with the new subcomponent v. The definition of live subprocesses makes use of $Act(E)$, an unlabelled set of actions in E which can happen autonomously (see Figure 8.3).

Note that $Act(E)$ never includes τ, the silent (or synchronized) move. A simple consequence of this definition is:

$$a \in Act(E) \quad \text{iff} \quad \exists F\colon E \overset{a}{- - \rightarrow} F.$$

Thus, Act is empty for a terminated, or blocked, process.

We now define $PL(E, A)$ (see Figure 8.4) to stand for the set of live concurrent subprocesses in E when the environment prevents the set of actions $A \subseteq Act$. We let $\overline{Act}(E)$ be the set $\{\bar{a}{:}a \in Act(E)\}$: that is, the set of co-actions of $Act(E)$.

The set A represents the actions restricted upon. Thus, $LP(a_u E,\ \{a\})$ is empty because the action a is prevented. Restriction increases the prevented set: $LP(E\backslash a, A)$ only includes subcomponents which are not prevented by $A \cup \{a,\bar{a}\}$. The possibility of synchronization reduces the prevention set. $LP(E \mid F,\ A)$ includes subcomponents of E and of F which

$$
\begin{aligned}
&Act(X) = Act(NIL) = Act(\tau E) = \varnothing\\
&Act(a_u E) = \{a\}\\
&Act(fix\ X.E) = Act(E)\\
&Act(E+F) = Act(E \mid F) = Act(E) \cup Act(F)\\
&Act(E\backslash a) = Act(E) - \{a, \bar{a}\}.
\end{aligned}
$$

Figure 8.3 $Act(E)$.

$$
\begin{aligned}
&LP(X_u, A) = LP(NIL_u, A) = \varnothing\\
&LP(m_u E, A) = \begin{cases} \{u\} & \text{if } m \notin A\\ \varnothing & \text{otherwise}\end{cases}\\
&LP(fix\ X.E, A) = LP(E, A)\\
&LP(E +_u F, A) = \begin{cases} \{u\} & \text{if } LP(E, A) \cup LP(F, A) \neq \varnothing\\ \varnothing & \text{otherwise}\end{cases}\\
&LP(E\backslash a, A) = LP(E, A \cup \{a, \bar{a}\})\\
&LP(E \mid F, A) = LP(E, A-\overline{Act}(F)) \cup LP(F, A-\overline{Act}(E)).
\end{aligned}
$$

Figure 8.4 Live concurrent subprocesses.

can synchronize with each other even though the individual synchronization partners may be prevented by A: for this to happen, there must be an $a \in Act(E)$ and and $\bar{a} \in Act(F)$. Here one can notice the difference in treatment w.r.t. Chapter 5. A move m_u contributes u to LP *independently* of the presence of $\overline{m}_v$ in LP. Thus, joint enabledness is not considered. The meaning of *live* is the *possibility* of contributing to a move.

Definition: $LP(E) \overset{def.}{=} LP(E, \emptyset)$.

For example, for $F = (a_u\bar{b}_{u1}NIL_{u11} \mid b_wNIL_{w1}) \backslash b$, $LP(F) = \{u\}$. The following lemma shows that LP captures the required set.

Lemma: (liveness)

i. If $u \in P(E) - LP(E)$ and $E \overset{m}{- - \rightarrow} F$ then $u \in P(F)$.

ii. If $u \in LP(E)$ then $\exists F, m$: $(E \overset{m}{- - \rightarrow} F$ and $u \notin P(F))$.

iii. If $E \overset{m}{- - \rightarrow} F$ then $\exists u \in LP(E)$: $u \notin P(F)$.

Example: We illustrate the meaning of the liveness lemma (see Figure 8.5) with the example F above.

The notion of subcomponent is dynamic: if a subcomponent contributes to a move then afterwards it no longer exists, as shown by u in F and $u1$, w in F_1. The first part of the liveness lemma, therefore, says that a non-live subcomponent must persist after the performance of a move: consider the component w in F. Consequently, a non-live subcomponent cannot currently contribute to a move. The second part of the liveness lemma says that if a component is live then it can contribute to a move–this is true of $u1$, w in F_1. Thus LP at most captures the live subprocesses of E. The final part of the liveness lemma states that if a process performs a move then some subcomponent must contribute to it–this is illustrated by the performance of a by F and τ by F_1. Clearly, if $LP(E) = \emptyset$ then E cannot perform any move and vice versa.

	P	LP
$F = (a_u\bar{b}_{u1}NIL_{u11} \mid b_wNIL_{w1}) \backslash b$	$\{u, w\}$	$\{u\}$
$\downarrow a$		
$F_1 = (\bar{b}_{u1}NIL_{u11} \mid b_wNIL_{w1}) \backslash b$	$\{u1, w\}$	$\{u1, w\}$
$\downarrow \tau$		
$F_2 = (NIL_{u11} \mid NIL_{w1}) \backslash b$	$\{u11, w1\}$	$\emptyset$

Figure 8.5 Illustration of the liveness lemma.

Given these definitions we are now in a position to define admissibility under fairness constraints.

Definition: For $\gamma = E_0 \overset{m_0}{--\rightarrow} E_1 \overset{m_1}{--\rightarrow} \cdots$ a finite or infinite *CCS* execution sequence:

(i) γ is *weak-admissible* iff $\forall u \forall i \exists k \geqslant i$: $u \notin LP(E_k)$
(ii) γ is *strong-admissible* iff $\forall u \exists i \forall k \geqslant i$: $u \notin LP(E_k)$.

Here weak-admissible (strong-admissible) means admissible under the weak (strong) fairness constraint. A sequence is weak-admissible just in case no subcomponent becomes live and then remains live throughout. A sequence is strong-admissible just in case no subcomponent is live infinitely often. Notice that a component cannot be live infinitely often and proceed infinitely often because of the dynamic labelling: as soon as a component contributes a move it "disappears". If a sequence is strong-admissible then it is also weak-admissible. Clearly, any finite execution sequence is admissible in both senses because the final process will have no live subcomponents. It is straightforward to check that the earlier examples of admissible and inadmissible sequences are deemed so by this definition.

Inadmissible execution sequences are allowed by the *CCS* rules because of the $\mid R$ and $\mid L$ rules. In effect, a use of either of these rules in a derivation involves an enforced delay of one or other of the subprocesses E, F in $E \mid F$. From small enforced delays lengthier delays can grow without limit: if either E or F has an infinite behaviour then there is nothing in the *CCS* rules to force the other to proceed (when it is able to).

A general method for controlling the length of delay is to use random assignment, as was done in Chapter 3. This is a very general, but very indirect, method of modeling both weak and strong fairness. However, it is not clear how it could be directly applied to *CCS* because it presupposes a fixed number of concurrent components. An alternative, more direct use of random assignment overcomes this problem [PL 82]. Plotkin offers rules for a fair $\mid$ by introducing a subsidiary set of parallel operators $\mid_n$, $\mid^n$, $n \in N$, in the case of a concurrent *while*-language (where there is distinction between weak and strong fairness): the rules for $\mid^n$ ensure that the left component proceeds no more than $n+1$ steps; a random choice of the maximum number of steps the right hand component may proceed is then made via the operators $\mid_n$. Although Plotkin's method works for *CCS* without restriction (where there is no distinction between weak and strong fairness) and, possibly, for weakly fair *CCS*, it is unclear how it can be generalized to strongly fair *CCS*.

The use of random assignment for capturing fairness is more a *simulation* than a *description* because of its involvement of *predictive choice* [M 82]. This forcing of choice in advance may have unhappy consequences:

under some definitions of program equivalence, for instance *bisimulation* [PA 81a], Plotkin's $|$ operator is not associative [CS 84]. Moreover, the analysis of the next section suggests that predictive choice is essential to a positive method of generating the strong-admissible *CCS* sequences but not the weak-admissible. The use of random assignment to simulate both masks this difference. The issue of predictive choice is further discussed later.

As inadmissible sequences arise due to the $|R$ and $|L$ rules, what is wanted are rules for $|$ which explicitly ensure that both components proceed (if they can) without at the same time enforcing synchrony. It is difficult to see how this can be achieved because standard operational semantics are based upon rules which show how programs may proceed in a single step where single step is tied to a notion of atomic action. In [CS 84] method is suggested to overcome this: to offer rules for sequences of actions, for *CCS* without restriction. An alternative, more general method, for both weak and strong fairness is presented in the next section, based on [CS 85].

8.3 Weak and Strong Fairness in *CCS*

8.3.1 Weakly fair *CCS*

A *CCS* execution sequence is weak-admissible provided that no process remains live almost always. For example, the following sequence is not admissible, where $E = fix\ X.aX$:

$$E \mid bc_u NIL \xrightarrow{b} E \mid c_u NIL \xrightarrow{a} E \mid c_u NIL \xrightarrow{a} \cdots$$

The subcomponent u becomes live and remains live throughout. In this subsection weak fair *CCS* rules are offered: rules for *CCS* which generate just the admissible execution sequences. The starting point is an alternative, more local, formulation of weak-admissible than its previous definition.

Definition: For $\gamma = E_0 \xrightarrow{m_0} E_1 \xrightarrow{m_1} \cdots$ a *CCS* execution sequence:

i. γ is *w-admissible at i* iff

$$\exists j \geqslant i\colon LP(E_i) \cap LP(E_{i+1}) \cap \cdots \cap LP(E_j) = \emptyset$$

ii. γ is *w-admissible* iff $\forall i\colon i \leqslant length(\gamma) \rightarrow \gamma$ is *w*-admissible at i.

The sequence γ is *w*-admissible at i just in case every live process of E_i eventually loses its liveness. Clearly, the following holds:

Proposition: γ is w-admissible at i iff $\forall j \leqslant i$: γ is w-admissible at j.

An execution sequence which is w-admissible at every i is weak-admissible and vice versa. This is the content of the following theorem.

Theorem: (characterization of weak admissibility) γ is w-admissible iff γ is weak-admissible.

Proof: By contradiction.

(Only-if) Suppose γ is not weak-admissible. Then by definition $\exists u \in LAB \exists i \geqslant 0 \forall k \geqslant i$: $u \in LP(E_k)$. Clearly, then γ is not w-admissible at i.

(If) Suppose $\exists i \geqslant 0$ such that γ is not w-admissible at i. By definition $\forall k \geqslant i$: $LP(E_i) \cap \cdots \cap LP(E_k) \neq \varnothing$. However $LP(E_i)$ is finite, hence $\exists u \forall k \geqslant i$: $u \in LP(E_k)$. Therefore γ is not weak-admissible. [ ]

The significance of this alternative definition of weak-admissibility is that it characterizes weak admissibility in terms of a localizable property and not just as a property of complete execution sequences. Moreover, it induces a straightforward strategy for generating any weak-admissible *CCS* sequence. Starting from E_0 one generates a derivation $E_0 \xrightarrow{m_0} E_1 \xrightarrow{m_1} \cdots \xrightarrow{m_n} E_{n+1}$ satisfying the admissibility at 0 condition; satisfaction of this condition is completely determinate. One then continues by generating a derivation $E_{n+1} \xrightarrow{m_{n+1}} E_{n+2} \xrightarrow{m_{n+2}} \cdots \xrightarrow{m_k} E_{k+1}$ which satisfies admissibility at $n+1$. By the proposition, the concatenation of these two derivations $E_0 \xrightarrow{m_0} \cdots \xrightarrow{m_n} E_{n+1} \xrightarrow{m_{n+1}} \cdots \xrightarrow{m_k} E_{k+1}$ guarantees the admissibility at j for any $j \leqslant n+1$. Clearly, the continuation of this process results in an admissible sequence. Following is a formalization of this strategy.

Definition: $E_0 \xrightarrow{m_0} E_2 \xrightarrow{m_1} \cdots \xrightarrow{m_n} E_{n+1}$ is a *B-step* just in case

i. B is a finite set of (process) labels;
ii. $B \cap LP(E_0) \cap \cdots \cap LP(E_{n+1}) = \varnothing$.

We abbreviate $E_0 \xrightarrow{m_0} E_1 \xrightarrow{m_1} \cdots \xrightarrow{m_n} E_{n+1}$ is a B-step to $E_0 \xrightarrow[B]{h} E_{n+1}$, where $h = m_0 \ldots m_n$.

The first part of the following B-step lemma shows that for any finite set of labels B and live process E there exists a B-step from E. The second part shows that any finite extension of a B-step is still a B-step: this clearly holds because of the second clause of the definition of a B-step.

Lemma: (B-step)

i. if $LP(E) \neq \emptyset$ then for every finite set of labels B there exist F, h, s.t. $E \overset{h}{\underset{B}{\dashrightarrow}} F$

ii. if $E \overset{h}{\underset{B}{\dashrightarrow}} F$ and $F \overset{k}{\dashrightarrow} G$ then $E \overset{h}{\dashrightarrow} \underset{B}{F} \overset{k}{\dashrightarrow} G$.

The definition of w-admissible at i means that a B-step from E, when $B = LP(E)$, is of special interest. An $LP(E)$-step from E is *locally* admissible: the live subprocesses of E have lost their liveness at some point in the step. For instance, Figure 8.6 is an $LP(E)$-step from E. The subprocess u and v synchronize and hence disappear whereas w loses its liveness (and regains it in E_2). Thus, $E \overset{\tau}{\dashrightarrow} E_1$ is also an $LP(E)$-step. On the other hand, Figure 8.7 is not an $LP(E)$-step from E, because v remains live throughout.

Definition: A *w-sequence* from E_0 is any *maximal* sequence of steps of the form $E_0 \overset{h_0}{\underset{LP(E_0)}{\dashrightarrow}} E_1 \overset{h_1}{\underset{LP(E_1)}{\dashrightarrow}} \cdots$

	P	LP
$E = (a_u b_{u1} a_{u11} F \mid (\bar{a}_v \bar{b}_{v1} c_{v11} G \mid \bar{a}_w H)) \backslash a$	$\{u, v, w\}$	$\{u, v, w\}$
$\downarrow \tau$		
$E_1 = (b_{u1} a_{u11} F \mid (\bar{b}_{v1} c_{v11} G \mid \bar{a}_w H)) \backslash a$	$\{u1, v1, w\}$	$\{u1, v1\}$
$\downarrow \tau$		
$E_2 = (a_{u11} F \mid (c_{v11} G \mid \bar{a}_w H)) \backslash a$	$\{u11, v11, w\}$	$\{u11, v11, w\}$

Figure 8.6 An $LP(E)$-step.

	P	LP
$E = (a_u a_{u1} a_{u11} F \mid a_v G)$	$\{u, v\}$	$\{u, v\}$
$\downarrow a$		
$E_1 = (a_{u1} a_{u11} F \mid a_v G)$	$\{u1, v\}$	$\{u1, v\}$
$\downarrow a$		
$E_2 = (a_{u11} F \mid a_v G)$	$\{u11, v\}$	$\{u11, v\}$

Figure 8.7 A non-*LP(E)*-step.

A w-sequence is simply a concatenation of *locally* admissible steps. If δ is a w-sequence then its associated *CCS* execution sequence is the sequence which drops all reference to the $LP(E_i)$s. The following *w-sequence* theorem shows that w-sequences are precisely the weak admissible sequences.

Theorem: (w-sequence) A *CCS* execution sequence is weak-admissible iff it is the sequence associated with a w-sequence.

Proof: A simple consequence of the definitions of w-sequence, weak admissibility and of the characterization of weak admissibility theorem. [ ]

Weak fair *CCS* rules

Operational rules are now offered for weak fair *CCS* based upon the *local* characterization of admissibility. Standard operational semantics are based upon rules which show how programs may proceed in a single step where single step is tied to some notion of atomic action: this is the case with the *CCS* rules offered in section 8.1, where the basic transition relation which appears throughout the rules is $\overset{m}{- - \rightarrow}$, $m \in Move$. In contrast, the analysis above of weak fairness appeals to the notion of a B-step: a finite sequence of moves satisfying a property. Thus, it is desirable to have rules involving a transition relation $\underset{B}{\overset{h}{\rightarrow}}$, satisfying the condition that $E \underset{B}{\overset{h}{\rightarrow}} F$ iff $E \underset{B}{\overset{h}{- - \rightarrow}} F$. Like $E \overset{h}{- - \rightarrow} F$, $E \overset{h}{\rightarrow} F$ is an abbreviation of a sequence of moves $E \overset{m_0}{\rightarrow} E_1 \overset{m_1}{\rightarrow} \cdots \overset{m_n}{\rightarrow} F$ with $h = m_0,\ldots,m_n$. The w-sequences will then be generable from such rules. Note that the significance of the B-step lemma in terms of rules involving $\underset{B}{\overset{h}{\rightarrow}}$ is that it expresses a *no stuck* property: for any live E and finite set of labels B the rules must allow a derivation of the form $E \underset{B}{\overset{h}{\rightarrow}} F$.

The way the rules are formulated is as an extension to the basic *CCS* rules of Section 8.1. This approach is successfully applicable to strong fairness as well.

We assume that the *CCS* rules take account of the labelled syntax. We merely add two new rules involving $\underset{B}{\overset{h}{\rightarrow}}$ to give weak fair *CCS* (see Figure 8.8). Here B, C are finite sets of labels. In the *Trans* rule $E \underset{B \cup C}{\overset{hm}{\longrightarrow}} G$ abbreviates $E \underset{B \cup C}{\overset{h}{\rightarrow}} F \overset{m}{\rightarrow} G$. The *Shift* rule allows one to derive any B-step involving a *single move* only. The *Trans* rule, on the other hand, allows

$$\textit{Shift}\quad \frac{E \overset{m}{-\,-\!\!\rightarrow} F}{E \underset{B}{\overset{m}{\rightarrow}} F} \qquad B \cap LP(E) \cap LP(F) = \varnothing$$

$$\textit{Trans}\quad \frac{E \underset{B}{\overset{h}{\rightarrow}} F \quad F \overset{m}{-\,-\!\!\rightarrow} G}{E \underset{B \cup C}{\overset{hm}{\longrightarrow}} G} \qquad C \cap LP(G) = \varnothing$$

Figure 8.8 Rules for weakly-fair *CCS*.

one to generate B-steps involving a sequence of moves. This is all that is needed to get the required result that $\underset{B}{\overset{h}{\rightarrow}}$ coincides with $\underset{B}{\overset{h}{-\,-\!\!\rightarrow}}$.

Theorem: (weak admissibility coincidence)

$$E \underset{B}{\overset{h}{-\,-\!\!\rightarrow}} F \text{ iff } E \underset{B}{\overset{h}{\rightarrow}} F.$$

Proof: By induction on $l = length(h)$, which by definition is greater than 0.

(Only-if) $l = 1$: Then $h = m$ and by definition of B-step $B \cap LP(E) \cap LP(F) = \varnothing$. Thus we can infer $E \underset{B}{\overset{m}{\rightarrow}} F$ from $E \overset{m}{-\,-\!\!\rightarrow} F$ using the *Shift* rule.

$l > 1$: Then $h = km$ and $E \overset{k}{-\,-\!\!\rightarrow} G \overset{m}{-\,-\!\!\rightarrow} F$ for some G. Let $C = B \cap LP(E) \cap \cdots \cap LP(G)$, and let $D = B - C$. Then clearly $E \underset{D}{\overset{k}{-\,-\!\!\rightarrow}} G$, and by the induction hypotheses $E \underset{D}{\overset{k}{\rightarrow}} G$. By definition of B-step $C \cap LP(F) = \varnothing$.

Hence we apply the *Trans* rule

$$\frac{E \underset{D}{\overset{k}{\rightarrow}} G \quad G \overset{m}{-\,-\!\!\rightarrow} F}{E \underset{D \cup C}{\overset{km}{\longrightarrow}} F}.$$

By definition $B = D \cup C$.

(If) $l = 1$: Then $h = m$ and $E \underset{B}{\overset{m}{\rightarrow}} F$. However, $E \underset{B}{\overset{m}{\rightarrow}} F$ must have been inferred from $E \overset{m}{-\,-\!\!\rightarrow} F$ using *Shift* rule and thus $B \cap LP(E) \cap LP(F) = \varnothing$. That is, $E \underset{B}{\overset{m}{-\,-\!\!\rightarrow}} F$.

$l > 1$: Then $h = km$ and $E \overset{h}{\underset{B}{\rightarrow}} F$. However $E \overset{h}{\underset{B}{\rightarrow}} F$ must have been inferred by *Trans* rule. Thus $B = D \cup C$ and $C \cap LP(F) = \emptyset$ for some C, D and $E \overset{k}{\underset{D}{\rightarrow}} G$ and $G \overset{m}{- - \rightarrow} F$ for some G.

By the inductive hypothesis $E \overset{k}{\underset{D}{- - \rightarrow}} G$. Thus,

$D \cap LP(E) \cap \cdots \cap LP(G) = \emptyset$, and

$B \cap LP(E) \cap \cdots \cap LP(G) \cap LP(F)$ is equal to

$$(D \cap LP(E) \cap \cdots \cap LP(G) \cap LP(F)) \cup$$

$$(C \cap LP(E) \cap \cdots \cap LP(G) \cap LP(F)).$$

But this set is $\emptyset$, and, hence, $E \overset{h}{\underset{B}{- - \rightarrow}} F$. []

Example: As an illustration of the use of these two rules consider the following example, where $K = (a_v G \mid \bar{a}_y c H)$ and

$$E_0 = (b_u cabF \mid K) \backslash a \qquad E_1 = (cabF \mid K) \backslash a$$

$$E_2 = (abF \mid K) \backslash a \qquad E_3 = (bF \mid (a_v G \mid cH)) \backslash a .$$

The set $LP(E_0)$ is $\{u, v, y\}$, and $LP(E_0) \cap LP(E_1) \cap LP(E_2) \cap LP(E_3) = \emptyset$. Hence, $E_0 \overset{b}{- - \rightarrow} E_1 \overset{c}{- - \rightarrow} E_2 \overset{\tau}{- - \rightarrow} E_3$ is an $LP(E_0)$-step. We show that this can be inferred from the two new rules in Figure 8.9.

The example suggests a way of choosing the sets of labels B and C in the two rules: in the case of the *Shift* rule let B be the largest subset of $LP(E)$ such that $B \cap LP(F) = \emptyset$; and in the case of the *Trans* rule let C also be the largest subset of $LP(E)$ such that $C \cap B = \emptyset$ and

$$\textit{Shift}\quad \frac{E_0 \overset{b}{- - \rightarrow} E_1}{E_0 \overset{b}{\rightarrow} E_1 \qquad E_1 \underset{\{u\}}{\overset{c}{- - \rightarrow}} E_2}$$

$$\textit{Trans}\quad \frac{}{E_0 \overset{b}{\rightarrow} E_1 \underset{\{u\} \cup \emptyset}{\overset{c}{\rightarrow}} E_2 \qquad E_2 \overset{\tau}{- - \rightarrow} E_3}$$

$$\textit{Trans}\quad \frac{}{E_0 \overset{b}{\rightarrow} E_1 \underset{\{u\} \cup \{v, y\}}{\overset{c}{\rightarrow}} E_2 \overset{\tau}{\rightarrow} E_3}$$

Figure 8.9 Using *Shift* and *Trans*.

$C \cap LP(G) = \varnothing$. This method of generating steps is merely a refinement of the strategy for constructing admissible sequences.

To generate all the admissible sequences from E it is not sufficient to be *rid* of the processes in $LP(E)$ as soon as possible. For instance, in the above example this would mean that instead of deriving $E_0 \overset{b}{\underset{\{u\} \cup \varnothing}{\rightarrow}} E_1 \overset{c}{\rightarrow} E_2$ one would derive $E_0 \overset{b}{\underset{\{u\} \cup \{v,\, y\}}{\rightarrow}} E_1 \overset{\tau}{\rightarrow} (cabF \mid (G \mid cH)) \backslash a$. The following admissible sequence makes this clearer, where $E = fix\ X.aX$

$$E \mid b_u NIL \overset{a}{- - \rightarrow} E \mid b_u NIL \overset{a}{- - \rightarrow} \cdots \overset{a}{- - \rightarrow} E \mid b_u NIL$$

$$\overset{b}{- - \rightarrow} E \mid NIL \overset{a}{- - \rightarrow} \cdots$$

There is no finite upper bound on how many a actions can be performed before u loses its liveness. This point is bound up with the issue of predictive choice, to which we return later. The *Shift* and *Trans* rules allow one to 'freely' generate steps at any point. Previous choices do not constrain future possibilities. This is in contrast to those analyses or simulations of admissibility which appeal to random assignment.

Definition: A *WFCCS execution sequence* is any sequence of the form:

$$E_0 \frac{h_0}{B_0}\!> E_1 \frac{h_1}{B_1}\!> \cdots$$

where $B_i = LP(E_i)$. The *CCS* execution sequence associated with it is the sequence which omits the B_is and replaces $\overset{m}{- - \rightarrow}$ for $\overset{m}{\rightarrow}$ throughout.

An immediate consequence of previous results is the following theorem.

Theorem: (*CCS* weak fairness characterization) A *CCS* execution sequence is weak-admissible iff it is the sequence associated with a WFCCS execution sequence.

8.3.2 Strongly fair *CCS*

In this section rules for strong fair *CCS* are offered. Recall that a *CCS* execution sequence is strong-admissible just in case no concurrent subcomponent is infinitely often live. As far as possible an analysis is developed, analogous to the weak case. However, there is an immediate problem. In the case of weak-admissibility, there is a localized definition. Recall that if a sequence is w-admissible at i then each live subcomponent at i eventually loses its liveness. Thus, if the sequence is also inadmissible then this cannot be due to a live process at i remaining live throughout the rest of the computation. This means that w-admissibility at i guarantees that no live subcomponent at i *remains* always live. A similar property in the case of strong-admissibility, *s-admissibility* at i, would guarantee that no (live) subcomponent at i is infinitely often live. But the following example shows that this is *not* a *localizable* property. Clearly, the sequence δ is strong-admissible, where $E = fix\ X.(aX + b(cNIL + dX)$ and $F = \bar{c}_u NIL$;

$$\delta = ((E + cNIL) \mid F) \backslash c \xrightarrow{a} (E \mid F) \backslash c \xrightarrow{a} \cdots$$

$$\xrightarrow{a} (E \mid F) \backslash c \xrightarrow{a} \cdots$$

The subcomponent u is initially live but loses its liveness once the action a is performed, and never regains it. However, at every point in δ there is the possibility of inadmissibility due to u being infinitely often live, because

$$(E \mid F) \backslash c \xrightarrow{b} ((cNIL + dE) \mid F) \backslash c \xrightarrow{d} (E \mid F) \backslash c \xrightarrow{b} \cdots$$

$$\xrightarrow{d} (E \mid F) \backslash c \xrightarrow{b} \cdots$$

Every initial segment of δ is also the initial segment of an inadmissible sequence whose inadmissibility is due to a process u which is live at 0 in δ. At no point in δ is it ever safe to conclude that u cannot be infinitely often live. Consequently, a definition of s-admissibility at i which guarantees that no subcomponent at i is infinitely often live needs to invoke the complete future segment of the sequence after i. This appears to be intrinsic to the difference between weak and strong fairness.

Definition: For $\gamma = E_0 \xrightarrow{m_0} E_1 \xrightarrow{m_1} \cdots$ a *CCS* execution sequence:

i. γ is *s-admissible at i* iff $\exists j \geqslant i\ \forall k \geqslant j$: $P(E_i) \cap LP(E_k) = \varnothing$.
ii. γ is *s-admissible* iff $\forall i \leqslant length(\gamma)$: γ is s-admissible at i.

γ is s-admissible at i just in case no subcomponent at i, whether live or not, becomes infinitely often live. The following results are analogous to their weak counterparts. The first says that s-admissibility at i implies s-admissibility at j for any $j \leqslant i$. (Notice that this result would not hold if $LP(E_i)$ replaced $P(E_i)$ in the first part of the above definition.) The second says that s-admissibility coincides with strong-admissibility.

Proposition: γ is s-admissible at i iff $\forall j \leqslant i$: γ is s-admissible at j.

Theorem: (characterization of strong admissibility) γ is s-admissible iff γ is strong-admissible.

Proof: Similar to the weak case and omitted. [ ]

The s-admissibility does not immediately suggest an analogue of a B-step. In fact, one can give analogues but they always appear to involve predictive choice: that is, one can *localize* strong-admissibility at the expense of predictive choice. One such method, based on a *queue* of labels, is suggested below. Another one, based on a *set* of labels, is discussed in [CS 85].

If B is a finite set of labels then let $Seq(B)$ be the set of permutations of elements in B: if $T \in Seq(B)$ then each element of B appears exactly once in T. conversely, if $T \in Seq(B)$ then $Set(T) = B$. We let T, U range over finite sequences of labels. The concatenation of two finite sequences $T \cdot U$ is defined in the usual way. If u and v are labels then $u \sqsubseteq v$ just in case $u = v$ or u occurs before v in T (and T is left implicit). Finally T/B is the sequence which results from deleting any label not in B from T.

The analogue of a B-step is a T-step. We are interested in $T \in Seq(P(E))$, and not just $T \in Seq(LP(E))$, because if we have a queue containing only live subcomponents of E, then at the end of a T-step from E, when T is updated, a subcomponent which has lost its liveness is deleted from the queue. But, an execution sequence is admissible if some subprocess infinitely often loses (and, thus, infinitely often regains) its liveness. The following definition does not enforce a strict queue discipline because it is too restrictive. Instead, the discipline used is given by the *min* condition in the definition. for simplicity we define a T-step from E_0 when $T \in Seq(P(E_0))$ and not for arbitrary T.

Definition: $E_0 \overset{m_0}{--\rightarrow} E_1 \overset{m_1}{--\rightarrow} \cdots \overset{m_n}{--\rightarrow} E_{n+1}$ is a *T-step* just in case

i. $T \in Seq(P(E_0))$.
ii. the following *min* condition holds: for every i, $0 \leqslant i \leqslant n$:

if $u \in P(E_0) \cap LP(E_i)$, then $\exists v\colon v \sqsubseteq u \wedge v \notin P(E_{i+1})$.

We abbreviate $E_0 \overset{m_0}{--\rightarrow} E_1 \overset{m_1}{--\rightarrow} \cdots \overset{m_n}{--\rightarrow} E_{n+1}$ in a T-step to $E_0 \overset{h}{\underset{T}{--\rightarrow}} E_{n+1}$, where $h = m_0 \ldots m_n$.

The *min* condition states that the live subcomponent of E_0 which is earliest in the queue must contribute to m_0 in preference to any other subprocess and, moreover, if at a later point, say E_j, in the derivation an even earlier process u in the queue becomes live then either u contributes to the mover m_j or E_j is E_{n+1}. Hence, the *min* condition guarantees that if

$E_0 \overset{m_0}{--\rightarrow} E_1 \overset{m_1}{--\rightarrow} \cdots \overset{m_n}{--\rightarrow} E_{n+1}$ is a T-step then so is $E_0 \overset{m_0}{--\rightarrow} E_1 \overset{m_1}{--\rightarrow} \cdots \overset{m_i}{--\rightarrow} E_{i+1}$ for each i, $0 \leqslant i \leqslant n$.

Example: We clarify this condition with an example. Let $T = <w, v, u>$ and let $E_0 = ((b_u c_{u1} F \mid d_v e_{v1} a_{v11} a_{v_3} G) \mid \bar{a}_w b_{w1} H) \backslash a$, where $v3 = v111$.

	P	LP
E_0	$\{u, v, w\}$	$\{u, v\}$
$\downarrow b$		
$E'_1 = ((c_{u1} F \mid d_v e_{v1} a_{v11} a_{v3} G) \mid \bar{a}_w b_{w1} H) \backslash a$	$\{u1, v, w\}$	$\{u1, v\}$

Both v and u are live in E_0 but u performs the move whereas v precedes u in the queue T. The derivation, therefore, is not a T-step. Nor is any extension of it a T-step. In contrast the pair of derivations $E_0 \overset{d}{--\rightarrow} E_1$, $E_0 \overset{de}{--\rightarrow} E_2$ are T-steps.

	P	LP
E_0	$\{u, v, w\}$	$\{u, v\}$
$\downarrow d$		
$E_1 = ((b_u c_{u1} F \mid e_{v1} a_{v11} a_{v3} G) \mid \bar{a}_w b_{w1} H) \backslash a$	$\{u, v1, w\}$	$\{u, v1\}$
$\downarrow e$		
$E_2 = ((b_u c_{u1} F \mid a_{v11} a_{v3} G) \mid \bar{a}_w b_{w1} H) \backslash a$	$\{u, v11, w\}$	$\{u, v11, w\}$

Note that $E_0 \overset{de}{--\rightarrow} E_2$ is a T-step even though u has still not contributed a move and even though w, which is earliest in T, has become live in E_2. The latter feature means that not every finite extension will also be a T-step. In particular, only those extensions were w immediately contributes a move remain a T-step. Thus, $E_0 \overset{de\tau}{--\rightarrow} E_3$ is a T-step whereas $E_0 \overset{deb}{--\rightarrow} E'_3$ is not a T-step.

	P	LP
E_2	$\{u, v11, w\}$	$\{u, v11, w\}$
$\downarrow \tau$		
$E_3 = ((b_u c_{u1} F \mid a_{v3} G) \mid b_{w1} H) \backslash a$	$\{u, v3, w1\}$	$\{u, w1\}$

E_2 $\{u, v11, w\}$ $\{u, v11, w\}$

$\downarrow b$

$E'_3 = ((c_{u1}F \mid a_{v11}a_{v3}G) \mid \bar{a}_w b_{w1}H) \backslash a$ $\{u1, v11, w\}$ $\{u1, v11, w\}$

Part i of the following T-step lemma (like part i of B-step lemma) expresses a "no-stuck" property: for any permutation T of $P(E)$ and live process E there is a move from E which amounts to a T-step. Part ii of the lemma says that a T-step is prefix closed. Moreover, it also says that if $E \overset{h}{- - \rightarrow} F$ is not a T-step then neither is any extension of it.

Lemma: (T-step)

i. If $LP(E) \neq \varnothing$ then $\forall T \in Seq(P) \exists F,m$: $E \underset{T}{\overset{m}{- - \rightarrow}} F$.

ii. If $E \overset{h}{- - \rightarrow} \underset{T}{F} \overset{k}{- - \rightarrow} G$ then $E \underset{T}{\overset{h}{- - \rightarrow}} F$.

In the example derivations from E_0 above it is clear that u must eventually contribute a move in any strong-admissible execution sequence from E_0. But, as noted, a T-step from E_0 can be achieved without a contribution from u. For this reason when T-steps are linked together to form a sequence of steps more machinery is necessary.

Definition: An *s-sequence* from E_0 is any *maximal* sequence of steps of the form

$$E_0 \underset{T_0}{\overset{h_0}{- - \rightarrow}} E_1 \underset{T_1}{\overset{h_1}{- - \rightarrow}} \cdots \quad \text{where for} \quad i \geqslant 0$$

$$T_{i+1} = (T_i/P(E_{i+1}))\cdot U, \quad \text{where } U \in Seq(P(E_{i+1}) - P(E_i)).$$

It is straightforward to check that $T_i \in Seq(P(E_i))$ for every i: $(T_i/P(E_{i+1}))$ is the sequence resulting from removing from T_i any subprocess not in $P(E_{i+1})$ and U is the permutation of the subcomponents of E_{i+1} which are not in E_i.

This linking together of steps in the definition of s-sequence means that any process in E_i which does not contribute a move will move towards the front of the queue. Thus, if it repeatedly becomes live then eventually by the *min* condition, it must contribute to a performance of a move. If δ is an s-sequence then its associated *CCS* execution sequence is the sequence which drops all reference to the T_i's. The following theorem shows that s-sequences are precisely the admissible ones.

Theorem: (s-sequence) A *CCS* execution sequence is strong-admissible iff it is a sequence associated with an s-sequence.

Proof:

(If) Let δ be the *s*-sequence in Figure 8.10.

Immediately from the definition of *s*-sequence and the *min* condition we get (*), where $T_i(j)$ is the j-th element of the queue T_i.

(*) If $u = T_i(j)$ for some i and j then $u \notin Set(T_{i+1})$ or $u = T_{i+1}(j')$ for $j' \leqslant j$. Moreover, if $u \in LP(E_k)$, $k_i \leqslant k < k_{i+1}$, and $u = T_{i+1}(j')$, then $j' < j$.

From (*) it follows that

(**) if for some i, $\forall j \geqslant i$: $u \in Set(T_j)$ then $\exists k \forall j \geqslant k$: $u \notin LP(E_j)$. The required result follows by contradiction from (**).

Suppose the sequence associated to δ is not strong admissible. Then, $\exists u \forall i \exists j \geqslant i$: $u \in LP(E_j)$. As $LP(E_j) \subseteq P(E_j)$, $\exists i' \forall j \geqslant i'$: $u \in P(E_j)$. Hence, $\forall j \geqslant i'$: $u \in Set(T_j)$. From (**) above we get $\exists k \forall j \geqslant k$: $u \notin LP(E_j)$, but this is a contradiction.

(Only-if) The proof is by construction. Suppose δ is strong-admissible. Then δ is *s*-admissible at 0 by the strong fairness characterization theorem. Hence, $\exists k \geqslant 0$ such that $\forall j \geqslant k$: $P(E_0) \cap LP(E_j) = \varnothing$. Let k_1 be the least such k.

Define T_0 s.t. $E_0 \overset{m_0}{\dashrightarrow} \underset{T_0}{\cdots} \overset{m_{k_1 - 1}}{\dashrightarrow} E_{k_1}$. By the liveness lemma (part iii), if $0 \leqslant i < k_1$ then $\exists u_i$ s.t. $u_i \in LP(E_i)$ and $u_i \notin P(E_{i+1})$. Let $U_0 = u_0 u_1 \cdots u_{k_1 - 1}$ and $T_0 = (U_0/P(E_0)) \cdot R_0$, where $R_0 \in Seq(P(E_0) - Set(U_0))$.

Clearly, $E_0 \overset{m_0}{\dashrightarrow} \underset{T_0}{\cdots} \overset{m_{k_1 - 1}}{\dashrightarrow} E_{k_1}$. Moreover, if $T'_1 = T_0/P(E_{k_1})$ and $u \in Set(T'_1)$ then $u \notin LP(E_j)$ for all $j \geqslant k_1$. By the definition of k_1, δ is also *s*-admissible at k_1.

Hence, again by the characterization theorem, $\exists k \geqslant k_1 \forall j \geqslant k$: $P(E_{k_1}) \cap LP(E_j) = \varnothing$. Let k_2 be the least such k and define U_1 analogously to U_0. (Note that $Set(T'_1) \cap Set(U_1) = \varnothing$). Let $T_1 = T'_1 \cdot (U_1/P(E_{k_1})) \cdot R_1$,

$$E_0 \overset{m_0}{\dashrightarrow} E_1 \cdots \overset{m_{k_1 - 1}}{\dashrightarrow} E_{k_1} \overset{m_{k_1}}{\dashrightarrow} \cdots \overset{m_{k_2 - 1}}{\dashrightarrow} E_{k_2} \overset{m_{k_2}}{\dashrightarrow} \cdots \overset{m_{k_i - 1}}{\dashrightarrow}$$
$$\text{- - - - - - - -}T_0\text{- - - - - - - -} \quad \text{- - - - - -}T_1\text{- - - - - - - -} \quad \cdots \quad \cdots$$

$$E_{k_i} \overset{m_{k_i}}{\dashrightarrow} \cdots \overset{m_{k_{i+1} - 1}}{\dashrightarrow} E_{k_{i+1}} \overset{m_{k_{i+1}}}{\dashrightarrow}$$
$$\text{- - - - - - - -}T_i\text{- - - - - - - -}$$

Figure 8.10 The *s*-sequence δ.

where $R_1 \in Seq(P(E_{k_1}) - Set(T'_1 \cdot U_1))$. Clearly,

$E_{k_1} \overset{m_{k_1}}{--\rightarrow} \underset{T_1}{\cdots} \overset{m_{k_2-1}}{--\rightarrow} E_{k_2}$.

In general, having reached E_{k_i}, we select $E_{k_{i+1}}$ and define T'_i, U_i, R_i, and T_i analogous to T'_1, U_1, R_1, T_1. [ ]

Strong fair *CCS* rules

We now offer operational rules for strong fair *CCS* based upon the notion of *T*-step. The method is analogous to weak fair *CCS*: two extra rules are added to standard *CCS* (see Figure 8.11), involving a transition relation $\underset{T}{\overset{h}{===>}}$, which coincides with $\underset{T}{\overset{h}{--\rightarrow}}$. If U is a non-empty sequence then $Hd(U)$ is the first member of U.

In the *Trans* rule $E \underset{T}{\overset{hm}{===>}} G$ abbreviates $E \underset{T}{\overset{h}{===>}} F \underset{T}{\overset{m}{===>}} G$. The *Shift* rule guarantees that the earlies live process in T contributes to the performance of m and, thereby, guarantees a T-step. The *Trans* rule, on the other hand, ensures that an extension of a T-step remains a T-step: If a process in $P(E)$ becomes live at F and is earlier in the queue T than any other process which has contributed to the sequence of moves h then it must contribute to the move m. Thus, together these two rules ensure that the *min* condition always holds. Consequently, $\underset{T}{\overset{h}{===>}}$ coincides with $\underset{T}{\overset{h}{--\rightarrow}}$.

Theorem: (strong admissibility coincidence)

$E \underset{T}{\overset{h}{--\rightarrow}} F$ iff $E \underset{T}{\overset{h}{===>}} F$.

Proof: By induction on $l = length(h)$.

(Only-if) $l = 1$: Then $h = m$ and by definition of T-step $E \overset{m}{--\rightarrow} F$ and $T = v_1 \cdots v_n u T'$ with $n \geqslant 0$, $v_1, \cdots, v_n \notin LP(E)$,

$$\textit{Shift} \quad \frac{E \overset{m}{--\rightarrow} F}{E \underset{T}{\overset{m}{===>}} F} \quad T \in Seq(P(E)) \text{ and } Hd(T/LP(E)) \notin P(F)$$

$$\textit{Trans} \quad \frac{E \underset{T}{\overset{h}{===>}} F \quad F \overset{m}{--\rightarrow} G}{E \underset{T}{\overset{hm}{===>}} G} \quad \forall u \in (LP(F) \cap P(E)) \; \exists v{:}\; v \sqsubseteq u \wedge v \notin \mathbf{P(G)}$$

Figure 8.11 Rules for strongly-fair *CCS*.

$u \in LP(E)$ and $u \in P(F)$. That is, $Hd(T/LP(E)) \cap P(F) = \varnothing$. Thus, $E \overset{m}{\underset{T}{==>}} F$ follows by *Shift* rule.

$l > 1$: Then $h = km$ and $E \overset{k}{--\rightarrow} G \overset{m}{\underset{T}{--\rightarrow}} F$ for some G. By the T-step lemma (part ii) $E \overset{k}{\underset{T}{--\rightarrow}} G$. Hence, by the induction hypothesis, $E \overset{k}{\underset{T}{==>}} G$. Since $E \overset{k}{\underset{T}{--\rightarrow}} G \overset{m}{--\rightarrow} F$, by *min* condition $\forall u \in P(E) \cap LP(G)\ \exists v$: $v \sqsubseteq u$ and $v \notin P(F)$. The result follows by the *Trans* rule.

(If) $l = 1$: Then $h = m$ and $E \overset{m}{\underset{T}{==>}} F$. However, $E \overset{m}{\underset{T}{==>}} F$ must have been inferred from $E \overset{m}{--\rightarrow} F$ using the *Shift* rule and $Hd(T/L)P(E)) \notin P(F)$. Hence, the *min* condition holds, and so $E \overset{m}{\underset{T}{--\rightarrow}} F$.

$l > 1$: Then $h = km$ and $E \overset{h}{\underset{T}{==>}} F$. This must have been inferred by the *Trans* rule. Hence, $E \overset{k}{\underset{T}{==>}} G$ and $G \overset{m}{--\rightarrow} F$ for some G with $\forall u \in (LP(G) \cap P(E))\ \exists v$: $v \sqsubseteq u$ and $v \notin P(F)$. By the induction hypothesis $E \overset{k}{\underset{T}{--\rightarrow}} G$, and by the condition on the *Trans* rule also $E \overset{km}{\underset{T}{--\rightarrow}} F$. []

There is an important difference between the workings of the weak and strong fair *CCS* rules. In the weak case one attempts to *achieve* a *B*-step, whereas in the strong case one attempts to *maintain* a *T*-step. *B*-steps are not, unlike *T*-steps, prefix closed: on the other hand any extension of a *B*-step, unlike a *T*-step, is still a *B*-step.

Example: We illustrate the use of the strong fair rules with the example in Figure 8.12. Note in this example that the choice of the queue $<v, u, y>$ (chosen when the *Shift* rule is applied) restricts the moves that can be performed. For instance, if $<v, y, u>$ were chosen instead then E_0 could not perform the action *a* first, because *y* is the earliest live process. Moreover, the initial choice of $<v,u,y>$ forces E_3 to synchronize because *v* which is earliest in the queue has then become live. Unlike the rules for weak fairness, these rules do not allow one to "freely" generate steps: the initial choice of the queue constrains future possibilities.

Definition: *A SFCCS execution sequence* is any *maximal* sequence of the form:

$$K = (\bar{d}_v G \mid \bar{b}_y H) \text{ and}$$
$$E_0 = (a_u bcdF \mid K) \backslash d \qquad E_1 = (bcdF \mid K) \backslash d$$
$$E_2 = (cdF \mid K) \backslash d \qquad E_3 = (dF \mid K) \backslash d$$
$$E_4 = (F \mid (G \mid \bar{b}_y H)) \backslash d.$$

$$\textit{Shift}\ \frac{E_0 \stackrel{a}{-\!\!\to} E_1}{E_0 \underset{<v,u,y>}{\overset{a}{\Longrightarrow}} E_1}$$

$$\textit{Trans}\ \frac{E_0 \underset{<v,u,y>}{\overset{a}{\Longrightarrow}} E_1 \qquad E_1 \stackrel{b}{-\!\!\to} E_2}{E_0 \overset{a}{\Longrightarrow} E_1 \underset{<v,u,y>}{\overset{b}{\Longrightarrow}} E_2}$$

$$\textit{Trans}\ \frac{E_0 \overset{a}{\Longrightarrow} E_1 \underset{<v,u,y>}{\overset{b}{\Longrightarrow}} E_2 \qquad E_2 \stackrel{c}{-\!\!\to} E_3}{E_0 \overset{a}{\Longrightarrow} E_1 \overset{b}{\Longrightarrow} E_2 \underset{<v,u,y>}{\overset{c}{\Longrightarrow}} E_3}$$

$$\textit{Trans}\ \frac{E_0 \overset{a}{\Longrightarrow} E_1 \overset{b}{\Longrightarrow} E_2 \underset{<v,u,y>}{\overset{c}{\Longrightarrow}} E_3 \qquad E_3 \stackrel{\tau}{-\!\!\to} E_4}{E_0 \overset{a}{\Longrightarrow} E_1 \overset{b}{\Longrightarrow} E_2 \overset{c}{\Longrightarrow} E_3 \underset{<v,u,y>}{\overset{\tau}{\Longrightarrow}} E_4}$$

Figure 8.12 Applying the strong fairness *CCS* rules.

$$E_0 \underset{T_0}{\overset{h_0}{\Longrightarrow}} E_1 \underset{T_1}{\overset{h_1}{\Longrightarrow}} \cdots$$

where the T_is satisfy the conditions of the definition of s-sequence.

The *CCS* execution sequence associated with an *SFCSS* sequence is the expected one. The following is an immediate consequence of preceding results.

Theorem: (*CCS* strong fairness characterization) A *CCS* execution sequence is strong-admissible iff it is the sequence associated with a *SFCCS* execution sequence.

Predictive choice

To end this section, we make precise the claim that *WFCCS*, unlike *SFCCS*, does not involve predictive choice. Consider the generation of an arbitrary *SFCCS* execution sequence from some live process E. Initially, a queue $T \in Seq(P(E))$ is chosen. This choice, however, may preclude the generation of some admissible sequences from E. For instance, if $T = <u, v>$ and $E = a_u F \mid b_v G$ then T prevents the generation of any admissible sequence from E whose initial move is b: $E \stackrel{b}{-\!\!\to} a_u F \mid G$ is not a T-step (and by the T-step lemma (ii) neither is any extension of it). This is a simple instance of predictive choice which is next generalized. Suppose $E_0 \underset{U}{\overset{h}{\Longrightarrow}} E_n$ by the *SFCCS* rules and suppose

$E_n \overset{m_n}{--\rightarrow} E_{n+1} \overset{m_{n+1}}{--\rightarrow} \cdots$ is a strong-admissible sequence. Then clearly, $\delta = E_0 \overset{h}{--\rightarrow} E_n \overset{m_n}{--\rightarrow} E_{n+1} \overset{m_{n+1}}{--\rightarrow} \cdots$ is also admissible. However, it may not be possible to generate an *SFCCS* sequence corresponding to δ starting with the derivation $E_0 \overset{h}{===>} E_n$: the choice of U may prevent extensions of $E_0 \underset{U}{\overset{h}{===>}} E_n$ which correspond to admissible *CCS* sequences. For example when $F = fix\ X.cX$ the derivation

$$(b_u(aNIL + F) \mid \bar{a}_v F) \backslash a \underset{<v,u>}{\overset{b}{===>}} ((aNIL + F) \mid \bar{a}_v F) \backslash a$$

cannot be extended so as to correspond to the admissible sequence

$$(b_u(aNIL+F) \mid \bar{a}_v F) \backslash a \overset{b}{--\rightarrow} ((aNIL+F) \mid \bar{a}_v F) \backslash a \overset{c}{--\rightarrow}$$

$$(F \mid \bar{a}_v F) \backslash a \overset{c}{--\rightarrow} (F \mid \bar{a}_v F) \backslash a \cdots$$

This cannot arise in the case of *WFCCS*.

WFCCS avoids predictive choice if every *WFCCS* derivation can be freely extended to any appropriate admissible sequence. Let us make this precise. we say that a *WFCCS* derivation $E \underset{B}{\overset{h}{--\rightarrow}} E_n$, when $B \subseteq LP(E)$, is *admissible closed* if whenever $\delta = E \overset{h}{--\rightarrow} E_n \overset{m_n}{--\rightarrow} E_{n+1} \overset{m_{n+1}}{--\rightarrow} \cdots$ is weak-admissible there exists a *WFCCS* execution sequence corresponding to δ whose first step $E \underset{LP(E)}{\overset{k}{--\rightarrow}} E_m$, $m \geqslant n$, is inferred from $E \underset{B}{\overset{h}{--\rightarrow}} E_n$ using the rules. Therefore, we take the following lemma to show that *WFCCS* does not involve predictive choice.

Lemma: (admissible closure)

If $B \subseteq LP(E)$ and $E \underset{B}{\overset{h}{\rightarrow}} F$ then $E \underset{B}{\overset{h}{\rightarrow}} F$ is admissible closed.

Proof: Let $\delta_i = E \overset{h}{--\rightarrow} F_0 \overset{m_0}{--\rightarrow} F_1 \overset{m_1}{--\rightarrow} \cdots$ be a weak-admissible sequence. Clearly, $\delta = F_i \overset{m_i}{--\rightarrow} F_{i+1} \overset{m_{i+1}}{--\rightarrow} \cdots$ is weak-admissible for any i. Let $C = LP(E) - B$. Two subcases arise:

i. $C = \varnothing$: Then $E \underset{LP(E)}{\overset{h}{--\rightarrow}} F_0$.

By the weak fairness characterization theorem there exists a *WFCCS* sequence $F_0 \underset{B_0}{\overset{h_0}{\rightarrow}} F_{i_1} \underset{B_1}{\overset{h_1}{\rightarrow}} \cdots$ with $B_j = LP(F_{i_j})$ corresponding to δ_0.

Hence, $E \underset{LP(E)}{\overset{h}{\rightarrow}} F_0 \underset{B_0}{\overset{h_0}{\rightarrow}} F_{i_1} \underset{B_1}{\overset{h_1}{\rightarrow}} \cdots$ corresponds to δ.

ii. $C \neq \emptyset$: Since δ_0 is w-admissible at 1 there exists $j > 1$ such that $LP(F_1) \cap \cdots \cap LP(F_j) = \emptyset$. Hence, clearly, $C \cap LP(F_1) \cap \cdots \cap LP(F_j) = \emptyset$. Let $C_k = \{u\colon u \in C$ and $u \notin LP(F_k)\}$ for $1 \leqslant k \leqslant j$.

Using repeated applications of the *Trans* rule, we can infer

$$E \underset{B}{\overset{h}{\rightarrow}} F_0 \underset{\cup\; C_1}{\overset{m_0}{\rightarrow}} F_1 \underset{\cup\; C_2}{\overset{m_1}{\rightarrow}} \cdots \underset{\cup\; C_j}{\overset{m_{j-1}}{\rightarrow}} F_j.$$

Clearly, $B \cup C_1 \cup \cdots \cup C_j = LP(E)$. As before, by the characterization theorem there exists a *WFCCS* sequence $F_j \underset{B_j}{\overset{h_0}{\rightarrow}} F_{j_1} \underset{B_{j_1}}{\overset{h_1}{\rightarrow}} \cdots$ with $B_j = LP(F_j)$ and $B_{j_i} = LP(F_{j_i})$ corresponding to δ_j.

Hence $E \underset{LP(E)}{\xrightarrow{hm_0 \ldots m_{j-1}}} F_j \underset{B_j}{\overset{h_0}{\rightarrow}} F_{j_1} \underset{B_{j_1}}{\overset{h_1}{\rightarrow}} \cdots$ corresponds to δ. [ ]

8.4 A Metric Characterization of *CCS* Fairness

8.4.1 Overview

One of the more challenging problems in modeling fairness properties is to reconcile infinite fair behaviours with approximations and limits. We would like a framework in which there are some notions of finiteness, approximation and limit, such that infinite behaviours are fully determined, via *countable limits* by their finite approximants. Now, fair infinite behaviours do not seem to fit into this pattern.

In [PA 79] Park provides a fixedpoint relational semantics for data-flow networks with a fair merge operator. In doing so he has to consider limits [*lub*'s and *inf*'s] of transfinite chains. the denotational semantics for a *while*-language with a fair parallel operator in [PL 82] also appeals to transfinite chains. Later, De Bakker and Zucker have proposed in [deBZ 83] metric spaces of processes where fair parallel operators can be interpreted using the standard notion of limit of (countable) sequences. Here, however, the finiteness of approximants is in question as fairness is achieved using the equivalent of random assignment. The same problem arises in the use of *oracles* in [PA 82].

A customary solution in such cases is to settle for less. Going in this direction, one realizes that the difficulties are not entirely due to the interaction of fairness on one side and the requirements, countable limits and finite approximations, on the other: the notion of *behaviour* plays its part. Some of the features that are considered most desirable become stumbling blocks. The most obvious one is *abstraction,* causing the removal of information which would allow to capture fairness easily. Another feature which, though desirable in general, becomes here an impediment is the consideration of global behaviours and their handling as a whole. For instance, in [PA 79] the behaviour of a network is its *input-output* relation; that of a program in [PL 82] is the set of its (*possible*) *results.* It is such a global entity that one tries to obtain through the limiting process.

In [DM 84], Degano and Montanari consider a notion of behaviour closely connected to the operational notion of step-wise evolution of a system. Then they can characterize some liveness properties, including fairness, of the *individual* entities which constitute the global behaviour of systems in terms of convergence properties in appropriate metric spaces.

Later, Costa [C 84] applied a similar characterization to (labeled) *CCS* and extended it to strong fairness also. The current presentation closely follows [C 84]. The basic idea is to define on the set of all derivations three *distances: da, dw, ds.* Then, infinite computations, taken individually, are fully determined as limits w.r.t. *da* of (countable) sequences of finite derivations (which play the role of finite approximants). The same result is obtained for infinite computations which are weakly, resp. strongly, fair using *dw,* resp. *ds.*

The origin of the *da* distance is from [AN 80], that of *dw* is [DM 84] and that of *ds* is [C 84]. the distance functions *dw* and *ds* are closely related to the characterization of fairness described in section 8.3.

8.4.2 The basic tools

In this subsection we introduce some notation and *lw, ls, LS*: the basic tools used in defining the distances for weak and strong fairness. We start by reviewing the basic concepts of metric spaces. More details can be found in any standard textbook on topology. A *metric space* (S, d) consists of a set S and a (real valued) *distance* function d, satisfying

i. $d(x,y) \begin{cases} = 0 & x = y \\ > 0 & x \neq y \end{cases}$

ii. $d(x,z) \leqslant d(x, y) + d(y, z)$ (the triangle inequality)

iii. $d(x, y) = d(y, x)$.

In our context we consider [0,1]-valued distance functions. Also, the distances d considered are *ultra distances,* namely

$$d(x, z) \leqslant \max\{d(x, y), d(y, z)\}.$$

A sequence (s_n), $n \leqslant 0$, is a *Cauchy sequence* iff for every $\epsilon > 0$ there exist $N(\epsilon)$, s.t.

$$m, n > N(\epsilon) \rightarrow d(s_n, s_m) < \epsilon.$$

Note that (s_n) being a Cauchy sequence depends on d. A sequence (s_n), $n \geqslant 0$, has a *limit* s (*converges to* s) iff for every $\epsilon > 0$ there exists $N(\epsilon)$, s.t. $d(s_n, s) \leqslant \epsilon$. A sequence (s_n), $n \geqslant 0$, is *quasi-constant* iff there exist N s.t. for every $n \geqslant N$ $s_n = s_N$.

Fact: A non-quasi-constant Cauchy sequence contains a subsequence (s_k) *without* repetitions which has the same limit (if any) as (s_n).

A subset $S' \subseteq S$ is *dense* in S iff for every $s \in S$ there exists a sequence (s'_n), $n \geqslant 0$, of elements in S', converging to s.

The main notion of interest in the sequel is that of the *completion.*

Definition: $(C(S), \bar{d})$ is the *completion* of (S, d) iff:

- $S \subseteq C(S)$.
- $\bar{d} \backslash S = d$ (i.e. d is the restriction of $\bar{d}$ on S).
- S is dense in $C(S)$.
- Every Cauchy sequence in $(C(S), \bar{d})$ converges (i.e. $(C(S), \bar{d})$ is *complete*).
- $(C(S), \bar{d})$ is *unique* up to isometric extensions of (S, d).

In the sequel we no not distinguish notationally between d and $\bar{d}$.

We now proceed in viewing *CCS* executions as metric spaces. It is convenient to concentrate initially on a fixed initial term. So, assume E_0 to be *fixed.* Later, this assumption is relaxed, and the initial term may range over the whole set of expressions. The following notations are used:

FD = the set of *finite derivations.*
D^{ω} = the set of *infinite derivations.*
$D = D^{\omega} \cup FD$.
$D^{\omega,w}$ = the set of *infinite weakly-fair derivations.*
$D^{w} = FD \cup D^{\omega,w}$.
$D^{\omega,s}$ and D^{s} are defined in a similar way.
If $Y \in D$ and $i \in Dom(Y)$ (which, by convention, always includes also 0), then:

$$Y(i) = \text{the } i\text{-th element of } Y;$$
$$Y[i] = \text{the initial segment of } Y \text{ of length } i: Y(1) \cdots Y(i).$$

By convention, $Y[0] = \epsilon$ (the null string).
The fixed parameter E_0, the initial term, is systematically omitted.

Let $Y = E_0 \overset{m_1}{\rightarrow} E_1 \overset{m_2}{\rightarrow} \cdots \overset{m_n}{\rightarrow} E_n \cdots$ be in D. The intuitive idea behind the definition of lw is to take the definition of w-fairness at i and read it backwards: $lw(Y, k)$ is the largest $i \leqslant k$ (if it exists) s.t. upon reaching E_k it is known that Y is w-fair at i.

Definition: For $k \in Dom(Y)$,

$$lw(Y, k) = \bigsqcup\{i: 0 \leqslant i \leqslant k \text{ and } LP(E_i) \cap \cdots \cap LP(E_k) = \varnothing\}.$$

From the definition we obtain immediately:

Proposition:

1. $lw(Y, n) \geqslant i$, for some $n \geqslant i$ iff Y is w-fair at i.
2. if $m \leqslant n$ then $lw(Y, m) \leqslant lw(Y, n)$.

The next result provides yet another characterization of infinite weakly-fair computations. Its proof is straightforward given the w-sequence theorem and the above proposition.

Lemma: **(lw-limit)** For $Y \in D^{\omega}$: Y is weakly fair iff $\lim \{lw(Y, n), n > 0\} = +\infty$.

We next define an appropriate correlate of s-fairness at i. Clearly, the difference between s- and w-fairness at i comes forward. A definition which mimics that of lw only provides with a convenient notation: ls below. The true correlate of s-fairness at i is LS, whose definition involves looking ahead in the derivation.

Definition: For $k \in Dom(Y)$:

$$ls(Y, k) = \bigsqcup \{i\colon 0 \leqslant i \leqslant k \text{ and } P(E_i) \cap LP(E_k) = \varnothing\}.$$

$$LS(Y, k) = \bigsqcup \{i\colon 0 \leqslant i \leqslant k \text{ and}$$

$$\forall n \geqslant k,\ n \in Dom(Y)\colon P(E_i) \cap LP(E_n) = \varnothing\}.$$

Clearly: $0 \leqslant LS(Y, k) \leqslant ls(Y, k) \leqslant lw(Y, k) \leqslant k$.

We now state the analogue proposition for LS. Its proof is immediate. Notice that neither part 1 nor part 2 hold for ls.

Proposition:

1. $LS(Y, n) \geqslant i$, for some $n \geqslant i$ iff Y is s-fair at i;
2. if $m \leqslant n$ then $LS(Y, m) \leqslant ls(Y, n)$.

The link between ls and LS is established by the LS–ls lemma below.

Lemma: **(LS–ls)**

$$LS(Y, k) = \min\{ls(Y, n), n \geqslant k \text{ and } n \in Dom(Y)\}.$$

Proof: Let $m = \min\{ls(Y, n), n \geqslant k$ and $n \in Dom(Y)\}$ and $L = LS(Y, k)$. The proof is by contradiction.

Suppose $L < m$. As $m \leqslant ls(Y, k) \leqslant k$ by definition, this implies, by definition of L:

$$\exists p \geqslant k\colon P(E_m) \cap LP(E_p) \neq \varnothing\,,$$

i.e.

$$\exists u \in P(E_m) \cap P(E_p) \text{ and } u \in LP(E_p)\,.$$

From the proposition: $\forall i\colon m \leqslant i \leqslant p \rightarrow u \in P(E_i)$. Let $j = ls(Y, p)$. By definition, $m \leqslant j$, $j \leqslant p$ and $P(E_j) \cap LP(E_p) = \varnothing$. But from above: $u \in P(E_j) \cap LP(E_p)$. Suppose now $m < L$. Then, by definition of m, $\exists p \geqslant k\colon ls(Y, p) < L$. By definition, $L \leqslant k$; hence, from above $P(E_L) \cap LP(E_p) \neq \varnothing$. This is against the definition of L. Note that $L \neq 0$, as $m < L$; hence $L = \max\{i\colon 0 \leqslant i \leqslant k$ and $\forall n \geqslant k\colon P(E_i) \cap LP(E_n) = \varnothing\}$. Thus, $L = m$. []

As expected, LS provides an alternative characterization of strong fairness. But this is also true of ls: taking the limit we overcome the weaknesses of ls. This is stated in the lemma below.

Lemma: (*LS*-limit) For $Y \in D^\omega$: Y is strongly fair

iff $\lim\{ls(Y, n), n \geqslant 0\} = +\infty$
iff $\lim\{LS(Y, n), n \geqslant 0\} = +\infty$.

Proof: Given the LS–ls lemma it suffices to prove the part concerning ls.
Y is strongly fair

iff $\forall i \geqslant 0$: Y is s-fair at i - by the s-sequence theorem.
iff $\forall i \geqslant 0 \exists k \geqslant i \forall n \geqslant k\colon P(E_i) \cap LP(E_n) = \varnothing$ –by definition.
iff $\forall i \geqslant 0 \exists k \geqslant i \forall n \geqslant k\colon ls(Y, n) \geqslant i$–by definition.
iff $\lim\{ls(Y, n), n \geqslant 0\} = +\infty$. []

8.4.3 A metric characterization of D and D^w

Next, we introduce two distances. The first, da, (a for *all*) is essentially a well known distance on strings. It allows to characterize *all* infinite computations as limits of sequences of finite derivations. Its analogue for infinite weakly fair computations is achieved using the second distance: dw.

The distances da and dw

Let Y and Z be two (finite or infinite) derivations s.t. $Y \neq Z$ and let P be their longest common prefix–as sequences– which is finite even if Y and

Z are not. The length of P provides a natural basis for a distance between Y and Z, without regard to fairness. Hence the definitions of $\#a$ and da below. The intuition behind lw and the Lw lemmas suggest that $lw(P, length(P))$ can play the same role w.r.t. a distance between Y and Z, which does take weak fairness into account. This motivates the definition of $\#w$ given below (notice that if $k \leqslant length(P)$ then $lw(P, k) = lw(Y, k) = lw(Z, k)$). Finally, dw is obtained from $\#w$ in the same way as da is obtained from $\#a$.

Definition: For $Y,Z \in D$ and $Y \neq Z$:

$$\#a(Y, Z) = \max\{i\colon Y[i] = Z[i]\},$$

$$\#w(Y, Z) = lw\{Y, \#a(Y,Z)\}.$$

Definition: For $Y, Z \in D$, $Y \neq Z$ and $x \in \{a, w\}$

$$dx[Y, Y] = 0;$$

$$dx[Y, Z] = [\#x[Y, Z] + 1]^{-1}.$$

Theorem: **(*a-w*-distance)** da and dw are distances on D. Moreover, for all Y and Z, $da(Y, Z) \leqslant dw(Y, Z)$.

Proof: The only non-trivial part is to show that the above inequality holds when $Y1 \neq Y2 \neq Y3 \neq Y1$. We show that $\#x[Y1, Y3] \geqslant \min\{\#x[Y1, Y2], \#x[Y2, Y3]\}$. Note that this is a stronger form of the *triangle inequality* which distances have to satisfy. First note that the following fact is immediate from the definitions and preposition about lw:

(*) $\#a(Y, Z'] \leqslant \#a[Y, Z'']$ implies $\#w(Y, Z'] \leqslant \#w[Y, Z'']$.

Assume that $\#a[Y1, Y2] \leqslant \#a[Y2, Y3]$. (In the other case the result follows by symmetry–interchanging $Y1$ and $Y3$.) Then, using (*), we have that

$$\#x[Y1, Y2] = \min\{\#x[Y1, Y2], \#x[Y2, Y3]\}.$$

Case $x = a$: Clearly, if $p = \#a[Y1, Y2]$ then $Y1[p] = Y3[p]$. Hence $\#a[Y1, Y3] \geqslant p$.
Case $x = w$: The result follows immediately from the line above and (*).

[]

We can now state the metric characterizations. The significant part of the a-metric theorem says that the infinite computations are fully determined by the finite derivations and the distance da. Any computation in D can be obtained as a limit of a sequence of finite derivations. Conversely, any sequence of (finite) derivations which is a *Cauchy sequence* w.r.t. *da* has a limit in *D*.

There is one side to this characterization which one might find unpleasant: it is impossible to get rid of (finite) derivations which are not computations. Indeed, they are needed as finite approximants to the infinite derivations, that is in *FD*, but then remain in the completion: any constant sequence $\{Y_n, n \geqslant 0, Y_n = Y\}$ is a Cauchy sequence and its limit is Y.

The same kind of comments apply to the *w*-distance theorem, concerning *dw* and weakly fair computations.

Notation: If D' is a subset of D and d is a distance on D, the restriction of d to D' (which is a distance on D') is also denoted by d. If $x \in \{a, w\}$, $\lim_x$ denotes a limit in D.

Theorem: (*a*-metric) The space (D, da) is (isomorphic to) the metric completion of (FD, da).

Proof:

Density: Consider $Y \in D$. It is clear that:

$$\text{if } Y \in FD \text{ then } Y = \lim\{Y, Y, Y \cdots\};$$

$$\text{if } Y \in D^\omega \text{ then } Y = \lim\{Y[n], n \geqslant 0\}.$$

Completeness: Let $S = \{Y_n, n \geqslant 0\}$ be a Cauchy sequence in (D, da). If S is quasi-constant then trivially it has a limit. Otherwise, we can assume it without repetitions. For $k \geqslant 0$ let $i(k)$ be the least index, s.t. $\forall p,q \geqslant i(k)$: $da(Y_p, Y_q) \leqslant (k+1)^{-1}$. S being without repetitions, we get: $\forall p > i(k)$: $\#a(Y_p, Y_{i(k)}) \geqslant k$. It follows that $Y_{i(k)}$ has length at least k and that $\forall p \geqslant i(k)$: $Y_p[k] = Y_{i[k]}[k]$. We can, therefore, define an infinite derivation, Z, by setting: $Z[k] = Y_{i[k]}[k]$, $k \geqslant 0$. Clearly, Z is well defined (i.e. it is indeed a derivation) and $Z = \lim S$. [ ]

As a by-product of the above proof we obtain two properties of *da*-limits, which will be useful in the sequel.

Lemma: (*da* properties) If $\{Y_n, n \geqslant 0\}$ is not quasi-constant and $Z = \lim\{Y_n, n \geqslant 0\}$ in (D,da), then:

1. $\forall k \geqslant 0 \exists i \geqslant 0 \forall n \geqslant i$: $Z[k] = Y_n[k]$;
2. if for some k, $i \geqslant 0 \forall n \geqslant i$: $Y_n[k] = Y_i[k]$, then $Z[k] = Y_i[k]$.

Lemma: (1st refinement) Let S be a Cauchy sequence in (D, dw); then:

1. S is also a Cauchy sequence in (D, da);
2. $\lim_w S$ exists and coincides with $\lim_a S$.

Proof: Let $S = (Y_n, n \geqslant 0)$ be a Cauchy sequence in (D, dw).

Part 1: We have to show that S is a Cauchy sequence w.r.t. *da*. But this is immediate as $\forall Y,Z$: $da(Y, Z) \leqslant dw(Y, Z)$.

Part 2: Let $Z = \lim_a S$—which exists by the *a*-metric theorem. We have to show that $Z = \lim_w S$. This is obvious when S is quasi-constant. Otherwise, we can assume S to be without repetitions. Hence $\exists m \forall p \geqslant m$: $Y_p \neq Z$. Consider $k \geqslant 0$. As S is a Cauchy sequence w.r.t. dw $\exists i \geqslant m$: $\forall p,q \geqslant i$: $dw(Y_p, Y_q) < (k+1)^{-1}$; hence $\forall p > i$: $\#a(Y_p, Y_i) \geqslant k$.

Let $r = \min\{\#n(Y_i, Y_p), p > i\}$. As S is without repetition, r is well defined; moreover, by the second *da*-property, $\forall p \geqslant i$: $Z[r] = Y_p[r] = Y_i[r]$.

Now, by definition of $\#w$ and the properties of *lw*, we have: if $Y \neq Y'$ and $Y[n] = Y'[n]$ then $\#w(Y, Y') \geqslant lw(Y, n)$. Hence $\forall p \geqslant i$: $\#w(Z, Y_p) \geqslant lw(Y_i, r)$. On the other hand, $\exists q > i$: $\#a(Y_i, Y_q) = r$. So, by definition: $\#w(Y_i, Y_q) = lw(Y_i, r)$. Therefore, $lw(Y_i, r) \geqslant k$. Hence $\forall p \geqslant i$: $\#w(Z, Y_p) \geqslant k$, i.e. $dw(Z, Y_p) \leqslant (k+1)^{-1}$. []

Lemma: (weakly-fair limit) If S is a sequence in *FD* and $\lim_w S = Y$ then $Y \in D^w$.

Proof: Let $S = \{Y_n, n \geqslant 0\}$ be a sequence in *FD* and $Y = \lim_w S$. We have to show that $Y \in D^w$. This is trivial if S is quasi-constant ($Y \in FD \subseteq D^w$). Otherwise, consider $k \in Dom(Y)$. Then $\exists i \geqslant 0$ $\forall n \geqslant i$: $dw(Y, Y_n) \leqslant (k+1)^{-1}$. As S is not quasi-constant, $\exists q \geqslant i$, s.t. $Y \neq Y_q$. Hence, $\#w(Y, Y_q) \geqslant k$. but $\#w(Y, Y_q) = lw(Y, \#a(Y, Y_q))$. So, $lw(Y, \#a(Y, Y_q)) \geqslant k$, hence Y is *w*-fair at k –(first part of *lw* proposition). From the proposition on *w*-admissibility we can conclude that Y is weakly fair. []

Theorem: (*w*-distance) The space (D^w, dw) is (isomorphic to) the metric completion of (FD, dw).

Proof: We first show that *FD* is dense in (D^w, dw) and then that (D^w, dw) is complete (by showing that each Cauchy sequence in *FD* has a limit in D^w).

Density: Let $Y \in D^w$. If Y is finite then $Y = \lim_w(Y, Y, Y, \ldots)$. Otherwise, $Y \in D^{\omega, w}$ and then $Y = \lim_w\{Y[n], n \geqslant 0\}$. Indeed, Y is weakly fair hence, and by the *lw*-limit lemma $\lim\{lw(Y, n), n \geqslant 0\} = +\infty$. But $dw\{Y, Y[n]\} = [lw(Y, n)+1]^{-1}$, hence the claim.

Completeness: Let S be a Cauchy sequence in (FD, dw). From the 1-st refinement lemma, S has a limit in (D, dw), say Y, and the weakly-fair limit lemma ensures that $Y \in D^w$. []

The distance *ds*

The distance for strong fairness is defined directly from LS, without an intermediate step analogous to $\#w$. A more fundamental difference w.r.t. dw is, however, the one inherited from the difference between LS and lw (and ls). Whilst $lw(Y, n)$ depends entirely on the initial segment of Y up to the n-th element, $LS(Y, n)$ depends also on the tail of Y after its n-th element. So, if $\#a(Y, Z) = n$ the distance dw uses lw to explore the common prefix of Y and Z while ds needs to know both $LS(Y, n)$ and $LS(Z, n)$.

Definition: For $Y,Z \in D$, $Y \neq Z$, and $n = \#a(Y,Z)$:

$$ds(Y, Y) = 0;$$

$$ds(Y, Z) = [LS(Y, n) + 1]^{-1} + [LS(Z, n) + 1]^{-1}.$$

Lemma: (*s*-distance) ds is a distance on D. Moreover, for any Z, Y:

$$da(Y, Z) \leqslant dw(Y, Z) \leqslant ds(Y, Z).$$

Proof: We only need to show that $ds(Y1, Y3) \leqslant ds(Y1, Y2) + ds(Y2, Y3)$ when $Y1 \neq Y2 \neq Y3 \neq Y1$. Let $n = \#a(Y1, Y3)$, $p = \#a(Y1, Y2)$ and $q = \#a(Y2, Y3)$. Then:

$$ds(Y1, Y3) = [LS(Y1, n) + 1]^{-1} + [LS(Y3, n) + 1]^{-1}$$

and

$$ds(Y1, Y2) + ds(Y2, Y3) =$$

$$[LS(Y1,p) + 1]^{-1} + [LS(Y2,p) + 1]^{-1}$$

$$+ [LS(Y2,q) + 1]^{-1} + [LS(Y3,q) + 1]^{-1}.$$

Assume $p \leqslant q$ (the other case follows by symmetry.) We can summarize the situation in a diagram (see Figure 8.13) showing also the two possible cases for n.

Clearly, $n \geqslant p$. Hence $LS(Y1, n) \geqslant LS(Y1, p)$, by the *ls*-proposition. If $n \geqslant q$, then also $LS(Y3, n) \geqslant LS(Y3, q)$ and the wanted claim follows. Otherwise, $p \leqslant n < q$. Then, by using the *LS–ls* lemma:

$$LS(Y3, n) = \min\{ls(Y3, i), i \geqslant n \textit{ and } i \in Dom(Y3)\}.$$

Let $j \geqslant n$ be s.t. $LS(Y3, n) = ls(Y3, j)$. If $j \geqslant q$, then also $LS(Y3, q) = ls(Y3, j)$ and we can conclude. Otherwise, $j < q$ and we have: $ls(Y3, j) = ls(Y2, j)$.

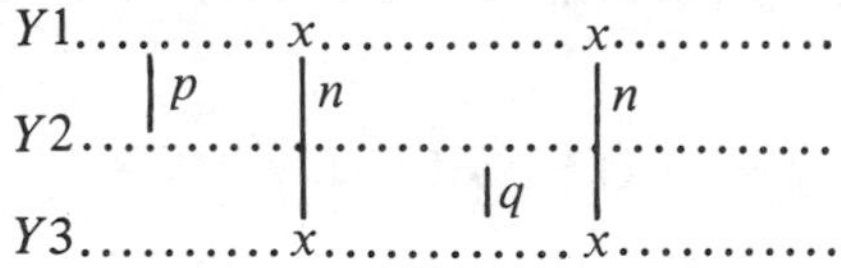

Figure 8.13 Two cases for n.

As $p \leqslant n \leqslant j$ we have also: $LS(Y2, p) \leqslant ls(Y2, j)$, using the $LS-ls$ lemma again. Therefore, $LS(Y3, n) \geqslant LS(Y2, p) \leqslant (Y2, p)$ and we can conclude. [ ]

Before stating the main s-limit theorem, we formulate (with proofs skipped, as they are similar to the weak metric case) the corresponding lemmata w.r.t. ds.

Lemma: (2nd refinement) If S is a Cauchy sequence in (D, ds), then:

1. S is a Cauchy sequence in (D, da) [and also in (D, dw)];
2. $\lim_s S$ exists and coincides with $\lim_a S$ [and also $\lim_w S$].

Lemma: (strongly-fair limit) If S is a sequence in FD and $\lim_s S = Y$ then $Y \in D^s$.

Theorem: (s-limit) The space (D^s, ds) is (isomorphic to) the metric completion of (FD, ds).

Proof:

Density: Let $Y \in D^s$. If Y is finite then $Y = \lim_s(Y, Y, \ldots)$. Otherwise, Y is infinite and strongly fair. We show that $S = \lim_s\{Y[n], n \geqslant 0\}$. From the LS-limit lemma,

$$\lim\{ls(Y, n), n \geqslant 0\} = \lim\{LS(Y,n), n \geqslant 0\} = +\infty.$$

Hence, $\forall k \geqslant 0 \ \exists i \geqslant 0 \ \forall n \geqslant i$: $ls(Y, n) \geqslant k$, $LS(Y, n) \geqslant k$.

Now, $ds(Y, Y[n]) = [LS(Y, n) + 1]^{-1} + [LS(Y[n], n) + 1]^{-1}$. But, by definition, $LS(Y[n], n) = ls(Y[n], n) = ls(Y, n)$, implying the claim.

Completeness: Similar to the weak distance case. [ ]

We now outline how to extend the main results to all derivations, relaxing the dependency on the initial term E_0.

Recall that $FD, D, \ldots$ have been used so far as explicit abbreviations for $FD(E_0)$, $D(E_0), \ldots$ Implicitly, dx too has been an abbreviation for $dx(E_0)$, $x \in \{a,w,s\}$. Now, we redefine $FD, D, \ldots$ and dx as follows.

If $\cup^+$ denotes disjoint union and *EXP* denotes the set of *CCS* expressions, then:

$$FD = \cup^+ \ \{FD(E)\colon E \in EXP\};$$

$$D = \cup^+ \ \{D(E)\colon \ E \in EXP\};$$

and so on.

Therefore, an element of D can be represented as a pair: $<E, Y>$, where $Y \in D(E)$. Now, on D we can define, for $x \in \{a, w, s\}$:

$$dx(<E, Y>, <E, Z>) = dx(E)(Y, Z)$$

$$dx(<E, Y>, <G, Z>) = 2, \quad \text{when } E \neq G.$$

The choice of 2 is arbitrary: any constant greater than 1 would do as well (1 is the diameter of $D(E)$ w.r.t. $dx(E)$). It is immediate to check that dx is a distance on D. Moreover, if $S = \{<E_n, Y_n>, n \geqslant 0\}$ is a sequence in D, then S is a Cauchy sequence in (D,ds) iff

$$\exists k \geqslant 0 \exists E \forall n \geqslant k\colon E_n = E$$

and $\{<E, Y_n>, n \geqslant k\}$ is a Cauchy sequence in $(D(E), dx(E))$.

It is clear then that the respective theorems (and the auxiliary lemmas) hold also when $FD, D, \ldots, da, dw, ds$ are those just defined.

This final "bringing everything together" should not mislead the reader. What has been shown here is that fair computations, taken individually, can be characterized as limits of finite derivations. Currently, it is not known whether this setting allows a similar characterization of the fairness of global behaviours keeping approximants finite.

Another interesting question is whether such results can also be obtained in the framework of ordered structures (posets, cpo's, . . .). It is not just a matter of having another characterization of fairness at hand. This can be seen comparing convergence in metric spaces with "convergence" (to $\sqcup$s) in ordered structures. Any "definite information" contained in an initial segment of a chain is also true of its $\sqcup$. The situation is entirely different when considering a sequence S in a metric space which converges to, say, y. If S' is an initial segment of S, it may well be that the information contained in S' is incompatible with that in y. Therefore, knowing S' only does imply anything about y. It seems that this fact alone is enough for preferring a characterization in terms of $\sqcup$'s of chains to one based on limits of sequences in metric spaces. But it can also explain why the former may be harder to obtain than the latter.

8.5 Finite Delay Operators

As mentioned before, the use of *CCS* provides an opportunity of handling another fairness-like operator, that of *finite* (but *unbounded*) *delay*. We conclude this chapter with a brief presentation based on ideas from [HE 83].

As it turns out, the natural context for studying delay operators is that of *tightly-coupled* systems. To this end another operator, that of *product*, denoted by $\times$, is introduced. Intuitively, $p_1 \times p_2$ is a new process which consists of two subprocesses p_1, p_2 tightly coupled together. It can only perform an action by *both* p_1 and p_2 simultaneously performing an individual action. For example, if p_1 performs a and p_2 performs b then $p_1 \times p_2$ performs an action we call $a \cdot b$. The $\cdot$ can be viewed as an operation on the action names ACT. It is useful to assume that $(ACT, \cdot)$ has certain properties. Suppose, for example, there is a distinguished element $1 \in ACT$ such that $(ACT, \cdot, -, 1)$ is a group. The action 1 may be viewed as *delaying*. Then, is p_1 performs a and p_2 performs its complement $\bar{a}$, the combined process $p_1 \times p_2$ performs 1, i.e. delays. This delay can be interpreted as an external reflection of an internal synchronization between the subprocesses p_1, p_2.

Fuller details about the usefulness of the structure imposed on ACT, as well as the more extensive treatment of *SCCS* (*synchronous CCS*), the tool for describing tightly coupled processes, may be found in [M 82a].

Consider a computation from $p_1 \mid p_2$. At each point in time each subprocess p_1, p_2, may perform an action or delay. We can interpret delay as performing a 1-action, so that at each point in time each process performs an action; it may be a real action or a delaying action. One can now reinterpret the various fairness notions in terms of restrictions on delaying. For example, unconditional fairness might be rendered as *no subprocess can delay forever.* In fact the different interpretations embodied in these fairness assumptions can be obtained by using different delay operators.

One such operator is ϵ, studied in [M 82, HE 82]. The process ϵp can *indefinitely* delay, i.e. perform a 1-action, but eventually it *must* perform an action from p. So for example, the process $fix\ X.\epsilon aX$ cannot perform an infinite number of 1-actions; it must always eventually perform an a-action. We can use ϵ to define very complicated processes. For example, consider the process defined by

$$Z \leftarrow (X \times Y) \backslash a, b$$

$$X \leftarrow \epsilon aX$$

$$Y \leftarrow \epsilon bY,$$

where a notational variation is used for the case of handling mutual recursion. Every infinite sequence of actions performed by Z must be a *fair merge* of the sequence a^ω, b^ω. Moreover, it can perform any infinite sequence of actions which is a fair merge of these sequences.

Another delay operator, denoted by γp, also takes into account enabledness of subprocesses of p, and is related to weak and strong fairness as ϵ is related to unconditional fairness.

The main task is the definition of admissible computations of processes involving delays. A study of the partial preorders associated with delay operators appears in details in [HE 83].

A simplicistic approach to the delay rules in the operational semantics might suggest using the following two rules:

$$WAIT \quad \epsilon p \overset{1}{-\,-\!\!\rightarrow} \epsilon p,$$

$$FULFIL \quad \frac{p \overset{a}{-\,-\!\!\rightarrow} p'}{\epsilon p \overset{a}{-\,-\!\!\rightarrow} p'}.$$

This approach immediately faces the same problem mentioned in the previous sections: repeating the *WAIT* rule ad infinitum is regarded as admissible. Thus, once again, some extra means is needed to render such sequences inadmissible. Again some more elaborate labeling may be employed, recording some information about the progress of a computation. So far, no rules have been suggested for directly generating all and only admissible computations for any *CCS* delay operator, in the spirit of the previous section.

References

The following abbreviations for journal names and conference names are used:

ACM-POPL—ACM Annual Symposium on Principles of Programming Languages
ACM-PODC—ACM Annual Symposium on Principles of Distributed Computing
ACM-STOC—ACM Symposium on Theory of Computation
ACM-TOPLAS—ACM Transactions On Programming Languages and Systems
CACM—Communications of the ACM
ICALP—International Colloquium on Automata, Languages and Programing (EATCS)
IEEE-FOCS—IEEE Symposium on Foundations of Computer Science
IEEE-TSE—IEEE Transactions on Software Engineering
IPL—Information Processing Letters
JACM—Journal of the ACM
JCSS—Journal of Computer and System Sciences
LNCS—Lecture Notes In Computer Science, Springer-Verlag
SCP—Science of Computer Programming
MFCS—Mathematical Foundation of Computer Science
TCS—Theoretical Computer Science

[A 84] K.R. Apt: "Ten years of Hoare's logic: a survey—part II: Nondeterminism", TCS 28: 83–109, 1984.

[AB 79] K. Abrahamson: "Modal logic for concurrent nondeterministic programs", Proc. Int. Symp. on Semantics of Concurrent Computations, Evian, July 1979. In: LNCS 70 (G. Kahn, ed.), Springer-Verlag, 1979.

[AC 85] K.R. Apt, P. Clermont: "Two normal form theorems for CSP programs", RC 10975, IBM T.J. Watson Research Center, Feb. 1985.

[AF 84] K.R. Apt, N. Francez: "Modeling the distributed termination convention in CSP", ACM-TOPLAS 6, 3: 370–379, July 1984.

[AFR 80] K.R. Apt, N. Francez, W.P. de Roever: "A proof system for communicating sequential processes", ACM-TOPLAS 2, 3: 359–380, July 1980.

[AN 80] A. Arnold, M. Nivat: "Metric interpretation of infinite trees and semantics of nondeterministic recursive procedures", TCS 11: 181–205, 1980.

[AO 83] K.R. Apt, E.R. Olderog: "Proof rules and transformations dealing with fairness", SCP 3: 65–100, 1983.

[AP 82] K.R. Apt, G.D. Plotkin: "Countable nondeterminism and random assignment", TR 82–7, LITP, University of Paris 7, February 1982. To appear in JACM.

[APS 84] K.R. Apt, A. Pnueli, J. Stavi: "Fair termination revisited with delay", TCS 33: 65-84, 1984. Also in: Proc. 2nd Conference on Foundations of Software Technology and Theoretical Computer Science (FST-TCS), Bangalore, India, Dec. 1982.

[B 82] H.J. Boom: "A weaker precondition for loops", ACM-TOPLAS 4, 4: 668–677, Oct. 1982.

[deB 80] J.W. de Bakker: *Mathematical Theory of Program Correctness,* Prentice-Hall, 1980.

[BA 83] R.J.J. Back: "A continuous semantics for unbounded nondeterminism", TCS 23: 187,283, 1983.

[BK 85] J.A. Bergstra, J.W. Klop: "Algebra of communicating processes", to appear in: Proc. CWI Symp. on Mathematics and Computer Science, and also as a CWI Tech. Report CS-R8421.

[BKS 83] R.J.J. Back, R. Kurki-Suonio: "Decentralization of process nets with centralized control", Proc. 2nd ACM-PODC Symposium, Montreal, Aug. 1983.

[BKS 84] R.J.J. Back, K. Kurki-Suonio: "Co-operation in distributed systems using symmetric multi-process handshakes", TR Abo Academy, Ser. A, 34, 1984.

[BMP 83] M. Ben-Ari, Z. Manna, A. Pnueli: "The temporal logic of branching time", ACTA Informatica 20: 207–226, 1983. Proc. 8th ACM-POPL, Williamsburgh, VA, Jan. 1981.

[BU 74] R.M. Burstall: "Program proving as hand simulation with a little induction", Proc. IFIP 74, pp. 308–312, North Holland, 1974.

[deBZ 83] J.W. de Bakker, J.I. Zucker: "Process and fair semantics for the ADA randezvous", Proc. 10th ICALP, Barcelona, July 1983. In: LNCS 154 (J. Diaz, ed.), Springer-Verlag, 1983.

[C 77] P. Cousot: "Asynchronous iterative methods for solving a fixed point system of monotone equations in a complete lattice", TR 88, L.A. 7, Univ. of Grenoble, 1977.

[C 84] G. Costa: "A metric characterization of fair CCS", TR CSR-169-84, Dept. of Comp. Sci., Edinburgh Univ., Oct. 1984.

[CE 81] E.M. Clarke, E.A. Emerson: "Design and synthesis of synchronization skeletons using branching time temporal logic", proc. Logics of Programs Workshop, CMU,1981. In: LNCS 131 (D. Kozen, ed.), Springer-Verlag, 1981.

[CES 83] E.M. Clarke, E.A. Emerson, A.P. Sistla: "Automatic verification of finite state concurrent systems", Proc. 10th ACM-POPL, Austin, TX., Jan. 1983.

[CS 84] G. Costa, C. Stirling: "A fair calculus of communicating systems", ACTA Informatica 21: 417–441, 1984.

[CS 85] G. Costa, C. Stirling: "Weak and strong fairness in CCS", TR CSR-16-85, Dept. of Comp. Sci., Edinburgh Univ., Jan. 1985.

[DIJ 68] E.W. Dijkstra: "Cooperating sequential processes", in: *Programming Languages* (F. Genuys, ed.), pp. 43–112, Academic Press, 1968.

[DIJ 75] E.W. Dijkstra: "Guarded commands, nondeterminacy and formal derivation of programs", CACM 18, 8, Aug. 1975.

[DIJ 76] E.W. Dijkstra: *A Discipline of Programming*, Prentice-Hall, 1976.

[DM 84] P. Degano, U. Montanari: "Liveness properties as convergence in metric spaces", Proc. 16th ACM-STOC, May 1984.

[EC 80] E.A. Emerson, E.M. Clarke: "Characterizing correctness properties of parallel programs using fixedpoints", Proc. 7th ICALP, Nordwijkerhout, July 1980. In: LNCS 85 (J.W. de Bakker, J. van Leuven, eds.), Springer-Verlag, 1980.

[EH 83] E.A. Emerson, J.Y. Halpern: "'Sometimes' and 'not always' revisited: on branching time versus linear time", Proc. 10th ACM-POPL, Austin, TX, Jan. 1983.

[EL 85] E.A. Emerson, D.L. Lei: "Modalities for model checking: branching time strikes back", Proc. 12th ACM-POPL, New Orleans, LA, Jan. 1985.

[F 76] N. Francez: "The analysis of cyclic programs", Ph.D thesis, Weizmann Institute of Science, Rehovot, July 1976.

[F 77] N. Francez: "A case for a forward predicate transformer", IPL 6, 6: 196–198, 1977.

[FH 84] Y. Feldman, D. Harel: "Probabilistic dynamic logic", JCSS 28: 193–215, 1984.

[FK 81] N. Francez, S. Katz: "Self-interpretability and nondeterminism", TR 105, IBM Israel Scientific Center, July 1981.

[FK 84] N. Francez, D. Kozen: "Generalized fair termination", Proc. 11th ACM-POPL , Salt Lake City, Jan. 1984.

[FL 67] R.W. Floyd: "Assigning meaning to programs", Proc. AMS Symp. in Applied Mathematics 19, 1967.

[FP 78] N. Francez, A. Pnueli: "A proof method for cyclic programs", ACTA Informatica 9: 133–157, 1978.

[FP 83] M.J. Fischer, M.S. Paterson: "Storage requirements for fair scheduling", IPL 17: 249–250, 1983.

[FR 80] N. Francez, W.P. de Roever: "Fairness in communicating processes" (extended abstract), unpublished memo, Computer Science Dept., Utrecht Univ., July 1980.

[FS 81] L. Flon, N. Suzuki: "The total correctness of parallel programs", SIAM J. of Computing 10, 1: 227–246, 1981.

[FW 82] R. Fagin, J.H. Williams: "A fair carpool scheduling algorithm", IBM J. of Research and Development 27, 2: 133–139, Mar. 1982.

[G 84] O. Grumberg: Ph.D. thesis, Computer Science Dept., Technion, Haifa , May 1984 (in Hebrew).

[GF 82] O. Grumberg, N. Francez: "A complete proof rule for weak equifairness", RC-9634, IBM T.J. Watson Research Center, Oct. 1982.

[GFK 83] O. Grumberg, N. Francez, S. Katz: "A complete proof rule for strong equifairness", Proc. 2nd Workshop on Logics of Programs, CMU, June 1983. In: LNCS 164 (E.Clarke, D.Kozen, eds.), Springer-Verlag, 1983. To appear in JCSS.

[GFK 84] O. Grumberg, N. Francez, S. Katz: "Fair termination of communicating processes", Proc. 3rd ACM-PODC, Vancouver, Aug. 1984.

[GFMR 81] O. Grumberg, N. Francez, J.A. Makowsky, W.P. de Roever: "A proof rule for fair termination of guarded commands", Proc. Int. Symp. on Algorithmic Languages, Amsterdam, Oct. 1981 (prelim. version); Inf. Contr. 66, 1/2:83–102, July/August, 1985.

[GPSS 80] D. Gabbay, A. Pnueli, S. Shelah, J. Stavi: "On the temporal analysis of fairness", Proc. 7th ACM-POPL, Las Vegas, NV, Jan. 1980.

[HA 79] D.Harel: *First order dynamic logic,* LNCS 68, Springer-Verlag, 1979.

[HA 84] D. Harel: "A general result on infinite trees and its applications", Proc. 16th ACM-STOC, May 1984.

[HE 82] M.C.B. Hennessy: "Axiomatizing finite delay operators", TR CSR-124-82, Dept. of Comp. Sci., Edinburgh Univ., 1982.

[HE 83] M.C.B. Hennessy: "Modeling finite delay operators", TR CSR-153-83, Dept. of Comp. Sci., Edinburgh Univ., Nov. 1983.

[HO 78] C.A.R. Hoare: "Communicating sequential processes", CACM 21, 8: 666–677, Aug. 1978.

[HO 78a] C.A.R. Hoare: "Some properties of predicate transformers", JACM 25: 461–480, 1978.

[HP 73] P. Hitchcock, D. Park: "Induction rules and termination proofs", Proc. 1st ICALP Symp. (M. Nivat, ed.), North-Holland, 1973.

[HP 79] M.C.B. Hennessy, G.D. Plotkin: "Full abstraction for a simple programming language", Proc. 8th MFCS, LNCS 74 (J. Becvar, ed.), Springer-Verlag, 1979.

[HSP 82] S. Hart, M. Sharir, A. Pnueli: "Termination of probabilistic programs", Proc. 9th ACM-POPL, Albuquerque NM, Jan. 1982.

[K 52] S.C. Kleene: *Introduction to metamathematics*, North-Holland, 1952.

[KO 27] D. König: "Uber eine schlussweise aus dem endlichen ins umendliche", Acta Litt. ac.sci. Univ. Allug. Fra Joseph, Section Sc. Math., 3: 121–130, 1927.

[KO 81] D. Kozen: "Semantics of probabilistic programs", JCSS 22: 328-350, 1981.

[KR 82] R. Kuiper, W.P. de Roever: "Fairness assumptions for CSP in a temporal logic framework", TC2 Working Conference on the Formal Description of Programming Concepts, Garmisch, June 1982.

[LA 74] L. Lamport: "A new solution of Dijkstra's concurrent programming problem", CACM 17: 453–455, 1974.

[LA 77] L. Lamport: "Proving the correctness of multiprocess programs", IEEE-TSE 3, 2: 125–143, 1977.

[LA 80] L. Lamport: " "sometimes" is sometime "not never" ", Proc. 7th ACM-POPL, Las Vegas, NV, Jan. 1980.

[LE 76] D. Lehmann: "Categories for fixed semantics", Proc. 17th IEEE-FOCS, 1976.

[LE 81] D. Lehmann: "Another proof for the completeness of a rule for the fair termination of guarded commands and another rule for their just termination", (preliminary version), Tech. Rep. IW 178/81, Mathematical Center, Amsterdam, Sept. 1981.

[LG 81] G. Levin, D. Gries: "Proof techniques for communicating sequential processes", ACTA Informatica 15: 281–302, 1981.

[LPS 81] D. Lehmann, A. Pnueli, J. Stavi: "Impartiality, justice and fairness: the ethics of concurrent termination", Proc. 8th ICALP, Acre, Israel, July 1981. In: LNCS 115 (O. Kariv, S. Even, eds.), Springer-Verlag, 1981.

[LPZ 85] O.Lichtenstein, A. Pnueli, L. Zuck: "The glory of the past", Proc. 3rd Logics of Programs Workshop, Brooklin College, June 1985, LNCS 193 (R. Parikh, ed.), Springer-Verlag, 1985.

[LS 83] D. Lehmann, S. Shelah: "Reasoning with time and chance", Proc. 10th ICALP, Barcelona, Jan. 1983.

[M 80] R. Milner: *A calculus for communicating systems,* LNCS 92, Springer-Verlag, 1980.

[M 82] R. Milner: "A finite delay operator in CCS", TR CSR-116-82, Dept. of Comp. Sci., Edinburgh Univ., 1982.

[M 82a] R. Milner: "Calculi for synchrony and asynchrony", TR CSR-104-82, Dept. of Comp. Sci., Edinburgh Univ., 1982.

[MA 74] Z. Manna: *Mathematical Theory of Computation*, McGraw-Hill, 1974.

[MO 74] Y. N. Moschovakis: *Elementary induction on abstract structures*, Studies in Logic and the Foundations of Mathematics series no. 77, North-Holland, 1974.

[MP 83] Z. Manna, A. Pnueli: "How to cook a temporal proof for your pet language", Proc. 10th ACM-POPL, Austin, TX, Jan. 1983.

[MP 84] Z. Manna, A. Pnueli: "Adequate proof principles for invariance and liveness properties of concurrent programs", SCP 4, 3: 257–290, Dec. 1984.

[MP ??] Z. Manna, A. Pnueli: A forthcoming book.

[OA 84] E.R. Olderog, K.R. Apt: "Transformations realizing fairness assumptions for parallel programs", TR 84-8, LITP, Univ. of Paris 7, Feb. 1984.

[OG 76] S. Owicki, D. Gries: "Verifying properties of parallel programs: An axiomatic approach", CACM 19, 5: 279–286, Aug. 1976.

[OG 76a] S. Owicki, D. Gries: "An axiomatic proof technique for parallel programs", ACTA Informatica 6: 319–340, 1976.

[OL 82] S. Owicki, L. Lamport: "Proving liveness of concurrent programs", ACM-TOPLAS 4, 3: 455–495, July 1982.

[PA 79] D. Park: "On the semantics of fair parallelism", Proc. Abstract Software Specification, 1979. In: LNCS 86 (D. Biorner, ed.), Springer-Verlag, 1980.

[PA 81] D. Park: "A predicate transformer for weak fair iteration", Proc. 6th IBM Symp. on Math. Foundation of Computer Science, Hakone, Japan, 1981.

[PA 81a] D. Park: "Cuncurrency and automata on infinite sequences", Proc. 5th GI conference, 1981. In: LNCS 104 (P. Deussen, ed.), Springer-Verlag, 1981.

[PA 82] D. Park: "The "Fairness" problem and nondeterministic computing networks", Proc. 4th Advanced School on Foundations of Computer Science—Distributed Systems', Amsterdam, June 1982.

[PF 77] G.L. Peterson, M.J. Fischer: "Economical solutions for the critical section problem in distributed systems", Proc. 9th ACM-STOC, Boulder, CO, May 1977.

[PL 76] G.D. Plotkin: "A power domain construction", SIAM J. of Computing 5, 3: 452–487, 1976.

[PL 81] G.D. Plotkin: "A structural approach to operational semantics", TR DAIMI-FN 19, Comp. Sci. Dept., Aarhus Univ., 1981.

[PL 82] G.D. Plotkin: "A power domain for countable nondeterminism", Proc. 9th ICALP, Aarhus, July 1982. In: LNCS 140 (M. Nielsen, E.M. Scmidt, eds.), Springer-Verlag 1982.

[PN 77] A. Pnueli: "The temporal logic of programs", Proc. 19th IEEE-FOCS, Providence, RI, Nov. 1977.

[PN 81] A. Pnueli: "The temporal semantics of concurrent programs", TCS 13: 45–60, 1981.

[PN 83] A. Pnueli: "On the extremely fair treatment of probabilistic algorithms", Proc. 15th ACM-STOC, Boston, April 1983.

[PR 79] V.R. Pratt: "Dynamic logic", in: Foundations of Computer Science III (J. van Leuven, J.W. de Bakker, eds.), Mathematical Center tracts 109, Amsterdam, 1979.

[QS 83] J.P. Queille, J. Sifakis: "Fairness and related properties in transition systems—a temporal logic to deal with fairness", ACTA Informatica 19, 195–220, 1983.

[R 84] W. Reisig: "Partial order semantics versus interleaving semantics for CSP-like languages and its impact on fairness", Proc. 11th ICALP, Antverpen, July 1984.

[deR 76] W.P. de Roever: "Dijkstra's predicate transformer, nondeterminims, recursion and termination", Proc. MFCS 1976, LNCS 45 (A. Mazarkiewicz, ed.), Springer-Verlag, 1976.

[deR 81] W.P. de Roever: "A formalism for reasoning about fair termination", Proc. 1st Workshop on Logics of Programs, Yorktown Heights, May 1981. In: LNCS 131 (D. Kozen, ed.), Springer-Verlag, 1981.

[RE 80] J.H. Reif: "Logics for probabilistic programs", Proc. 12th ACM-STOC, Los Angeles, CA, May 1980

[RO 67] H. Rogers, Jr.: *Theory of recursive functions and effective computability,* McGraw-Hill, 1967.

[S 78] M. Smyth: "Power domains", JCSS 16, 1: 23–36, 1978.

[SH 67] J.R. Shoenfield: *Mathematical logic,* Addison-Wesley, 1967.

[SI 83] A.P. Sistla: "Theoretical issues in the design and verification of distributed systems", Ph.D. thesis, Carnegie-Mellon Univ., Aug. 1983.

[SdRG 84] F.A. Stomp, W.P. de Roever, R.T. Gerth: "The μ-calculus as an assertion language for fairness arguments", TR RUU-CS-84-12, Utrecht, Nov. 1984.

[ST 77] J. Stoy: *Denotational semantics: the Scott-Strachey approach to programming language theory,* MIT Press, 1977.

[TA 55] A. Tarski: "A lattice-theoretical fixed point theorem and its applications", Pacific J. of Mathematics, 5, 1955.

[TM 83] M. L. Tiomkin, J. A. Makowsky: "Probabilistic propositional dynamic logic", TR #305, Comp. Sci. Dept., Technion, Nov. 1983.

List of Proof Rules

$UFAIR_2$	Rule for proving unconditionally-fair termination for *GC* programs (with two directions) using the explicit-scheduler method **63**
SIM-$UFAIR_2$	A simplified version of **$UFAIR_2$** **63**
UFAIR	Rule for proving unconditionally-fair termination for *GC* programs using the explicit-scheduler method **69**
WFAIR	Rule for proving weakly-fair termination for *GC* programs using the explicit-scheduler method **76**
SFAIR	Rule for proving strongly-fair termination for *GC* programs using the explicit-scheduler method **77**
SIM-$SFAIR_2$	A simplified version of **SFAIR** for two-directional programs **78**
FAIR-IF	Rule for proving termination under (strong) ''all-levels'' fairness for (deterministic-iterations) *GC* programs, using the explicit-scheduler method **82**
UEFT	Rule for proving unconditionally-equifair termination for *GC* programs **98**
SEFT	Rule for proving strongly-equifair termination for *GC* programs **106**
F-UFT	Rule for proving unconditionally **F**-fair termination for *GC* programs (**F**—a generalized fairness property) **115**
F-WFT	Rule for proving weakly **F**-fair termination for *GC* programs (**F**—as above) **116**
F-SFT	Rule for proving strongly **F**-fair termination for *GC* programs (**F**—as above) **117**
Γ-UXFT	Rule for proving unconditionally Γ-extremely-fair termination for *GC* programs (Γ—a countable set of state properties) **123**
Γ-SXFT	Rule for proving strongly Γ-extremely-fair termination for *GC* programs (Γ—as above) **124**
I-CFAIR	Rule for proving relativized (strongly-) fair termination of a CSP program (using the helpful directions method) **142**
INIT	Rule for deducing temporal invariance from initial preconditions **207**
TRNS	Rule for deducing temporal properties of a single transition **208**
INV	(Derived) rule for temporal invariance proofs **208**
F-WIND	Rule for proving fairness-independent temporal liveness properties **208**
Temp-WFAIR	Rule for proving temporal weak-fairness liveness properties **209**
Temp-SFAIR	Rule for proving temporal strong-fairness liveness properties **209**
Temp-WWELL	Rule for proving temporal weak-fairness liveness properties using well-foundedness (the temporal analog **WFT**) **210**

Author Index

Entries in this index refer also to implicit reference to a name through reference to her/his work.

Subject Index

Texts and Monographs in Computer Science

Suad Alagić
Relational Database Technology

Suad Alagić and Michael A. Arbib
The Design of Well-Structured and Correct Programs

S. Thomas Alexander
Adaptive Signal Processing: Theory and Applications

Michael A. Arbib, A. J. Kfoury, and Robert N. Moll
A Basis for Theoretical Computer Science

Michael A. Arbib and Ernest G. Manes
Algebraic Approaches to Program Semantics

F. L. Bauer and H. Wössner
Algorithmic Language and Program Development

Kaare Christian
The Guide to Modula-2

Edsger W. Dijkstra
Selected Writings on Computing: A Personal Perspective

Nissim Francez
Fairness

Peter W. Frey, Ed.
Chess Skill in Man and Machine, 2nd Edition

R. T. Gregory and E. V. Krishnamurthy
Methods and Applications of Error-Free Computation

David Gries, Ed.
Programming Methodology: A Collection of Articles by Members of IFIP WG2.3

David Gries
The Science of Programming

A. J. Kfoury, Robert N. Moll, and Michael A. Arbib
A Programming Approach to Computability

E. V. Krishnamurthy
Error-Free Polynomial Matrix Computations

Franco P. Preparata and Michael Ian Shamos
Computational Geometry: An Introduction

Brian Randell, Ed.
The Origins of Digital Computers: Selected Papers

Arto Salomaa and Matti Soittola
Automata-Theoretic Aspects of Formal Power Series

Jeffrey R. Sampson
Adaptive Information Processing: An Introductory Survey

William M. Waite and Gerhard Goos
Compiler Construction

Niklaus Wirth
Programming in Modula-2